HISTORY AND HISTORIOGRAPHY IN CLASSICAL UTILITARIANISM, 1800–1865

This first comprehensive account of the utilitarians' historical thought intellectually resituates their conceptions of philosophy and politics, at a time when the past acquired new significances as both a means and object of study. Drawing on published and unpublished writings – and set against the intellectual backdrops of Scottish philosophical history, German and French historicism, Romanticism, positivism, and the rise of social science and scientific history – Callum Barrell recovers the depth with which Jeremy Bentham, James Mill, George Grote, and John Stuart Mill thought about history as a site of philosophy and politics. He argues that the utilitarians, contrary to their reputations as ahistorical and even antihistorical thinkers, developed complex frameworks in which to learn from and negotiate the past, inviting us to rethink the foundations of their ideas, as well as their place in – and relationship to – nineteenth-century philosophy and political thought.

CALLUM BARRELL is Associate Professor of Political Thought at New College of the Humanities, Northeastern University. He teaches undergraduate and postgraduate political thought and the history of philosophy.

IDEAS IN CONTEXT

Edited by DAVID ARMITAGE, RICHARD BOURKE and JENNIFER PITTS

The books in this series will discuss the emergence of intellectual traditions and of related new disciplines. The procedures, aims and vocabularies that were generated will be set in the context of the alternatives available within the contemporary frameworks of ideas and institutions. Through detailed studies of the evolution of such traditions, and their modification by different audiences, it is hoped that a new picture will form of the development of ideas in their concrete contexts. By this means, artificial distinctions between the history of philosophy, of the various sciences, of society and politics, and of literature may be seen to dissolve.

A full list of titles in the series can be found at: www.cambridge.org/IdeasContext

HISTORY AND HISTORIOGRAPHY IN CLASSICAL UTILITARIANISM, 1800–1865

CALLUM BARRELL

New College of the Humanities
at Northeastern University

CAMBRIDGE
UNIVERSITY PRESS

Shaftesbury Road, Cambridge CB2 8EA, United Kingdom

One Liberty Plaza, 20th Floor, New York, NY 10006, USA

477 Williamstown Road, Port Melbourne, VIC 3207, Australia

314–321, 3rd Floor, Plot 3, Splendor Forum, Jasola District Centre, New Delhi – 110025, India

103 Penang Road, #05–06/07, Visioncrest Commercial, Singapore 238467

Cambridge University Press is part of Cambridge University Press & Assessment, a department of the University of Cambridge.

We share the University's mission to contribute to society through the pursuit of education, learning and research at the highest international levels of excellence.

www.cambridge.org
Information on this title: www.cambridge.org/9781009001366

DOI: 10.1017/9781009004718

First published 2021
First paperback edition 2023

A catalogue record for this publication is available from the British Library

ISBN   978-1-316-51907-3   Hardback
ISBN   978-1-009-00136-6   Paperback

For Loy

There are only two ways of acquiring knowledge about human affairs – through the perception of the particular, or through abstraction; the latter is the method of philosophy, the former of history.[1]

[1] Leopold von Ranke, 'A fragment from the 1830s' in F. Stern (ed.), *The varieties of history: from Voltaire to the present* (New York: Meridian, 1956), pp. 58–59.

Contents

Acknowledgements

This project began life as a doctoral thesis at Queen Mary University of London in 2011, and I have incurred many debts in the decade since. I must begin with my supervisor, Georgios Varouxakis, whose insights, friendship, and unfailing generosity have been indispensable to the book's completion.

I had not one but two brilliant supervisors. Gareth Stedman Jones encouraged me to undertake a PhD in 2010 and provided invaluable advice that makes even more sense now. Richard Bourke has also been instrumental to my development, and I am thankful for his conversation and guidance.

I have profited from conversations with many people over the years, but special thanks must go to Antis Loizides, who helpfully commented on an early draft; Brian Young; Stuart Jones; my PhD examiners, Philip Schofield and Richard Whatmore; Paul Cartledge, who ignited my passion for the history of philosophy and political thought; Allegra Fryxell, who provided intellectual and moral support; and my colleagues at New College of the Humanities at Northeastern University, especially Diana Bozhilova, A. C. Grayling, David Mitchell, and Christoph Schuringa.

I regret being unable to mention them by name, but my thanks go to the unfailingly helpful archivists at Johns Hopkins University; Yale University; Trinity College, Cambridge; University Library, Cambridge; The Bodleian Library, Oxford; Somerville College, Oxford; The British Library; The London Library; The National Library of Scotland; Senate House Library, University of London; and University College London Library.

I am deeply grateful to Liz Friend-Smith, the Editorial Board, and the anonymous readers who helped to embolden and clarify my ideas. I cannot thank them enough.

Thanks to my friends who suffered the process with me, especially Briony FitzGerald and Pascal Porcheron. Julia Nicholls has been there through all of it, from Cambridge to Queen Mary and beyond.

Leo, Mark, and Peggy have done more for me than they could possibly imagine. This is their book, too. As for my mum, Jan, thanks don't even come close. She is my greatest source of humility, sarcasm, and strength. I am grateful for you all.

Conventions

Footnote Abbreviations

CW: J. S. Mill (eds. J. M. Robson and others), *The collected works of John Stuart Mill* (Toronto: University of Toronto Press, 1963–1991), 33 vols.

CPB: J. Mill (ed. R. A. Fenn), *James Mill's commonplace books* (2010), 5 vols., www.intellectualhistory.net/mill, last accessed on 23 May 2017.

HBI: J. Mill, *The history of British India* [1817] (London: Baldwin, Cradock, and Joy, 1826), 6 vols.

HG: G. Grote, *History of Greece; from the earliest period to the close of the generation contemporary with Alexander the Great* [1846–1856] (Boston: J. P. Jewett & Co, 1851–1857), 12 vols.

Works: J. Bentham (ed. J. Bowring), *The works of Jeremy Bentham* (Edinburgh: William Tait, 1838–1843), 11 vols.

MMO: J. S. Mill (eds. E. D. Pionke and E. A. Wilson), *Mill's marginalia online* (2016), 151 vols., www.millmarginalia.org, last accessed on 1 June 2018.

Transcriptions

I have standardised spelling where possible, except in titles of works where the original is given. Square brackets have been employed to expand on otherwise unclear prose.

Translations

Translations are my own unless otherwise stated. I have allowed my sources to speak in their original language where possible.

Introduction

John Stuart Mill (1806–1873) in his autobiography recalled that 'a voluntary exercise to which I was throughout my boyhood much addicted was
what I called writing histories'. These histories were composed in 'imitation' of his father, James (1773–1836), whose *History of British India* had
been published to widespread acclaim in 1817.[1] Given his reputation as an
abstract moral and political theorist, it is tempting to see John's addiction
to 'writing histories' as a passing phase that precipitated other, more
significant interests for which he is better known today.[2] While some
have read into his essays a rhetoric or doctrine of progress, his philosophy
of history has been reconstructed only sporadically and without the exegetical vigour which his writings otherwise command.[3] Its place in the
intellectual history of utilitarianism is even less clear. John's engagement in
the 1830s and 1840s with Romantic, historicist, and positivist conceptions
of history is usually regarded either as insignificant – to the extent that it
altered only theoretically his approach to political problems – or as something that undermined utilitarianism's deductive simplicity. His attempt
to reconcile utilitarianism with a broadly conceived historicism was thus
either unserious or nonsensical, and in both cases its intellectual significance is called into question.[4] These conclusions, however, leave

---

[1] *CW*, I, p. 28. John Stuart Mill is sometimes referred to as 'John' and James Mill as 'James' to avoid
confusion.
[2] On the tendency to view the utilitarians as 'abstract moral and political theorists', see E. Stokes, *The
English utilitarians and India* (Oxford: Clarendon Press, 1959), p. vii.
[3] One notable exception is the now classic collaboration between Stefan Collini, Donald Winch, and
John Burrow: *That noble science of politics: a study in nineteenth-century intellectual culture*
(Cambridge: Cambridge University Press, 1983). Another is J. M. Robson, *The improvement of
mankind: the social and political thought of John Stuart Mill* (Toronto: University of Toronto Press,
1968).
[4] For example, George Cornewall Lewis (1806–1863) questioned Mill's intention to unite political
theory and history. 'It follows', he concluded, 'that, in the attempt to unite in one work political
history and political theory, both are spoiled': *A treatise on the methods of observation and reasoning in
politics* (London: John W. Parker and Son, 1852), I, p. 315.

I

precariously open the question of why John turned to history as a method and site of politics, and what he hoped to achieve by doing so.

The tendency to treat the utilitarians as abstract theorists has privileged critical over exegetical analysis, because of which commentators have thought either casually or not at all about their intentions in writing formal histories ('historiography') or in developing historical methods and philosophies of history ('history') whose purpose was to inform, frame, accelerate, or slow down politics; and yet, it is only by examining their political thought historically that their commitments to history come fully into view.[5]

In the early nineteenth century, for example, Jeremy Bentham (1748–1832) and James Mill suffered two potent strains of criticism, the first of which came from Whig custodians of the Scottish Enlightenment, and the second from a historically-inflected Romanticism whose disciples included William Hazlitt (1778–1830) and Samuel Taylor Coleridge (1772–1834). In both cases the utilitarians were portrayed as dogmatists who ignored and even disdained the past, and whose inability to draw lessons from experience disqualified them from the kind of empirical science on which their political radicalism was theoretically based. These attacks inspired especially in James and John Stuart Mill, but also in George Grote (1794–1871), a willingness to either reformulate or reconsider the ways in which utilitarianism and its political adjunct, Philosophic Radicalism, addressed themselves to history. A richer understanding of these debates will help to better grasp their intentions as political actors, and to understand more deeply the ways in which they related politics to history, at a time when history acquired new significances as both a means and object of study.

My intention is not to reconstruct a classical utilitarian 'idea' of history comparable to Duncan Forbes's liberal Anglicans' or Herbert Butterfield's Whigs'.[6] To hypostasise their writings into an analytically coherent theory, shorn of historical context, would be to obscure the individual motives which carried them into historical reflection. It is better to treat them individually, and even my use of the term 'utilitarian' has less to do with its

[5] Elijah Millgram recently conceded that context 'tends to go missing', but he persisted anyway with 'the practice of analytic history of philosophy': *John Stuart Mill and the meaning of life* (Oxford: Oxford University Press, 2019), pp. 5, 13. On utilitarianism as a doctrine, see T. Mulgan, *Understanding utilitarianism* (London: Routledge, 2014); M. D. Bayles (ed.), *Contemporary utilitarianism* (New York: Anchor Books, 1968); R. Goodin, *Utilitarianism as a public philosophy* (Cambridge: Cambridge University Press, 1993).
[6] D. Forbes, *The liberal Anglican idea of history* (Cambridge: Cambridge University Press, 1952); H. Butterfield, *The Whig interpretation of history* [1931] (London: W. W. Norton, 1961).

history as an idea than with a network of thinkers – Bentham, Grote, and the two Mills – whose reflections on history emerged out of a shared goal to reform British society and build on utilitarian foundations, however so constructed, a new science of morality and politics. Their writings were often richly intertextual, and their attitudes towards the forms and functions of historical knowledge emerged out of common intellectual heritages and debates. While there is a case for extending my analysis to John Sterling (1806–1844), John Austin (1790–1859), Henry Sidgwick (1838–1900), and John Hill Burton (1809–1881), and perhaps even to Adam Smith (1723–1790), Joseph Priestley (1733–1804), and David Hume (1711–1776), I have limited its scope to a series of intellectual exchanges whose reconstruction does not require me to pronounce on who or what counts as utilitarian. The book's chronology, which stretches from roughly 1800 to 1865, corresponds to the period in which these thinkers developed their historical thought, usually in response to their opponents and each other. If, however, these exchanges were as important as I claim, then why has it taken so long for a study to materialise?

In one sense the answer is obvious: neither Bentham nor his 'direct heir', John, published a work of history that was recognised as such by their contemporaries.[7] It would be easy, therefore, to assume either that their historical interests were irrelevant to their philosophy and political thought, or that they never held such interests in the first place. Bentham's so-called 'ignorance of history' has steadily acquired the status of a truism, despite the dissenting voices of Mary Mack and R. O. Preyer.[8] While John has fared slightly better in this respect, C. W. Bouton argued over fifty years ago that his philosophy of history remains the obscurest feature of his liberalism, a sentiment that has been echoed more recently by John Gibbins and Inder Marwah.[9] Given that neither Bentham nor John wrote formal works of history, it has been assumed that they bequeath little

[7] H. R. West, *An introduction to Mill's utilitarian ethics* (Cambridge: Cambridge University Press, 2004), p. 8. As Stefan Collini put it, 'there weren't many books Mill didn't write. A work of history, however, is a conspicuous absentee': *English pasts: essays in history and culture* (Oxford: Oxford University Press, 1999), p. 138.

[8] A. W. Benn, *The history of English rationalism in the nineteenth century* (London: Longmans and Green, 1906), I, pp. 302–303; M. P. Mack, *Jeremy Bentham: an odyssey of ideas, 1748–1792* (London: Heinemann, 1962), p. 157; R. O. Preyer, *Bentham, Coleridge, and the science of history* (Bochum-Langendreer: Verlag Heinrich Pöppinghaus, 1958), pp. 1, 3.

[9] C. W. Bouton, 'John Stuart Mill on liberty and history', *Western Political Quarterly* 18 (1965), p. 569; J. Gibbins, 'J.S. Mill, liberalism, and progress' in R. Bellamy (ed.), *Victorian liberalism. Nineteenth-century political thought and practice* (London: Routledge, 1990), pp. 91–110; I. S. Marwah, 'Complicating barbarism and civilisation: Mill's complex sociology of human development', *History of Political Thought* 32.2 (2011), pp. 345–366.

to scholars of nineteenth-century historiography whose interests are typically confined to the forms and functions of narrative historical prose, and that they paid little attention to history when forming and expressing their ideas.

This answer, for equally obvious reasons, carries us only so far. It hardly needs pointing out that John's father, James, was a renowned historian of British India about whom an abundance of scholarship has since materialised, or that Grote published a major history of Greece through which he enjoyed lasting fame in Europe and America.[10] Grote in the last decade or so has enjoyed a revival of interest in his political but especially his historical writings, while James's *History of British India* remains a focal point for historiographies of nineteenth-century imperialism.[11] While they have been overshadowed in the literature by the likes of Thomas Carlyle (1795–1881), Thomas Macaulay (1800–1859), James Froude (1818–1894), E. A. Freeman (1823–1892), William Stubbs (1825–1801), and J. R. Green (1837–1883), it would be disingenuous to claim that their contributions to historiography have been entirely overlooked.[12] The problem, rather, is that we do not fully understand the ways in which they related history to other intellectual and political commitments. That they have this in common with Bentham and John provides further grist to my argument.

This book is interested not only in historiography as a mode of political discourse, or how the telling of history can be politically telling, but also in philosophical uses of the past which unveil problems of logic and method. J. G. A. Pocock has persuasively argued that the philosophy of history must be seen as an 'enquiry into the logical character of historical explanation', the outcome of which is not necessarily 'a reproduction or reconstruction' of what historians actually do.[13] Mark Salber Phillips has likewise insisted on a 'liberal definition' of historical writing 'that does not limit us to one or two prestigious genres', or to a 'peculiar kind of present-mindedness that narrows our sense of earlier traditions and flatters the professionalism of our own times with a false sense of its own distinctive accomplishments'.[14] For

[10] E. A. Freeman called Grote's history one of the 'glories of our age and country': *Historical essays* (London: Macmillan and Co, 1873), II, p. 147.
[11] See T. Koditschek, *Liberalism, imperialism, and the historical imagination: nineteenth-century visions of a greater Britain* (Cambridge: Cambridge University Press, 2011), p. 82.
[12] Even so, one recent survey mentions John Stuart Mill and Bentham only briefly, while James Mill and Grote are ignored altogether: A. Tucker (ed.), *A companion to the philosophy of history and historiography* (London: Wiley-Blackwell, 2009).
[13] Quoted in E. A. Clark, *History, theory, text: historians and the linguistic turn* (Cambridge: Harvard University Press, 2004), p. 37.
[14] M. S. Phillips, *Society and sentiment: genres of historical writing in Britain, 1740–1820* (New Jersey: Princeton University Press, 2000), p. xi.

the purposes of this book, therefore, I define historical enquiry elastically as a purposive engagement with the past, which is conducted either formally through the interpretation of historical evidence and the writing of narrative prose (historiography), or informally through the articulation of historical laws, generalisations, and methods (history). These liberalisations will help us to understand the utilitarians on their own terms and in their proper contexts, whereas the tendency at present is to reproduce categories of analysis into which they simply do not fit, especially in histories of historical writing. I will address this literature first before putting into historical perspective their place in nineteenth-century philosophy and political thought.

Historians of historiography have eyes mostly for established conventions of historical writing which can be parsed into the *isms* of conjecturalism, Whiggism, Romanticism, liberalism, and so on, and which further the idea that the past in the nineteenth century was used as a mirror for contemporary fears. Angus Hawkins, for example, has argued that the intellectual 'cross currents' of Malthusianism, evangelicalism, and British and Irish Radicalism produced a 'persistent anxiety' about the future, which, in turn, encouraged 'partisan visions of the past'.[15] I offer three reasons for why the utilitarians do not fit neatly into this picture, and why, in many instances, their historical writings have been completely overlooked. The first corresponds to the extent to which a historian or philosopher of history is considered as representative of a particular mode of thought or 'master narrative'; the second relates to the truth or falsity of the historical argument in question (how it strikes us critically as modern readers); and the third concerns our regard or disregard for the skill of the historian whose work we study.[16]

First, the classical utilitarians have been overshadowed in the literature by the historiographies of nationality which flourished in the early to mid-nineteenth century. R. J. Smith has examined the so-called 'Gothic bequest' in England between 1688 and 1863, while John Burrow has explored nineteenth-century encounters with the English past in the work of Stubbs, Green, Freeman, and Froude.[17] Furthermore,

---

[15] A. Hawkins, *Victorian political culture: 'habits of heart and mind'* (Oxford: Oxford University Press, 2015), pp. 219, 2.

[16] R. Price, 'Historiography, narrative, and the nineteenth century', *Journal of British Studies* 35.2 (1996), p. 220.

[17] R. J. Smith, *The Gothic bequest: medieval institutions in British thought, 1688–1863* (Cambridge: Cambridge University Press, 2002); J. W. Burrow, *A liberal descent: Victorian historians and the English past* (Cambridge: Cambridge University Press, 1981).

Butterfield's research into the germination of 'Whig' historiography continues to influence our understanding of national history in the century's
early decades.[18] These accounts explore the correlation between political,
social, and economic transformation and what T. W. Heyck called the
desire to 'establish continuities with the past' in the search for
a mythologised national identity.[19] On this account, the onset of new
political and social realities, exemplified by radical demographic change,
industrialisation, the French Revolution, and the clamour for domestic
political reform, helps to explain the predominantly national focus of
nineteenth-century historiography.[20] In support of this view we might
point to the growth in the 1770s of a new Saxonist radicalism, led by
Major Cartwright (1740–1824); to the Gothicism of Henry Hallam (1777–
1859), John Allen (1771–1843), and Francis Palgrave (1788–1861); to the
nineteenth-century revival (or, depending on one's view, the survival) of
a 'Burkean' organicism; or, finally, to Macaulay's Whiggish narratives of
progress.

   The connection between history and a mythologised national identity,
rooted in contemporary experiences of political, social, and economic
transformation, remains a salient one, and while it is not my intention to
undermine the enduring importance of these studies, I do want to explain
how, if at all, the utilitarians relate to them. The scholarship repeatedly
attests to history's mythologising purpose, and how, in the early nineteenth
century, the past was used either to affirm or delegitimise existing political
identities and institutional bequests. Michael Bentley has contended that
the past was moved deliberately 'towards the present' to 'show how the
English people came into being and what they can learn from their
journey', while T. N. Baker has claimed that 'nineteenth-century Britons
who investigated the past almost invariably searched it for answers to
contemporary political and social troubles'.[21] The writing of history,

---

[18] See H. Butterfield, *The Englishman and his history* (Cambridge: Cambridge University Press, 1944),
     p. 73.
[19] T. W. Heyck, *The transformation of intellectual life in Victorian England* (London: Cromo Helm,
     1982), pp. 122–123.
[20] See B. Melman, 'Claiming the nation's past: the invention of an Anglo-Saxon tradition', *Journal of
     Contemporary History* 26 (1991), p. 575. According to Reinhart Koselleck, '[h]istoricism's axiom that
     everything in history is singular . . . is the epiphenomenon of the primary experience that ever since
     the French and Industrial Revolutions, history has in fact seemed to be continuously changing at an
     accelerated rate: to this extent, nothing was comparable and everything singular': *Sediments of time:
     on possible histories*, trans. S. Franzel and S. Hoffman (Stanford: Stanford University Press, 2018),
     p. 113.
[21] M. Bentley, *Modernising England's past: English historiography in the age of modernism, 1870–1970*
     (Cambridge: Cambridge University Press, 2005), p. 25; T. N. Baker, 'National history in the age of

therefore, was invariably didactic.[22] Unlike Hume in the previous century, and thanks to the rise of various Romantic and counter-Enlightenment influences, early nineteenth-century readers of history wanted to feel alive in the English past, whether it was the Norman Conquest, the Reformation, or the Glorious Revolution of 1688.[23]

The utilitarians with whom I am concerned rivalled this under-standing of history in at least two ways. First, they criticised the translation of England's contested political origins into an ideology of historical continuity. James Mill, for instance, regarded nationality as a prejudice because it derived political legitimacy from a principle of self-government in which the 'nation' was endowed with an intrin-sic but essentially arbitrary value.[24] The Christian Socialist F. D. Maurice (1805–1872) even reproached the Benthamites for seeing 'national distinctions' as mere deviations from universal specimens, a line of argument that was by no means unique.[25] Whereas John took a more nuanced stance towards the issue of nationality, it was certainly not the case that he intended to use history as a conduit for his own theory of Englishness.[26] He conceded in *Considerations on Representative Government* (1861) that the 'strongest of all is identity of political antecedents; the possession of a national history, and conse-quent community of recollections'; and yet 'none of these circum-stances, however, are either indispensable or necessarily sufficient by themselves'.[27]

Second, the utilitarians disagreed that the past meaningfully reflected the present. Insofar as they have been analysed as historical thinkers, it has been with the assumption that they confronted the past as political actors first and foremost; James's *History of British India* thus becomes a recondite argument for utilitarian civility, while John and Grote's writings on Athens reveal an 'ancient equivalent of the modern British liberal state'.[28] The

Michelet, Macaulay, and Bancroft' in L. Kramer and S. Maza (eds.), *A companion to Western historical thought* (London: Blackwell, 2002), p. 193.
[22] See A. Brundage and R. A. Cosgrove, *British historians and national identity* (London: Routledge, 2014), p. 195.
[23] On Hume and historical distance, see M. S. Phillips, *On historical distance* (New Haven: Yale University Press, 2013), pp. 12–13.
[24] N. Urbinati, 'The many heads of the hydra: J.S. Mill on despotism' in N. Urbinati and A. Zakaras (eds.), *J.S. Mill's political thought: a bicentennial reassessment* (Cambridge: Cambridge University Press, 2007), p. 75n.
[25] Quoted in H. S. Jones, 'The early utilitarians, race, and empire: the state of the argument' in B. Schultz and G. Varouxakis (eds.), *Utilitarianism and empire* (Oxford: Lexington, 2005), p. 179.
[26] See G. Varouxakis, *Mill on nationality* (London: Routledge, 2002).   [27] *CW*, XIX, p. 546.
[28] A. D. Culler, *The Victorian mirror of history* (New Haven: Yale University Press, 1985), p. 18.

utilitarians, however, opposed this present-mindedness with an increasingly stringent historicism; anyone, John argued in 1853, can 'scrawl over the [historical] canvas with the commonplaces of rhetoric or the catchwords of party politics'.[29] They did not simply map onto their respective visions of the past a utilitarian, Radical, or liberal philosophy of history in the hope of adding a sheen of historical legitimacy. Like Hume and Smith in the eighteenth century, they sought to claim the higher ground by dismissing those historians who, through distortions of evidence and feints of rhetoric, defended their party shibboleths.[30] While it is true that almost all historians throughout the eighteenth and early nineteenth centuries appealed to the Tacitean virtues of honesty and impartiality, this should mask neither the sincerity of the utilitarians' method nor the critical paradigms with which they scrutinised texts.[31] That they defined themselves against partisan historiographies is itself an intellectual artefact worthy of recovery, not least because it connects them more strongly to the rise of historicism in hermeneutics, historiography, political science, and jurisprudence – a theme to which I will return shortly.

Our second problem concerns the ways in which scholars criticise and evaluate historiographical approaches. This approach tends to sublimate an author's intentions into a model of historical writing which is then judged according to its perceived merit or veracity; in short, to determine its relevance to our present. Bruce Mazlish has confronted what he saw as the 'present-mindedness' of James's *History*, while Christopher Herbert has claimed that Grote's scientific methodology failed to engender 'a pose of disinterested value-free objectivity' that corresponds to the ways in which we define objectivity today.[32] In a widely celebrated lecture from 1952, for instance, Arnaldo Momigliano alerted his audience to recently discovered evidence of which Grote knew 'practically nothing', and claimed that the 'limits and

---

[29] *CW*, XI, p. 330.

[30] Whereas Viscount Bolingbroke (1678–1751) dismissed 'mere antiquaries and scholars' as 'parting pedants', Hume cautioned against historical prolepsis: 'injustice' and 'violence', he argued, becomes 'in time legal and obligatory', and 'transfers to its predecessors and ancestors that right, which it naturally ascribes to their posterity, as being related together'. H. Bolingbroke, *Letters on the study and use of history* (Basil: J. J. Tourneisen, 1791), p. 35; D. Hume (eds. S. D. Warner and D. W. Livingston), *Political writings* (Indiana: Hackett, 1994), p. 73. Adam Smith issued similar warnings against party-political historians: A. Smith (ed. J. C. Bryce), *Lectures on rhetoric and belles lettres* (Oxford: Oxford University Press, 1983), ii. 40.

[31] See V. E. Pagán, *A companion to Tacitus* (Wiley-Blackwell, 2012), p. 105; L. Okie, *Augustan historical writing: histories of England in the English Enlightenment* (New York: University Press of America, 1991), p. 63.

[32] B. Mazlish, *James and John Stuart Mill. Father and son in the nineteenth century* (London: Hutchinson, 1975), p. 120; C. Herbert, *Victorian relativity: radical thought and scientific discovery* (Chicago: University of Chicago Press, 2001), p. 228.

shortcomings' of Grote's *History* were 'only too obvious' to modern readers.[33] Intellectual history, however, prioritises authorial intent over critical analysis, which means that I am interested less in their arguments' tenability than the contexts in which they developed.

This brings me onto my third problem, which in many ways exemplifies the issues to which I have already alluded. Hayden White's now classic *Metahistory: The Historical Imagination in Nineteenth-Century Europe* (1973) continues to challenge our attitudes towards the functions of historical knowledge, as well as the verbal and aesthetic structures in which historical narratives are produced. However, White's cast of historians was assembled for literary as opposed to historical reasons, effectively deracinating them from their historical contexts. The period between 1821 and 1868, he observed, 'produced the works which still serve as the models of modern historical accomplishment, for professionals and amateurs alike'.[34] White acknowledged that while Grote ought to be remembered as one of 'the great classical historians', he could not lay claim to 'the authority and prestige of the four masters, Michelet, Ranke, Tocqueville, and Burckhardt'.[35] Along with Auguste Comte (1798–1857), Henry Buckle (1821–1862), Ludwig Feuerbach (1804–1872), and others, Grote was dismissed as an anachronism of 'modern historical consciousness'.[36] White was interested less in the epistemic value of nineteenth-century historiography than in its aesthetic endowments to a decidedly modern historical consciousness, of which his 'four masters' were upheld as archetypes.[37]

For these distinct but related reasons, the classical utilitarians have been marginalised by historians of historiography. Their reputation for historical ignorance runs deeper than that, however, and I want to sketch out here some arguments that will recur in the following chapters. The first is that the utilitarians have been accused of reasoning in a historical vacuum, an argument which forms an almost unbroken line of criticism from the early nineteenth to the mid-twentieth centuries, and whose authors include, amongst others, James Mackintosh (1765–1832), Francis Jeffrey (1773–1850), William Hazlitt, Thomas Macaulay, Leslie Stephen (1832–1904), Elie Halévy (1870–1937), and A. A. Mitchell. Halévy argued that 'the

[33] A. Momigliano, 'George Grote and the study of Greek history' (1952) in G. W. Bowersock and T. J. Cornell (eds.), *A. D. Momigliano: studies on modern scholarship* (London: University of California Press, 1994), pp. 25, 27.
[34] H. White, *Metahistory: the historical imagination in nineteenth-century Europe* (Baltimore: Johns Hopkins University Press), p. 140.
[35] Ibid., p. 141.   [36] Ibid.
[37] I am inclined to agree with Salber Phillips that the 'boldness' of *Metahistory* 'also worked against its claim to be considered as a history of historical writing': *Society and sentiment*, p. 9.

idea of a philosophy of history' was 'totally foreign' to the Benthamites, while Mitchell suggested that the utilitarians' neglect of history 'must have been on principle'.[38] The utilitarians, they argued, arrived at political conclusions by reasoning down from universal and thus transhistorical principles, chief amongst which was human nature's abiding governance by pleasure and pain. Writers in the *Edinburgh Review* attacked the utilitarians for arguing, either, that pleasures and pains were relative almost to the point of tautology – to say that one pursues pleasure is to say nothing except that individuals will do what they will do – or, worse, that human beings have universal appetites and aversions whose formation is prior to their experiences in history.

There can be no doubt that the utilitarians rejected on political as well as methodological grounds what they called 'vulgar' appeals to history, the goal of which, they suspected, was to equate political reform with reckless revolution.[39] Bentham positioned the utility principle as a rational alternative to common law in which historical precedents were valued seemingly for their own sake, and whose purpose, therefore, was to serve as an external standard against which all actions could be judged, regardless of where or when they were performed. The same applied to political institutions whose legitimacy stemmed solely from their ancientness. History on its own, Bentham reasoned, could not justify existing political and legal arrangements, let alone anticipate or prescribe the future.[40] This position, I suggest in Chapter 1, can be read as a kind of inverted historicism, as a plea for the past's irreducibleness against those who searched it tirelessly for precedents and customs; and it was from arguably historical premises that Bentham emphasised the differences between past and present, as well as the 'folly of our ancestors'.[41] More important still is the claim, implicit in Bentham's remarks, that arguments from history foment an intractable conservatism towards established institutions. The worship of 'dead men's bones', he opined in *The Book of Fallacies* (written roughly between 1809 and 1811), elicits 'pride, anger, obstinacy, and overbearingness'.[42]

The utilitarians did not ignore history, but they were sceptical about the method of extensive induction as favoured by the philosophic Whigs or

---

[38] E. Halévy (trans. M. Morris), *The growth of Philosophic Radicalism* (London: Faber and Faber, 1972), p. 273; A. A. Mitchell, 'Bentham and his school' in B. C. Parekh (ed.), *Jeremy Bentham: critical assessments* (London: Routledge, 1993), I, p. 301.

[39] For John's comments, see *CW*, I, pp. 89–137.

[40] J. Bentham (eds. J. H. Burns and H. L. A. Hart), *An introduction to the principles and morals of legislation* (Oxford: Oxford University Press, 2005), p. 11.

[41] J. Bentham (ed. P. Schofield), *The book of fallacies* (Oxford: Oxford University Press, 2015), p. 170.

[42] Ibid., p. 144.

'Whig Conservatives'.[43] They were clear that history required complementary or even controlling principles drawn from other fields of knowledge – usually psychology and philosophy – if it was to help discriminate between good and bad arrangements. They did not theorise into thin air the differences between one society and another, but nor did they offer prescriptions for specific times and places; and while they refused to appeal normatively to historical precedents, traditions, and customs, it is wrong to argue that they comprehensively rejected history. The past, they acknowledged, helps us to understand why we behave in the ways that we do; why certain civilisations developed in certain ways instead of others; and how, at any given point in a society's development, utility can be introduced for its benefit and progress.

This is not to justify their 'rigid' civilisational hierarchies, or to disconnect their historical vocabularies from a distinctly liberal imperialism which deprecated non-European cultures.[44] That they saw themselves as engaged in a more sophisticated enterprise, rooted not in ignorance but in consultation of history, is to say nothing of their successes or failures in doing so. My contribution, rather, is to situate their views on historical difference (as they did) within fundamental questions of theory, method, and logic. Consider, for example, their prevalent but widely overlooked distinction between matter and form. Forms were universal but their matter was not, and it was the philosopher's business, they argued, to discriminate effectively between the two. Differences in matter – the actual substance of laws and institutions – far exceeded correspondences in form: beyond a 'few capital points', Grote argued, the world 'is all peculiarity and diversity: on which each age and each national clings to tenets of its own'.[45] The challenge, therefore, was to elaborate a moral and political science that could negotiate historical difference without fatally succumbing to it.

The utilitarians were not alone in this pursuit. Romantic critics, including Coleridge, attempted to balance political principles with historical diversity.[46] They conscripted Vico (1688–1744) and the relevant strands of German historicism into the war against the eighteenth century, whose prosecution

[43] George Grote to John Austin, February 1838: H. Grote, *The Philosophic Radicals of 1832* (London: Savill and Edwards, 1866), p. 41.
[44] Inder Marwah has acknowledged increasing disillusionments with utilitarianism for precisely this reason. John's conception of historical diversity, he countered, was richer than his critics have supposed: *Liberalism, diversity, and domination: Kant, Mill, and the government of difference* (Cambridge: Cambridge University Press, 2019), pp. 1, 2, 4, 5.
[45] G. Grote (ed. A. Bain), *Fragments on ethical subjects* (London: John Murray, 1876), p. 18.
[46] See P. Edwards, *The statesman's science: history, nature, and law in the political thought of Samuel Taylor Coleridge* (New York: Columbia University Press, 2004), p. 157.

rested on an overstated if not entirely false distinction between a mechanical utilitarianism and a modern, anti-Enlightenment historical consciousness.[47] Paul Hamilton has pithily summarised Vico's intentions as the desire to evolve a 'new science which could accommodate historical variety without the loss of principle', and who, in John's words, 'conceived the succession of historical events as subject to fixed laws, and endeavoured to discover these laws by an analytical survey of history'.[48] Both the utilitarians and their Romantic opponents were faced with what Stefan Collini, Donald Winch, and Stefan Collini have called the 'time-honoured' problem of separating historical essences from accidents: time-honoured, because it can be read backwards into the Scottish, French, and German Enlightenments; forwards into mid-century debates about the science of history and historical methods of politics; and forwards again into the battles between Austin's analytic jurisprudence and Henry Maine's (1822–1888) legal historicism.[49] While they met this challenge in radically different ways, the fault lines between the utilitarians' approach to history and the Romantic counter-Enlightenments have been too clumsily sketched, determined, more often than not, by the Romantics' misrepresentation of and perceived emancipation from the eighteenth century.

The philosophic Whigs, no less than the Romantics, exaggerated their differences with the utilitarians to consolidate their political positions, and, more importantly, to discredit the Philosophic Radicals' push for reform in the years leading up to 1832. The utilitarians, like the Whigs, claimed the virtues of a slow, cautious empiricism whose methods could be traced back to Bacon and Newton. That was why Macaulay in the 1820s and 1830s attacked James, successfully but unfairly, for privileging theory above practice and the phantoms of scholasticism above concrete historical experience. James, like Bentham in the *Book of Fallacies*, denied the opposition between theory and practice because he saw their relationship as logically apodictic; the issue was whether the theory was formed cautiously and well, or rashly and erroneously.[50] Theory, the utilitarians agreed, was inescapable because it served as a compass with which to navigate our individual and collective experiences, including historical events lacking in direct evidence. As Bentham put it, the necessity of

---

[47] D. Forbes, '*Historismus* in England', *The Cambridge Journal* 14 (1951), p. 396. See also A. McCalla, 'Romantic Vicos: Vico and providence in Michelet and Ballanche', *Réflexions historiques* 19.3 (1993), pp. 389–408.
[48] *CW*, VIII, p. 913; P. Hamilton, *Historicism* (London: Routledge, 2003), p. 30.
[49] Collini, Winch, and Burrow, *That noble science of politics*, p. 148.
[50] J. Mill, 'Theory and practice: a dialogue', *The London and Westminster Review* 25 (1836), p. 223.

'general principles' meant that there can be no 'good foundation for the opposition betwixt Theory and Practise [sic]'.[51] Without theory, he argued, we are liable to mistake origins for reasons.

The utilitarians' reputation as theorists who privileged universal principles above historical evidence was largely a polemical construction, and this construction masked the nuances of their historical thought, as well as their proximity to other thinkers and discourses. The Whigs exaggerated the tension between Bentham's professed empiricism (which relied on history) and his rationalism (which did not), while even sympathetic Romantics like Sterling turned to Niebuhr's historicist *History of Rome* (1812) as a way out of 'the slough of Benthamism'.[52] These polemical oppositions, between a cautious Whig empiricism and a trite utilitarian rationalism, and again between an ahistorical utilitarianism and a historically rich Romanticism, have provided the focal points for much of the commentary; and while the utilitarians may have failed to successfully mediate between general principles and actual historical events – a failure best illustrated by John's abandoned science of ethology – the problem was neither uniquely theirs nor limited to historical writing. John, for example, reasoned that political economy did not presume to reflect human beings' actual behaviour in observable social conditions. As with other social sciences, it prioritised certain aspects of human experience and proceeded hypothetically from there. It deduced from the principle of economic self-interest the likely effects of pursuing such a goal, but it did not assert that human beings always acted in this way. Theory was a prism, not a mirror. It strove to refract rather than simply reflect human experiences, in the hope of revealing something that simple observation could not.[53]

Karl Marx (1818–1883) had no truck with this logic when he traduced 'the arch-Philistine, Jeremy Bentham, that insipid, pedantic, leather-tongued oracle' for assuming that the parochial interests of the typical English shopkeeper accounted for all of human nature in times 'past, present, and future'.[54] Marx criticised Bentham for believing that human nature was impervious to modification by material forces, and that one type of person could serve even hypothetically as a model for the rest. This critique, or versions of it, remains popular among critics of liberal

---

[51] J. Bentham, 'Bentham papers', University College London Library, box 97, f. 5.
[52] Quoted in Forbes, '*Historismus* in England', p. 394.
[53] For analysis, see Collini, Winch, and Burrow, *That noble science of politics*, p. 136.
[54] K. Marx (ed. F. Engels, trans. S. Moore and E. Aveling), *Capital* [1867] (New York: International, 1967), I, p. 609n.

individualism, who, like Marx in *Das Kapital* (1867), reprimand the utilitarians for lifting individuals out of history and out of culture, reconstituting them, in turn, as *homines economici*.[55] But it was John, ironically, who raised the most serious and immediate objections to Bentham's conception of human nature. In an anonymous appendix to Edward Bulwer-Lytton's *England and the English* (1833), he questioned Bentham's assumption that 'mankind are alike [sic] in all times and all places . . . [and] that if the same institutions do not suit them, it is only because in the more backward stages of improvement they have not wisdom to see what institutions are most for their good'.[56] This comment must be taken at face value, first, because John toned down his criticism elsewhere, and, second, because it misrepresents Bentham's actual position (see Chapter 1). It is more profitable to ask why John chose to depict Bentham in this way and to reconstitute the contexts in which he did so.

One explanation lies in John's peculiar understanding of utility, which, in certain fundamental respects, differed from Bentham's own. John in *On Liberty* (1859) redefined utility as that which furthers the 'permanent interests of man [considered] as a progressive being'.[57] According to John Rawls, this implied 'the possibility of a more or less continual improvement in human civilisation, arriving finally at the normal and natural state of society as one of full equality'.[58] The introduction of 'progressiveness' to the principle of utility suggests that John strove to redress a perceived imbalance in Bentham's thinking, in which historical diversity played second fiddle to a world-levelling jurisprudence. John in his essay on Bentham from 1838 seemed to anticipate this view. In it he argued that Bentham was largely oblivious to the historical processes which animated the work of his near contemporaries, including Claude Helvétius (1715–1771).[59] He returned to this line of criticism in 1852 when he asked whether Bentham had in fact overlooked 'what Dr. Whewell calls the historical element of legislation' as an accessory of jurisprudence.[60]

However, John in subsequent writings defended Bentham not just from the charges levelled against him by Whewell, but also from the charges which he himself had levelled against Bentham in the appendix to Lytton's volume from 1833. Mill in his 1838 essay argued that Bentham had never

[55] See, for example, C. W. R. Fitzgerald, 'Needs and wants: an ontological or historical problem?' in C. W. R. Fitzgerald (ed.), *Human needs and politics* (Oxford: Pergamon Press, 1977), p. 29.
[56] *CW*, X, p. 16.   [57] Ibid., XVIII, p. 224.
[58] J. Rawls (ed. S. Freeman), *Lectures on the history of political philosophy* (Cambridge: Harvard University Press, 2007), p. 301.
[59] *CW*, X, p. 110.   [60] Ibid., p. 195.

intended to propose 'one uniform suit of ready-made laws' to suit all times and places, while in the later essay from 1852 he claimed that an attentiveness to the origins of laws did not change 'what was desirable to be done, but only what could be done'.[61] Bentham may have been only passingly familiar with history, but this did not mean that he was wholly insensitive to historical and cultural differences, or that his inability to explain laws' origin and evolution undermined his case for reform. But John's ambiguity is striking. If a fuller understanding of the past had almost no bearing on what needed to be done, then what was its value? What did it mean to bring history meaningfully into jurisprudence, ethics, and politics? How could Bentham be blind to history and at the same time untouched by his blindness? The problem, once again, is that we do not fully understand how the utilitarians drew and redrew – and constructed logical bridges between – the boundary between historical explanation and normative judgement.

This raises additional questions. How serious was John's attempt to make utilitarianism more substantively historical, in the light of the attacks made on Bentham and his father? His historicism in the 1830s and 1840s was both methodological and ontological, in the sense that he conceptualised man as a historical being whose character was shaped by the laws of progress. He agreed with Comte that we must devise appropriately historical methods if we are to fulfil the promise of positive sociology, but the legacy of this commitment is unclear. What did John's concessions to historicism, Romanticism, and positivism ultimately amount to, and what are we to make of the claims made by Sidgwick and others that, by the late 1850s and early 1860s, he had reverted to a method of direct deduction in which history was overtaken by psychology and abstract political theory? What does this say about the relationship between the utilitarians' political logic and the rise in Germany, France, and Britain of an increasingly prominent but variegated historicism? In response to these questions I wish to outline three additional arguments, after which I will briefly explain the book's structure.

The first recovers the utilitarians' indebtedness to the enlightened historicisms of the eighteenth century.[62] This oversight may have

---

[61] Ibid., pp. 104, 196.

[62] Jonathan Knudsen contrasted historicism with a 'one-dimensional and shallow utilitarianism', while Mark Bevir recently argued that although historicism was 'unquestionably dominant throughout the Victorian era, there were alternatives ... [one of which] was the utilitarian tradition': J. Knudsen, 'The historicist Enlightenment' in K. M. Baker and P. Reill (eds.), *What's left of Enlightenment? A postmodern question* (Stanford: Stanford University Press, 2001), p. 39;

something to do with historicism's 'troublesome semantic ambiguity', but
it also has something to do with the sources of the utilitarians' reputation.[63]
We have too readily agreed with their critics that utility was systematically
ahistorical, when in fact it was circumstantially and thus historically
relative. This is significant for a number of reasons, not least because it
reinforces the increasingly accepted view that the eighteenth-century
Enlightenments had historicist proclivities of their own and cannot, therefore, be separated neatly from the Romantic and historicist counter-
Enlightenments.

While Grote and John were more deeply cognisant of German developments in hermeneutics, historiography, and philology, Bentham was
also enduringly sceptical of legal and political essences, and he drew on
the likes of Montesquieu (1689–1755) and Cesare Beccaria (1738–1794) to
develop a critical jurisprudence that accommodated variations in time
and space.[64] Furthermore, his arguments against transcendent political
fictions – natural law, sociability, the social contract – issued from
arguably historical premises, and he repeatedly attempted to integrate
history into a systematic moral, legal, and political science. An attentiveness to history, therefore, was not something that was added to utilitarianism later by Grote or John. It was there from the beginning, and this
partly explains why the utilitarians experimented freely with other historical approaches, from Scottish philosophical history and Romanticism
to German historicism and Comtean positivism.

It is important not to obscure the differences between the utilitarians
and the various historicists from whom they took inspiration, or to
characterise all of their historical undertakings as paradigmatically
historicist.[65] Even so, scholars have too readily presented utilitarianism
and historicism as parallel rather than intersecting lines.[66] The problem is

M. Bevir, 'Historicism and the human sciences in Victorian Britain' in M. Bevir (ed.), *Historicism and the human sciences in Victorian Britain* (Cambridge: Cambridge University Press, 2017), p. 17.
[63] J. Burrow, 'Historicism and social evolution' in B. Stuchtey and P. Wende (eds.), *British and German historiography 1750–1950: traditions, perceptions, and transfers* (Oxford: Oxford University Press, 2000), p. 251. See also J. Kent Wright, 'History and historicism' in T. M. Porter and D. Ross (eds.), *The Cambridge history of science: the modern social sciences* (Cambridge: Cambridge University Press, 2003), p. 114.
[64] See, for example, J. P. Cléro, 'Bentham et Montesquieu', *Revue Française d'histoire des idées politiques* 35 (2012), pp. 171–182.
[65] Furthermore, nineteenth-century historicism did not achieve a total victory over other forms of historical enquiry: B. W. Young, 'History' in Bevir (ed.), *Historicism and the human sciences*, p. 154.
[66] For a classic account, see F. Meinecke, *Historism: the rise of a new historical outlook* (New York: Herder and Herder, 1972), pp. liv–lxi. See also O. G. Oexle, *Geschichtswissenschaft im Zeichen des Historismus: Studien zu Problemgeschichten der Moderne* (Göttingen: Vandenhoeck and Ruprecht,

aggravated by the need to define historicism without smoothing over its historical ambiguities, or without prioritising certain strands above others. It has deep interweaving roots in German philology, hermeneutics, and Biblical exegesis; nominalist and naturalist philosophy; histories *raisonnée* and *approfondie*; Vico's humanist historiography in the *Scienza Nuova* (1725); and Montesquieu's *De l'esprit des lois* (1748), to take a few examples.[67] Since it cannot be regarded as a coherent intellectual tradition, Frederick Beiser has suggested that our working definition must be commodious and fairly general, if we are to negotiate its often stark internal differences (between, for example, Whig, Romantic, and positivist historicism).[68]

With this in mind, I wish to follow Peter Reill in suggesting that the tenets of historicism were minimally twofold: the first stressed the past's individuality and uniqueness – and the importance of reconstituting that uniqueness *wie es eigentlich gewesen* – and the second offered an idea of development whose full-blooded pursuit sat in tension with, and perhaps even contradicted, the first.[69] This tension, between the animating principles of uniqueness and development, gives context to some enduring complexities in the utilitarians' thought, and those complexities further enrich our understanding of nineteenth-century historicism. Reill and others have rightly disabused the idea, for which Karl Popper is partly responsible, that historicism's intellectual essence resided in one rather than both of those principles, and that its 'metaphysical theories' of development made a nonsense out of 'vastly dissimilar' conditions.[70] John saw things differently. His combination of historical relativism (Chapter 5) and universal history (Chapter 6) may have been intellectually unstable – if we're thinking philosophically – but it was also deliberate, and this further consolidates Reill's and others' revisionism. It also loses much

1996), p. 98; E. Fuchs, 'Conceptions of scientific history in the nineteenth-century west' in E. Wang and G. G. Iggers (eds.), *Turning points in historiography: a cross-cultural perspective* (Rochester: University of Rochester Press, 2002), p.148; R. D'Amico, 'Historicism' in Tucker (ed.), *Companion to the philosophy of history and historiography*, pp. 243–253; G. G. Iggers, 'Historicism: the history and meaning of the term', *Journal of the History of Ideas* 56.1 (1995), pp. 129–152.

[67] Beiser, *The German historicist tradition*, pp. 256–257. See also P. H. Reill, 'Barthold Georg Niebuhr and the Enlightenment tradition', *German Studies Review* 3 (1980), pp. 9–26; H. P. Liebel, 'The Enlightenment and the rise of historicism in German thought', *Eighteenth-Century Studies* 4.4 (1971), pp. 359–385.

[68] F. C. Beiser, 'Historicism' in M. Rosen and B. Leiter (eds.), *The Oxford handbook of continental philosophy* (Oxford: Oxford University Press, 2009), p. 159.

[69] P. H. Reill, *The German Enlightenment and the rise of historicism* (Berkeley: University of California Press, 1975), p. 214. See also G. G. Iggers, *The German conception of history: the national tradition of historical thought from Herder to the present* (Connecticut: Wesleyan University Press, 1968), p. 29.

[70] K. Popper, *The poverty of historicism* [1957] (London: Routledge, 2004), p. 102.

of its strangeness when we consider historicism's intellectual continuities with the eighteenth century, where we also find seemingly paradoxical commitments to the past's uniqueness and the laws of its progress. The intellectual histories of utilitarianism and historicism, when placed in their formative eighteenth-century contexts, were more delicately entwined than commentators have acknowledged.

My second argument traces the shifting boundaries between history, politics, and philosophy. These boundaries were porous but not equally or consistently so.[71] John's conception of progress, for example, is often seen to have permeated 'the political' as a distinct field of study.[72] While they agreed unanimously with Hume that we must detach the political 'ought' from the historical 'is', and agreed, therefore, that history lacked a normative apparatus of its own (i.e., utility), they otherwise disagreed on the logical boundaries between the historical and the political. My reading of their work suggests two camps, in the first of which I place Bentham and Grote (and perhaps also Austin, Burton, and Sidgwick), both of whom conceptualised historical and political enquiry as methodologically distinct but complementary enterprises. 'These are two distinct lines of enquiry', Grote argued, 'which may be pursued separately, and which ought not to be confounded'.[73] This demarcation made history the invaluable accessory of political science, whereas in the second camp, in which I place James and John Stuart Mill, the division of labour was intentionally less clear-cut. James spoke about history as the real business of philosophy, while John in *A System of Logic* (1843) appeared to collapse politics into a philosophy of human progress, a move that caused difficulties and no shortage of criticism.

My final argument recovers the critical paradigms with which the utilitarians theorised and practised history, and with which they developed an indigenous language of historical objectivity. This language appealed to the usual Tacitean virtues of impartiality, but it was specifically elicited by the utilitarians' reflections on the recovery, examination, and presentation of historical texts. Its distinguishing feature, I claim, was an analogy between the historian and the judge. Leslie Stephen in his classic work

---

[71] These disciplines (as academic disciplines) crystallised later in the century with the growth of institutional and professional bodies: S. M. den Otter, 'The origins of a historical political science in late Victorian and Edwardian Britain' in R. Adcock, M. Bevir, and S. C. Stimson (eds.), *Modern political science: Anglo-American exchanges since 1880* (Princeton: Princeton University Press, 2007), pp. 37–66.

[72] See Collini, Winch, and Burrow, *That noble science of politics*, p. 129.

[73] Grote, *Fragments on ethical subjects*, p. 31.

went as far as to argue that Grote's 'model history ... embodied the utilitarian spirit' because it 'resembled an ideal judge investigating evidence in a trial'.[74] Bentham in his published and unpublished writings made explicit connections between the 'historiographer' and the judge, both of whom resisted easy didacticism by dispassionately scrutinising evidence. James's *History of British India* made an almost identical argument, while Grote and John co-opted the analogy into a critical idiom which borrowed heavily from German *Historismus*.

The book is loosely chronological and proceeds thinker by thinker. This allows me to recover their similarities and differences whilst remaining sensitive to their individual contexts and intentions. The chapters are organised around the arguments listed above, but different thinkers require different kinds of analysis; in the chapters on James and Grote, for instance, my analysis is more substantively exegetical because they wrote multi-volume histories whose arguments repay close attention. Their writings on the methods of historical enquiry must be accompanied by a study of those methods in action. Likewise, John's writings on history and historiography are spread across three chapters because he thought the most extensively about historical criticism; the logic of historical explanation; and history's place in a comprehensive social science. This decision is further justified by John's role in shaping the utilitarians' legacy. He was a feverish commentator on the others' work, and he set out to redress the shortcomings of the utilitarian method as laid bare by the philosophic Whigs.

The chapters are organised into three parts. Part I, 'Enlightened Historicisms', situates Bentham and James within eighteenth-century views on historical difference.[75] Part II, 'Historicism and Historiography', relates John's and Grote's historiography to German historicism and early-nineteenth century ideas of historical uniqueness. Part III, 'Sciences of History', claims that these ideas, for John and other historicists, coexisted with – rather than contradicted – the pursuit of historical laws and universal histories of progress.

The chapters are structured as follows. Chapter 1 examines contemporary responses to utilitarianism as a political tradition, and, contrary to accepted wisdom, argues that Bentham's theory of utility was circumstantially and thus historically relative. Chapter 2 reappraises James's logic of historical

---

[74] L. Stephen, *The English utilitarians* [1900] (London: Continuum, 2005), III, p. 338.
[75] This phrase is indebted to Bevir, who regarded Ferguson and Smith as 'Enlightenment historicists': 'Historicism and the human sciences in Victorian Britain', p. 4.

explanation, which has been widely misunderstood by nineteenth- and twentieth-century commentators. It takes seriously his praise of David Hume's *History of England* (1754–1761) and argues that, as a keen reader of Francis Bacon (1561–1626), James tried to narrow the gap between theory (as philosophy) and practice (as history). Chapter 3 explores the nexus between politics and historicism in Grote's *History of Greece* (1846–1856) and, using his unpublished and lesser known writings, recovers the ways in which he used the past to reassess longstanding utilitarian assumptions about liberty, obligation, and happiness; these interventions, I suggest, help to more fully comprehend his historicism and *vice versa*. Chapters 4, 5, and 6 are devoted to John, in accordance with the three interconnected perspectives from which he approached the study of history. The first offered a progressive theory of historical criticism; the second outlined the principles of historical relativism; and the third (and least acknowledged) drew on a resurgent French tradition of universal history. Mill's historical writings, I argue, championed both an individualising and a progressive historicism, in keeping with the arguments outlined above. The conclusion addresses these arguments to utilitarianism's intellectual history, complicating the frequently polemical – and, indeed, aesthetic – divide between the eighteenth and nineteenth centuries.

PART I

Enlightened Historicisms

CHAPTER I

Jeremy Bentham on Historical Authority

The Historical Bentham

Our business is not with antiquities but with jurisprudence. The past is of no value but by the influence it preserves over the present and the future. ... Let us reflect that our first concern is to learn, how the things that are in our power *ought to be.*[1]

Jeremy Bentham is never thought of as a historian, or as a thinker who expressed an interest in the origins and growth of political society. He dedicated much of his life to the development of a *pannomion*, a complete judicial code with which he intended to reform civil, procedural, and constitutional law. His ambition intensified in the late 1770s and persisted until his death in 1832. The codification project was vast in scope and cosmopolitan in outlook. Its central goal was to elaborate 'un corps de loix complet' in which citizens could determine their political and moral obligations through rationally explicable laws.[2] The principle of utility, whose philosophical origins could be traced to Beccaria, Hume, Helvétius, and William Paley (1743–1805), was to do precisely that by enabling a systematic theory of jurisprudence and ethics with a view to practical application. Given the comprehensiveness of Bentham's intended reforms, it is unsurprising that Duncan Forbes, Michael Oakeshott, R. G. Collingwood, Herbert Butterfield, and others have identified Bentham's thought as a paradigm of Enlightenment rationalism whose outlook was fundamentally unhistorical, unburdened by the sorts of commitments made by 'Burkean' organicists and Whigs, or, later,

---

[1] J. Bentham (eds. J. H. Burns and H. L. A. Hart), *A comment on the Commentaries and A fragment on government* (Oxford: Oxford University Press, 1977), p. 314.
[2] See D. Armitage, 'Globalising Jeremy Bentham', *History of Political Thought* 32.1 (2011), pp. 63–82; E. de Champs, *Enlightenment and utility: Bentham in French, Bentham in France* (Cambridge: Cambridge University Press, 2015), p. 4.

by Romantics, historicists, and Coleridgean idealists.[3] This interpretation, which I offer up for reassessment, has cast a long shadow over
Bentham's political thought and the Benthamite tradition, and in this
section, I wish to examine in greater depth the reasons for its persistence.

The publication in 1776 of *A Fragment on Government*, followed by the
appearance in 1778 of *A View of the Hard-Labour Bill*, marked Bentham's
emergence as a political and legal reformer. The *Fragment* was an offshoot
of an extensive but unfinished commentary on William Blackstone's
Commentaries on the Laws of England (1765–1769), which was published
posthumously in 1928 as *A Comment on the Commentaries* and only recently
recomposed by Bentham's present-day editors. In those works, Bentham
attacked natural and common law theorists for illegitimately using
history.[4] If natural law was a historical phantom which manufactured
political authority out of nowhere, then common law facilitated the
abuse of historical precedents by lawyers, judges, and political representatives who conflated historical authority with rational judgement.[5] His
critique of Blackstone (1723–1780) memorably dismissed the 'trammels of
authority and ancestor-wisdom' as burdens on the shoulders of the living –
as the dead weight of history.[6] Elsewhere, he reduced to logical and
political absurdity the 'mechanical veneration for antiquity' that was so
common to his contemporaries, excoriating Blackstone for believing that
'everything is as it should be'.[7] This withering contempt for custom, which
extended beyond his critical jurisprudence to his theory of government and
ethics, was almost certainly indebted to Helvétius, whose posthumous
Treatise on Man called for a 'reformation in manners, laws, and government', even though it may 'displease old men, those that are weak and
slaves to custom'.[8]

Ross Harrison has argued that Bentham's opposition to common law,
and all *lex non scripta*, reflected his belief that arguments from history were
fundamentally opposed to reason, and that historical truths were categorically distinct from the necessary truths of reason. The purpose of critical

---

[3] For analysis, see Preyer, *Bentham, Coleridge, and the science of history*, p. 1. As an example, see
R. G. Collingwood, *Speculum mentis* (Oxford: Clarendon Press, 1924), p. 172.

[4] Bentham, *A comment on the Commentaries*, p. 195. The natural law tradition of Grotius, Pufendorf,
and Burlamaqui was 'an obscure phantom' that confused 'manners' with what the law should be: *An
introduction to the principles and morals of legislation*, p. 298n.

[5] R. Harrison, *Bentham* (London: Routledge, 1983), p. 175.   [6] Bentham, *Works*, I, p. 260n.

[7] Bentham, *A comment on the Commentaries*, pp. 399, 201. See R. A. Posner, 'Blackstone and Bentham',
The Journal of Law and Economics 19.3 (1976), pp. 569–606.

[8] C. Helvétius (trans. W. Hooper), *A treatise on man: his intellectual faculties and his education*
(London: Albion Press, 1810), II, p. 336.

jurisprudence was to scrutinise all authorities that were unaccountable to the external standard of utility, including what Harrison called 'mere history'. To perceive 'something to be good, more is needed than the fact that it has sometimes, or even always, happened in that way'.[9] As Bentham remarked in *Defence of Usury* (1787), 'it is one thing to justify a law' but another thing entirely 'to account for its existence'.[10] His objection to arguments from history can therefore be seen as a part of an on-going attempt to demystify the law through legal codification, whose principles were to be determined not by historical accidents but by their timeless utility.

Utility was timeless to the extent that human nature was empirically consistent; as he put it in an early manuscript, it is more profitable to dive 'at once unto the recesses of the human understanding with Locke, and with Helvétius' than to wander 'the maze of history in search of particular facts'.[11] It is plausible, then, that Bentham's utilitarianism was not a theory in which legal, moral, or political issues could be worked out historically, still less a doctrine in which the past assumed a normative or even rhetorical significance; indeed, the happiness principle took as its measure of right and wrong the 'greatest happiness of the greatest number' of living or future persons, and within this framework there could be no place for the prejudicial ties of custom, or, as John Burrow put it, for pasts 'untouchable by the reforming hand'.[12] Bentham in the *Introduction to the Principles and Morals of Legislation* (1789, hereafter referred to as *IPML*) and *The Book of Fallacies* made this point in typically grandiloquent terms: we must not, he argued, sacrifice 'the real interests of the living to the imaginary interests of the dead'.[13]

History disclosed neither our present and future obligations nor the rational truths which made possible a systematically utilitarian body of law. It would be amiss, however, to mark out Bentham as uniquely sceptical about history's political and legal functions. He would have been aware of Aristotle's distinction in the *Poetics* between philosophical and historical knowledge, and of Hobbes's suggestion in *Leviathan* (1651) that the

[9] Harrison, *Bentham*, p. 175. See also H. L. A. Hart, *Essays on Bentham: studies in jurisprudence and political theory* (Oxford: Clarendon Press, 1982), pp. 21–40; D. Lieberman, *The province of legislation determined* (Cambridge: Cambridge University Press, 1989), pp. 219–240.

[10] Bentham, *Works*, III, p. 15.

[11] 'Bentham papers', University College London Library, box 27, f. 95.

[12] Bentham, *A comment on the Commentaries*, p. 393. See also J. Burrow, *Evolution and society: a study in Victorian social theory* (Cambridge: Cambridge University Press, 1966), p. 41; P. Schofield, *Bentham: a guide for the perplexed* (London: Continuum, 2009), p. 105.

[13] Bentham, *Book of fallacies*, p. 174.

historical origin of states, or whatever 'examples may be drawn out of history', had no place in a deductive science of politics.[14] Even Edmund Burke (1729–1797), whose political theory made allowances for 'the stable prejudice of time', or practically formed habits, argued in 1791 that one 'can never plan the future by the past'.[15] Bentham was distinguished, perhaps, by the vehemence with which he criticised arguments from custom, but this did not amount to a political, moral, or legal science which proclaimed independence from the past. As with Locke in his *Essay Concerning Human Understanding* (1689), Bentham was only too aware that legal and political authorities were typically derived from custom and reinforced by habit, and that legislators must take into account society's attachment to existing laws and institutions.[16] Why, then, have scholars argued that Bentham was both an *anti-historical* thinker, that is, someone who rejected arguments from historical authority, and an *ahistorical* thinker, that is, someone whose philosophy failed to engage with the events of the past and interpretations thereof?[17] In search of an answer it is useful to examine the political contexts in which Bentham articulated and disseminated his ideas, especially from the 1790s onwards, a period in which representations of the past became freshly significant in the wake of the French Revolution.

Elie Halévy and Bertrand Russell argued that Bentham's conversion to political radicalism during 1809–1810 marked a significant turning point in his career.[18] This is undoubtedly true, although his affinities with political reform date back further to a brief period in which he supported the revolutionary cause in France, from 1789 to 1790.[19] Melissa Lane has argued that Bentham, like the Jacobins and the Paineite Radicals, wanted to

[14] See S. Carli, 'Poetry is more philosophical than history: Aristotle on *mimêsis* and form', *The Review of Metaphysics* 64.2 (2010), pp. 303–326; T. Hobbes (ed. R. Tuck), *Leviathan* (Cambridge: Cambridge University Press, 1996), p. 373.

[15] E. Burke, *The works of the Right Honourable Edmund Burke* (London: Henry G. Bohn, 1856), VI, p. 33; II, p. 557.

[16] Boyd Hilton has argued that Bentham 'was aware that much knowledge about the world is handed down from generation to generation and serves to guide conduct much of the time': *A mad, bad, and dangerous people? England 1783–1846* (Oxford: Oxford University Press, 2006), p. 330.

[17] J. H. Burns, 'The light of reason: philosophical history in the two Mills' in J. Robson and M. Laine (eds.), *James and John Stuart Mill/Papers of the centenary conference* (Toronto: Toronto University Press, 1976), p. 3. Wilfried Nippel recently claimed that Bentham 'was not really very interested in history . . . as a resource for experience and argument': *Ancient and modern democracy: two concepts of liberty?* (Cambridge: Cambridge University Press, 2015), p. 251.

[18] See M. Mack, *Jeremy Bentham: an odyssey of ideas 1748–1792* (London: Heinemann, 1962), pp. 17, 416, 432–440.

[19] See J. R. Dinwiddy, 'Bentham's transition to political radicalism, 1809–10', *Journal of the History of Ideas* 36.4 (1975), pp. 683–700; J. H. Burns, 'Bentham and the French Revolution', *Transactions of the Royal Historical Society* 16 (1966), pp. 95–114.

liberate the future from 'the benighted imposters of the past'.[20] Drawing on his *Anarchical Fallacies*, which were composed between 1795 and 1796, Lane suggested that for Bentham the 'authority of rational judgment invokes a tolerably though not necessarily absolutely predictable sense of the future, in order to banish the dead hand of the past', and that he shared with Thomas Paine (1737–1809) a contempt for Burke's slavishly historical politics.[21] But his views on the revolution quickly shifted, and he accused the revolutionaries of prioritising political liberty above the proper ends of government, which were security and equality.[22] In a series of three rudiment sheets from 1795, he distanced himself from their 'absurd and dangerous' proposals but kept up his attack on Burke, whose *Reflections on the Revolution in France* (1790) subjugated 'the well-informed to the ill-informed *ages*'.[23] Perhaps this serves as a litmus test of Bentham's views on history, because even in his most virulently anti-Jacobin writings, he denounced the pious traditionalism with which Burke invoked *mos maiorum* and Britain's ancient political fabric.

It is not surprising that Bentham's attacks on Blackstone and Burke have been read as interventions into what Steven Blakemore has called that 'great ideological war over the significance of the past', which took place throughout the 1790s in pamphlets, books, and parliamentary debates.[24] Both sides of this war exaggerated their claims for maximum political impact, thanks to which the nuances of Bentham's position have been lost. The bifurcation of political thought into Benthamite and Burkean 'traditions' gathered steam in the following century, when Bentham's arguments were simplified once again to suit specific rhetorical needs.[25] As early as 1804, Francis Jeffrey in the *Edinburgh Review* criticised Bentham's 'vulgar distinctions of right and wrong' for ignoring 'the nature

---

[20] M. Lane, 'Political theory and time' in P. N. Baert (ed.), *Time in contemporary intellectual thought* (Amsterdam: Elsevier, 1999), p. 242–243.

[21] Ibid., p. 243.

[22] See C. Blamires, *The French Revolution and the creation of Benthamism* (London: Palgrave, 2008), pp. 132–181.

[23] J. Bentham (eds. P. Schofield, C. Pease-Watkin, and C. Blamires), *Rights, representation, and reform: nonsense upon stilts and other writings on the French Revolution* (Oxford: Oxford University Press, 2002), p. lix.

[24] S. Blakemore, *Intertextual war: Edmund Burke and the French Revolution in the writings of Mary Wollstonecraft, Thomas Paine, and James Mackintosh* (London: Associated University Presses, 1997), p. 15.

[25] Hedva Ben-Israel agreed that Bentham and Burke represented 'truly polar traditions in nineteenth-century England': *English historians on the French Revolution* (Cambridge: Cambridge University Press, 1968), p. 14. The gap between 'Bentham' and 'Benthamism' is a pervasive problem in the scholarship: D. Lieberman, 'From Bentham to Benthamism', *The Historical Journal* 28.1 (1985), pp. 199–224.

or origin of these distinctions', a view popularised by the philosophic Whigs.[26] A similar objection was raised in John's essay on Bentham from 1838, to which he added a companion piece on Coleridge in 1840. Bentham and Coleridge served as mouthpieces for rivalling philosophical moods. Coleridge was cast as an insurgent against the ahistorical spirit of the eighteenth century, while Bentham represented the 'philosophy of mechanism'.[27] Bentham, unlike Coleridge, had made only one contribution to 'the elucidation of history', which was to illustrate the ways in which 'any set of persons who much mix together and have a common interest, are apt to make that common interest their standard of virtue'. The rest of history, John concluded, 'except so far as this explained it, must have been entirely inexplicable' to him.[28]

The rifts between these rivalling moods, which are often construed as a battle between 'organic' and 'mechanical' metaphors, were severe and long-lasting.[29] James Mackintosh famously declared that he felt as though he lived 'in two different countries, and conversed with people who spoke two different languages'.[30] Thomas Carlyle in 1829 lamented what he called the 'age of machinery, in every outward and inward sense of that word', which referred to the seemingly insuperable forces of industrialisation as well as to the mechanisation of man's inward life.[31] William Wordsworth (1770–1850) acknowledged these rifts as late as 1850, when he pitted Burke's defence of 'social ties' and 'custom' against the countervailing claims of 'upstart theory'.[32] It is possible, therefore, to establish continuities between the pamphlet, book, and parliamentary wars of the 1790s and early nineteenth-century debates about the past's practical significance, which intensified further in the years leading up to 1832. These debates, Boyd Hilton has argued, stemmed from the French Revolution and Romantic counter-Enlightenments.[33] The evangelical revival, abetted by Newtonianism and William Paley's natural theology, also played its part by presenting grace and sin in fundamentally mechanical terms – as levers

[26] W. Hazlitt, 'Bentham, Principes de législation, par Dumont', The Edinburgh Review 4 (1804), p. 11.
[27] CW, X, p. 125.   [28] Ibid., p. 110. My emphasis.
[29] See L. Stewart, 'A meaning for machines: modernity, utility, and the eighteenth-century British public', The Journal of Modern History 70.2 (1998), pp. 259–294.
[30] J. Mackintosh (ed. R. J. Mackintosh), Memoirs of the life of the Right Honourable Sir James Mackintosh (London: Edward Moxon, 1835), II, pp. 391–392.
[31] From 'Signs of the times' (1829): G. Himmelfarb (ed.), The spirit of the age: Victorian essays (Yale: Yale University Press, 2007), p. 34.
[32] From the final version of The Prelude (1850): W. Wordsworth (eds. J. Wordsworth, M. H. Abrams, and S. Gill), The Prelude: 1799, 1805, 1850 (New York and London: Norton, 1979), p. 255.
[33] Hilton, A mad, bad, and dangerous people?, p. 312.

pulling downwards and upwards the precarious souls of the living.[34] Bentham, at least in the eyes of his critics, was the mechanical philosopher par excellence. He often imagined himself as the author of a *Novum Organon Juris* whose goal was to replicate for the legal and moral worlds what Bacon had done for the natural world; and, as these fissures widened, Benthamism became synonymous with the mechanical and historically ignorant philosophy of the eighteenth century.[35]

Bentham's reputation as an ahistorical thinker was further solidified by the debates surrounding the publication of James Mill's 'Essay on Government' in 1820, from which he remained largely aloof (see Chapter 2). This reputation has cast a long shadow over the secondary literature, even though it stems more from his opponents' rhetoric than sound exegesis. There are at least two assumptions here. The first is that Bentham was the custodian of an unhistorical and universalising Enlightenment. The second is that his rejection of historical authority – that is, arguments from tradition – implied an unwillingness to conceptualise politics historically.[36] This gave rise to a powerful mode of critique in which Bentham's empiricism and rationalism were set irrevocably at odds, hence Leslie Stephen's remark that the utilitarians were paradoxically committed to both 'experience' and an 'indifference to history'.[37] Bentham's method was thus inherently contradictory, based, on the one hand, on concrete observable experiences (or on evidence that could be reduced to such experiences), and, on the other, on a willingness to escape the 'maze' of historical facts. This interpretation, I wish to argue, overlooks the ways in which Bentham related historical exposition to normative criticism. Unlike the early German historicists, with whom he was distantly familiar, he was concerned less with the present's imposition on the past – although he cautioned against this, too – than with the past's

---

[34] See D. W. Bebbington, *Evangelicalism in modern Britain: a history from the 1730s to the 1980s* (London: Routledge, 2003), pp. 20–151.

[35] See M. Hoesch, 'From theory to practice: Bentham's reception of Helvétius', *Utilitas* 30.3 (2018), p. 298.

[36] J. H. Burns concluded that Bentham's theory of society was 'essentially a-historical', while 'in later life he could be brashly anti-historical in his dismissal of history both as a subject of study and of historical argumentation': 'Jeremy Bentham and the political science of his time', Institute of Intellectual History archive, http://arts.st-andrews.ac.uk/intellectualhistory, last accessed on 12 January 2018. R. J. Smith also concluded that for Bentham and the Benthamites 'historical argument was actively harmful': Smith, *The Gothic bequest*, p. 132. The only substantive revisionist study was written in 1958 by R. O. Preyer, who suggested that Bentham 'rejected the whole idea of a science of history' but defended the past's utility when it furnished 'examples of the arts by which ideas and principles become effective in the real world': Preyer, *Bentham, Coleridge, and the science of history*, pp. 3, 51, 61.

[37] Stephen, *The English utilitarians*, III, p. 317.

imposition on the present; both claims rested on a distinct view of the historian's task in relation to critical jurisprudence and politics, as well as a sensitivity to the past's uniqueness.

Bentham was clear that history could not independently furnish the materials for a law-giving political or legal science, and thus he distinguished throughout his career between expository and critical jurisprudence: to the 'province of the Expositor', he argued in the *Fragment*, 'belongs to explain to us what, as he supposes, the Law is' and how it has been formed, while the province of 'the Censor, [is] to observe to us what he thinks it ought to be'.[38] Grote saw these as mutually complementary enterprises, just as Bentham in *IPML* remarked that the 'common and most useful object of a history of jurisprudence' was to 'exhibit the circumstances that have attended the establishment of laws actually in force … [in order] to furnish examples for the art of legislation'.[39] Furthermore, he argued in the unfinished *Constitutional Code* (1822–1832) that those 'by whom the powers of government are exercised' always seek to maximise their happiness, evidence for which could be found in the 'principle of human nature' and 'particular experience, as brought to view by the history of all nations'.[40] History thus considered the different sets of circumstances which produced different sets of laws, and these, in turn, enlarged the legislator's stock of experiences. The consequences of this position were twofold. First, it meant that Bentham could not simply ignore history or the methods with which it was reconstructed. In *Not Paul, but Jesus* (written for the most part in 1817), he compared the historian to a judge and the study of history to the examination of judicial evidence, while in *Rationale of Judicial Evidence* (written between 1802 and 1812), he argued that judges must employ historical techniques because a 'history of any kind may come to be required for evidence'.[41]

Second, it meant that Bentham could not gloss over the exigencies of time and place in the pursuit of a systematic legal code. Taking his cue from Montesquieu (and, to a lesser extent, from Smith, Ferguson, and Kames), he argued only that the *form* of laws could aspire to something approaching universality, whereas the *matter* of laws – that is, their specific formulation or contents – would vary according to time and place.[42] It was

---

[38] Bentham, *A comment on the Commentaries*, p. 398.
[39] Bentham, *Introduction to the principles and morals of legislation*, p. 298.
[40] Bentham, *Works*, IX, p. 9.
[41] Ibid., VI, p. 386. A new edition of *Rationale of judicial evidence* is forthcoming from Oxford University Press and the Bentham Project. Hereafter, *Not Paul, but Jesus* will be referred to as '*Not Paul*'.
[42] See Cornewall Lewis, *A treatise on the methods of observation and reasoning in politics*, II, p. 35.

Kames who provided him with a 'very ingenious and instructive view of the progress of nations', while Montesquieu combined normative legal principles with a history of 'the reasons which may have influenced the legislators'.[43] History, therefore, was hardly a trivial pursuit. It provided the material with which a political and legal science could be empirically constructed, and this alone required Bentham to think seriously about the examination of historical evidence and its relationship to other branches of knowledge.

The Past on Trial

Hume in 1770 famously opined that 'this is the historical age and this [is] the historical nation', in an attempt to capture the century's astonishing range and depth of historical writing.[44] Edward Gibbon's (1737–1794) 'allusions to history', as Bentham wryly called his *History of the Decline and Fall of the Roman Empire*, appeared in six volumes between 1776 and 1789.[45] Hume's own *History of England* went through numerous editions throughout the period and paved the way for the philosophical histories of the Scottish Enlightenment, including Adam Ferguson's *Essay on the History of Civil Society* (1767), William Robertson's *The History of America* (1777), and John Millar's *Historical View of the English Government* (1787). Bentham was by no means oblivious to the historical temper with which Hume, looking back, associated his age and nation. Leslie Stephen remarked that Bentham from a young age was 'plunged in historical studies', first at Westminster and then at Oxford (he also had access to a vast library at Browning Hill).[46] Those early influences included Sallust and Clarendon's *The History of the Rebellion* (1702–1704), as well as Voltaire's *Histoire de Charles XII* (1731), an 'essence of history' that provided a 'just view of things'.[47] These early studies extended beyond national and biographical histories to treatises that turned hypothetically to the past in the pursuit of political origins – to Grotius (1583–1645), Pufendorf (1632–1694), and Burlamaqui (1694–1748) – all of whom, Bentham later argued, moved fallaciously from the historical 'is' to the

---

[43] Bentham, *A comment on the Commentaries*, p. 430. Montesquieu, however, was too concerned with explaining rather than critically examining the 'chaos of laws': Bentham, 'Of promulgation of the laws', *Works*, I, p. 162.

[44] Hume to William Strahan, August 1770: J. Y. T. Greig (ed.), *The letters of David Hume* [1932] (Oxford: Oxford University Press, 2011), II, p. 230.

[45] Bentham, *Works*, VII, p. 402.   [46] Stephen, *The English utilitarians*, I, p. 170.

[47] Bentham, *Works*, I, p. 11. Bentham also wrote and reflected on Voltaire's philosophical history: 'Bentham Papers', University College London Library, box 73, f. 92.

normative 'ought'.[48] Where, he demanded in the *Fragment on Government*, is 'that page of history' which empirically verifies the social contract?[49]

Bentham, as we shall see, was wary of collapsing philosophical questions into historical ones, but he did expect historians to bestow an instructive knowledge of their subject. He considered Paul de Rapin's *L'histoire d'Angleterre* (1724–1727) to be of 'little advantage in a moral point of view', but he extolled James Mill's *History of British India* for its legal and political profundities.[50] In a letter to José Joaquin de Mora from 1820, he praised Mill for combining 'the amusement that history affords us' with 'political instruction'. It was a 'complete history' and 'by far the most *instructive* history that has ever seen the light anywhere' because it exposed the 'misconduct of English functionaries' in the colonies.[51] Likewise, Kames and Daines Barrington (1727–1800) provided 'instructive' histories for the arts of legislation and politics.[52] 'A rational enquirer', Kames argued in the second edition of his *Historical Law-Tracts* (1758), 'is not less entertained than *instructed*, when he traces the gradual progress of manners, of laws, of arts, from their birth to their perfect maturity'.[53] Bentham simply developed existing distinctions between instructive histories and uninstructive annals whose function was primarily descriptive.

Before Gibbon and the Scottish philosophical historians, the writing of history was widely considered as second-rate, the preserve of what the Scottish rhetorician Hugh Blair (1718–1800) called 'dull compilers'.[54] These compilers were typically antiquarians who used material objects to assert the past's existence in the face of a revived Pyrrhonian skepticism, but Bentham had little time for these 'monkish Chroniclers'.[55] By the end of the century, however, Blair was able to observe a deepening philosophical interest in the past, characterised by an interest in *moeurs* and a desire to lift historical writing above the shoulders of a prosaic, leaden antiquarianism – to the extent that Britain was almost level with the burgeoning historical cultures of France and Italy.[56] The emergence of philosophical history in Scotland, in particular, fomented a new historical consciousness in

---

[48] See P. Schofield, *Utility and democracy: the political thought of Jeremy Bentham* (Oxford: Oxford University Press, 2006), p. 6.

[49] Bentham, *A comment on the Commentaries*, p. 440n.   [50] Bentham, *Works*, I, p. 12.

[51] Ibid., IX, pp. 78–79. History, as for Hume, was relevant as a source of pleasure: Ibid., II, p. 253.

[52] Bentham, *A comment on the Commentaries*, p. 430.

[53] H. H. Kames, *Historical law-tracts* (Edinburgh: A. Kincaid and J. Bell, 1861), p. v. My emphasis.

[54] H. Blair, *Lectures on rhetoric and belles lettres* (Philadelphia: Robert Aitken, 1784), p. 341.

[55] From a miscellaneous fragment: Bentham, *A comment on the Commentaries*, p. 317.

[56] J. G. A. Pocock, 'Adam Smith and history' in K. Haakonssen (ed.), *The Cambridge companion to Adam Smith* (Cambridge: Cambridge University Press, 2006), p. 272.

which greater attention was paid to commerce, industry, manners, arts, and agriculture, and not just to monolithic political forces and the *vita activa*.[57]

Alongside these debates over the methods and objects of historical enquiry, historians offered new perspectives on its political importance. Hume with uncharacteristic immodesty considered himself the only historian to have neglected 'the cry of popular prejudices'.[58] The so-called rage of party, which split along the intersecting lines of Whig and Tory, Court and Country, was a characteristic feature of British politics between the Revolution of 1688 and the Hanoverian accession. As Laird Okie notes, these 'dogmatically partisan' perspectives influenced the ways in which history was written, with the effect that pasts, both real and imagined, were invoked to defend or bring to account Britain's ancient constitution.[59] Bentham was certainly cognisant of the great ideological battles between Bolingbroke and Walpole, many of which were proxy battles over England's recent political past.[60] He confessed to opening Bolingbroke's *The Idea of a Patriot King* (c. 1738) 'with eagerness' but shut it 'with disappointment', having found nothing in it but 'general maxims for the distributions of favours'.[61] Bolingbroke's broadside was less a historical survey of kingship than a call for its theoretical perfection, according to which, Bolingbroke argued, the past can be said to 'render manifest . . . a certain form of government'.[62] Historical writing in Bentham's formative years was thus shaped by political conflict, and those conflicts alerted him to historians' political allegiances; he acknowledged, for example, that William Mitford's *History of Greece* (1784–1810) was effectively a stricture against republicanism and the 'pestilence of our times' (see Chapter 3), while as late as 1820 he referred to the enduring discords between 'Whig' and 'Tory History'.[63]

---

[57] See Salber Phillips, *Society and sentiment*, p. 29.

[58] D. Hume, *The life of David Hume* (London: Hunt and Clarke, 1826), p. 5. Bentham read and enjoyed Hume's *History*, which he called 'a great treat': *Works*, X, p. 40.

[59] Okie, *Augustan historical writing*, p. 212.

[60] See P. Jupp, *The governing of Britain, 1688–1848: the executive, Parliament, and the people* (London: Routledge, 2006), p. 65.

[61] Bentham, *Works*, X, p. 72. See D. Armitage, 'A patriot for whom? The afterlives of Bolingbroke's Patriot King', *The Journal of British Studies* 36.4 (1997), p. 406.

[62] H. Bolingbroke, *The patriot king; and, an essay on the spirit of patriotism* (London: John Brooks, 1831), p. 100.

[63] J. Bentham (ed. A. T. Milne,), *The correspondence of Jeremy Bentham* (London: UCL Press, 2017), V, p. 362; Bentham, *Works*, VIIII, p. 473n. E. J. Eisenach has observed how Bentham used Locke, Hume, and Ferguson to highlight the relationship between 'legitimating historical myths' and the command of 'political loyalties': 'The dimension of history in Bentham's theory of law' in Parekh (ed.), *Critical assessments*, III, pp. 140–141.

Bentham thought deeply, especially towards the end of his career, about the relationships between different branches of knowledge. These branches, he argued, exhibited logical relations and priorities within a single 'tree'.[64] Spurred on by d'Alembert's classification of the sciences in the *Encylopédie*, he outlined in *Chrestomathia* (1817) a curriculum for a new secondary school founded on the principles of *eudæmonics*, in which history was defined in its 'narrowed and most usual sense' as 'an account of states of things and events, as they are *supposed* to have had existence in times past'.[65] The adjective 'supposed' alluded to the partisanship of contemporary historical writing, and also to Hume's point that we experience the past indirectly through mental impressions, which are established by association.[66] Bentham expanded on this definition in an appendix to *Chrestomathia*, which was re-edited and translated into French by his nephew, George Bentham (1800–1884), in 1823. In that volume – *Essai sur la nomenclature et la classification des principles branches d'art-et-science* – Bentham divided history into five sub-branches (*civile, ecclésiastique, naturelle, profane*, and *sacrée*) but argued that in its 'acception plus ordinaire ... [e]lle doit faire partie de toutes les branches qui ont pour sujet une entité réelle, matérielle, ou immatérielle', including 'le domaine ... de l'Ethique'.[67]

History, according to Bentham, was foundational to other branches of knowledge, including ethics and the art of government, because it examined 'la description des événements et des états des choses qui ont eu lieu dans les temps passés'.[68] Statements of history were unphilosophical essentially by definition: '[o]n dit aussi Sciences historiques par opposition à Sciences philosophiques pour désigner celles dont l'étude exerce plus l'observation que la réflexion'.[69] They purported only to recount events and states of things as they were supposed to have happened – although the term 'Sciences historique' implied much more than observation, devoid of

---

[64] See E. de Champs, 'The place of Jeremy Bentham's theory of fictions in eighteenth-century linguistic thought', *Journal of Bentham Studies* 2 (1999), pp. 1–28.

[65] J. Bentham (eds. M. J. Smith and W. H. Burston), *Chrestomathia* (Oxford: Oxford University Press, 1983), pp. 181, 169. My emphasis. Earlier, in 1775, he argued that '[a] passage of history is but a set of signs serving to communicate the belief of the historian concerning a point in history': J. Bentham, (eds. D. G. Long and P. Schofield), *Preparatory principles* (Oxford: Oxford University Press, 2016), p. 84.

[66] As an empiricist, Bentham defined history as a fictitious entity whose existence could only be confirmed through *paraphrasis*, that is, by translating it into a real physical entity such as pleasure or pain. See Bentham, *Works*, VIII, pp. 120–130; Schofield, *Utility and democracy*, pp. 8, 28. On Bentham's psychological theories, which drew on Hume and David Hartley (1705–1757), see F. Rosen, *Classical utilitarianism from Hume to Mill* (London: Routledge, 2003), p. 82.

[67] J. Bentham (ed. and trans. G. Bentham), *Essai sur la nomenclature et la classification des principles branches d'art-et-science* (Paris: Bossange, 1823), p. 208.

[68] Ibid.   [69] Ibid., pp. 208–209.

logical or linguistic abstraction – whereas philosophy enquired into the past's utility.[70] Along with Grote, the utilitarian John Hill Burton shared Bentham's commitment to empirical history in which the evidence shaped and constrained the historian's reflections.[71] In his *History of Scotland*, published in nine volumes between 1853 and 1870, he argued that the 'philosophy of history', which supposedly expunged from the past all 'picturesque and venerable fables, have been apt to substitute others of their own'. Philosophies of history, he observed, were allegedly products of 'learning and sagacity', but 'in search of fact they are not less unreal than the old fables'.[72]

This did not mean that history was inapplicable to other branches of knowledge and *vice versa*; in *A Comment on the* <u>Commentaries</u>, for example, Bentham attacked Robertson for substituting 'philosophical penetration' for 'poetical graces', while in the *Essay on Logic* he argued that '[u]nder the direction of an attentive [i.e., philosophical] observer, geography serves, in some sort, for supplying the gaps left by history. The description of nations exhibiting themselves on different levels in the scale of improvement, or, to speak more precisely, having before them fields of observation of different extent, serve, when put together, to exhibit a simultaneous view of no inconsiderable portion of the history of the human race'.[73] History on its own provided scant political guidance.[74] It furnished 'delusive notions' inverse to 'the progress of true knowledge and morality' – showing how far history had strayed from the path of utility – but it also provided the materials with which other disciplines furnished practical maxims.[75] True history, he argued in *Rationale of Reward* (1825), must afford 'instruction applicable to morality, or any other branch of useful or agreeable knowledge', otherwise the discipline in question is not history but rather the 'study of antiquities'.[76]

Leslie Stephen grasped Bentham's point that we must treat history *as history* before judging its utility. The utilitarians, Stephen argued,

---

[70] As Leslie Stephen put it, '[s]tick to bare fact and you can only write annals. History proper begins as you introduce causation, and the mere series is transformed into a process. It is impossible to get a bare fact without some admixture of theory': *The English utilitarians*, III, p. 342.

[71] Burton helped Bowring to edit Bentham's works and wrote various prefaces and introductions.

[72] J. H. Burton, *The history of Scotland from Agricola's invasion to the Revolution of 1688* (Edinburgh: William Blackwood and Sons, 1867), I, p. 84.

[73] Bentham, *A comment on the* <u>Commentaries</u>, p. 317; Bentham, *Works*, VIII, pp. 265–266.

[74] As he put it in a letter to his father, Jeremiah (1712–1792), on 16 January 1786: 'how uncertain must be the lights that can be derived from even the most rational and best attested histories?': J. Bentham (ed. I. R. Christie), *The correspondence of Jeremy Bentham* (London: UCL Press, 2017), III, p. 444.

[75] Bentham, *Chrestomathia*, p. 30. For an almost identical argument see *Book of fallacies*, pp. 126, 170.

[76] Bentham, *Works*, II, p. 253.

abandoned 'the mischievous didacticism of older historians' by placing the 'question of fact' everywhere before 'the question of right'.[77] The close ties between history and philosophy required Bentham to think at length about the critical, interpretive, and literary paradigms with which the past is recovered; and although he never published a work of history that was immediately received as such, he did think seriously, if somewhat prosaically, about the historian's craft. He even published in 1823, under the pseudonym of Gamaliel Smith, a work of ecclesiastical history called *Not Paul, but Jesus*, which appeared five years after *Church-of-Englandism and its Catechism Examined*, and one year after Grote edited and prepared for publication his *Analysis of the Influence of Natural Religion on the Temporal Happiness of Mankind*. In this widely overlooked work, the second and third volumes of which are to be published shortly by Oxford University Press, Bentham set out to undermine through Biblical exegesis the asceticism of St. Paul that had spread throughout the Christian world since late antiquity.[78] Its published first volume was heavily criticised by pastors and men-of-letters, including David Bowker Wells, who criticised the distortion of 'facts relating to the history of the Apostles'.[79]

Bentham in *Not Paul* testified to his own impartiality as a 'historiographer' who scrutinised the 'materials with which history has furnished us'.[80] At the beginning of volume one, he stated his intention to critically examine the evidence and uncover 'the truth of the story [about Paul]'.[81] The task of historical enquiry, therefore, was to establish as forensically and dispassionately as possible what had happened at a particular time and place, even if the evidence was partial or incomplete. While he was sceptical that historians could be scientifically objective, he declared in his commentary on Blackstone that they must nevertheless divest themselves of 'habitual prejudice' and 'dogma'.[82] In *Not Paul*, he celebrated the 'manner' and 'principles' of profane history for especially this reason, and his criticism of ecclesiastical authority often resulted in thinly-veiled attacks on religious historians – including the 'clerical historian' Robertson – because their profession 'debarred' them from 'entering

[77] Stephen, *The English utilitarians*, III, p. 342.
[78] 'Bentham papers', University College London Library, box 139, ff. 348, 464, 469.
[79] D. B. Wells, *St. Paul vindicated: being part one of a reply to a late publication by Gamaliel Smith* (T. Sevenson: Cambridge, 1824), p. i. See J. E. Crimmins, *Secular utilitarianism: social science and the critique of religion in the thought of Jeremy Bentham* (Oxford: Oxford University Press, 1990), pp. 2, 227–254.
[80] 'Bentham papers', University College London Library, box 139, f. 445; J. Bentham (ed. F. Place), *Not Paul, but Jesus* (London: John Hunt, 1823), p. viii.
[81] Bentham, *Not Paul, but Jesus*, p. 59.   [82] Bentham, *A comment on the Commentaries*, p. 317.

into just reflexions'.[83] As he put it in the *Fragment on Government*, '[n]o man should dare to write history who is not free to choose his notions'.[84] While he could forgive the 'wanderings of an imagination' or the embellishments of prose, he could not excuse Robertson's 'didactic' and 'rhetorical exclamations against experience'.[85]

The historian, then, must strive for objectivity in the same way that judges do, but this raises questions about what was to be judged and how, and whether or not this amounts to an autonomously historical exercise.[86] Bentham's arguments in *Not Paul* and *Chrestomathia* allow us to flesh out some tentative points. First, the task of *sciences historiques* was to scientifically observe the past, while *sciences philosophiques* reflected on those observations by estimating their utility. The forensic criticism of evidence thus made possible the normative judgements from which the past derived its utility, hence his admiration for Kames, Barrington, Voltaire, and Mill's *History of British India*. If that latter work put to shame the misconduct of English functionaries, then *Not Paul* set out to prove that Paul was 'guilty' of dissimulation and 'obtaining money on false pretences'.[87] Second, the criteria with which the evidence was judged were intentionally modern; as Bentham remarked in volume two, 'whatsoever be the subject in question on which a judgment is to be passed – in the case of a narrative, trustworthiness ... one proper object of reference – one proper standard of comparison – ought never to be out of mind: this is the state of things, this is as part and parcel of that state the nature of man, as it manifests itself in these our times'.[88] The facts of 'universal experience', Bentham argued, tell us that Paul was incapable of the miracles commonly ascribed to him, and that his contemporaries were more inclined to believe 'marvellous' or supernatural testimonies.[89] *Sciences historiques* deployed what we know about 'the nature of man' as a tool of critical analysis, thereby laying the foundations for *sciences philosophiques* and the judgement of past events.[90]

---

[83] Bentham, *Not Paul, but Jesus*, pp. xiii–xiv; Bentham, *A comment on the Commentaries*, pp. 318n, 317.

[84] Bentham, *A comment on the Commentaries*, p. 317n.

[85] Quoted in J. H. Burns, 'Bentham and the Scots', *Journal of Bentham Studies* 7 (2004), p. 8.

[86] Carlo Ginzburg has argued that this metaphorical way of thinking about the relationship between history and historical truth gained momentum only in the late nineteenth and early twentieth centuries: 'Checking the evidence: the judge and the historian', *Critical Enquiry* 1 (1991), p. 80.

[87] Bentham, *Not Paul, but Jesus*, p. 400.

[88] 'Bentham papers', University College London Library, box 161, f. 20.

[89] Bentham, *Not Paul, but Jesus*, p. 339.

[90] The necessity of having 'a critical principle to guide reflection on the historical record' was a hallmark of rationalist historiography: White, *Metahistory*, p. 58.

The *Digest of Justinian* (22.3.2) decreed that 'ei incumbit probatio qui dicit, non qui negat' (the burden of proof is on he who declares, not on he who denies).[91] Bentham adapted this legal maxim to the assessment of historical evidence. The Acts of the Apostles, he argued in volume one of *Not Paul*, 'has a claim to be provisionally taken for true', much like 'any other history ancient or modern'.[92] Similarly, in *Rationale of Judicial Evidence*, he observed that the burden of proof was greater in times of remote antiquity because, 'in the track of experience and civilisation, the further back we go, the greater the proportion of incorrectness as well as mendacity, the greater the ratio of fable to history, till at last it is all pure fable. In distant times, histories melt at last into fables, as, in distant plains, hills do into clouds. It is with the infancy of the species, as with the infancy of the individual: dreams mix themselves with realities'.[93] For this reason the historian ought to adopt modern standards of enquiry rather than trust testimonies which contradicted universal experience and the 'nature of man'. The capacity to faithfully record historical events, to 'present each fact in its genuine and proper colours', was a hallmark of modern civilisation.[94]

The early Christian world was particularly difficult to study because of the paucity and fallibility of its records. The further one receded in time, the harder it was to recover basic empirical facts, but with the development of language and philosophy came fuller and more accurate accounts of the past. By contrast, 'other and anterior times' were those 'in which the nature of things, including the nature of man, were not so well known'.[95] Modern history, then, was clearly a more plausible undertaking than ancient history, a theme that surfaced in the *Rationale of Judicial Evidence*: 'the more remote the antiquity', he argued, 'the less clear, the less correct, the less complete are the accounts which we have of those times' – so much so that 'imagination is called in ... and the business which, to be well done, could only have been done by the instructive faculty, is executed by its delusive substitute [imagination]'. Whereas an 'epic poem' may have once passed for testimony, an 'historical work', by contrast, implied the study of what was actually said by persons who, 'at the time at which it [the testimony] was written ... were still either in existence or in remembrance'.[96] The discriminating principle,

---

[91] W. Blackstone, *Commentaries on the laws of England* (London: W. Strahan and T. Cadell, 1783), III, p. 366.
[92] Bentham, *Not Paul, but Jesus*, p. 60.   [93] Bentham, *Works*, VII, p. 90.
[94] 'Bentham papers', University College London Library, box 139, f. 446.   [95] Ibid., box 161, f. 21.
[96] Ibid., box 139, f. 522. James Mill made the same argument five years later in *HBI* when he discussed 'fable' standing 'in the place of fact', and 'imagination' in the place of 'memory': I, p. 140.

again, was a rather vague appeal to 'the nature of man' and the standard of knowledge 'in these our times'.[97]

Bentham believed that historians were better placed to understand history, especially ancient history, than at any time before. As he put it in the *Rationale of Judicial Evidence*, it is now possible to scrutinise testimonies *a priori* because 'universal experience' has 'established that the course of nature is uniform', and that 'the more widely an alleged event differs from the ordinary course of nature', the 'smaller is the probability of its being true'.[98] In other words, we can judge evidence probabilistically, based on what we have come to rationally know about the world (and this, needless to say, is based on a wider stock of observations than a single testimony). The issue, as for James Mill, was that historians were rarely philosophers who drew on 'universal experience' and the 'ordinary course of nature', and who understood what it meant to examine the 'state of society and the character of the human mind'.[99] Both thinkers appealed to universal experience as a tool of historical criticism, which, in Bentham's case, allowed him to forensically debunk Paul's authority and the tradition of Christian asceticism. These accumulated experiences also allowed the historian to penetrate more deeply into past events. As Bentham put it towards the end of volume one of *Not Paul*, 'to those particulars, which composed no more than the surface of the business, *their* knowledge was confined; while *we*, thought at the distance of more than seventeen centuries, know more or less of the inside of it'.[100]

Dead Men Have No Rivals

Bentham, I have argued, was by no means oblivious to the historical age in which he formulated some of his most significant political and legal ideas.[101] While it is problematic to read into his writings the emergence of a definitively utilitarian historiography, not least because it presupposes a consistency and depth of intention that simply wasn't there, it is also surprising that *Not Paul* and the *Rationale of Judicial Evidence*, alongside his critical exegeses of Blackstone and *Chrestomathia*, have failed to unsettle his reputation as a doctrinaire rationalist who ignored the enduring

---

[97] 'Bentham papers', University College London Library, box 161, f. 20.
[98] Bentham, *Works*, XI, p. 243.
[99] 'Bentham papers', University College London Library, box 139, f. 447.
[100] Bentham, *Not Paul, but Jesus*, p. 399.
[101] A 'dead man has no rivals', he argued, because in 'whose ever way he may have stood when living, no sooner is the breath out of his body, he stands not any longer in any body's': *Book of fallacies*, p. 174.

questions of historiography: how and with what tools should history be
written, and how can it be made instructive without imposing the author's
political or religious views? Bentham's anti-clericalism, I have suggested,
informed precisely these questions. The historian must abandon 'one's
notions' and keep methodologically separate the tasks of explanation and
judgement, otherwise history could not accurately inform philosophy.
There is an irony, perhaps, in Bentham's unwillingness to contemplate
his own philosophical presentism – normative judgements always boiled
down to questions of utility, a point to which I will return shortly – but it is
nevertheless difficult to sustain the view that he was 'indifferent' to history,
or that he underestimated the perils of didacticism.

One problem is that we have conflated Bentham's rejection of historical
authority, or arguments that leapt from the explanatory 'is' to the normative 'ought', with a rejection of history *per se*. It is important, therefore, to
examine in greater depth Bentham's opposition to history as a structuring
principle of politics and jurisprudence. It is worth noting that Dugald
Stewart (1753–1828), several of whose pupils contributed to debates
between the philosophic Whigs and Philosophic Radicals, argued in
*A General View of the Progress of Metaphysical, Ethical, and Political
Philosophy* (1817) that Bentham's argument against historical authority
was perfectly compatible with Montesquieu's 'historical disquisitions' in
De l'esprit des lois (1748), and that the argument itself was not necessarily
ahistorical; rather, it was a rebuke to those for whom 'the very existence of
a legal principle, or of an established custom, becomes an argument in its
favour'.[102] As Bentham's project to codify the law intensified, he attacked
this fallacy within the context of critical jurisprudence, reserving his most
forceful criticisms for Blackstone. His most developed thoughts, however,
are to be found in *The Book of Fallacies*, the relevant books and chapters of
which were written between 1810 and 1811, with minor revisions added in
1819.[103]

One strategy of *The Book of Fallacies*, as in *A Comment on the
Commentaries*, was to construe utility and custom as incompatible principles of critical jurisprudence. The former was a method of rational
philosophical enquiry based on the laws of human nature, while the latter
derived its normative force from legal precedents, customs, and a habitual
attachment to existing institutions. Even though *The Book of Fallacies* was

---

[102] D. Stewart, *The works of Dugald Stewart* (Cambridge: Hilliard and Brown, 1829), VI, p. 179. On
Stewart's pupils and their exchanges with the Philosophic Radicals, see Collini, Winch, and
Burrow, *That noble science of politics*, pp. 91–127.
[103] Bentham, *Book of fallacies*, pp. lvii–lix.

written in the early 1800s, it belongs thematically to his writings from the 1790s, especially *Nonsense upon Stilts*, which, in the Bowring edition of his works, appeared under the title of *Anarchical Fallacies*. Bentham in both *The Book of Fallacies* and *Nonsense upon Stilts* examined the fallacies of political debate surrounding the French Revolution. Both republicans and conservatives, he argued, had used the past in philosophically illegitimate ways; article 12 of the *Déclaration des droits de l'homme et du citoyen de 1789*, for example, confused questions of utility, that is, what ought to be the case, with statements of historical fact. The author of that document, Bentham suggested, mistook 'a declaration of what he supposes was or is the state of things' for 'a declaration of what he conceives ought to have been or ought to be'.[104] Burke, Blackstone, Burlamaqui, Grotius, and Pufendorf had all made similar errors; as he put it in the preface to the *Fragment*, they had mistaken the province of the 'Censor' for that of the 'Expositor' who enquired into the law's development without pronouncing on its utility.[105]

The Humean distinction between 'is' and 'ought' provided a lasting fulcrum for Bentham's normative critiques. Prior to his death in 1832, he attacked in progressively emphatic terms the so-called historical school of law, which disingenuously used history to formulate prescriptive legal arguments. He periodically revived his argument from *The Book of Fallacies* that 'blind custom' prevented the law from attaining 'general utility' because it substituted a rational defence of existing laws and institutions for the dogma of historical authority.[106] These arguments sprung from the same convictions as his diatribes against Blackstone, Burke, and the authors of the *Déclaration,* but they were redeployed against legal historicists in Germany and France for whom the past seemed to possess an intrinsic philosophical value; in his exhortation to Lafayette from 1830, for example, Bentham defended Anton Thibaut (1772–1840) from Friedrich von Savigny's (1779–1861) critique of legal universalism in *Vom Beruf unserer Zeit für Gesetzgebung und Rechtswissenschaft* (1814), which drew on Johann Gottfried von Herder's (1744–1803) idea of *Volksgeistlehre.*[107]

---

[104] Bentham, *Rights, representation, and reform*, p. 364. See, for analysis, Schofield, *Utility and democracy*, p. 66.

[105] Bentham, *A comment on the Commentaries*, p. 397.

[106] Bentham, *Book of fallacies*, p. 428. On Savigny's historicism, see F. C. Beiser, *The German historicist tradition* (Oxford: Oxford University Press, 2011), pp. 214–253.

[107] Bentham, *Works*, IV, p. 425. See also J. Le Rider, 'La codification, objet de la controverse Thibaut-Savigny' in G. Kamecke and J. Le Rider (eds.), *La codification: perspectives transdisciplinaires* (Paris: Librairie Droz, 2007), pp. 161–169.

According to Bentham, the 'historical school, à la mode de l'Allemagne', and of which 'Herr Savigny' was 'schoolmaster', replaced 'law itself' with the 'history of law', which dictated 'the political conduct of men in that same country'.[108] While he exaggerated his familiarity with German jurisprudence, his opposition to it was characteristically strident. In an unpublished sheet from the same year, he attacked the 'jurists of the historical school' for seeking in customary law a timeless precedent or standard, even though their duty was to legislate presently for security and happiness.[109] A contemporary of Bentham's, Pellegrino Rossi (1787–1848), erstwhile professor of law at Bologna and émigré in Geneva, was one of the first to publicly associate Bentham with analytical jurisprudence. The analytical method, Rossi argued, opposed the historical method by arguing that the law's spirit was endogenous to society and thus a product of its history.[110] Eugène Lerminier (1803–1857), a French lawyer who sympathised with Savigny, likewise reprimanded Bentham for neglecting legal history in the *Traité de législation civile et pénale* (1802).[111] This interpretation soon found its way to Britain, where, towards the end of the century, the jurist and historian Henry Maine numbered Bentham among the analytic jurists who had 'failed to see a great deal which can only be explained in history'.[112]

Bentham's response to Savigny preserved the distinction between philosophy and history that I have been exploring, but it had even deeper roots in his arguments against authority and tradition. His lifelong distrust of lawyers, for example, stemmed from a rejection of unwritten legal systems, a suspicion of discretion and authority, and a belief that lawyers profited from the mystification of law at the expense of others; as he quipped to James Mackintosh (another of Stewart's pupils) in 1808, 'the power of the lawyer is in the uncertainty of the law'.[113] The deference to historical authority amounted to more than an error of reasoning. The 'worship of dead men's bones', he argued in *The Book of Fallacies*, encouraged 'the affections and even passions the most opposite to humility – pride, anger, obstinacy, and overbearingness'.[114] The spectre of religious idolatry was never far from his mind, and his remarks were blatantly anti-clerical; indeed, the text was composed during a period in which he repeatedly attacked ecclesiastical

---

[108] Bentham, *Works*, IV, p. 425.
[109] 'Bentham papers', University College London Library, box 83, f. 157.
[110] See J. R. Dinwiddy, 'Early-nineteenth-century reactions to Benthamism', *Transactions of the Royal Historical Society* 34 (1984), pp. 47–69; P. Schofield, 'Jeremy Bentham and nineteenth-century English jurisprudence', *The Journal of Legal History* 12.1 (1991), pp. 58–88.
[111] J. R. Dinwiddy, *Radicalism and reform in Britain, 1780–1850* (London: Hambledon, 1992), p. 347.
[112] Eisenach, 'The dimension of history in Bentham's theory of law', p. 152.
[113] Bentham, *Works*, X, p. 429.   [114] Bentham, *Book of fallacies*, p. 144.

authority.[115] In *Influence of Religion on the Temporal Happiness of Mankind* (1822), for example, he examined the ways in which different historical mythologies had become institutionalised 'in a particular class of persons incurably opposed to the interests of humanity'.[116] Likewise, in *The Book of Fallacies*, he associated with 'the religion of Budha, of Brama, of Foe, of Mahomet, of Jesus' the worship of idols and dead men's bones, the 'probative force' of which stemmed not from their utility but from the 'number of persons joining in'.[117]

Bentham's challenge to authority applied equally to the political sphere as it did to the ecclesiastical and legal. In Book I, Part II of *The Book of Fallacies*, which exposed fallacies of political rhetoric, he opined that 'as the world grows older, if at the same time it grows wiser ... the influence of authority will in each situation, and particularly in Parliament, become less and less'.[118] As things stood, however, authority took precedence over independent 'reasoning', and parliamentarians turned typically 'to some other man or set of men of whom he knows little or nothing, except that they lived so many years ago – that is that the time their existence was by so much anterior to his own time; by so much anterior, and consequently possessing for its guidance so much the less experience'.[119] *The Book of Fallacies* was composed during a period of increasingly vocal radicalism, during which he consolidated his friendship with James Mill. Over the next two decades, his opposition to authority informed the arguments and rhetoric of the Philosophic Radicals, whose growth as a concerted political force occurred against the backdrop of unprecedented political developments in the late 1820s and early 1830s, including the repeal of the Test and Corporation Acts in 1828; the Swing Riots in the summer of 1830; the fall of the Pittite regime in November 1830; and the agitation for political reform in Parliament, which culminated in the passing of the Reform Act in 1832, one day after Bentham's death.[120]

Bentham's strictures against authority thus mapped onto growing discontents within England's *ancien régime*, and, more broadly, onto what the historian Walter Houghton called the 'rise of the critical spirit'

---

[115] J. E. Crimmins, 'Bentham on religion: atheism and the secular society', *Journal of the History of Ideas* 47.1 (1986), pp. 95–110.
[116] Eisenach, 'The dimension of history in Bentham's theory of law', p. 150. See also C. Fuller, 'Bentham, Mill, Grote, and An analysis of the influence of natural religion on the temporal happiness of mankind', *Journal of Bentham Studies* 10 (2008), pp. 1–15.
[117] Bentham, *Book of fallacies*, p. 145. [118] Ibid., p. 152. [119] Ibid., p. 144.
[120] J. E. Crimmins, *Utilitarian philosophy and politics: Bentham's later years* (London: Continuum, 2011), p. 4.

and the crisis of established political authority.[121] As Bentham put it in his *Plan for Parliamentary Reform* – published in 1817 but written for the most part in 1809 – agitations for reform were typically dismissed as 'theoretical, visionary, utopian, impracticable', and injurious to the 'pride of ages'. This 'yoke of custom', he argued, was the blind tyrant whom 'all other tyrants make their slave'.[122] His preferred example, as elsewhere, was China. In Book I, Part II, Chapter 3 of *The Book of Fallacies*, he brought to his readers' attention to the so-called 'Chinese' or 'Ancestor-Worshipper's Argument' in which a 'supposed repugnancy' is stated 'between the proposed measure and the opinions of men by whom the same country was inhabited in former times: these opinions collected either from the direct evidence as contained in the express words of some writer living at the period of time in question, or from the laws or institutions that were at that time in existence'.[123]

Bentham's assault on historical authority shaped his conception of progress.[124] In *The Book of Fallacies*, for instance, he radically subverted the conventional appeal to history with an innovative piece of literalism. Appeals to historical authority, he argued, wrongly inferred that 'the true mother of wisdom is, not experience, but inexperience'.[125] This was a self-abolishing notion, an absurdity so glaring that he struggled to explain its prevalence.[126] History in Bentham's mind went by the false appellation of 'old time', when in fact it was not old at all.[127] What 'in English, as well as in Latin . . . a portion of time which, with reference to the present, ought to have been called *young*, and is sometimes called *early*, is in possession of being dignified with the name of *old*.[128] This claim was repeated in *Chrestomathia*, in which he criticised the perceived equivalence between

---

[121] W. Houghton, *The Victorian frame of mind 1830–1870* (New Haven: Yale University Press, 1957), p. 94.

[122] J. Bentham, *A plan for parliamentary reform in the form of a catechism, with reasons for each article, with an introduction, shewing the necessity of radical, and the inadequacy of moderate, reform* (London: R. Hunter, 1817), pp. ix, cxcviii. Looking back, J. S. Mill agreed that Bentham had helped to break 'the yoke of authority': *CW*, X, p. 78.

[123] Bentham, *Book of fallacies*, p. 166. In the *History* James Mill considered this a measure of a civilisation's rudeness: 'rude nations seem to derive a peculiar gratification from pretensions to a remote antiquity': I, p. 133.

[124] See Bentham, *A comment on the Commentaries*, p. 393.

[125] Bentham, *Book of fallacies*, p. 166. On Bentham's rejection of sentimentalism, see F. Rosen, *Jeremy Bentham and representative democracy: a study of The constitutional code* (Oxford: Clarendon, 1983), p. 30.

[126] He had argued in *A comment on the Commentaries* that the true 'natural course of things . . . is for the world to increase in wisdom as it comes on in age': *A comment on the Commentaries* p. 212.

[127] Bentham, *Book of fallacies*, p. 168.   [128] Ibid., p. 167.

history and 'what was preposterously termed ancient times'.[129] Nothing, he argued, was to be learnt from classical antiquity because 'modern and English authors' had preserved and surpassed its knowledge.[130]

Bentham's inversion of early and old times was neither a rhetorical conceit nor linguistically pedantic; rather, it was an attempt to substantively redefine the terms on which societies learnt from the past. It allowed him to oppose historical authority whilst keeping theoretically intact the idea of intellectual progress. He offered the following example in *The Book of Fallacies*: 'but now take the case of persons taken at the same age (fifty) and considered as living or having lived in two different portions of time ... Here, at the same age, you have, for objects of comparison, the inhabitant of modern time and the inhabitant of ancient time: will any one take upon him to pronounce, as between them, that the probable superiority of wisdom is on the side of him whose situation in the scale of time past is the more distant from our own? No'.[131] If time was to be seen as the measure of improvement, did it follow that there was nothing to be learnt from the past, that we ought to 'live and talk ... as if we had never had any ancestors?' Bentham's answer, laced with mock surprise, was 'Oh, no'. Our ancestors suffered 'as we suffer' and 'their practice forms part of our own experience'.[132]

Bentham drew attention to history's importance in other ways, even though he questioned its claim to political authority. Shortly after completing *The Book of Fallacies*, he argued in a letter to James Madison (1751–1836) that America's laws, much like England's, were invariably founded on 'some random decision ... pronounced in this or that barbarous age, almost always without any intelligible reason, under the impulse of some private and sinister interest'.[133] Laws were products, or perhaps even victims, of the times in which they were passed.

> Law which being, in so far as it could be said to be *made*, made at a multitude of successive periods, and for the use and governance of so many different generations of men, imbued with notions, habituated to modes of life, differing more or less widely from each other, as well as from those which have place at present, would, even if it had been well adapted to the circumstances and exigencies of the times, in which its parts respectively came into existence, have, to a considerable extent, been thereby rendered not the better adapted, but by so much the worse

---

[129] Bentham, *Chrestomathia*, p. 73. See J. H. Burns, 'Bentham's critique of political fallacies' in Parekh (ed.), *Critical assessments*, III, p. 692.
[130] Bentham, *Chrestomathia*, p. 40.   [131] Bentham, *Book of fallacies*, p. 168.   [132] Ibid., p. 178.
[133] J. Bentham (ed. S. Conway), *The correspondence of Jeremy Bentham. Volume 8* (Oxford: Clarendon Press, 1988), p. 188.

adapted, to the notions and manners now prevalent, – to the state of things at present in existence.[134]

Bentham undermined history's authority by embracing its role in the formation of positive laws, and by arguing that the law must be adapted to 'things at present in existence', that is, to a state of society in which greater progress had been made. Progress, therefore, implied a rejection of historical authority because societies accumulated wisdom through time. While Bentham was typically reluctant to divulge his influences, it is possible to detect traces of Helvétius's critique of natural law as an innate property of the social world. Natural law, Helvétius had claimed, was proportioned to 'the progress of the human mind', because of which we must stress 'time, experience, and reason' over a transcendent or natural conception of law.[135] Indeed, Bentham's own views on progress precluded the kind of world-levelling rationalism of which he was frequently accused. Utility provided a framework in which to rationally accommodate historical differences, and to ensure that utility was maximised irrespective of civilisational progress. Evidence for this can be traced to the mid-1770s, when, in the *Preparatory Principles*, he asserted that expository treatises of 'universal jurisprudence', if they are to reflect 'actually subsisting' matters of fact

> cannot but be applied to some state in particular: and the state it is most natural for a man to apply it to, is that state of which he is himself a member. I say to some state in particular: for as applied to all states in general, it would be nothing. Some assignable rights there may be, some powers, some duties, some restraints, that subsist alike in all states. But in point of number they would be few … So broken, in short, would be the thread of connection between the parts of such a universal system, that, unless the gaps were filled up by materials taken from some particular system, it would probably be utterly unintelligible and useless …[136]

Since historical and cultural differences precluded 'such a universal system', Bentham argued forcefully for a critical jurisprudence whose guiding principle – utility – could be applied to all times and places. Rather than supplying universal laws, the goal was to provide a framework in which to objectively measure their utility. The utility principle, he reasoned, did not posit universal essences or systems of law – in other words, it did not require him to establish common legal features – because it maximised happiness within varied

[134] Ibid., p. 196.
[135] Helvétius, *A treatise on man*, I, p. 247. See De Champs, *Enlightenment and utility*, p. 123.
[136] Bentham, *Preparatory principles*, p. 136–137.

historical and cultural contexts. Its claim to universality rested not on the 'broken' and 'unintelligible' expositions of universal jurisprudence, but rather on the fundamental laws of human nature. Bentham therefore embraced historical variation as a feature of political and legal systems, hence his scepticism regarding the uniformity of legal 'powers', 'duties', and 'restraints'.[137] This is not to say that he was deeply sensitive to cultural difference; that he solved rather than reproduced the problem of universalism; or that he embraced the kind of historicism which reduced to mere exposition the normative judgement of laws and institutions. At the same time, his emphasis on the past's fundamental distinctness, alongside his rejection of natural law and other metaphysical fictions – he criticised Montesquieu for entertaining 'pseudo-metaphysical sophistry' – reveals a view of history based less on the elimination of historical difference than on its explicit acknowledgement.[138]

Time, Place, and Progress

Bentham reduced to logical absurdity the reverence and authority which legislators conferred on the past, and while he saw little difference between Savigny's legal historicism and Blackstone's and Burke's arguments from tradition, this did not mean that his political thought was systematically unhistorical. R. O. Preyer has argued that Bentham's essay *On the Influence of Time and Place in Matters of Legislation*, which first appeared in Etienne Dumont's edition of his works in 1802, was historicist to the extent that it formally connected the art of legislation to the demands of time, place, and circumstance.[139] He overeggs the claim by reading into *Time and Place* Savigny's historicising language of *Volksgeist*, even though Bentham reprimanded Savigny for appropriating Niebuhr's 'historical method' to the 'forces of legal reaction'. While Niebuhr and other philologists had 'made historical truth more clear', this did not eliminate the need for criticism.[140] There is, however, something to be said for Preyer's argument. Bentham did not

---

[137] Bentham in *IPML* softened his position. It was still 'as ineligible as it is impossible' that 'the laws of all nations, or even of any two nations, should coincide in all points', but there were at least 'some leading points' according to which the 'laws of all civilised nations might, without inconvenience, be the same': *An introduction to the principles and morals of legislation*, p. 295. See G. Postema, 'The expositor, the censor, and the common law', *Canadian Journal of Philosophy* 9.4 (1979), pp. 643–670.

[138] Bentham, *A comment on the Commentaries*, p. 56n.

[139] Hereafter referred to as *Time and place*. See Preyer, *Bentham, Coleridge, and the science of history*, p. 58.

[140] Bentham, *Works*, X, p. 562.

believe in an absolutely relative approach to legal and political questions – all laws and institutions were to be judged according to their utility – but nor was he a legal universalist. He understood that societies developed in different ways and at different speeds, invoking utility as a compass with which to navigate, rather than transcend, historical difference.

Bentham in several of his writings, including *IPML*, the *Constitutional Code* (1822–1832), and the *Rationale of Judicial Evidence*, conceded that civilisations do not emerge uniformly from barbarous origins.[141] He was less clear on what those differences might look like, possibly because he assumed readers' familiarity with Smith's four-stage account of the changing modes of subsistence, or with the idea of material and intellectual progress generally.[142] He was more concerned with whether or not laws should accommodate societies' unique routes to progress, and, if so, to what extent. His fullest discussion of the issue occurred in the essay on *Time and Place*, a work that has confused and divided scholars. The confusion, it seems, arises from the difficulty of squaring Bentham's relativism regarding the *matter* of laws with his universalism regarding their *form*; as Cornewall Lewis put it in 1852, systems of law which attempted to 'universalise the matter, as well as the form of law' were 'fallacious', a remark directed specifically at Bentham.[143] The essay itself, Burrow noted, can 'by selective quotation' be used to support the view that Bentham was either a universalising rationalist, or, as in Preyer's account, a thinker who wrangled with historical diversity.[144] This conundrum has wider significances within Bentham scholarship, not least because it maps onto contemporary debates about his credentials as a value-pluralist liberal, or, conversely, as a parochial (and Eurocentric) thinker who wanted to homogenise social norms.[145]

Burns observed that the circumstantial relativism of *Time and Place* owed a debt to Montesquieu and, less straightforwardly, to Kames and

---

[141] On the *Constitutional code*, see Rosen, *Jeremy Bentham and representative democracy*, p. 24. For this argument in *Rationale of judicial evidence*, see Bentham, *Works*, VI, p. 329.

[142] Bentham occasionally referred to Smith's four stages and the 'pastoral state' in the 'scale of civilisation': *Works*, VIII, p. 256. Similarly, in a footnote to Book I, Part II, Chapter 3 of *The Book of Fallacies*, he asserted that the 'savages and barbarians of the present period exhibit to us our ancestors in anterior periods': *Book of fallacies*, p. 168n. For context, see D. Spadafora, *The idea of progress in eighteenth-century Britain* (New Haven: Yale University Press, 1990), p. 381.

[143] Cornewall Lewis, *A treatise on the methods of observation and reasoning in politics*, II, p. 35. At least some of the confusion stems from Bentham's early editors. In the Bowring edition of *Time and Place*, Bentham is made to argue that while laws 'need not be of the wild and spontaneous growth of the country to which they are given . . . prejudice and the blindest custom' must also be 'humoured': *Works*, I, p. 180.

[144] Burrow, *Evolution and society*, p. 38.

[145] See G. Hoogensen, *International relations, security and Jeremy Bentham* (London: Routledge, 2005), pp. 23–24.

Barrington.[146] 'Before Montesquieu', Bentham opined in 1776, 'all was unmixed barbarism'. Grotius, Pufendorf, and Burlamaqui were illiberal because their respective conceptions of natural law reproduced, either explicitly or accidentally, the metaphysical barbarisms of religion. Montesquieu thus divided the pure barbarism of natural law from his own 'mixed' barbarism in *De l'esprit des lois*, but even he could slip into 'pseudo-metaphysical sophistry'.[147] It is an interesting coincidence, if nothing more, that a number of German historians and jurists saw Montesquieu as a precursor to their own historicism and a key figure, therefore, in the break with natural law and Christian universal history.[148] It is well known that Bentham decried the idea of sovereignty as 'abstract dogma' because it had no basis in historical and thus empirical fact, and these shared demarcations are significant to the extent that both Bentham and the German historicists questioned transcendental systems of interpretation which downplayed historical difference.[149] The impulse in both cases was to reject the universalising frameworks in which these political and legal fictions – natural law, the social contract, the idea of sovereignty, and so on – claimed legitimacy.

Burns concluded, ultimately, that Bentham constructed a legislative science on the universal principles of Condillac and Hartley, rather than on Montesquieu's 'circumstantial empiricism', and that he was not a thinker who seriously understood, let alone legislated for, the kinds of historical, cultural, and ethnographic differences which Montesquieu had emphasised.[150] The thrust of Burns's argument is undoubtedly correct: Bentham's historical understanding was clearly shallow. Given what I have been arguing here, however, it is not immediately obvious that those universal principles, which provided laws with their timeless form, trivialised the question of time and place. It is a matter of how far, exactly, we want to push Bentham's concessions to historical, geographic, and cultural contexts – not whether we push them – and, perhaps more importantly, of

---

[146] Bentham mentioned to Bowring that Montesquieu, along with Helvétius and Beccaria, 'set me on the principle of utility': *Works*, X, p. 54.

[147] Bentham, *A comment on the* <u>*Commentaries*</u>, p. 444n.

[148] Meinecke argued that Montesquieu was instrumental to later historicisms: *Historism*, pp. 106–111. Montesquieu in *De l'esprit des lois* (1748) claimed that 'laws should be relative' to the 'spirit and the passions of the heart' in 'various climates': C. de Montesquieu (ed. A.M. Cohler), *The spirit of the laws* (Cambridge: Cambridge University Press, 1989), p. 231. James Mill also alluded to Montesquieu in *HBI*: I, p. 412.

[149] Quoted in Burns, 'Jeremy Bentham and the political science of his time', http://arts.st-andrews.ac.uk/intellectualhistory, last accessed on 12 January 2018.

[150] Ibid.

how we measure their significance. John Hill Burton in the introduction to Bentham's *Works* observed that '[h]is expositions in politics are divided into two distinct classes'; the first belonged to 'a people, supposed to have thrown off all prejudice and established custom', whereas the second belonged to a people who operated within the 'existing machinery of established institutions and opinions'. The former could only ever represent an 'ultimate end of gradual change', which meant that much of Bentham's political thinking inevitably took place in the latter, in the world of 'distinct circumstances'.[151] As we shall see in Chapter 4, John Stuart Mill made a similar distinction regarding his own work.

The essay on *Time and Place* offered a more substantively historical conception of society than commentators have generally acknowledged.[152] Its arguments for legal uniformity applied more to the form of laws – that is, to the normative framework of utility – than to their substantive contents.[153] A cosmopolitan legal code could account only for our natural susceptibility to pleasures and pains, without dogmatically asserting what was universally pleasurable and painful.[154] 'Before Montesquieu', Bentham observed, 'a man who had a distant country given him to make laws for would have made short work of it' by assuming that his own manners, tastes, and religion were universal.[155] The laws of one society, therefore, were not readily exportable to another, but this did not mean that their form should be relative as well. One common objection, articulated by Cornewall Lewis, is that Bentham's distinction between the form and matter of laws was conceptually bogus.[156] The criticism may be valid, but either way we must not lose sight of why Bentham made the distinction in

---

[151] J. H. Burton, 'Introduction to the study of Bentham's Works', *Works*, I, p. 47.

[152] In the years since I began this project, this reading of Bentham's political and legal thought has steadily gained traction. See, for example, R. Loring, 'The role of universal jurisprudence in Bentham's legal cosmopolitanism', *Revue d'études benthamiennes* 13 (2014), http://journals .openedition.org/etudes-benthamiennes/749, last accessed on 7 June 2017; P. Rudan, 'Society as a code: Bentham and the fabric of order', *History of European Ideas* 42.1 (2016), pp. 39–54. On the other hand, the interpretation of *Time and place* as unhistorical has proved resilient: S. G. Engelmann and J. Pitts, 'Bentham's "place and time"', *La revue Tocqueville* 32.1 (2011), p. 56.

[153] Burns pointed to Bentham's remark in the *Fragment* that the law ought to be 'a great degree the same' in different times and places, but even here the implication is that these uniformities would extend only to the form of laws; either way, Bentham's qualification – 'to a great degree the same' – is at best ambiguous: 'Jeremy Bentham and the political science of his time', http://arts.st-andrews.ac.uk/intellectualhistory, last accessed on 12 January 2018.

[154] The edition of *Time and place* to which I refer has been arranged according to Bentham's manuscripts: J. Bentham (ed. S. G. Engelmann), *Selected writings* (New Haven: Yale University Press, 2011), p. 155.

[155] Ibid., p. 156.

[156] Cornewall Lewis, *A treatise on the methods of observation and reasoning in politics*, II, p. 35.

the first place; his intention, however misguided, was to make room for precisely those factors which he allegedly ignored – the circumstances of time and place – and, more importantly, to ensure that utility provided a happiness-maximising framework in which to rationally consider them.

I am not trying to exonerate Bentham from well-deserved charges of narrowness, or to suggest that his political and legal sciences were explicitly historicist. He did, however, understand that laws varied historically, and that the circumstances of time and place must be addressed by the legislator. The distinction is slight but significant, and it is obvious from my analysis so far that Bentham could not entertain a relativism more ambitious than that, not least because his criticisms of Blackstone, Burke, and the legal historicists distinguished between exposition and criticism. It was simply impossible to dissolve questions of utility into explanations of laws' origins and development, but we should not take this to mean that for Bentham the circumstances of time and place were irrelevant. If we had no way of discriminating between good and bad laws – an undertaking that cannot rely on irreducibly historical methods – then we might as well conclude that 'rude nations' in 'barbarous ages' deserved rude or barbarous laws.[157] In a lecture delivered over Bentham's remains, the physician and sanitary reformer Thomas Southwood Smith (1788–1861) extolled this aspect of Bentham's thought, and expressed regret that the principle of utility had not been adopted sooner in less advanced civilisations, so great were its services to 'the progress of time' and 'civilisation'.[158]

As Bentham put it in *Time and Place*, it cannot be the case that 'rude nations' deserved 'simple, that is, imperfect laws', or that the laws of a 'civilised nation' cannot guide, to some degree, 'a rude and ignorant nation'.[159] It is difficult to gauge Bentham's commitment to this idea, largely because his writings do not yield a definite answer; nevertheless, it is worth pointing out that even his more stridently universalist claims were not wholly deaf to local circumstances. In the *Codification Proposal* (1822), for example, he averred that 'in comparison of the *universally-applying*, the extent of the *exclusively-applying* circumstances will be found very inconsiderable ... The great outlines ... will be found to be the same for every territory, for every race, and for every time'.[160] Likewise, in the much

---

[157] Bentham, *Selected writings*, p. 179. This line of argument also appears in *Rationale of judicial evidence*, in which he claimed that the 'writing of good judicature' was indispensable to 'the progress of civilisation': *Works*, VI, p. 328.

[158] Bentham, *Works*, XI, pp. 83–84.   [159] Bentham, *Selected writings*, p. 218.

[160] J. Bentham (eds. P. Schofield and J. Harris), *Legislator of the world: writings on codification, law, and education* (Oxford: Oxford University Press, 1998), p. 291. Before revising his perspective, John

earlier *Fragment*, he claimed that the laws of different nations may, over time, become 'to a great degree the same'.[161] It is not obvious in these texts, either, that the identification of 'great outlines' reduced to a mere technicality their application to specific times and places, or that utilitarian laws would simply abolish historical difference; in *Time and Place*, for example, he conceded that it may be impossible to define property universally, which, as Robert Loring has pointed out, was practically to 'give up on universality' altogether.[162]

One way of addressing the problem is to think about the relationship between universal laws and their local enforcement. In *Time and Place*, for example, he argued that penal codes ought to vary according to the civility of the place in question, and that in a 'very rude' age 'it is possible that punishments in point of quantity might require to be somewhat greater than it were necessary they should be in a civilised one'.[163] Furthermore, he endorsed the idea that different stages of civilisational development required different kinds of sanctions.[164] In 'a rude age', he observed, 'the moral sanction has less force than in a civilised one', just as the 'religious sanction has commonly given but little assistance to the political' because 'the people are not yet broke in to the habit of lending spontaneously their assistance to the laws'.[165] The dichotomy between rude and civilised ages lacked the sophistication of a more finely graded stadial theory, but it pointed to the gradual establishment of a political community in which individuals could live peacefully without the threat of physical or religious punishment. This meant that laws, once codified, should not be immutable or static in the face of change: only the utilitarian 'grounds of law' should be permanent, not the 'laws themselves'.[166]

Bentham did recognise the need to reconcile his legal cosmopolitanism with the principle of historical difference, and thus to square the universal form of law with its circumstantially relative contents. This concern

criticised Bentham for failing to understand that 'the same institutions will no more suit two nations in different stages of civilisation, than the same lessons will suit children of different ages': J. S. Mill, *CW*, X, p. 16. On Bentham's science of legislation, see U. Mehta, *Liberalism and empire: a study in nineteenth-century British liberal thought* (Chicago: University of Chicago Press, 1999), p. 92.

[161] Bentham, *A comment on the Commentaries*, p. 398.
[162] R. Loring, 'The role of universal jurisprudence in Bentham's legal cosmopolitanism', *Revue d'études benthamiennes* 13 (2014), http://journals.openedition.org/etudes-benthamiennes/749, last accessed on 7 June 2017.
[163] Bentham, *Selected writings*, p. 200.
[164] I owe this observation to Mary Mack: *Jeremy Bentham: an odyssey of ideas*, p. 157.
[165] Bentham, *Selected writings*, p. 200. Mill made the same argument in *HBI*, V, p. 528.
[166] Bentham, *Selected writings*, p. 200.

became increasingly pronounced in the 1810s and 1820s, culminating in the essay on *Time and Place* and the publication in 1822 of his ambitious *Codification Proposal*, which addressed itself, tellingly, to all nations professing liberal opinions. He argued in the *Proposal* that, while the *pannomion* would necessarily vary at the local level, especially in regard to offences against reputation and property, this would not undermine its universality; it was perfectly possible, he reasoned, to achieve 'variation within uniformity'.[167] It is right, perhaps, to suspect Bentham of having his cake and eating it, but the more urgent point is that he did not sense the contradiction, hence, *inter alia*, his distinction between genus and species.[168] The genus referred to a general category of law within which different species co-existed, so that a single form of law could be applied to various historical and cultural contexts. This, essentially, was a reformulation of Hume's point in the *Treatise* that the universal principles of human nature were not cancelled out by the circumstances in which they were placed, and that it was possible, therefore, to identify both uniformity and variation within social phenomena.[169]

The utility principle, Bentham argued, made room for society's historically acquired manners, tastes, customs, and laws; and if we take seriously Burton Hill's point that Bentham wrote in two different contexts, one of which presupposed advanced moral and political progress while the other did not, then these accommodations certainly matter.[170] Paola Rudan has made perhaps the strongest case for seeing Bentham's conception of society as the logical and historical space of politics.[171] Legislators on this account do not call society into being *ex nihilo*, but they do make prudent calculations about the prospective benefits and drawbacks of change, especially when the society in question is strongly attached to its existing laws and institutions. In the earlier *Comment on the Commentaries*, Bentham was even more explicit. Man, he proclaimed, was unquestionably 'formed for society' because 'he is in it'.[172] There was no Archimedean standpoint outside history or society.

---

[167] Bentham, *Legislator of the world*, p. 292.

[168] Ibid. See also Bentham Loring, 'The role of universal jurisprudence in Bentham's legal cosmopolitanism', *Revue d'études benthamiennes* 13 (2014), http://journals.openedition.org/etudes-benthamiennes/749, last accessed on 7 June 2017.

[169] See D. Forbes, *Hume's philosophical politics* (Cambridge: Cambridge University Press, 1985), pp. 102–125; M. Watkins, *The philosophical progress of Hume's essays* (Cambridge: Cambridge University Press, 2019), p. 64.

[170] Burton Hill, 'Introduction to the study of Bentham's works', p. 47.

[171] Rudan, 'Society as a code: Bentham and the fabric of order', p. 40.

[172] Bentham, *A comment on the Commentaries*, p. 34.

Bentham's theory of human nature was more fluidly historical than his critics have acknowledged, but even so the 'universal system of human actions' that drove his legal cosmopolitanism is still widely regarded as a determining principle, and not, as I wish to suggest, a framework in which to navigate (rather than transcend or eradicate) historical difference.[173] Marx's strident reproof in *Das Kapital* was arguably the most memorable, but the immediate damage was dealt by moderate and philosophic Whigs in the early decades of the nineteenth century.[174] Jeffrey's complaint in 1804 of Bentham's 'vulgar' distinctions between right and wrong set the tone for other Whigs who rejected utilitarian morality and logic. Bentham did believe that, over time, these historical differences would become increasingly less significant; and it is also true that he assigned to his 'universal system of human actions' an essentially timeless significance. The principle of self-preservation, he argued, was embedded in human nature and civil society, a fact which he, like Hobbes and Locke, could only establish hypothetically. On this basis E. J. Eisenach has argued that, according to Bentham, 'law should be based on the universal motives of and desire for the means of self-preservation', and that in future these historical differences would dissolve into a 'timeless and universal science of politics' in which we are bound by 'self-interest and the fear of death'.[175]

In a more immediate context, however, the legislator's task was to weigh up the utility of abandoning established laws and customs, and while it would be an overstatement to argue that for Bentham the relationship between human nature and history was meaningfully co-constitutive, he denied that our conceptions of pleasure and pain were universal, beyond very basic aversions such as the fear of death. As Simon Evnine has shown in the case of David Hume, it is important to distinguish between substantive and methodological uniformity; the former implies that individuals always pursue what they think is good, whereas the latter implies that notions of the good change according to time and place.[176] This distinction

---

[173] J. Bentham (ed. P. Schofield), *Of the limits of the penal branch of jurisprudence* [1780–1782] (Oxford: Oxford University Press, 2010), p. 130.

[174] Marx, *Capital*, I, p. 609n.

[175] Eisenach, 'The dimension of history in Bentham's theory of law', p. 151. On the debate between Dinwiddy and David Lyons over the harmony of interests in Bentham's thought, see J. Dinwiddy (ed. W. Twining), *Bentham: selected writings of John Dinwiddy* (Stanford: Stanford University Press, 2004), pp. 132–138.

[176] S. Evnine, 'Hume, conjectural history, and the uniformity of human nature', *Journal of the History of Philosophy* 31.4 (1993), p. 591. See D. Hume (ed. E. Steinberg), *An enquiry concerning human understanding* (Indianapolis: Hackett, 1993), p. 55; see also Forbes, *Hume's philosophical politics*,

opens up a space in Bentham's thought for the study of history as an illustration of what different societies regarded as pleasurable and painful, as well as the contexts in which those preferences were shaped. In *Deontology, or the Science of Morality* (1834), for instance, he made a distinction between original and derivative utility, within which he conceptualised pleasures and pains as historically informed expectations.[177]

Bentham's language of progress strove, in part, to explain the transformation of human nature over time, not because the desire for pleasure and fear of pain were historically contingent, but because the objects of those desires and fears were determined, in part, by cultural, geographical, and historical conditions.[178] In *The Book of Fallacies*, for example, he argued that history attested to the 'gradual melioration of the mental frame' of even the most barbarous communities.[179] His distinction between civility and barbarism, however, did not imply a teleological view of progress comparable with Condorcet's (1743–1794) or Turgot's (1727–1781), or even Smith's in *Lectures on Rhetoric and Belles Lettres* (1762–1763, henceforth *LRBL*). Unlike them, Bentham denied that progress was inexorable especially in politics and law, a fact to which his own political experiences attested. Consider the preface to the second edition of the *Fragment* from 1828, in which he recalled Lord Camden's opposition to William Eden's unsuccessful attempt to clear the statute book of 'antique rubbish'.[180] His conversion to political radicalism in 1809-1810 further entrenched his view that political progress depended on the transformation of established attitudes and norms, amongst which he included the appeal to history. As he put it in *The Book of Fallacies*, in 'no other department of the field of knowledge' other than politics 'do leading men of the present times' appeal 'to the wisdom of our ancestors'.[181]

Social progress for Bentham was more akin to what David Spadafora has called the doctrine of pliability, whose origins can be traced to David Hartley's *Observations on Man* (1749), a text with which Bentham was

---

p. 103. Variations in preferences also occurred amongst individuals of the same age: P. Schofield, 'Bentham on taste, sex, and religion' in X. Zhai and M. Quinn (eds.), *Bentham's theory of law and public opinion* (Cambridge: Cambridge University Press, 2014), p. 93.

[177] J. Bentham (ed. A. Goldworth), *Deontology together with A table of the springs of action and Article on utilitarianism* (Oxford: Oxford University Press, 1983), pp. 89–90; Schofield, *Utility and democracy*, p. 31.

[178] The unpublished second volume of *Not Paul* charted the progression from barbarism to civility. '[A]s we recede farther and farther from present time', he argued, 'we find the mind of man in a still ruder and ruder state': 'Bentham papers', University College London Library, box 161, f. 23.

[179] Bentham, *Book of fallacies*, p. 301. Likewise, in the second volume of *Not Paul*, he contended that his age was 'an age not only of prodigiously superior intellectual power, but even of comparative probity': 'Bentham papers', University College London Library, box 139, f. 460.

[180] Bentham, *Works*, I, p. 242.   [181] Bentham, *Book of fallacies*, p. 52.

familiar, and to other eighteenth-century writings on education and psychology.[182] Progress on this account was neither inevitable nor imminent; on the contrary, it resembled the art of medicine in which the patient's health depended as much on the physician's skill as on scientific principles. The physician, in other words, was to the patient what the legislator was to the body politic. The pliability of the patient, or their amenability to treatment, allowed the physician to administer 'medicine for the soul'; and, as Mary Mack has shown, Bentham's hitherto unpublished writings make frequent comparisons between the arts of legislation and medicine, the purpose of which was to emphasise the fragility of progress and the need for constant vigilance and redress.[183] 'In short', Bentham declared, 'what the physician is to the natural body, the legislator is to the political: legislation is the art of medicine exercised upon a grand scale'.[184] An unassailable faith in progress could have deleterious effects on the actual course of development. By positing an analogy between the physician and the legislator, however, Bentham stressed the importance not just of fundamental scientific principles, but of knowing how to put those principles effectively into practice. Political bodies, just like natural bodies, require individual treatment.

Bentham was more optimistic about the possibilities of intellectual and scientific progress, on the back of which he called for equivalent revolutions in morality and politics: '[the] moral world', he argued in the 1780s, still awaited its Bacon or Newton, a role which he undoubtedly intended to fulfil.[185] Likewise, in *Rationale of Judicial Evidence*, he contrasted the vertiginous progress of natural science with the slower, more fragmented progresses of the moral and legal sciences. He described how the scientific mind had advanced 'with uninterrupted and continually accelerated progress towards the pinnacle of perfection', unlike 'moral science' and the 'field of law'.[186] There has been much debate over the extent and significance of his political optimism. His oft-quoted declaration in the *Fragment* that scientific knowledge was advancing 'rapidly towards perfection' implied that the same might happen for politics; however, as Warren Roberts has argued, Bentham exhibited a recurring pessimism in this respect.[187] 'Perfection', he opined in an unpublished manuscript, 'is not

---

[182] Spadafora, *The idea of progress in eighteenth-century Britain*, pp. 177–178.
[183] Mack, *Jeremy Bentham: an odyssey of ideas*, p. 264.
[184] Bentham, 'Bentham papers', University College London Library, box 32, f. 138.
[185] In D. G. Long, 'Censorial jurisprudence and political radicalism: a reconsideration of the early Bentham', *The Bentham Newsletter* 12 (1988), p. 8.
[186] Bentham, *Works*, VI, p. 205.   [187] Bentham, *A comment on the Commentaries*, p. 393.

the lot of human nature' because it required a 'utopia to plant it in'.[188] It was possible that the art of legislation could be elevated to the point at which a theoretically perfect legal code existed, but beyond that even the most rational laws could not legislate out of existence all human sources of mischief and pain.[189]

Conclusion

Bentham, I have argued, defied his own stereotype by engaging with history and historiography in the contexts of jurisprudence, ethics, and politics. While he denied that history possessed an independent value that could determine or even effectively structure politics, we should not mistake these arguments for an unwillingness to contemplate politics historically, or to make occasionally significant concessions to time and place. Bentham's point, rather, was that historical truths were categorically distinct from philosophical truths, and that _sciences historiques_ observed the past while _sciences philosophiques_ appraised it. He reproached Blackstone, Burke, and Savigny for inadequately distinguishing between history and philosophy, and for attempting to resolve politics through exclusively historical methods. This made him paradoxically more but also less of a historian: more, in the sense that he stressed the past's distinctness above the metaphysical abstractions of religion and natural law, something he shared, coincidentally, with the early German historicists; less, in the sense that he opposed historical approaches to legislation and government for the very same reason. The laws, beliefs, and institutions of one time and place could not serve _a posteriori_ as prescriptions for another.

F. C. Beiser has argued that historicism at its most fundamental can be interpreted as a plea for history's autonomy, conceived in a spirit of rebellion from political and religious authorities.[190] Bentham's tree of knowledge in _Chrestomathia_ likewise called for history's separation from philosophy, and this, I suggest in Chapter 3, directly influenced Grote. Finally, I have explored Bentham's reception of the enlightened historicisms of the eighteenth century, including Montesquieu, Kames, Smith, and Barrington. Montesquieu's 'circumstantial empiricism' broke with the barbarisms of religion and natural law, and it too viewed history in

---

[188] Bentham, 'Bentham papers', University College London Library, box 62, f. 188. See W. Roberts, 'Bentham's conception of political change: a liberal approach' in Parekh (ed.), _Critical assessments_, III, p. 955.

[189] Roberts, 'Bentham's conception of political change', p. 955.   [190] Beiser, 'Historicism', p. 156.

particular rather than universal or transcendent terms.[191] Bentham wished merely that Montesquieu had gone further, and this re-reading, I wish to suggest, has at least two implications for my central argument. The first is that utility was conceived as circumstantially and thus historically relative, and not, as later Whig and Romantic writers claimed, as a framework in which to eradicate historical difference. The second is that, if utility was indeed anti-historical but not ahistorical, then it is not altogether surprising that the two Mills experimented with political methods in which history and progress were more boldly stated, or that Grote's *History of Greece* has been read as both utilitarian and historicist. These thinkers, as we shall see, did not regard their historical endeavours as contrary to the aims of utility.

---

[191] Burns, 'Jeremy Bentham and the political science of his time', http://arts.st-andrews.ac.uk/intellec tualhistory, last accessed on 12 January 2018.

CHAPTER 2

James Mill and the Real Business of Philosophy

The Unhistorical Historian

James Mill in *A Fragment on Mackintosh* (1835) denied that Bentham had ignored 'the circumstances which distinguish any people for whom a particular [legal] code is designed'.[1] Mackintosh's errors were numerous. He had confused 'jurisprudence' with 'legislation' and criticism with exposition; he had failed to distinguish adequately between the matter and form of laws; and he had misunderstood the relationship between theory and practice.[2] The Benthamite tone of these remarks is clear enough, but the context in which they were written lends them extra weight. The *Fragment on Mackintosh* was Mill's last significant work and its preoccupation with time and place is telling. 'The only men who can appreciate the circumstances which are accidental to this or that particular people', he observed, 'are the men who best understand that far more important part of the circumstances constituting their condition, which they have in common with the men of other communities'.[3] A profound knowledge of universal circumstances helped the philosopher to understand local contexts, while so-called practical men neglected both general and particular conditions by transplanting 'the laws of their own country'.

[1] J. Mill, *A fragment on Mackintosh: being strictures on some passages in the dissertation by Sir James Mackintosh prefixed to the Encyclopædia Britannica* [1835] (London: Longman, Green, Reader, and Dyer, 1870), p. 142. For the initial criticism, see J. Mackintosh, *Dissertation on the progress of ethical philosophy, chiefly during the seventeenth and eighteenth centuries* [1830] (Edinburgh: Adam and Charles Black, 1862), p. 241.
[2] Mill, *A fragment on Mackintosh*, pp. 141, 146. See Mackintosh, *Dissertation on the progress of ethical philosophy*, pp. 257, 263. Mill even contemplated writing a history of English law in which he would trace 'the expedients of the several ages to the state of the human mind, and the circumstances of society of those ages, and to show their concord or discord with the standard of perfection': Mill to Napier, 5 August, 1818 in A. Bain, *James Mill: a biography* (London: Longmans, Green, and Co., 1882), p. 173.
[3] Mill, *A fragment on Mackintosh*, p. 143.

It was not the utilitarians, therefore, who constructed a legislative science on 'pure mathematics'. 'Did Sir James not know that the business of philosophy', as defined by Bacon, was to ascend from particulars to general laws, and then to descend from general laws to particulars?[4]

Mill's defence of Bentham was also self-defence, and the similarities between their respective conceptions of history are not entirely surprising. Both scoffed at the chronicler who wandered history without philosophy as a torch and guide, and both rejected arguments from historical authority.[5] In his *Commonplace Books*, which were compiled mostly in the 1810s and 1820s, Mill protested against 'blind custom, alias experience, alias practice, alias wisdom of ancestors'.[6] His conversion to utilitarianism in 1809 only deepened a resolve that can be traced to Dugald Stewart's (1753–1828) lectures at Edinburgh. 'Custom', Mill wrote, afforded no 'proof of utility' because it illustrated merely the doing of certain things at certain times, usually by a vested interest.[7] As in Bentham's case, however, his opposition to arguments from tradition did not prevent him from thinking historic-ally about politics. His *History of British India*, conceived as an 'introduc-tion to the study of civil society in general', demonstrates his ambition in this respect.[8] But his logical construction of the relationship between philosophy and history preceded his utilitarianism – he argued in 1805 that no 'scheme of government' can 'happily conduce to the ends of government, unless it is adapted to the state of the people for whose use it is intended' – and scholars have generally overlooked two important influences in this respect.[9] The first is Francis Bacon and the second is David Hume, both of whom encouraged Mill to think more deeply about the relationship between general and special causes.

Mill in 1803 praised Hume's *History of England* for exhibiting 'the complete union of history and philosophy' and for showing that, whereas the 'common historian' simply recounted events, one after the other, the philosophical historian examined society's governance and customs. For the first time 'philosophical delineation' had triumphed over the bare facts of history to reveal 'the manner in which the principles of human nature operated in conjunction with the circumstances in which the people were

---

[4] Ibid., pp. 144, 296.
[5] 'It is remarkable', he observed, 'that all men whose minds in the field of morals and legislation have benefited their species, have been abused as contemners [sic] of authority. Luther, Bacon, Locke, Bentham': *CPB*, III, ch. 4.
[6] Ibid., ch. 9.   [7] Ibid., ch. 4.
[8] James Mill to David Ricardo, 19 October 1817 in D. Ricardo (ed. P. Sraffa), *The works and correspondence of David Ricardo* (Cambridge: Cambridge University Press, 1951), VII, p. 195.
[9] J. Mill, 'William Dawson's thoughts on public trusts', *Literary Journal* 5.12 (1805), p. 1311.

placed, to produce the political changes; and thus to refer particular facts to general laws'. This, Mill maintained, was 'the real business of philosophy', a phrase which reappeared in the *Fragment on Mackintosh* in praise of Bacon.[10] Whereas Bentham had drawn strict boundaries between philosophy and history, Mill followed Hume and Bacon in establishing porous boundaries between the two. His essay on 'Theory and Practice' (1836) presented this argument in the form of a Socratic dialogue, while his *History of British India* (1817) – and to a lesser extent his essay 'On Government' (1820) – demonstrated in more practical terms the affinities between philosophical and historical knowledge, as well as the importance of observation, experiment, and induction.[11]

The reception of Mill's political writings in the 1820s and 1830s did not faithfully reflect the scope of his ambitions. His essay 'On Government' was the subject of fierce attacks by Whigs and Tories in the *Edinburgh Review*, the most devastating of which came from Mackintosh and Macaulay.[12] As with Bentham, he was accused of developing a political science in which abstract principles trumped historical facts. This line of argument was an effective rhetorical strategy, crafted by the 'enemies of all reform', in which attention was shifted away from the content and onto the logic of his arguments.[13] The language of practice was mobilised against the language of theory, deduction, and general principles, a fact to which Mill privately admitted when he disparaged those 'who condemn theory'.[14] Likewise, his friend David Ricardo (1772–1823) complained in 1811 of those who are 'all for fact and nothing for theory'.[15] The utilitarians, in turn, were seen by the likes of William Hazlitt as peddlers of 'theories' as 'little addressed to the head as to the heart'.[16] To their adversaries, theory was a dirty word that indicated a kind of Hobbesian geometry in which assertion predominated over concrete empirical analysis, and, as Crimmins noted, their reputation as theorists was 'particularly harmful to the public perception of utilitarianism' and its vituperations against the British state.[17]

---

[10] J. Mill, 'An historical view of the English government by J. Millar', *The Literary Journal* 2.6 (1803), pp. 325–326.

[11] See A. Loizides: 'Induction, deduction, and James Mill's "Government"', *Modern Intellectual History* (2015), pp. 1–29.

[12] See also J. Lively and J. Rees (eds.), *Utilitarian logic and politics* (Oxford: Clarendon Press, 1978).

[13] Mill, *A fragment on Mackintosh*, p. 147. [14] Ibid., p. 140; Mill, *CPB*, I, ch. 8.

[15] D. Ricardo, *Reply to Mr. Bosanquet's observations on the report of the bullion committee* (London: John Murray, 1811), p. 32.

[16] W. Hazlitt, 'The new school of reform: a dialogue between a rationalist and a sentimentalist' [1826] in W. Hazlitt (ed. W. C. Hazlitt), *The plain speaker: opinions on books, men, and things* (London: Bell and Daldy, 1870), p. 257.

[17] Crimmins, *Utilitarian philosophy and politics*, p. 25.

These Whig and Tory counterstrategies were well established by the time Mill's essay 'On Government' appeared in 1820. An anonymous Tory in 1817 had denounced Bentham's *Plan of Parliamentary Reform* (1817) as a specimen of unhistorical 'theory' that eviscerated 'the bowels of experience'.[18] Sir James Mackintosh and Henry Brougham (1778–1868) hurled similar accusations at Bentham's proposals for 'representative', 'pure', and 'total' democracy.[19] Mackintosh reverted to the well-worn language of experience, while Brougham accused Bentham of dealing in 'books' rather than 'men'.[20] The strategy, more often than not, was to attack the first principles from which the utilitarians deduced their political and moral views. Joseph Sortain (1809–1860), a nonconformist minister and avowed disciple of Bacon, dismissed Bentham's moral science as an elaborate fiction which addressed only one part of human nature: the Hobbesian tendency to oppress others.[21] The subtleties of Mill's logic were glossed over by Whigs and Tories who opposed his calls for annual elections, the secret ballot, qualified universal suffrage, and the compulsory rotation of MPs; falling back on debates from the 1790s, they attacked theory's philosophical and revolutionary pretensions and its disregard for concrete experience.[22]

Mill's methodology in the *History of British India* suffered similar attacks. The first Professor of Sanskrit at Oxford, Horace H. Wilson (1786–1860), wrote a preface to the 1840 edition of the *History* in which he recounted Mill's controversial decision not to visit India in person.[23] An advertisement in the *Edinburgh Review* for that very edition lamented Mill's 'deficiencies' and 'sweeping conclusions'.[24] When pressed on the issue by Sir James MacDonald (1784–1832) at a parliamentary Select Committee in 1831, Mill admitted that he could only speak about India 'generally, because my reason is an inference from all I know, from all I have heard, and all I have read about the people'.[25] This argument was

---

[18] [Anon.], 'Parliamentary reform', *British Review and London Critical Journal* 11/22 (1818), p. 308. Quoted in Loizides, 'Induction, deduction, and James Mill's "Government"', p. 25.

[19] Bentham, *A plan for parliamentary reform*, pp. xli–xlii.

[20] Loizides, 'Induction, deduction, and James Mill's "Government"', p. 5.

[21] J. Sortain, 'Bentham's *Science of morality*', *The Edinburgh Review* 61 (1835), pp. 368, 371.

[22] Bentham hardly banished the ghost of 1789 when he argued in the *Plan* that his proposals were the only possible remedy 'revolution apart': *Plan for parliamentary reform*, p. lvi. Mill was alive to the issue. In his *Commonplace Books*, he agreed with Condorcet that the French Revolution had not been caused by philosophers: *CPB*, III, ch. 5.

[23] H. H. Wilson, 'Preface' in J. Mill, *The history of British India* (London: James Madden, 1840), I, p. ii.

[24] *The Edinburgh Review* 71 (1840), p. 37.

[25] *British Parliamentary Papers* 5 (1831), pp. 396–399. Quoted in J. Chen, *James Mill's History of British India in its intellectual context*, PhD dissertation, University of Edinburgh (2000), p. 1.

consistent with what he had argued elsewhere, most notably in a letter to Alexander Walker from 1819. 'The immediate results of the recollection of gentlemen from India', he reasoned, 'are the materials by which I can best supply the disadvantage of not having been there'.[26] Mill's critics, including Francis Jeffrey, were quick to equate the *History's* utilitarian epistemology with that of 'a theorist, a bigot, or a partisan', and in this respect the charges levelled against Mill's *History* were not entirely dissimilar to those levelled against his essay 'On Government'; in both instances he was accused of eschewing empirical knowledge for a deductive science of politics.[27]

These critical receptions helped to shape Mill's legacy, even amongst some of his more sympathetic commentators. Henry Sidgwick and Alexander Bain (1810–1877) characterised his essay 'On Government' as an ahistorical exercise in deduction, while John in *A System of Logic* (1843) criticised his father for failing to combine inductive and deductive reasoning as a comprehensive logical method.[28] John in his *Autobiography* fulminated against the so-called method of 'pure geometry' because of its narrow premises and 'small number of general truths', and he remained sceptical that his father's essay 'On Government' had proved anything beyond the necessity of artificially aligning political interests through representative government.[29] At the same time, he argued that the 'accusations against the Benthamic theory of *being* a theory, of proceeding *à priori*, by way of general reasoning, instead of Baconian experiment, shewed complete ignorance of Bacon's principles, and of the necessary conditions of experimental investigation'.[30] John, as we shall see, gave succour to both sides of the debate by developing a 'historical' method of inverse deduction (Chapter 5).

My immediate purpose is to rescue James Mill from the reputation handed to him by his Whig and Tory opponents.[31] I wish to develop my earlier claim that Bentham's circumstantial relativism enabled precisely the

---

[26] James Mill to Alexander Walker, 6 November 1819, 'Walker papers', National Library of Scotland, MSS. 13724, f. 178.

[27] F. Jeffrey, *Contributions to the Edinburgh Review* (London: Longman, Brown, Green, and Longmans, 1844), p. 298.

[28] H. Sidgwick, *The elements of politics* [1891] (Cambridge: Cambridge University Press, 2012), p. 8n; Bain, *James Mill*, pp. 217–218; *CW*, VIII, p. 889–894. See also Loizides, 'Induction, deduction, and James Mill's "Government"', p. 3.

[29] J. S. Mill, *CW*, I, p. 168. [30] Ibid., p. 165.

[31] This reappraisal of Mill, which arguably began with Donald Winch, has been continued by Antis Loizides. See D. Winch (ed.), *James Mill's economic writings* (London: Oliver and Boyd, 1966), p. 368; Loizides, 'Induction, deduction, and James Mill's "Government"', pp. 1–29.

kind of methodological innovation for which the *History* is renowned, although its label as a philosophical history has often been applied for the wrong reasons. It is still widely assumed that the *History's* utilitarian logic was fundamentally at odds with its historical subject matter. I suggest, by way of counterargument, that we must take seriously Mill's distinction between philosophy and empiricism, whose roots he traced to Bacon and Hume, and that these influences were equal to his utilitarian and Scottish ones.[32] I end by re-examining his essay on 'Theory and Practice' from 1836, in which he replied to his critics in a dialogic style reminiscent of the Socratic *elenchus*, and denounced as illegitimate the partisan distinction between theory and practice. This frequently neglected essay, when placed alongside his other late writings, points to an increasing concern with the role of contingent historical, cultural, and geographic contexts in political science, 'the most important of all sciences'.[33]

Contextualising *The History of British India*

> I wish to see you thoroughly acquainted with, the course which human affairs, upon the great scale, have hitherto taken, the causes of their taking these different courses, the degree in which these courses have severally departed from the best course, and by what means they can best be made to approximate to that course.[34]

It is clear from even the shallowest of readings that Mill set out to write a philosophical history of British India. As William Thomas observed, one of its ambitions was to distil into as few propositions as possible the experiences and practical lessons of the past.[35] But what did this process of distillation involve, exactly?[36] In what form did the past suggest its lessons and how could the historian discover them? The literature has provided only limited answers to these questions, and we still lack a thorough account of the ways in which the *History* connected

---

[32] See, for example, J. Pitts, *A turn to empire: the rise of imperial liberalism in Britain and France* (Princeton: Princeton University Press, 2005), p. 121.

[33] Mill, 'William Dawson's thoughts on public trusts', p. 1311.
For analysis, see A. Loizides, *James Mill's utilitarian logic and politics* (London: Routledge, 2019), p. 182.

[34] James Mill to David Ricardo, 19 October 1817 in Ricardo, *Works*, VII, p. 196.

[35] Quoted from an introduction to an abridged edition of the *History*: J. Mill (ed. W. Thomas), *The history of British India* (Chicago: University of Chicago Press, 1975), p. xi.

[36] His *Analysis of the phenomena of the human mind* (1829) strove to reduce to its simplest elements the manifold complexities of mental states; to assign laws to those states; and to disclose the laws of their combination: J. Mill (eds. J. S. Mill, A. Bain, A. Findlater, and G. Grote), *Analysis of the phenomena of the human mind* (London: Longman, Green, Reader, and Dyer, 1878), p. x.

historiography to inductive logic and an 'Enlightenment' *science de l'homme*. Mill's ambition to do so was evident as early as 1803, when he praised Hume's *History of England* for relating the laws to the circumstances of human nature.[37] The preface to the *History* stated nakedly his own ambitions in this respect; it is, he argued, 'the business of the historian not merely to display the obvious outside of things', to chronicle 'institutions' and 'ordinances', but to penetrate into the causes of phenomena and discern 'natural tendencies', as well as the 'circumstances likely to operate either in combination with these natural tendencies, or in opposition to them'.[38] These tendencies gave context to India's history and disclosed opportunities for its reform.

Mill's civilisational grammar led to egregiously simplistic claims about India's state of society. One of his targets in this respect was the philologist Sir William Jones (1746–1795), whose founding of the Asiatic Society in 1784 encouraged a sympathetic if fleeting orientalism.[39] Mill in articles from 1807 onwards castigated Jones and the Orientalists for overestimating India's civility, and it is unsurprising that the *History* incited passionate responses from other Orientalists, including Vans Kennedy (1784–1846).[40] One source of disagreement was Mill's attempt to establish a theory of civilisation that went further than Bentham's in using historical and cultural differences to inform political decisions.[41] His goal wasn't simply to depict or denounce Indian society, but rather to provide the stimulus for its reform.[42] The 'happiness and rapid improvement of the people of India', he insisted, was a guiding priority, and, as Javeed Majeed observed, the utility principle served as a tool with which to measure the rudeness of

---

[37] Mill, 'An historical view of the English government by J. Millar', pp. 325–326.

[38] Mill, *HBI*, I, pp. xvii–xviii.

[39] Ibid., V, p. 513. See also Mehta, *Liberalism and empire*, p. 89; M. J. Franklin, *'Orientalist Jones': Sir William Jones, poet, lawyer, and linguist, 1746–1794* (Oxford: Oxford University Press, 2011), p. 340; Pitts, *A turn to empire*, p. 60.

[40] J. Rendall, 'Scottish orientalism: from Robertson to James Mill', *Historical Journal* 25.1 (1982), p. 43; H. M. Höpfl, 'From savage to Scotsman: conjectural history in the Scottish Enlightenment', *Journal of British Studies* 17.2 (1978), p. 45. These debates were made more urgent by the controversies surrounding the East India Company and Britain's apparatus of rule in India, both of which had come under scrutiny during the trial of Warren Hastings in the 1780s and 1790s. Mill met these charges, albeit with reservations, in volumes five and six of the *History*: V, pp. 433–513; VI, pp. 11–52.

[41] Stokes, *The English utilitarians and India*, p. 48; W. Thomas, *The Philosophic Radicals: nine studies in theory and practice, 1817–1841* (Oxford: Clarendon Press, 1979), p. 98; Mazlish, *Father and son*, pp. 118, 120.

[42] As Mill put it in a letter from 1819, 'I am not prejudiced against them [the Hindus] ... but I am convinced that a true estimate of the state of their civilisation, & of the stage which they reached in the progress from simplicity & rudeness to refinement is an essential condition to the adoption of the manners which are best calculated to do them good': Mill to Alexander Walker, 6 November 1819, 'Walker papers', National Library of Scotland, MSS. 13724, ff. 132–133.

India's civilisation, with a view to introducing a 'comprehensive code of law' based on a universal notion of utility.[43] But Mill's gaze was only ever half-fixed on India, and he was equally at pains to expose the shortcomings of British rule.[44] In volume three, for example, he scorned the idea that English law was 'the pure extract of reason, adapted to the exigencies of human nature itself', when actually it was 'arbitrary' and 'ill-adapted to the general ends which it is intended to serve'.[45] The two issues went together. India's reform depended on the reform of Britain's own political, civil, and legal institutions, because only then would there be a perfect standard with which to accelerate India's progress.[46] Utility, in this respect, accelerated history.

Mill employed utility as a framework in which to discriminate between civilised and non-civilised societies, and the *History* assimilated into the utility principle a theory of civilisational development which hearkened back to the late Scottish Enlightenment and the Edinburgh of his youth.[47] We know that he was influenced by Stewart's lectures on moral philosophy, which made him, according to John, the 'last survivor of this great school'.[48] In reality this 'great school' comprised several disparate schools spread across two generations at Edinburgh, Glasgow, and Aberdeen; and yet Stewart's lectures on Smith, Hume, and Thomas Reid (1710–1796) solidified Mill's 'tastes' and 'pursuits'.[49] Scholars have since claimed that he inherited from Stewart a 'theoretical' or 'conjectural' approach to historiography, a term which Stewart coined and then retrospectively applied to Smith's *Dissertation on the Origin of Languages* (1761), Hume's *Natural History of Religion* (1757), and *histoire raisonnée*.[50] The *History* does bear

[43] Mill, *HBI*, V, p. 490. On the link between happiness and education, see J. Mill (ed. T. Ball), 'Education', *Political writings* (Cambridge: Cambridge University Press, 1992), p. 139; J. Majeed, *Ungoverned imaginings: James Mill's The history of British India and orientalism* (Oxford: Oxford University Press, 1992), p. 133.

[44] See D. Forbes, 'James Mill and India', *The Cambridge Journal* 5.1 (1951), pp. 19–33.

[45] Mill, *HBI*, III, p. 446.

[46] See Collini, Winch, and Burrow, *That noble science of politics*, p. 116.

[47] See Bain, *James Mill*, p. 16; K. Grint, *James Mill's common place books and their intellectual context, 1773–1836*, PhD dissertation, University of Sussex (2013), p. 9; Chen, *James Mill's History of British India in its intellectual context*, p. 191.

[48] John Stuart Mill to Auguste Comte, 28 January 1843 in O. A. Haac (ed.), *The correspondence of John Stuart Mill and Auguste Comte* (London: Transaction, 1995), p. 129.

[49] Mill to Macvey Napier, 10 July 1821, British Library [BL] Additional Manuscript [Add. MS] 34612, f. 428; Rendall, 'Scottish orientalism', p. 43. See J. G. A. Pocock, *Barbarism and religion. Volume one. The enlightenments of Edward Gibbon, 1737–1764* (Cambridge: Cambridge University Press, 1999), p. 3.

[50] A. Smith (ed. D. Stewart), *Essays on philosophical subjects* (Dublin: Wogan, Byrne, Moore, Colbert, Rice, Jones, Porter, and Folingsby, 1795), p. liii. By the time Mill wrote the *History*, however, the conjectural method was already in decline: M. Schmidt, 'Dugald Stewart, "conjectural history" and

traces of these influences, but it is important to separate conjectural history from the philosophical history which Mill actually practised.

The conjectural method was philosophical because it inferred otherwise unknowable parts of history from the principles of human nature and the circumstances of man's environment.[51] This allowed the historian to tabulate civilisation's development within the progress of civil society and commerce, and to supersede hypothetical accounts of man's exit from the state of nature, both of which had far-reaching political implications.[52] Stewart encouraged the use of travellers' reports and anthropological data gathered from the observation of pre-political communities, a technique to which even Bentham had approvingly referred.[53] Stewart assumed that contemporary societies could replace missing links in the historical sequence, but Mill in the *History* practised this technique only sporadically.[54] He shared Stewart's vision of history as a systemic development for the same reason that Bentham feared the 'maze' of historical facts, and he agreed on the importance of sifting them with general principles, but he agreed with Ferguson that historians were too frequently tempted into the 'boundless regions' of 'conjecture'.[55]

Mill in an article on China from 1809 qualified his otherwise effusive praise for Millar's *Origin of the Distinction of Ranks* (1778) by lamenting that 'philosophers have not as yet laid down any very distinct canons for ascertaining the principal stages of civilisation'. While he endorsed the division of history into epochs of increasing civility, he believed that

the decline of Enlightenment historical writing in the 1790s' in U. Broich, H. T. Dickinson, E. Hellmuth, and M. Schmidt (eds.), *Reactions to revolutions: the 1790s and their aftermath* (Berlin: Verlag, 2007), p. 233. Frank Palmeri recently argued against this chronology by tracing continuities in the nineteenth century: *State of nature, stages of society: Enlightenment conjectural history and modern social discourse* (New York: Columbia University Press, 2016), p. 12.

[51] Smith (ed. Stewart), *Essays on philosophical subjects*, p. lii. See Mill to Macvey Napier, 10 July 1821, British Library [BL] Additional Manuscript [Add. MS] 34612, f. 428. On the scholarship, see Rendall, 'Scottish orientalism', p. 43.

[52] See I. Hont, 'The language of sociability and commerce: Samuel Pufendorf and the theoretical foundations of the four stages theory' in A. Pagden (ed.), *The languages of political theory in early modern Europe* (Cambridge: Cambridge University Press, 1987), pp. 227–299.

[53] Bentham, *Works*, VIII, pp. 265–266. See A. Meyer, 'Ferguson's "appropriate stile" in combining history and science: the history of historiography revisited' in Heath and Merolle (eds.), *Adam Ferguson: history, progress and human nature*, p. 234.

[54] Mill, *HBI*, I, p. 258; II, p. 424.

[55] 'It is of more importance', Stewart argued, 'to ascertain the progress that is most simple, than the progress that is most agreeable to fact … [for the latter] may have been determined by particular accidents, which are not likely again to occur': Smith (ed. Stewart), *Essays on philosophical subjects*, p. lviii; A. Ferguson, *An essay on the history of civil society* (Philadelphia: A. Finley, 1819), p. 138. On Hume's criticism of conjectural history, see G. H. Sabine, 'Hume's contribution to the historical method', *Philosophical Review* 15 (1906), pp. 17–38.

previous theories of civilisational progress were 'vague in the extreme. All they do is, to fix on one or two of the principal nations of Europe as at the highest point of civilisation; and wherever, in any country, a few of the first appearances strike them as bearing a resemblance to some of the most obvious appearances in these standards of comparison, such countries are at once held to be civilised'. To be considered civilised, a society needed merely 'crowded streets' and a 'bustle of people'.[56] The utility principle provided a more thorough litmus test, leading him to a view of historical development in which local variations were seen to deviate from an ideal standard. The appearance of civility often proved deceiving. Only philosophy could dissolve the mirage.

More recently, Mill has been accused of oversimplifying the Scottish model of civilisation by combining it with a utilitarian epistemology, whose purpose, ironically, was to render more rational and accurate the stages of historical development. Jennifer Pitts, for example, has argued that Mill's synthesis of Scottish conjectural history and utilitarianism was conceptually 'ill-advised'.[57] Whereas Duncan Forbes had seen Mill as a largely faithful disciple of the Scottish conjectural historians, Pitts saw him as altering 'both Bentham's thought and the conjectural histories in directions incompatible with the views of his predecessors'.[58] Moreover, Adam Knowles has observed that Mill transformed Ferguson, Millar, and Smith's theories of civilisation into a crude dichotomy between civility and barbarism, into whose mix we should add Francis Jeffrey's notion of 'semi-barbarism', through which Mill subsumed India's cultural achievements into a story of limited legal evolution, religious superstition, and irrationalism.[59] Even his more sympathetic readers doubted that he had constructed a coherent theory of civility, as he undoubtedly intended to do. In a reply to a letter from Alexander Walker in 1819, Mill conceded that 'we have no standard of civilisation, & of course no precise & accurate ideas, or language in which to convey them'. It was 'not impossible', he

---

[56] James Mill, 'Voyages à Peking, Manille et l'île de France. Par M. de Guignes', *The Edinburgh Review; or Critical Journal* 28 (1809), p. 413.

[57] Pitts, *A turn to empire*, p. 121. Bain claimed that Mill combined the 'sociological writers of the eighteenth century' with Benthamism and his own 'independent reflections': *James Mill*, p. 177.

[58] Pitts, *A turn to empire*, p. 123. For similar arguments see A. Knowles, 'Conjecturing rudeness: James Mill's utilitarian philosophy of history and the British civilising mission' in C. A. Watt and M. Mann (eds.), *Civilising missions in colonial and postcolonial South Asia* (London: Anthem, 2011), p. 42; J. Regan, 'No "nonsense upon stilts": James Mill's The History of British India and the poetics of Benthamite historiography' in P. Fermanis and J. Regan (eds.), *Rethinking British Romantic history* (Oxford: Oxford University Press, 2014), p. 72.

[59] On Jeffrey's influence, see Chen, *James Mill's History of British India in its intellectual context*, p. 35.

continued, that he had judged the Hindus harshly, although it is telling that subsequent editions declined to reflect this.[60]

Mill appeared to invoke the 'rude state' of the Hindu mind as both the premise and conclusion of his argument.[61] The Hindu mind, he asserted, was rude because it neglected utility and it neglected utility because it was rude, and this circular reasoning provided him with a pretext for sweeping reform. It was not entirely in jest that Bentham imagined Mill as the 'living executive' and himself as the 'dead legislative of British India', and it is clear that India served as an example with which to demonstrate utility's global reach.[62] In an appendix on Sanskrit algebra in volume two of the *History*, Mill claimed that 'exactly in proportion as *Utility* is the object of every pursuit, may we regard a nation as civilised' and conversely so for 'barbarous' nations.[63] As with Bentham in *Time and Place*, utility became the yardstick against which to measure civilisational progress, as well as a prognostic and curative device.[64] Knowles put it this way: if utility could become the 'benchmark for measuring rudeness', then it might be possible to codify the exigencies of time and place and thus reduce civilisational difference to minor variations within a determined pattern.[65]

Some of Mill's readers, including Javed Majeed and Uday Mehta, have taken this to mean that Mill employed historical analysis only to practically dismiss it.[66] According to Mehta, there would be no need to 'engage with the facts of history' once 'it had been established that the savage was listless and indolent under every climate'.[67] Likewise, for Majeed, Mill's 'disregard for the past in assessing cultures and their institutions' was a quintessentially utilitarian blindness originating in Bentham's logic.[68] This flagrant disregard for cultural difference, they alleged, stemmed from Mill's intention to undermine conservative appeals to history.[69] He is seen,

---

[60] He held onto his conclusions nevertheless: James Mill to Alexander Walker, 6 November 1819, 'Walker papers', National Library of Scotland, MSS. 13724, f. 178.

[61] Knowles, 'Conjecturing rudeness', p. 42.

[62] Bentham, *Works*, X, p. 450. On the possible links between the *History* and Bentham's essay on time and place, see Majeed, *Ungoverned imaginings*, p. 125; Halévy, *Growth of Philosophic Radicalism*, p. 251.

[63] Mill, *HBI*, II, p. 134.

[64] Knowles, 'Conjecturing rudeness', p. 52. According to Donald Winch, utility became for Mill 'a universal principle for judging all societies at all times': Winch, *James Mill: selected economic writings*, p. 390.

[65] Knowles, 'Conjecturing rudeness', p. 42. See also J. Majeed, 'James Mill's The History of British India: a re-evaluation' in Moir, Peers, and Zastoupil (eds.), *J. S. Mill's encounter with India*, p. 61.

[66] According to William Thomas, Mill 'avoided … empirical enquiry': 'James Mill's politics: a rejoinder', *Historical Journal* 14.4 (1971), p. 750.

[67] Mehta, *Liberalism and empire*, p. 93.

[68] Majeed, 'James Mill's The History of British India: a re-evaluation', p. 55.   [69] Ibid., p. 61.

like Bentham, as a universalising reformer, blasé about time and place, and, like the late writers of the Scottish Enlightenment, as a thinker who anticipated the colonial civilising mission by seeing the extra-European worlds as problems to be solved, rather than as societies to comprehend.[70] There is much to be said for these arguments, but they also rest on two assumptions which do not fully capture Mill's intentions.

The first is that, through an elaborate synthesis of utilitarianism and conjectural history, Mill made hyperbolic judgements about Indian society and its place in the scale of civilisations; the second is that he flattered history only to deceive it, providing him with a platform from which to dismiss India's achievements. With respect to the first point, Mill's attitudes towards conjectural history, as we have seen, were more ambivalent than is commonly acknowledged. His conversion to utilitarianism in 1809 reflected but also deepened this ambivalence, and led him to question further the accuracy with which the likes of Millar had delineated the stages of civilisation. The pressing issue, however, is not whether Mill's approach was fundamentally Scottish or Benthamite, or a muddied synthesis of the two; rather, it is to situate those approaches within his understanding of inductive logic, according to which he attempted to surpass the vague ideas of civilisation promulgated by previous thinkers. This understanding owed more to Hume and Bacon than it did to Bentham, Smith, Robertson, and Millar, but he also regarded these distinct influences as practically compatible, and the goal must be to understand, or at least attempt to understand, how he intended this compatibility. These Scottish and Benthamite lenses, when used on their own, do not bring sufficiently into focus his complex and sometimes inconsistent views on the relationship between philosophy and history.

Furthermore, Mill's association with Scottish philosophical history has overshadowed his arguably more significant claims about the nature of historical reality, which drew on the psychological theories of Hartley and Hume. Mill, like Hume and Bentham, believed that the study of history proceeded from the study of the human mind, whose associations produced irresistible beliefs in past events. This meant that there was no such thing as *the past*, only contiguous associations of historical impressions which we interpret *as* the past. With respect to the second point – that Mill wrote history only to ignore it – he did not claim that philosophy could effectively substitute historical evidence, or that it was possible to establish from a few limited cases generalisations about human nature from which

[70] Knowles, 'Conjecturing rudeness', p. 37.

conclusions could be drawn *a priori*; it was the empiricist, not the theorist, who produced rash general laws through a cursory examination of individual cases. We may reasonably assert the opposite – that his historical method both reflected and reinforced his deprecation of otherness – but this, clearly, is not how he saw it. Ocular or sensory reasoning, he argued in the *History*, failed to produce generalisations that applied universally or even generally. He contrasted this unphilosophical empiricism with Bacon's method of 'philosophic induction', which generated from the facts of history insights into the deeper order of things. This, he believed, was the real business of philosophy.[71]

The Surface of Things

> As the surface of history affords, therefore, no certain principle of decision, we must go beyond the surface, and penetrate into the springs within.[72]

Isaiah Berlin regarded James Mill as one of the last 'great *raisonneurs* of the eighteenth century', a rationalist in an increasingly Romantic world. [73] His indifference to Romanticism can be explained, perhaps, by the vestiges of a strict Presbyterianism, into which he was almost ordained, or, as is likelier, by the lingering influence of Edinburgh.[74] Mill was certainly typical of those eighteenth-century (predominantly Scottish and French) historians who believed, as Pocock put it, that 'all history was produced by the workings of the human mind', and that there was a '*science de l'homme* to which any *science de l'histoire* was at best ancillary'.[75] The disciplines were genetically linked. Drawing on Hume and Hartley's theory of association, Mill developed an ontology of history based on the laws of mental activity, rejecting in the process an objectively 'real' conception of the past.

Hume in his *A Treatise of Human Nature* (1739) and *An Enquiry Concerning Human Understanding* (1748) associated historical enquiry with a form of casual reasoning in which we judge the probability of past

---

[71] Mill, *CPB*, I, ch. 8. See also Loizides, 'Induction, deduction, and James Mill's "Government"', p. 9.
[72] Mill, 'On government', *Political writings*, p. 11.
[73] I. Berlin, 'John Stuart Mill and the ends of life', *Four essays on liberty* (Oxford: Oxford University Press, 1969), p. 175. See also P. Fermanis and J. Regan, 'Introduction' in Fermanis and Regan, *Rethinking British Romantic history*, p. 14.
[74] See V. Wallace, 'Benthamite radicalism and its Scots Presbyterian contexts', *Utilitas* 24.1 (2012), pp. 1–25.
[75] Pocock, *Barbarism and religion. The enlightenments of Edward Gibbon*, p. 146.

events based on their extant evidence. The most reliable form of evidence was usually textual because it established on 'the unanimous testimony of historians' a train of narratives traceable to 'those who were eye-witnesses and spectators of the event'.[76] The challenge, Hume claimed, was to sustain the vivacity and immediacy of those events despite our increasing remoteness from them. We only believe in the evidential force of testimonies because of custom and casual reasoning; in other words, we believe them because we are accustomed to doing so. This means that we merely generate beliefs in historical events based on an inclination to regard human testimony as a form of evidence, rather than as expressions of the imagination. As Hume put it in the *Treatise*, 'I form an idea of *Rome*, which I neither see nor remember; but which is connected with such impressions as I remember to have received from the conversation' of numerous historians.[77]

Mill in his *Analysis of the Phenomena of the Human Mind* followed Hume's 'hardy scepticism' and agreed that the past could only be understood as a belief rather than as a sequence of events processed empirically by the senses.[78] The law of association, which he extended into our emotions, ethics, and aesthetic sensibility, described the ways in which we process, evaluate, and hand down to subsequent generations an idea or impression of the past.[79] A testimony or a piece of evidence 'calls up the idea of the reality of the event' even though the idea 'is a *Belief*. 'It is in this way', he continued, 'that belief in History is to be explained. It is because I cannot resist the evidence; in other words, because the testimony calls up irresistibly the idea' through continuity, repetition, or similarity 'that I believe in the battle of Marathon, in the existence of the Thirty Tyrants of Athens, in that of Socrates, Plato, and so on'.[80] The *Analysis* developed the idea, first hinted at in the *History*, that the past existed only within a solipsistic consciousness of ideas, the associations of which produced irresistible beliefs in the realness of historical events, and these associations, he contended in the *History*, formed an 'important law of human nature'.[81]

Contrary to what W. H. Burston argued, the reduction of past events to psychological laws did not automatically rule out history as a form of

---

[76] D. Hume, *A treatise of human nature* [1738–40] (London: Thomas and Joseph Allman, 1817), I, p. 122. See C. Schmidt, *David Hume: reason in history* (Pennsylvania: Pennsylvania State University Press, 2003), pp. 379–380, 103.

[77] Hume, *Treatise*, I, p. 156.   [78] J. Mill, *Analysis of the phenomena of the human mind*, p. xii.

[79] Ibid., p. viii.   [80] Ibid., p. 386.

[81] Mill, *HBI*, I, p. xiv. John made the same argument in 1867: 'our conception of the past is not drawn from its own records, but from books written about it ... [and the] knowledge they give is upon trust': *CW*, XXI, p. 227.

knowledge.[82] It did, however, prompt Mill into thinking lengthily about historical judgement, a problem over which Bentham had merely skirted.[83] He declared in the preface to the *History* that historians must take into account 'disagreeable objects' and 'proofs', and avoid judging the evidence prematurely according to the mind's 'preferences', 'prepossessions', and 'false notions'.[84] He called this 'critical' or 'judging' history. But what, he asked, 'does it judge?' 'It is evident', he continued, that there are only two kinds of 'historical judgements'. The first is 'the matter of statement, the things given by the historian, as things really done, really said, or really thought. The second is, the matter of evidence, the matter by which the reality of the saying, the doing, or thinking, is ascertained'.[85] Criticism, therefore, was not confined to matters of evidence in which the 'pursuit of truth' triumphed over prejudice.[86] The historian was required to distinguish between real and apparent causes, as well as between real and apparent effects, and this, Mill acknowledged, was an irreducibly philosophical exercise which required inductions of 'considerable length'. The reader could decide whether or not those inductions were logically valid, but 'they are, indisputably, in place'.[87]

Mill was perhaps overly optimistic about the transparency of his inductions, but he believed resolutely in their necessity. He agreed with d'Alembert that the historian should not 'abstain from reflections', but what sorts of reflections should the historian make and how should they make them?[88] One answer is to be found in Mill's contempt for sensory evidence, which has confounded and often irked his readers.[89] He notoriously rejected the benefits of visiting India in person, as if doing so would have deepened his understanding of the sources. Of 'so extensive and complicated a scene as India', he argued, 'how small a portion would the whole period of his life enable any man to observe!'[90] His point, repeated elsewhere, was that simple observation produced rash judgements, first, because it offered only a narrow and incomplete view of its subject,

---

[82] W. H. Burston, *James Mill on philosophy and education* (London: Athlone Press, 1973), p. 162.

[83] On judgement as distinct from belief, see Mill, *Analysis of the phenomena of the human mind*, p. 387. Writing in the 1880s, Alexander Bain observed that Mill's 'higher function' as a historian was to 'criticise, and to apportion praise and blame': *James Mill*, p. 179.

[84] Mill, *HBI*, I, p. xiv. [85] Ibid., p. v–vi. [86] Ibid., p. xxvi.

[87] Ibid., p. vi. This, he argued, was the only way to 'learn wisdom by experience': Mill, *HBI*, V, p. 503.

[88] Mill, *CPB*, III, ch. 5. This was a more radical position than Bacon's, who had argued that the historian should leave 'the observations and conclusions thereupon to the liberty and faculty of every man's judgement': F. Bacon (ed. W. A. Wright), *The advancement of learning* [1605] (Oxford: Clarendon Press, 1876), p. 97.

[89] See, for example, Knowles, 'Conjecturing rudeness', p. 38. [90] Mill, *HBI*, I, p. xi.

and, second, because it ignored the laws of human nature. Instead of this unruly empiricism the historian should appeal to the 'science of human nature' because it demanded evidence from many sources as opposed to a few isolated observations.[91] This meant that the historian's task was properly philosophical: to exhibit the 'powers of combination, discrimination, classification, judgment, comparison, weighing, inferring, inducting, [and] philosophising'.[92] 'Mere observing' would 'render the conception of the whole erroneous'.[93]

Deductions from the laws of mind, far from cancelling out historical evidence, were themselves products of induction. In a footnote to Charles de Villers's *An Essay on the Spirit and Influence of the Reformation of Luther* from 1805, Mill dissented from the 'metaphysical philosophy of Kant' because it proceeded on 'hypothesis and theories' at the expense of 'induction' and could not, therefore, bear an 'enlightened' analysis of its subject.[94] Antis Loizides in a recent article has recovered the nuances of his views regarding generalisation, induction, and deduction, showing how, in various articles and marginalia, he defended philosophy as a remedy for observation. The difference between philosophy and observation, on this account, was the extent to which they employed the laws of human nature.[95] The so-called 'theoretical man' never believed his eyes above his knowledge, and, in contrast to the 'practical man', generalised 'slowly and cautiously' from 'a full induction of particular cases'. A visit to India would have served no purpose, he believed, other than to suggest general rules from specific cases.[96] Utility's foundation in human nature helped to situate and rank historical differences, but not, crucially, to ignore them.[97]

Mill had read Stewart's *Elements of the Philosophy of the Human Mind* (1792–1827) and internalised its cautionary tale against the 'rash application of general principles'.[98] He agreed that arguments from 'theory' were no less grounded in experience than those which professed an allegiance to empiricism, but it was Bacon who had alerted him to the danger of 'the

---

[91] Ibid.   [92] Ibid., p. xii.   [93] Ibid., pp. xii, xiii.

[94] C. Villers (trans. and ed. J. Mill), *An essay on the spirit and influence of the Reformation of Luther* (London: Baldwin, 1805), p. 318n.

[95] Loizides, 'Induction, deduction, and James Mill's "Government"', pp. 1–29.

[96] Mill, *CPB*, I, ch. 8. Mill levelled at Burke the accusation of generalising directly from particulars: *HBI*, V, pp. 246–247.

[97] Halévy, *Growth of Philosophic Radicalism*, p. 251.

[98] J. Mill, 'Elements of the philosophy of mind, by Dugald Stewart', *British Review and London Critical Journal* 6 (1815), p. 181. For analysis see Loizides, 'Induction, deduction, and James Mill's "Government"', p. 7.

mind's premature and precipitate haste, and its leaping or flying to general statements and the principles of things'.[99] In letters to Napier and in the preface to the *History*, Mill heralded Bacon's method of philosophic induction as a signal of intellectual progress, and he suggested in volume two, rather pointedly, that 'the propensity to abstract speculations' was 'the natural result of the state of the human mind in a rude and ignorant age'.[100] In the same volume, he drew conclusions about Hindu society from the 'preceding induction of particulars', which he extended to its religion, laws, government, manners, arts, sciences, and literature. On this basis he offered 'correct judgement[s]' of Hindu civilisation by comparing it with others.[101]

Mill's application of inductive logic was prone to the sort of rashness and simplicity to which it was supposedly immune, and yet his method was by no means a deliberate exercise in historical effacement.[102] F. D. Maurice criticised Mill for failing to see that every nation had 'within itself the germs ... of those institutions which are the most likely to produce its happiness', but Mill disagreed that a nation's history provided a sound basis for induction.[103] The double process of observation and cogitation guarded against the errors of enumerative induction in which the observation of local regularities suggested general or perhaps even universal laws. Mill in his *Commonplace Books* stated plainly the difference between the two: 'philosophical induction', he argued, in contrast to enumerative or empirical induction, examined particulars with a pervading mind that 'separates, and combines; that goes beyond, in short, to something more extensive and noble'.[104] This kind of induction 'goes through the matters of detail, with a view to draw from them general rules', whereas those 'hackneyed mechanical merchants' simply go through details 'as a horse goes round in a mill' and 'with a mind that never stirs'.[105] Only once this extensive process of observation and cogitation had taken place could there be sufficient grounds for establishing a principle or law.[106]

Once again, Mill's argument drew on the laws of association. In a 'cursory survey', he argued, 'the mind' falls in 'with the current of its own thoughts; those which accord with its former impressions' and 'confirm its previous ideas'.[107] The connection between empiricism and

---

[99] F. Bacon (eds. L. Jardine and M. Silverthorne), *The new organon* [1620] (Cambridge: Cambridge University Press, 2008), p. 52; Mill, *CPB*, I, ch. 8. John in the *Logic* (1843) agreed that Bacon had abolished deductions from 'premises hastily snatched up, or arbitrarily assumed': *CW*, VII, p. 482.
[100] Mill, *HBI*, II, p. 70.   [101] Ibid., pp. 135–136.   [102] See Mazlish, *Father and son*, p. 135.
[103] Quoted in Loizides, *James Mill's utilitarian logic and politics*, p. 26.   [104] Mill, *CPB*, I, ch. 8.
[105] Ibid.   [106] Ibid.   [107] Mill, *HBI*, I, p. xiv.

prejudice was hardly esoteric in its indebtedness to Bacon, whose *Novum Organum* (1620) had taken issue with orthodox Aristotelian logic in which axioms or first principles were established directly from empirical particulars and then employed as the basis of deduction.[108] The problem for Bacon, as for Mill, was that the highest generalisations should form the end, not the beginning, of scientific inference, and the purpose of philosophy was neither to take the world as one found it (the fault of empiricism), nor to reason solely from within the confines of pre-existing modes, assumptions, and patterns of thought (the fault of what Bacon called mere 'Reasoners').[109] The solution was to combine empiricism and reasoning as a comprehensive logical method.[110]

The union between reasoning and observation was Hume's and the *History's* 'real business', and it enabled him to marry his theory of induction to Bentham's judicial historiography.[111] The 'situation', he remarked, was 'very analogous to that of the judge, in regard to the witnesses who give their evidence before him'.[112] On the one hand, the historian must cross-examine the evidence and particular events, but on the other she or he must not trust the senses above the highest generalisations, according to which it is possible to separate general from special causes.[113] In search of this *via media* the philosophical historian transcended the 'obvious outside of things' to elaborate the 'causes', 'consequences', and 'natural tendencies' of historical development. As with Stewart and Hume, the value of philosophical history resided in its ability to specify the 'circumstances likely to operate either in combination with these natural tendencies, or in opposition to them'.[114] This allowed Mill to assert that philosophical history provided a good 'introduction to civil society in general' while affirming d'Alembert's (and, more importantly, Bentham's) distinction between a philosophically enlightened 'science of history' and mere 'historical knowledge', which 'tells us only that a thing can be or occur, and not why it can be or occur'.[115]

---

[108] M. Peltonen, 'Introduction' in M. Peltonen (ed.), *The Cambridge companion to Bacon* (Cambridge: Cambridge University Press, 2012), p. 16.

[109] See P. Rossi, 'Bacon's idea of science' in Peltonen (ed.), *The Cambridge companion to Bacon*, p. 29.

[110] Ibid.   [111] Mill, 'An historical view of the English government by J. Millar', p. 326.

[112] Mill, *HBI*, I, p. xv. The language employed by Mill to describe the nature of historical evidence and judgement may well have been influenced by Bentham, on whose manuscripts he worked intermittently between 1811 and 1812.

[113] Hence R. G. Collingwood's characterisation of Mill as a 'Cartesian' historian who championed the cross-examination of sources and the relation of specific cases to known events: *The idea of history* (Oxford: Oxford University Press), p. 62.

[114] Mill, *HBI*, I, pp. xvii–xviii.

[115] The original quotation was from d'Alembert's *Mélanges de littérature, d'histoire et de philosophie* (1767): Mill, *CPB*, III, ch. 5.

The *History* proposed to examine the 'laws of human nature, which is the end, as well as the instrument, of every thing . . . [as well as] the whole field of legislation, the whole field of judicature, the whole field of administration'.[116] This wide command of human affairs had been a *sine qua non* for philosophical historians at least since the publication in 1728 of Christian Wolff's *Philosophia Rationalis Sive Logica*, to which Mill referred in his *Commonplace Books*: things 'which we know philosophically', by which he meant an understanding of 'conditions', are 'applied to the problems of human life with greater success than the things which we know only historically'.[117] Philosophical history, therefore, separated generals from particulars, and extracted from the ineffable complexities of the past a clear image of its development.[118] It was, he continued, 'necessary for the historian . . . to appreciate the counteraction which the more general laws of human nature may receive from individual or specific varieties'.[119] Mill's more sympathetic reviewers, such as the Benthamite Walter Coulson (1795–1860), declared his victory in this respect.[120]

To re-contextualise the *History* as an exercise in philosophic induction is to say nothing of its successes or failures in doing so, but it does allow us to historically explain what postcolonial scholars, with good reason, have identified as Mill's disregard for cultural difference.[121] In volume one, for instance, he argued that India had remained in a 'stationary' condition since Alexander's invasion in 326 BCE.[122] This forced him, *prima facie*, to explain away India's cultural achievements of the preceding two millennia, especially the Hindus', whose religion and services to 'human nature' he ranked below the Muslims'.[123] On closer inspection it is clear that Mill was restating in practical historical terms the methodological warnings of the preface. In an explicit attack on Jones and the Orientalists, he claimed that India's outward progress concealed its inner barbarism, and that again the source of the error was a philosophically impoverished empiricism which trusted more to first appearances than to the laws of human nature.

Mill observed that the 'gentleness of Hindu manners has usually impressed their European visitors, with a high conception of their progress in civilisation'. This was, perhaps, a 'ground of presumption' but

---

[116] Mill, *HBI*, I, p. xviii.   [117] Mill, *CPB*, I, ch. 8.
[118] See Dugald Stewart on the 'political empiric': *Elements of the philosophy of the human mind* in *The works of Dugald Stewart*, I, p. 172.
[119] Mill, *HBI*, I, p. xviii.
[120] W. Coulson, 'Mill's British India', *Edinburgh Review* 41 (1818), p. 3.
[121] For a brief discussion, see Koditschek, *Liberalism, imperialism, and the historical imagination*, p. 84.
[122] Mill, *HBI*, I, p. 146.   [123] Ibid., p. 362; II, pp. 424, 429.

'fallacious if taken as a proof'.[124] The Hindus' hospitality had only disguised their barbarism, since it 'commonly happens ... that in a rude period of society, the virtue of hospitality, generously and cordially displayed, helps to cast into the shade the odious passions which adhere to man in his uncultivated state'.[125] Empiricism was again the undisputed source of the error. Drawing on volume two of Robertson's *History of America*, Mill made analogies with the Spanish settlement of Mexico in the sixteenth and seventeenth centuries, and, quoting Robertson, he explained how the conquistadors had been 'struck with the appearance of attainments in policy and in the arts of life,' even though the Mexicans were 'less civilised' than their appearance suggested.[126] Since the Europeans had discovered India at the same time as America, the Hindus had been 'compared with the savages of America; the circumstances in which they differed from that barbarous people, were the circumstances in which they corresponded with the most cultivated nations; other circumstances were overlooked; and it seems to have been little suspected that conclusions too favourable could possibly be drawn'.[127]

That mild manners were compatible with the rudest violence, and civility with the most despotic barbarism, was conveniently clear only to those who were capable of 'close inspection'.[128] Jones, by contrast, had written about India from a few casual observations, rather than from a comprehensive view of the state of society: its manners, character, practices, social arrangements, arts, creeds, form of government, and so on.[129] His idea of civilisation was so crude that not even 'the rhapsodies of Rousseau on the virtue and happiness of the savage life' could surpass them.[130] In a passage reminiscent of his article on China from 1809, Mill acknowledged the difficulty of accurately determining the general course of civilisational development, and of locating nations within its scale.

> It is not easy to describe the characteristic of the different stages of social progress. It is not from one feature, or from two, that a just conclusion can be drawn. In these it sometimes happens that nations resemble which [sic] are placed at stages considerably remote. It is from a joint view of all the great circumstances taken together, that their progress can be ascertained; and it is from an accurate comparison, grounded on these general views, that a scale of civilisation can be formed, on which the relative position of nations may be accurately marked.[131]

---

[124] Ibid., I, p. 399.   [125] Ibid., p. 405.   [126] Mill quoting Robertson: *HBI*, II, p. 144n.
[127] Ibid., p. 143.   [128] Ibid., p. 139n.   [129] Ibid., I, p. 147.   [130] Ibid, II, p. 139.
[131] Ibid., p. 138–9.

Jones, Mill speculated, had been ensnared by India's superficial progress in the arts but blinded to the backwardness of its political economy, government, religion, and prose.[132] His misfortune was to have written in ignorance of 'all that modern philosophy had performed for the elucidation of history'.[133] Only Millar, into whose works 'it is probable Sir William had never looked', had begun to establish the laws of social progress with any concreteness, and even then his conclusions were formed from 'detached considerations applied to particular facts, and not a comprehensive induction leading to general conclusions'.[134] With the same logic Mill dismissed the possibility that the Hindus had once enjoyed 'a high state of civilisation ... from which they had fallen through miseries of foreign conquest, and subjugation'. This was merely a theory 'invented to preserve as much as actual observation would allow to be preserved, of a pre-established and favourite creed. It was not an inference from what was already known. It was a gratuitous assumption. It preceded enquiry, and no enquiry was welcome, but that which yielded matter for its support'.[135] What Mill sought was a 'rational inference' from the experience of 'human nature, and the phenomena which are exhibited under its manners, attainments, and institutions'.[136]

Mill's method of philosophic induction remained optimistic about social progress, which meant that India's stagnation neither contradicted nor slowed humanity's natural progressiveness. More importantly, India's peculiarities (the features which were unique to it) did not undermine the case for a universal legal code based on the principle of utility. He mused in volume two that on 'close inspection' the laws of progress revealed similarities between certain nations – here he referred to the 'Hindus, the Persians, the Arabians, the Turks, and Chinese of the present day' – notwithstanding 'the dissimilarity in some of the more obvious appearances'.[137] This wide-ranging induction allowed him to suggest that laws possessed a universal form whose matter ought to vary according to the 'obvious appearances' of society. Like Bentham and the Italian jurist Gaetano Filangieri (1752–1788), whose work he reviewed in 1806, Mill believed that the purpose of legislation was to establish the 'general principles of law, detached from its accidental and national forms', and at the same time to produce a 'code of laws, in which the principles of substantial justice shall be accurately adapted to the circumstances of the society'.[138] The only way of reconciling these two

---

[132] Ibid., pp. 156–186.   [133] Ibid., p. 139.   [134] Ibid., p. 139n.   [135] Ibid., p. 144.
[136] Ibid., pp. 156–157.   [137] Ibid., II, p. 139n.
[138] On Filangieri see Bain, *James Mill*, p. 58; Mill, *HBI*, III, p. 446; J. Mill, 'Affairs of India', *The Edinburgh Review* 16 (1810), p. 156.

ambitions was through philosophic induction: to generalise slowly from particulars and thus codify into law the exigencies of time and place.

Theory and Practice

Mill's intellectual and literary life in the 1820s was markedly different to the previous decade. Galvanised by the *History*'s financial success and his role at the East India Company, he became an important Radical figure until his death in 1836. He co-founded the *Westminster Review* in 1823 and helped to form the Philosophic Radicals, a 'school' with which he complemented Bentham's 'philosophy'.[139] The high watermark of his political celebrity came with the publication in 1820 of his essay 'On Government'. Even though it is seen now as the political blueprint for Philosophic Radicalism, few of its proposals were new.[140] Mill advocated shorter parliaments, the rotation of MPs, the secret ballot, and an extension of the franchise, and if anything his arguments were blunted by a determination to appear as a moderate champion of 'good government'.[141] He remained conspicuously silent on the endeavours of popular Radicalism – he declined to mention the massacre at Peterloo, even though he had begun the essay only weeks afterwards – and his arguments were couched in relatively moderate terms.[142] Even if we take into consideration the backlash to the Caroline affair and the Cato Street conspiracy, in whose immediate aftermath 'On Government' appeared, we can scarcely account for the captious intensity of its reception.

The reaction to Mill's essay, as with the *History*, was rooted in its method and logic, a fact to which he privately attested: the 'business of legislation', he contended, 'is wholly theoretical, because it consists wholly in making general rules' and in 'marking individual and special differences'.[143] The issue had less to do with his political than his philosophic Radicalism, a defining feature of which was the belief, repeated *ad nauseam*, that 'theory' was synonymous with 'systematised experience'.[144] To Macaulay, his most outspoken critic, the essay violated Bacon's principles of inductive logic and thus the very epistemology of historical experience.[145] It has also been pointed out by Collini, Winch, and

---

[139] Halévy, *Growth of Philosophic Radicalism*, p. 251.
[140] See W. Thomas, 'James Mill's politics: the essay on government and the movement for reform', *History Journal* 12.2 (1969), pp. 249–284.
[141] Ibid., p. 258.   [142] Ibid.   [143] Mill, *CPB*, I, ch. 8.   [144] Ibid.
[145] T. B. Macaulay, *Miscellaneous writings of Lord Macaulay* (London: Longman, Green, Longman, and Roberts, 1869), I, p. 284.

Burrow that the essay adopted an altogether different method than his
'introduction to civil society' in the *History*, and that the discrepancy
between the two cast sharply into relief the former's deductive qualities.
The main source of controversy, therefore, was whether Mill's essay
followed experience and wisdom, or whether it theorised out of thin air
a deductive science of politics. As Mill put it in his *Commonplace Books*, the
debate was between 'empiricism' on the one hand and 'theory' – the
method of the 'truly inductive philosopher' – on the other.[146] Into his
cause he enlisted Bacon, Wolff, Aristotle, and Paley, all of whom had
understood that 'all men generalise', and that the objects of their knowledge are 'laid up in parcels' either large or small.[147]

Macaulay's infamous diatribe, published in March 1829 in the
Edinburgh Review, was a late intervention into a series of exchanges
heralded by the publication of Mill's essay 'On Government'. While the
thrust of Macaulay's criticism is well known, it merits the briefest of
treatments here. His main line of attack was to accuse Mill of assuming
'certain propensities of human nature' *a priori*, from which 'the whole
science of politics' was 'synthetically deduced'.[148] He excoriated Mill for
elaborating only one half of human nature, which was the Hobbesian
tendency to 'oppress and despoil others'. By taking 'the other half of
human nature' – the half which impelled men to 'benefit' rather than
'injure' their neighbours' – we can, Macaulay insisted, 'bring out a result
diametrically opposite to that at which Mr. Mill has arrived'.[149] He was
incredulous at Mill's vision of a society in which self-interested individuals
freely observed the principle of utility, because such a society implied either
that human nature was capable of other-regarding action, which would
disprove the proposition that they were self-interested in the first place, or
else it proved that Mill's philosophy of human nature rested on the
tautology that agents will do what they will do.[150] Macaulay's point was
that our knowledge of human nature consists entirely of observations of
individuals in social contexts, and that any attempt to explain their behaviour by inference from universal propositions was intellectually quixotic.[151]

Macaulay in 1829 posited a similar objection to Bentham's happiness
principle. 'Where has this principle been demonstrated?' he opined. 'It is
not our fault that ... the subtlety of nature, in the moral as in the physical
world, triumphs over the subtlety of syllogism'.[152] He thus set out to defend

[146] Mill, *CPB*, I, ch. 8.   [147] Ibid.   [148] Macaulay, *Miscellaneous writings*, I, p. 285.
[149] Ibid., p. 295.   [150] Ibid., p. 317.   [151] A. Ryan, *J. S. Mill* (London: Routledge, 1974), p. 38.
[152] Macaulay, *Miscellaneous writings*, I, p. 386.

Baconian induction from the encroachments of syllogistic logic, which is
why, in his critique of 'On Government', he depicted Mill as an
Aristotelian scholastic 'born out of due season' whose philosophy was
mired by logical illusions – a 'hubbub of unmeaning words' – and
a blindness to 'the real state of the world'.[153] Macaulay's logical objections
to the essay were prior to, and even shaped, the political dimensions of his
attack. He reasoned that 'to quote history' would be a 'waste of time'
because Mill refused the 'help of either history or experience'.[154] It followed
that 'the happiness of mankind', which was the very thing to which Mill
aspired, could only be achieved by a 'method of induction – by observing
the present state of the world' and by 'assiduously studying the history of
past ages'.[155]

Mill replied to Macaulay indirectly in his *A Fragment on Mackintosh* in
1835, and John, looking back, wished that his father had made clear his
intention to legislate only for 'England or the United States', and not, as
Macaulay had alleged, for all 'mankind'.[156] If the essay had been presented
as a historically specific argument for political reform, then the whole issue
of universality could have been factored out; however, as Crimmins noted,
Mill believed that the universal science of human nature was 'the only valid
foundation upon which a comprehensive theory of government could be
built'.[157] In his *Commonplace Books*, he quoted John Moore's (1729–1802)
story about the medical student who, having used a salt herring to successfully cure an Englishman of fever, killed a Frenchman with the same.[158]
The scientific analogy was deliberate: the political theorist, as with the
natural scientist, did not determine laws from only a handful of cases; thus,
he praised Bacon's *De Augumentis Scientarium* (1623) for arguing that
politics was best suited to those who could see beyond 'the circumstances
of the case' to the 'rules' of which it was either an example or an 'exception';
as he put it in the *Fragment*, 'the whole nature of man must be taken into
account, for explaining the "immense variety" of historical facts'.[159] The
implication was that the *History* and the essay shared a historical method,
notwithstanding differences in emphasis and rhetorical style. Whereas the
History's inductions were lengthier and more transparent, the essay
addressed an English political context whose relative progress required
a different style of argument.

---

[153] Ibid., pp. 285, 299, 290.   [154] Ibid., pp. 303, 302.   [155] Ibid., p. 321.   [156] *CW*, I, p. 164.
[157] Crimmins, *Utilitarian philosophy and politics*, p. 49.   [158] Mill, *CPB*, I, ch. 8.
[159] Ibid; Mill, *A fragment on Mackintosh*, p. 293.

The question, of course, was how to effectively mediate between the highest generalisations and actual historical facts, and Mill throughout his corpus employed different terminologies to illustrate this problem. Theory was referred to variously as 'speculation', 'abstraction', and 'philosophy', while its opposite was referred to most commonly as 'practice', but also as 'empiricism' and 'Misologia'.[160] It is clear, furthermore, that he became increasingly concerned with the mediation between theory and practice.[161] His essay on the corn bounty (1804) attacked the political economist James Anderson (1739–1808) for appealing to unmitigated experience over theory, and in 1836, the year of his death, he published two dialogues defending the scientific bases of political economy and government.[162] In the first of those, 'Whether Political Economy is Useful?', he claimed that *theoria* gave a comprehensive 'view' of *scientia*, or complete knowledge.[163] In the second, 'Theory and Practice', he defended his conception of inductive logic. Even though he had addressed the subject in the *Analysis*, where he drew on Thomas Brown's (1778–1820) distinction between theory and hypothesis, he had not yet disseminated his ideas to a wider audience.

The political turbulences of 1835 added to Mill's resolve. The Melbourne Whigs had returned to government in February 1835 with a weaker but still commanding majority, the upside of which, Mill observed in an article for *The London Review*, was the palpable 'strength of the spirit of reform'.[164] The 'permanency' of that spirit, however, hinged on the 'philosophical principles of government' and the defence of 'speculation' against 'practice'.[165] The dialogue on 'Theory and Practice' was thus intended to bolster the Radical cause, and its two interlocutors, Y and X, debated the differences between theory and practice until, in true Socratic fashion, one participant conceded defeat in the face of a definitive objection. The first interlocutor, Y, represented Mill, while X embodied in a single speaker a range of anti-reform voices, although only Burke and William Pitt (1759–1806) were mentioned by name.[166] Y thus attempted to counter the anti-reformers by bringing under the aegis of theory the vaunted wisdoms of history and practice, while X declared that 'in following experience we follow facts; in following theory we follow fancy',

---

[160] Mill, *CPB*, I, ch. 8.

[161] R. A. Fenn explored the distinction in *James Mill's political thought* (London: Garland, 1987), p. 128.

[162] J. Mill, *An essay of the impolicy of a bounty on the exportation of grain* (London: C. and R. Baldwin, 1804), p. 6. See Winch, *James Mill's economic writings*, p. 367.

[163] J. Mill, 'Whether political economy is useful?', *The London and Westminster Review* 30 (1836), p. 562.

[164] J. Mill, 'The state of the nation', *The London and Westminster Review* 25 (1835), p. 1.

[165] Ibid., pp. 5, 18.   [166] Mill, 'Theory and practice', p. 232.

'speculation', and the 'vortices of Descartes'.[167] The importance of experience was accepted by both sides, and what ensued was a debate about precisely how 'knowledge of the past becomes a guide of the future', since all knowledge is 'of the past' and all action 'regards the future'.[168]

The past, Y asserted, could not serve as a guide to the future because 'a past act is a thing done, and cannot be revived'.[169] That 'a man died last week' or that 'a bird flew in the air' are 'events' but not examples, 'meaning by an example an act to be repeated'.[170] These solitary acts yielded 'no guidance' to the future because it 'is an admitted principle that from an individual instance no conclusion can be drawn'. To jump out of a tower because someone else had done so without suffering injury might cost one 'dear for being so practical a man'.[171] Mill's point was twofold: first, that the consequences of an action must be 'agreeable' to warrant their imitation, and, second, that the sequence of consequences must be constant.[172] From Y's *reductio ad absurdum*, it followed that only a theorem could differentiate between irregularities and 'cases of constancy', and that all rational practice was founded on an accurate 'observation of the past'.[173] An error of practice was necessarily an error of theory, a point to which Bentham had alluded in *The Book of Fallacies*: bad practice, he had argued, was really 'bad in theory', and those who disparaged theory but exalted practice were contradictory 'no-thinkers'.[174]

In Mill's dialogue, Y persuaded his interlocutor that 'practice' necessarily implied theory and could not be divorced from it. If 'there is no practice without theory', Mill reasoned, then 'it is altogether absurd to set practice in opposition to theory'.[175] The only thing left to decide, therefore, was what constituted good theory and good practice. To this Mill answered that, whereas a hypothesis might offer predictions from a solitary event, a good theory is 'always the more valuable the greater the extent of sequence which it correctly announces. This, in reality, is neither more nor less than saying that more knowledge is better than less'. Consequently, good practice reposed on the accuracy of the sequence inferred: if the theory was correct, then so too was the practice 'founded on it'.[176] By collapsing *praxis* into *theoria*, Mill avoided one of the central dilemmas of Kant's *Kritik der Urteilskraft* (1790), which claimed that the relationship between theory and practice could be determined only by an act of judgement for which we lack clear rules of engagement. Since

[167] Ibid., p. 223.   [168] Ibid., p. 226.   [169] Ibid., p. 225.   [170] Ibid.   [171] Ibid.   [172] Ibid.
[173] Ibid.   [174] Bentham, *Book of fallacies*, p. 226.   [175] Mill, 'Theory and practice', p. 229.
[176] Ibid., p. 231.

judgement itself requires rules – that is, some sort of theory – then we become stuck in what István Hont called a situation of 'infinite regress'.[177]

For Mill, however, the goal was to prove that theory was instrumental to practice, and to argue, like Aristotle, for permeable boundaries between thinking and doing.[178] If, according to Mill, a good theory revealed an extended sequence of agreeable consequences, then a useful theory existed 'in proportion as the sequences of which they [the theories] are the expression have much or little influence on human life'.[179] The very purpose of philosophy was to 'discover these sequences' by distilling into a 'few propositions' the higher generalisations of human nature.[180] By condensing human nature into as few laws as possible, Mill hoped to eradicate 'mistaken practice', and yet it was in putatively reductive statements like these that his critics discovered a different Mill, one who deduced a universal science of politics from a few narrow premises.[181] That human nature could be accounted for in a small number of propositions was nonsense to Macaulay and Mackintosh; indeed, Mackintosh wrote to Napier in disbelief at Mill's 'erroneous' application of Bacon's principles. If Mill did consult experience it was only 'partially or superficially', much like ancient philosophers whom he held in high esteem.[182] Perhaps, as John later reflected, it was strategically unwise for his father to argue that 'experience and theory are the same', but either way James's critics were more concerned with undermining than faithfully representing his intentions, in both the *History* and the essay.[183]

Conclusion

It is significant that a major intellectual battle of the 1820s and 1830s was waged by two historians who thought philosophically about politics. Both Macaulay and Mill extolled the virtues of induction, but it was Macaulay who successfully tethered to the 'authority of Bacon' his progressive and self-professedly noble 'science of politics'.[184] Mill's dogmatic rhetoric in

---

[177] I. Hont, 'Adam Smith's history of law and government as political theory' in R. Bourke and R. Geuss (eds.), *Political judgement: essays for John Dunn* (Cambridge: Cambridge University Press, 2009), p. 132.
[178] D. Ebery, 'Introduction', in D. Ebery (ed.), *Theory and practice in Aristotle's natural science* (Cambridge: Cambridge University Press, 2015), p. 2.
[179] Mill, 'Theory and practice', p. 230.   [180] Ibid., p. 232.
[181] Ibid. John discussed the issue in *CW*, I, p. 165.
[182] In Collini, Winch, and Burrow, *That noble science of politics*, p. 99.
[183] Mill, 'Theory and practice', p. 223.
[184] T. B. Macaulay in Lively Rees (eds.), *Utilitarian logic and politics*, p. 128.

'On Government' and his rejection in the *History* of ocular and narrowly empirical methods, when seen against the febrile political backdrop of the early 1830s and the hostile reception of Bentham's *Plan of Parliamentary Reform*, was a gift to utilitarianism's opponents; however, his defence in *A Fragment on Mackintosh* of Bentham's jurisprudence and moral philosophy, when placed in the context of his other late writings, suggests a different intention. In both his historical and political works, he pursued the 'real business of philosophy' in which general principles illuminated social phenomena and laid bare the emptiness of Whig empiricism.[185] Only the 'speculative man' could appreciate the past's distinctness by separating general from special causes, and Mill's indebtedness to Bacon and Hume is evident in this respect. His attractions to Benthamite utilitarianism and Scottish philosophical history were variously deepened and underpinned by his readings of Bacon and Hume, and those readings were possibly encouraged by Dugald Stewart at Edinburgh.[186]

Mill's disciple, George Grote, praised the *History* for proceeding from a 'conscientious criticism' of the evidence to circumstances 'far removed from his [Mill's] personal experience'. But his praise concealed as much as it revealed. Grote's early ambition to do for the Greeks what Mill had done for India – by establishing 'the comparative degree of civilisation which their habits and institutions evinced them to have reached' – was left unrealised as he developed interests in 'conscientious criticism' and German *Historismus*. Philosophy did have an illuminative function, but only when it 'enlightened' historical evidence.[187] By praising Mill's understanding of distant circumstances, Grote asserted the compatibility between philosophical history and historicist ideas of distinctness, and it is telling that he sidestepped Mill's more speculative arguments; indeed, Grote was generally dismissive of speculative philosophies of history even though he himself was a celebrated philosophical historian, a curiosity which may explain his interest in the Greek origins but not the development of Western civilisation. One attraction of historicism was that it sharpened Bentham's distinction between history and philosophy, and proved, in Leslie Stephen's words, that 'the utilitarian who was faithful to his most vital principles was especially qualified to be a historian'.[188]

---

[185] Mill, *CPB*, I, ch. 8.

[186] Collini, Winch, and Burrow saw Stewart as a formative influence: *That noble science of politics*, p. 95.

[187] See an exchange of letters between Grote and Cornewall Lewis in 1851: H. Grote (ed.), *The personal life of George Grote. Compiled from family documents, private memoranda, and original letters to and from various friends* (London: John Murray, 1873), pp. 203–204.

[188] Stephen, *The English utilitarians*, III, p. 338.

PART II

Historicism and Historiography

CHAPTER 3

George Grote and Historismus

Philosophic Radicalism

George Grote was introduced to James Mill and Bentham in the late 1810s and his political and literary careers took off shortly thereafter.[1] He published in 1821 a short pamphlet on parliamentary reform, in which he attacked Mackintosh and restated the philosophical case for Radicalism.[2] A second pamphlet followed ten years later, and from 1832 to 1841 he served as a Radical Member of Parliament for the City of London.[3] He also edited Bentham's *Analysis of the Influence of Natural Religion on the Temporal Happiness of Mankind* (1822) and collaborated with John and Bain on a revised edition of James Mill's *Analysis of the Phenomena of the Human Mind* (1869). His philosophical and ethical essays, written shortly after his time in Parliament, addressed many of the themes to which I have already alluded. Bentham's distinction between matter and form informed his idea of ethical sentiment, while the distinction between criticism and exposition provided a framework in which to think about history's practical significance.[4] His utilitarianism was so devout that even John complained of its narrowness, and Grote, in turn, did little to divest himself of the parochialism implied by Mill's remark.[5] As he argued in an unpublished manuscript, 'there is but one single method of making your behaviour &

---

[1] Grote was probably introduced to James Mill by David Ricardo in March 1819. See a letter from Grote to George Warde Norman from May 1819 in Bain, *James Mill*, pp. 180–181.

[2] G. Grote, *Statement on the question of parliamentary reform* (London: Baldwin, Cradock, and Joy, 1821).

[3] G. Grote, *Essentials of parliamentary reform* (London: Baldwin, Craddock, 1831).

[4] Grote claimed that writers 'have paid more attention to the *Matter*' of sentiments than to their '*Form*, and have considered the latter as if it were something subordinate to and dependent upon the former': *Fragments on ethical subjects*, p. 19.

[5] J. S. Mill to Carlyle, 2 August 1833: *CW*, XII, p. 170. As late as January 1862, John confided to Grote that he could not match his optimism about 'converting opponents' to utilitarianism: Mill to Grote, 10 January 1862: *CW*, XV, p. 763.

89

intentions throughout systematic & well-principled: & that is, by adopting in its full extent what Bentham has termed the doctrine of utility'.[6]

Grote's twelve-volume *History of Greece*, published in ten volumes between 1846 and 1856, is usually interpreted in one of two ways. It is read, on the one hand, as a species of political theory whose commitment to historicism was either disingenuous or superficial, and whose true intention was to appropriate Athenian democracy to Philosophic Radicalism.[7] As James Turner put it, Grote offered a 'present-minded agenda' of 'Benthamite liberalism' with which he countered prevailing criticisms of Athenian democracy.[8] Underlying this interpretation is a belief that the *History* set out to demonstrate the edifying effects of political participation within a modern liberal framework. If James Mill situated India within a utilitarian locus of civility, then Grote – or so the argument goes – projected onto classical Athens his own ideals of democracy, individuality, and liberty. To many of critics, therefore, his new approach to ancient history looked uncannily like the old. A. D. Lindsay (1879–1952) criticised him for superimposing 'the passions and prejudices of modern politics', while Karl Julius Beloch (1854–1929) attacked his eagerness to dress the ancient Greeks in the clothes of modern Englishmen.[9] It is now orthodox to identify continuities between Grote's political allegiances and the 'audacious historical voice' with which he championed Athenian democracy.[10] More orthodox still is the argument that Grote, for all his methodological austerities, was, like the two Mills, just another Greece-intoxicated man.[11]

---

[6] G. Grote, 'Grote papers', University College London [UCL] Additional Manuscripts [Add. MS], A2, f. 10.

[7] K. N. Demetriou, 'In defence of the British constitution: theoretical implications of the debate over Athenian democracy in Britain, 1770–1850', *History of Political Thought* 27.2 (1996), p. 295. The argument is frequently extended to John: R. O. Preyer, 'John Stuart Mill on the utility of classical Greece', *Browning Institute Studies* 10 (1982), p. 46; T. H. Irwin, 'Mill and the classical world' in J. Skorupski (ed.), *The Cambridge companion to Mill* (Cambridge: Cambridge University Press, 1998), p. 414.

[8] J. Turner, *Philology: the forgotten origins of the modern humanities* (Princeton: Princeton University Press, 2014), p. 206.

[9] A. D. Lindsay, 'Introduction' in G. Grote (ed. A. D. Lindsay), *History of Greece* [1846–1856] (London: Dent, 1906), I, p. vii; Beloch quoted in J. Kierstead, 'Grote's Athens: the character of democracy' in Demetriou (ed.), *Brill's companion to George Grote*, p. 201.

[10] Ian Macgregor Morris has claimed that 'Grote, as did his predecessor [Mitford], read his prejudices into his work': I. Macgregor Morris, 'Navigating the Grotesque; or, rethinking Greek historiography' in J. Moore, I. Macgregor Morris and A. J. Bayliss (eds.), *Reinventing history: the Enlightenment origins of ancient history* (London: Institute of Historical Research, 2008), p. 254.

[11] Bain, *James Mill*, p. 94.

On the other hand, the *History* has been singled out for its contributions to historicism and the 'scientific study of Greek history'.[12] Mark Bevir recently credited Grote with introducing into English the verb 'historicise', which appears in the *History* no less than nine times, and he repeatedly defended a historicist *Wissenschaft* whose reconstruction of the past *wie es eigentlich gewesen* undermined the kind of didacticism and anachronism of which he is frequently accused.[13] His indebtedness to *Historismus* was evident as early as 1826, when he attacked the Tory historian William Mitford (1744–1827) for denouncing the violent excesses of 'free government' in his anti-Jacobin *History of Greece* (1784–1810).[14] Drawing on the science of source criticism (*Quellenkritik*), Grote questioned the integrity of Mitford's scholarship and, by implication, the credibility of his political conclusions.[15] Mitford was a man of 'bias' and 'prejudice' whose 'scattered political remarks' deprived the Greeks of their 'peculiarity' and 'grand determining circumstances', and for whom the past was a convenient anachronism, a rhetorical tool with which to denigrate democracy.[16] Thus, the historiography attests to two George Grotes, one who used the past to theorise and illustrate his politics, and another who emphasised the past's inimitability above its contemporary significance.

My goal is to construct a bridge between these interpretations by paying close attention to Grote's published and unpublished essays and the intellectual contexts in which he wrote them. I argue that the *History* was written neither as a 'political pamphlet' nor as a work of criticism whose significance was narrowly historical, and that Grote's historicism allowed him to discredit Mitford's Tory historiography whilst claiming historical exactness for himself.[17] His defence of Athenian democracy, I suggest, was not intended as a defence of democracy *tout court*, but it did undermine the historical basis of many anti-democratic invectives.[18] The 'very attempt to

[12] T. B. Jones, 'George Grote and his History of Greece', *The Classical Weekly* 29.8 (1935), p. 61.

[13] Bevir, 'Historicism and the human sciences in Victorian Britain', p. 1. For an example, see Grote, *HG*, II, p. 58.

[14] W. Mitford, *The history of Greece* (London: T. Cadell, 1838), IV, pp. 96–97.

[15] G. Grote, 'Clinton's Fasti Hellenici: The civil and literary chronology of Greece', *Westminster Review* 5 (1826), p. 281.

[16] Ibid., pp. 284, 287, 270.

[17] See Jones, 'George Grote and his History of Greece', p. 60; F. M. Turner, *The Greek heritage in Victorian Britain* (Yale: Yale University Press, 1980), pp. 205–214.

[18] As he remarked in a commentary on Aristotle's logic, the 'appeal to various separate cases is the only basis on which we can rest for testing the correctness of all these maxims proclaimed as universal': G. Grote (ed. A. Bain), *Aristotle* (London: John Murray, 1872), I, pp. 212–213n.

criticise', he argued in an essay on ethics, implied a subjective 'standard of judgement' which failed the tests of historicism.[19] It was John who did much of the heavy political lifting in articles for *The Spectator* and the *Edinburgh Review*.[20] Mill praised Grote for reversing 'what we are so often told about the entire sacrifice, in the ancient republics, of the liberty of the individual to an imaginary good of the state', the political significance of which prompted Mill to alter his views on ancient liberty.[21] By placing the *History* in these varied contexts, I hope to further demonstrate, in the sage but forgotten words of Leslie Stephen, that 'the utilitarian position was no disqualification for writing history', and that Grote did not see historicism and utilitarianism as obvious antitheses.[22]

From Bacon to Historicism

Sciences 'which have real truth for their object', Grote argued in an early unpublished essay, cannot lay down their principles *a priori*, but must evolve 'step by step, & by gradually widening . . . [their] induction'.[23] His political pamphlets from 1821 to 1831 mounted a familiar defence of 'principle and philosophy' against the fallacies of practice, and elsewhere he echoed James's contempt for the use of 'particular phenomena' as 'omens and signs of the future'.[24] He saw himself, like James, as an assiduous disciple of Bacon, in whose name he condemned 'conjecture' and inferences from 'scanty' evidence.[25] From this he generated a critical logic with which to counter Tory attacks on Athenian democracy.[26] In a review of Mitford's *History of Greece* from 1826, he restated the problem of

---

[19] Grote, *Fragments on ethical subjects*, p. 70.

[20] For the influence of Mill's *Logic* on Grote, see G. Grote, *Plato and other companions of Socrates* (London: John Murray, 1867), I, pp. 379, 380, 382. For the influence of *On liberty*, see *Companions of Socrates*, II, pp. 142–143n. See also P. Liddel, 'Liberty and obligation in George Grote's Athens', *Polis* 23 (2006), p. 139; J. Riley, 'Interpreting Mill's quantitative hedonism', *The Philosophical Quarterly* 53 (2003), pp. 410–418.

[21] *CW*, XI, p. 319. See P. Spahn, 'George Grote, John Stuart Mill und die antike Demokratie' in U. Gähde and W. H. Schrader (eds.), *Der klassische Utilitarianismus* (Berlin: Akademie Verlag, 1991), p. 155; W. Nippel, *Antike oder moderne Freiheit? Die Begründung der Demokratie in Athen und in der Neuzeit* (Berlin: Fischer Taschenbuch Verlag, 2008), pp. 246–266; N. Urbinati, *Mill on democracy: from the Athenian 'polis' to representative government* (London: University of Chicago Press, 2002), pp. 1, 4, 10, 153.

[22] Stephen, *The English utilitarians*, III, p. 338.

[23] G. Grote, 'George Grote. Four notebooks', Senate House Library MS429 [SHL Add. MS], III, f. 8.

[24] Grote, *Essentials of parliamentary reform*, pp. v–vi; Grote, *Fragments on ethical subjects*, p. 19.

[25] G. Grote, 'Notes relating to Grecian history 1818–1831', British Library Additional Manuscript [BL. Add MS] 29514, f. 149.

[26] Nippel has discussed 'die Tory-Sicht auf Athen': *Antike oder modern Freiheit?*, pp. 246–248.

drawing 'excessive inferences from single facts' and of 'stating as certain that which is doubtful, or at best only probable'.[27] The classical historian, Grote insisted, must be wary of the 'scantiness of the original documents' whilst providing an accurate report of the 'facts' and a 'full view of the phenomena of society'.[28] James's illumination of special circumstances by general laws had a lasting impact, but it is significant that Grote's *History of Greece* effectively dropped his mentor's concern with the scale and progress of civilisations.[29] As Forbes put it, Grote came to realise that the 'ever-swelling spate of German monographs' made these abstract schematic histories increasingly untenable.[30]

Bacon, Grote argued in 1821, had drawn back the 'perverted doctrine' of politics to 'the laws of human nature and experience', and those same laws illuminated history.[31] In the article on Mitford from 1826, he claimed that 'philosophy and research' were the historian's most indispensable tools, and that without the 'principles of human nature' it would be impossible to penetrate the surface of things and reveal society's hidden 'mechanism'.[32] Those principles were the 'true connecting links of the moral & political phenomena'. They consisted of and also helped to navigate the past, whereas those who inferred general truths from special circumstances did so through 'false' and 'superficial application[s] of philosophy', as when Mitford condemned Athenian democracy in the light of French republicanism.[33] Mitford's contributions to 'political science' and 'the science of government' confirmed his own preconceptions; relied too heavily on anti-democratic authorities; and lacked 'analytical' rigour.[34] In other words, he had failed to logically address history to politics.

Ian Hesketh has argued that the leap from Baconian induction to German historicism was a small one, and it is not surprising that Grote consistently defended both. Two of the historicists' most celebrated figures, Leopold von Ranke (1795–1886) and Wilhelm von Humboldt (1767–1835), were canonised by their contemporaries as Bacon's successors in historical science who, much like the Kantians, rejected both blind empiricism and the empty speculations of scholastic rationalism.[35] Ranke, like

---

[27] Grote, 'Fasti Hellenici', p. 307.   [28] Ibid., pp. 307, 281, 304.

[29] See Grote, *Minor works*, p. 283.   [30] Forbes, '*Historismus* in England', p. 399.

[31] Grote, *Statement on the question of parliamentary reform*, pp. 5, 7.

[32] Grote, 'Fasti Hellenici', pp. 280, 331. As he put it in the *History*, the historian – in true utilitarian fashion – must employ the 'language of the judge' and the principles of human nature to make credible 'conjectures and inferences': *HG*, I, p. vii.

[33] Grote, 'Notes relating to Grecian history 1818–1831', BL Add. MS 29514, f. 149.

[34] Grote, 'Fasti Hellenici', p. 286.

[35] I. Hesketh, *The science of history in Victorian Britain: making the past speak* (Oxford: Routledge, 2016), pp. 3–4; Beiser, *The German historicist tradition*, p. 168.

Bacon, proceeded from lower historical generalisations to intermediate axioms and, finally, to the highest and most universal level of historical explanation. In both cases history's explanatory power was to be found in an artfully struck balance between observation and reasoning, much in the same way that Grote in 1826 called for a union between philosophy and research. As Ranke put it in his *Englische Geschichte* (1859–1869), Bacon's triumph was to approach philosophy as a combination of 'wide observation and calm wisdom'.[36] Grote even met Ranke in 1857, one year after the publication of the *History's* twelfth and final volume, but we know precious little about their interaction, except that Grote had read and admired Ranke's *The Ecclesiastical and Political History of the Popes of Rome During the 16th and 17th Centuries* (1840) and that they debated the problem of historical objectivity at dinner with Macaulay.[37]

Grote in the preface to the *History* acknowledged his debts to Barthold Georg Niebuhr (1776–1831), August Böckh (1785–1867), and Karl Otfried Müller (1797–1840), the latter of whom had pioneered a new science of antiquity, *Altertumswissenschaft*, in his unfinished *Geschichten hellenischen Stämme und Städte* (1820, 1824).[38] He praised the critical approaches to historical texts in the decades 'since Mitford', especially in Germany where 'philological studies' had achieved 'remarkable success'.[39] He argued in 1826 that this methodological revolution had not yet taken place in England, where the historian must be 'painfully sensible of the difference between the real knowledge of the ancient world possessed or inquired for by a German public, and the appearance of knowledge which suffices here'; and, as with Blair and the British historians of the previous century, the Continent was presented as a ray of light in an otherwise dark historiographical landscape, iridescent with the possibilities of science.[40] It is worth pointing out that Grote's reception of historicism emphasised its critical, hermeneutic, and philological strands but not its developmental or progressive ones (as in German idealism, for instance).[41] As he put it in 1842, we 'regard Niebuhr with reference to erudition alone – copious, accurate, and available erudition', and to his 'ingenuity', 'piercing eye', and

---

[36] Quoted in H. G. Wormald, *Francis Bacon: history, politics, and science, 1561–1626* (Cambridge: Cambridge University Press, 1993), p. 12.

[37] A. D. Bolt, *Leopold von Ranke: a biography* (London: Routledge, 2019), p. 206.

[38] Grote, *HG*, I, pp. iv, 354. See K. Nickau, 'Karl Otfried Müller, Professor der Klassischen Philologie 1819–1840' in C. J. Classen (ed.), *Die Klassische Altertumswissenschaft an der Georg-August-Universität Göttingen* (Göttingen: Vandenhoeck & Ruprecht, 1989), pp. 27–53.

[39] Grote, *HG*, I, p. iv.   [40] Grote, 'Fasti Hellenici', p. 281.

[41] See Young, 'History', pp. 176–185.

'separation of leading points of evidence from that crowd ... under which they often lie concealed'.[42]

Shortly after his review of Mitford, Grote received a letter from Niebuhr, whose revolutionary work of historicism, *Römische Geschichte*, had appeared in German in 1812 and in English in 1827. Despite holding a professorial chair at Bonn, Niebuhr confided to the amateur that 'we may both be conscious, without personal acquaintance, that there exists between our principles and our views of history such a congeniality that we are called upon to become acquainted, and to connect our labours'.[43] Grote in later life recalled wading through Niebuhr's 'distressingly difficult volumes' and yet 'found him magisterially passing sentence on the works of authors which have perished, describing their excellences or defects'.[44] Niebuhr's 'moral nature', Grote insisted, 'was distinguished not only by a fearless love of truth ... [but] by a hearty sympathy with the mass of the people' and a tendency to 'treat their sentiments and motives with respect'.[45] At the start of his career, Niebuhr had focused primarily on Roman agrarian law with the aim of extracting wisdoms for the modern world, but the particularity of Roman conditions prompted him to develop an reconstructive science of history with which to probe the veracity of ancient sources. Contrary to what one might expect, this aspiration only deepened his interest in history's practical value.[46] As the past became less like the present, new possibilities emerged for moral and political reflection, and presumably Grote had something like this in mind when he argued that 'the liberal spirit of criticism' had made the 'poets, historians, orators, and philosophers of Greece ... both more intelligible and more instructive' than in the previous century.[47]

With the 'inestimable aid of German erudition', Grote sought to provide a remedial narrative of ancient Greek history, freed from Mitford's errors, as well as a 'general picture' of Greek society whose illustrations were 'suggestive and improving to the reason'.[48] This provided the *History* with a practical but not a partisan significance. The historian E. A. Freeman, in a review from 1856, commended Grote's 'practical bearing' as a historian whose 'fair examination of Grecian history' fully justified the conclusion 'that this mob clothed with executive functions made one of the

---

[42] Grote, *Minor works*, p. 75.   [43] Grote, *The personal life of George Grote*, p. 52.
[44] G. Grote, 'Early Roman history', *Eclectic Review* 10 (1855), p. 173.
[45] Grote, *Minor works*, pp. 75–76.
[46] U. Muhlack, 'German Enlightenment historiography and the rise of historicism' in S. Bourgault and R. Sparling (eds.), *A companion to Enlightenment historiography* (Leiden: Brill, 2013), p. 302.
[47] Grote, *HG*, I, p. iv.   [48] Ibid.

best governments which the world ever saw'.[49] Freeman disagreed with
Grote on several smaller points but he agreed that the *History*'s political
implications were compatible with its 'conscientious' scholarship.
'Mr. Grote's political views', he continued, '[do] colour his judgements,
but they in no way colour his statements. He always argues, and never
assumes or insinuates. He always fully and fairly sets forth the whole
evidence, and places elaborately before his reader the grounds of his own
judgement'.[50] John had made a similar point in an earlier review, in which
he celebrated Grote's 'simple veracity' and 'conscientious scrupulousness
in maintaining the demarcation between conjecture and proof'.[51]

Mitford had long been a thorn in the utilitarians' side, and James Mill in
conversations with his son, John, had decried his 'Tory prejudices' and
'perversions of facts' for the 'blackening of popular institutions'.[52] Grote's
articles were similarly emphatic but his intention in writing the *History*
wasn't simply to inveigh against old Tory prejudices, but to redefine
philosophical history within the context of historicism.[53] His distinction
between philosophical and abstract history addressed precisely this.
A 'philosophical history', he argued to George Cornewall Lewis in 1851,
could never be, *pace* Auguste Comte, an 'abstract history' independent of
'time, place, and person' because it would bear no relation to the '*facts* of
history'.[54] Comte had imposed onto Athens and Rome his own 'standard'
of morality, whose emphasis on individual prudence was akin to the
'Catholic divines of the present day'. Abstract history, as distinct from
philosophical history, allowed Comte to denounce under the vague aus-
pices of progress the 'comparative corruption' of the ancient world, without entertaining even the slightest 'study of the evidence'.[55] Cornewall
Lewis replied in kind: 'I have come to the conclusion (particularly after
reading your four volumes) that an enlightened commentary upon historical data, well ascertained . . . would be the best foundation and preparation
for a really scientific treatment of politics and morals'.[56]

If philosophical history was not 'abstract', as Comte suggested, then
what was it? In the letter to Cornewall Lewis, Grote suggested that there
existed 'certain general conditions and principles, common to all particular

---

[49] Ibid., p. 158.   [50] Ibid., p. 143.   [51] *CW*, XV p. 511; XI, p. 330.
[52] Ibid., I, p. 14. Bentham knew Mitford from Oxford and thought little of him: *Works*, X, p. 40.
[53] Grote, *HG*, I, p. iii.
[54] Grote, *The personal life of George Grote*, p. 203. Comte could be disparaging towards 'history proper'
because of its 'methodological emphasis on the unique and the individual': Kent Wright, 'History
and historicism', p. 128.
[55] Grote, *The personal life of George Grote*, p. 204.   [56] Ibid., p. 181.

histories, and which are essential to enable us to explain and concatenate the facts of every particular history'.[57] Evidently Comte had gone too far in delineating the course of history from its intellectual and social progress, but at the same time the past could not be explained solely by philology and textual criticism. General principles, which were themselves informed by history, helped to illuminate the past's uniqueness, and, by insisting on an empirical concreteness to those principles – that is, on their manifestation in time, place, and person – Grote guarded against the kind of prejudice that he identified in Mitford and, in a different way, in Comte. That historians should not speculate on the bases of personal belief, or theorise abstractly, were recurring themes in Niebuhr's lectures: 'our own personal views and opinions can be of little avail in history, if they are not in accordance with things and relations which really existed', and the historian must rely instead on a profound 'knowledge of human and political affairs'; of 'social relations in general'; and of 'occurrences which have taken place at different times and in different nations, according to the same or similar laws'.[58] Grote's reception of Niebuhr complemented his reading of James Mill, both of whom illuminated particular facts with general laws.

Grote's philosophical history set him apart from other ancient historians who took inspiration from Niebuhr and the critical philologists. Connop Thirlwall (1797–1875), a contemporary of Grote's at Charterhouse, published his own *History of Greece* between 1835 and 1847, and, along with Julius Hare (1795–1855), translated Niebuhr's *Römische Geschichte* into English. Thirlwall disabused Mitford of countless factual errors and questioned the historical basis of his anti-democratic views, arguably setting his sights no higher than that.[59] Grote modestly remarked that Thirlwall's *History* had blunted the impact of his own, but the two works scarcely compare.[60] Looking back, John remarked that Thirlwall had produced a 'critical' but not a 'philosophical history', whereas Grote had combined a critical approach to ancient texts with philosophical insights into the causes, reality, and distinctness of historical phenomena.[61] As Grote put it in the *History*, the illumination of human nature under its 'diverse modifications' helped to form 'generalisation[s] ... hardly less applicable to other political societies, far distant in both time and place'.[62] History must

---

[57] Ibid., p. 204.

[58] B. G. Niebuhr (trans. W. Smith and L. Schmitz), *The history of Rome* (Philadelphia: Lea & Blanchard, 1844), III, p. 51.

[59] Thirlwall in volume three attacked those 'polemical' historians of Greece who 'distorted' the facts: *A history of Greece* (London: Longman, Brown, Green, and Longmans, 1842), III, p. 463.

[60] Grote, *HG*, I, p. iii.   [61] *CW*, XI, p. 275.

[62] Grote, *HG*, VI, pp. 279, 278. He believed that this kind of 'perfect' and 'philosophical' history had been made possible only in 'the last century': *HG*, I, p. 357.

always be a 'series of true matters of fact, exemplifying the laws of human nature
and society', and enlarging our knowledge of them for purposes of future
inference'.[63]

The philosophical historian, then, was concerned exclusively with matters
of fact, whereas philosophers of history tended to 'pass unconsciously' from
exposition to criticism.[64] The plea for history's autonomy, which is comparable with both Bentham's and Niebuhr's, is consistent throughout Grote's
writings. In an essay on the idea of ethical sentiment, written in the 1840s or
early 1850s, he reiterated Bentham's point that the functions of exposition
and criticism were erroneously 'confounded ... [when] a man explains the
historical origin of certain dispositions and sentiments, and thinks that by
doing so he has justified them critically; or he expatiates upon the value of
certain dispositions and sentiments, and thinks that by doing so he has
justified them critically'.[65] He was less clear about the ways in which history
could rationally inform politics, but the same ambiguity plagued the early
German historicists, many of whom prevaricated over antiquity's moral and
political value; indeed, Beiser has argued that their contradictory emphasis
on the principles of historical distinctness and development help to explain
historicism's enduring ambiguity, and it is worth noting that John's own
historical writings were similarly conflicted (see Chapters 5 and 6).

Using the case of Wilhelm von Humboldt, Beiser argued that historicism
can be split into two camps, the first of which exalted antiquity's exemplary
status, while the second denied that exemplarity by conceptualising the past as
unique. Humboldt, Beiser tells us, was intellectually stranded between
Gotthold Lessing's (1729–1781) aesthetic neo-Hellenism and Friedrich
Wolf's (1759–1824) philology. Friedrich Schiller (1775–1805) and Karl
Dalberg (1744–1817) even interrogated Humboldt about his contradictory
approach to history, which defended both a historicist *Eigenthumlickheiten*
and a prescriptive neo-classicism.[66] Grote's sympathies were similarly split,
especially in his early private writings. While the *History* defended what
Alexandra Lanieri has called a 'historicist *Wissenschaften*', which challenged
'exemplary uses of antiquity and its quick identification with modern practices', Grote elsewhere could be strikingly equivocal.[67] This, for the reasons
I have outlined, situates him even more firmly within the context of early
nineteenth-century historicism.

[63] Ibid., V, p. 7n.   [64] Grote, *Fragments on ethical subjects*, p. 70.   [65] Ibid.
[66] Beiser, *The German historicist tradition*, pp. 183–192.
[67] A. Lanieri, 'Unfounding times: the idea and ideal of ancient history in Western historical thought'
in Lianeri (ed.), *The western time of ancient history: historiographical encounters with the Greek and
Roman pasts*, p. 21.

Grote in private acknowledged the 'utility of the ancient authors, in guiding the thoughts & reasonings [sic] of the moderns', and in another manuscript he argued that the Athenian constitution was the 'purest model of democracy'.[68] Elsewhere, he attacked presentism for robbing the past of its distinctness. In a manuscript written at roughly the same time as the article on Mitford, he observed how in England 'modern history' was 'commonly considered under the points of comparison with ancient [history]', even though the past, properly understood, was unfamiliar and even dissonant.[69] The historian, he argued, must be 'superior to [the] prejudices of his own age & country: if he is not so, he will ascribe all the calamitous phenomena, which history exhibits to such institutions as are contrary to the prejudices which he has imbibed, all the favourable phenomena to institutions conformable to these prejudices'.[70] A similar argument can be found in the *History*, which complained of the 'false colouring' commonly attached 'to the political feeling of recent days to matters of ancient history, such as the Saxon Witenagemote [sic], the Great Charter, the rise and growth of the English House of Commons, or even the Poor Law of Elizabeth'.[71]

For Grote, therefore, philosophical history fell somewhere between the dry, technical pursuits of antiquarianism, whose practitioners rarely sought to explain or generalise facts, and Comte's 'Catholic' abstractions. Indeed, his commitments to Baconian induction and historicism shared a disdain for wild speculation and prejudice, both of which were longstanding utilitarian bugbears. In 1851, for example, a debate broke out between the classicist Richard Shiletto (1809–1876) and George's brother, the Cambridge moral philosopher John Grote (1813–1866). Shiletto condemned the *History* with 'the prejudice of one not ashamed to call himself a Tory against one not ... ashamed to call himself a Republican', while John retorted that his brother should be seen not as a 'Republican', but rather as a 'historian anxious to produce, according to his conscientious views, a faithful history'.[72] In an

---

[68] Grote, 'Notes relating to Grecian history 1818–1831', BL Add. MS 29514, f. 17; Grote, 'Notes relating to Grecian history 1826–1832', BL Add. MS 29517, f. 71. He also made an analogy between the Swiss cantons and Athenian democracy in an exchange with Tocqueville: G. Grote, *Seven letters concerning the politics of Switzerland, pending the outbreak of the civil war in 1847* (London: John Murray, 1876), pp. x, 37. He praised Thucydides in volume one of the *History* for understanding that 'the true scheme of the historian, common to him with the philosopher, [is] to recount and interpret the past, as a rational aid towards the prevision of the future': *HG*, I, p. 197–8.

[69] Grote, 'Notes relating to Grecian history 1818–1831', BL Add. MS 29514, f. 149.   [70] Ibid.

[71] Grote, *HG*, II, p. 401.

[72] R. Shilleto, *Thucydides or Grote?* (Cambridge: John Deighton, 1851), p. 1; J. Grote, *A few remarks on a pamphlet by Mr. Shilleto, entitled "Thucydides or Grote?"* (Cambridge: John Deighton, 1851), p. 79.

unpublished letter written in the aftermath of this exchange, Grote suggested to his brother that Shiletto's polemical style would do 'more harm to his own cause than to me' and that 'by no means ... should [he] be attacked'.[73] He refused to fight Shiletto at the level of political principle, and instead allowed others to contrast his historicism with Shiletto's brazen partialities.

It is worth noting that Grote was attacked for defending Athenian democracy even by some of his German readers, one of whom, Emil Müller, argued in 1857 that the 'English historian has been accused of allowing his own democratic partisanship an unwarranted influence upon the historical account', while Grote accused the German philologists of being 'prejudiced against Greek democracy, and against the Athenian *demos* in particular'.[74] I do not wish to entirely dismiss these claims, or to argue that Grote's historiography was unprecedently objective and separate from his politics; at the same time, his articles, essays, and memoranda do help to clarify his intentions as a philosophical historian. The aim of philosophical history was to illuminate the past with general facts, in keeping with his historicism, and to recover the past's uniqueness. His defence of Athenian democracy was not intended as a fulcrum for liberal politics, and this invites us to reconsider the ways in which he deduced lessons for 'our own world'.[75] Those lessons emphasised the resemblances as well as the 'contrast[s] with the better-known forms of modern society' and applied less to the institutions than to the sentiments of democracy.[76] Those sentiments had universal forms but historically specific contents, and the sentiments of modern society, he observed, were largely incompatible with those of a flourishing democracy. It is this disparity which gives context to the *History's* substantive political claims and Mill's reception of them.

Sentiments of Democracy

Athenian democracy could not serve as a blueprint for representative government, whose uniquely modern benefits Grote outlined in an unpublished essay from the 1820s.[77] The principles of a 'well constituted

---

[73] George Grote to John Grote, 31 May 1857: Trinity College, Cambridge, 'Papers of the Mayor and related families', ADD. MS C12/53.

[74] Quoted in Nippel, *Ancient and modern democracy*, p. 269. Grote argued that, while Niebuhr was sometimes mistaken in his judgements, they were always founded on truthful examinations: Grote *Minor works*, p. 75.

[75] The quotation is from John: *CW*, XI. p. 274.   [76] Grote, *HG*, I, p. v.

[77] The distinction between democracy and representative had become increasingly prevalent: W. Nippel, *Ancient and modern democracy. Two concepts of liberty?* (Cambridge: Cambridge

representative system', he observed, were 'unknown' to the ancient republics, and this characteristically utilitarian distinction found its way into the *History*.[78] Bentham in *A Plan for Parliamentary Reform* had praised 'representative' but not ancient 'self-acting' democracies, while Grote in an unpublished essay on Harrington's *Commonwealth of Oceana* (1656) followed James Mill in insisting that 'the real guarantee for good behaviour on the part of both assemblies is, that they are elected by the people for short periods'.[79] The institutional parallels between ancient and modern democracy were few, but both relied on ethical sentiment to reconcile political freedom with individual restraint. As Grote put it in volume four of the *History*:

> This coexistence [in Athens] of freedom and self-imposed restraint ... may be found in the aristocracy of England (since about 1688) as well as in the democracy of the American United States: and because we are familiar with it, we are apt to suppose it a natural sentiment; though there seem to be few sentiments more difficult to establish and diffuse among a community, judging by the experience of history. We may see how imperfectly it exists at this day in the Swiss cantons; and the many violences of the first French revolution illustrate, among various other lessons, the fatal effects arising from its absence ...[80]

Elsewhere, in an essay on ethics, he argued that to 'collect and compare different societies' helps to 'purify the character of ethical sentiment, and to disengage those great principles which are common to all ages and nations from the capricious adjuncts which are peculiar to this or that portion of the globe'.[81] All societies were held together by an ethical sentiment whose

University Press, 2015), p. 116; J. G. A. Pocock, 'Perceptions of modernity in early modern historical thinking', *Intellectual History Review* 17 (2007), p. 58; K. O'Brien, *Narratives of Enlightenment: cosmopolitan history from Voltaire to Gibbon* (Cambridge: Cambridge University Press, 1997), p. 11.

[78] G. Grote, 'Notes relating to Grecian history 1818–1831', BL Add. MS 29514, f. 322; Grote, *HG*, IV, p. 157.

[79] Bentham, *A plan of parliamentary reform*, p. xliii; G. Grote, 'Grote papers, 1818–1822', BL Add. MSS 29529, ff. 5, 9.

[80] Grote, *HG*, IV, p. 157. Several political theorists have interpreted Grote's utilitarianism as a form of classical republicanism, even though there is little evidence to suggest that he did so himself. Others have suggested, again without concrete proof, that Grote defended 'ancient' liberty from the criticisms levelled at it by Benjamin Constant in his essay *De la liberté des anciens comparée à celle des modernes* (1819). See K. N. Demetriou, *Studies in the reception of Plato and Greek political thought in Britain* (Surrey: Ashgate, 2011), p. viii; A. W. Saxonhouse, *Free speech and democracy in ancient Athens* (Cambridge: Cambridge University Press, 2006), p. 85; Demetriou, 'The spirit of Athens: George Grote and John Stuart Mill on classical republicanism' in Demetriou and Loizides (eds.), *Mill: a British Socrates*, p. 179; P. Liddel, *Civic obligation and individual liberty in ancient Athens* (Oxford: Oxford University Press, 2007), pp. 7–8. This misreading also applies to Mill's theory of liberty. See J. Lachs : 'Mill and Constant: a neglected connection in the history of the idea of liberty', *History of Philosophy Quarterly* 9 (1992), p. 87.

[81] Grote, *Fragments on ethical subjects*, p. 77.

form was universal but whose matter varied; thus, by examining the
sentiments which prevented the Athenians from excessively indulging
their freedom, he hoped to parry Mitford's (and others') attacks on
democracy.[82] In the 1780s and 1790s, diatribes condemning Athenian
democracy had provided the intellectual lineaments of a furious anti-
Jacobinism. Historians including John Gillies (1747–1836), Oliver
Goldsmith (1728–1774), and Mitford – in keeping with the anti-
democratic bias of extant sources – inferred from the Athenian example
that democracies were fickle, violent, and despotic.[83] These denunciations
were fuels for conservatism, and Grote in the *History* mounted a defence of
the Athenians' ethical sentiment, first, by demonstrating that extensive
political participation by a mass of citizens undermined neither the community's competence nor moral integrity; second, by demonstrating the
ways in which the Athenians' individual and collective interests spontaneously aligned; third, by articulating a theory of liberty in which individuals cultivated themselves in accordance with the general good; and,
finally, by arguing that the Athenians promoted individuality through
the ritualised performance of obligations. These points merit a lengthier
exegesis, especially of the *History's* fourth, fifth, and sixth volumes.

Grote rehabilitated the popular assemblies by emphasising their capacity
for rational deliberation, and by characterising as 'reasonable changes of
opinion' what Gillies and Mitford had interpreted as a familiar form
of democratic fickleness.[84] He argued in volume four that the appearance
of volatility in Athens was amplified by the publicness of the Pnyx, *ekklesia,*
boule, and *agora*.[85] He concluded volume seven by playing down the
volatility of the *demos* and underscoring the corruption of the oligarchs,
amongst whom, he claimed, reason frequently succumbed to 'self-
delusion', 'pride, power-seeking', 'party-antipathy', and 'love of ease'.[86]
While he acknowledged that people – as *the* people – had occasionally
sanctioned bad laws, he also observed that it 'was not the maxim at Athens

---

[82] Mitford's political bias is manifested 'especially in those parts of it which were written subsequently to the French Revolution': Grote, 'Fasti Hellenici', p. 286; see Mitford, *The history of Greece*, II, p. 166.

[83] J. Gillies, *The history of ancient Greece, its colonies, and conquests, from the earliest accounts to the division of the Macedonian Empire in the East* [1786] (London: T. Cadell and W. Davies, 1801), I, p. iii; O. Goldsmith, *The history of Greece from the earliest state, to the death of Alexander the Great* [1774] (London: Rivington, 1823), I, pp. 396–397; Mitford, *The history of Greece*, IV, p. 361. See also J. T. Roberts, *Athens on trial: the antidemocratic tradition in Western thought* (Princeton: Princeton University Press, 1994), p. 237.

[84] Gillies, *The history of ancient Greece*, I, p. iii; Mitford, *The history of Greece*, IV, p. 361.

[85] Grote, *HG*, IV, pp. 376–378.   [86] Ibid., VII, p. 401.

to escape the errors of the people, by calling in the different errors, and the sinister interest besides, of an extra-popular or privileged few . . . Beyond the judgment of the people the Athenians felt there was no appeal'; and thus 'their grand study' was to establish 'the best preservatives against haste, passion, or private corruption'.[87] In 1823, shortly after his conversion to utilitarianism, he had written to his brother-in-law, Francis Lewin, to illustrate this very point: 'no one', he argued, 'ever concluded that the people make no mistakes; what is contended is, that the people are right upon the long run . . . & above all, that they have no interest in going wrong'.[88]

Demagogy posed one of the greatest challenges to the rehabilitation of Athenian democracy, hence his now famous defence of Cleon; less known, however, is his identification of the family and household as important checks on the assembly.[89] Even though a demagogue could incite a 'formidable mass of private hatred', the threat of dishonour, alongside the legal sanction of ostracism, encouraged the Athenians to solve their problems socially, outside of formal political institutions.[90] When 'the assembly broke up, when the citizen, no longer wound up by sympathising companions and animated speakers in the Pnyx, subsided into the comparative quiescence of individual life, when the talk came to be, not about the propriety of passing such a resolution, but about the details of executing it, a sensible change and marked repentance became presently visible'.[91] The private life and the active life were seen by Grote as reciprocal elements of a community in which the laws were permeated by the virtues of the *oikos*, thus curbing the irrationality, passion, and susceptibility to rhetoric of the collected crowd. He defended this view further in a letter to his publisher, John Murray, in which he claimed that the 'true character' of the *dikastery* and *demos* 'was to be open-minded & susceptible of multifarious impulses not at all exclusively wrathful & jealous'.[92]

The exercise of one's conscience in the assembly and law-courts strengthened the reciprocity between individuals' and the city's interests: 'each man', Grote argued, 'felt that he exercised his share of influence on the decision, [but] identified his own safety and happiness with the vote of

---

[87] Ibid., IV, p. 157. [88] Grote to Lewin, 27 January 1823: UCL Add. MS 266 A2, f. 10.
[89] Mill agreed and quoted Grote in a review: '*Demos* sitting in the Pnyx was a different man from *Demos* at home': *CW*, XXV, p. 1127.
[90] Grote, *HG*, VI, p. 486. In an early manuscript, Grote argued that moments of 'excitement' and 'violent proceedings' were 'cases of exception': 'Notes relating to Grecian history 1818–1831', BL Add. MS 29514, f. 17.
[91] Grote, *HG*, VI, p. 249.
[92] Grote to Murray, 15 May 1850: Bodleian Library Oxford [BOD] Additional Manuscript [Add. MS], Eng.Let.d.122, f. 92.

the majority'.[93] In classic utilitarian fashion, citizens located their self-interest in the aggregate interest of the community, but whereas Bentham had artificially aligned the interests of the rulers and the ruled, Grote showed how one's conscience, both publicly and privately formed, could willingly prioritise the interests of the city.[94] This prepared the way for a new kind of liberty, central to which was a rejection of oligarchy and passive acquiescence. In a private manuscript written during the composition of the *History*, he proclaimed that 'the character of a citizen, as modern politicians would mould it, is far too passive, mercenary & unpatriotic to form a flourishing city in the circumstance of ancient Greece'.[95] Basic acts of political obligation, such as electing representatives, paying one's taxes, and following the laws, were seen as necessary but not sufficient conditions of political virtue.[96] Like Hume, Locke, and von Humboldt – the latter of whom he effusively praised in 1857 for giving a 'low comparative estimate' of 'passive imitation and submission' – Grote saw acquiescence as the death of active citizenship.[97] The Athenians, by contrast, had 'kept alive in the bosom of each individual resident a constant feeling of union with all his fellow citizens' so that the 'obligations rendered towards the community became inseparably connected in his mind with rights which he was entitled to claim from them'.[98]

The politically active life underpinned Grote's philosophy of education, which he set out in a brief unpublished essay in the early 1820s. His central claim, as with James and John, was that education promoted utility through the development of character, that is, through its ability to shape preferences and habits. As an autodidact and champion of liberal education, freed from the clutches of the church, he was acutely aware that education, in its baser forms, could encourage habits of obedience and blind citizens to their political maltreatment. His boldest example was Sparta's pedagogy of *agoge*, which, he claimed, fostered patriotism at the expense of sharing in political rule and fomented an equality 'not of power,

---

[93] Grote, *HG*, IV, p. 139.
[94] See P. Schofield, 'Bentham on the identification of interests', *Utilitas* 8 (1996), p. 227.
[95] Grote, 'Fragments of Mr. Grote's handwriting', BOD, Add. MS. c. 208, f. 49.
[96] Grote, 'Grote papers', BL Add. MS 29520, f. 65.
[97] H. Grote, *The personal life of George Grote*, p. 237. In an unpublished essay written between 1826 and 1832, he claimed that the democratic assemblies raised 'the character of the people' by 'preventing that tame submission & apathy under injustice' and 'magnifying ... the sympathy of their fellow citizens': G. Grote, 'Notes relating to Grecian history etc. 1826–1832. Newspaper cuttings on the ballot 1833', BL Add. MS 29517, f. 38.
[98] Grote, 'Fasti Hellenici', p. 272. See also Grote, 'Grote papers, 1818–1822', BL Add. MS 29529, ff. 16–17.

but of subjection to a higher influence'.[99] Against this stood the writings of Aristotle and Plato, in whose absence 'nothing is done in modern education to create any extensive sympathies for fellow-citizens, or any strong sense of right or obligation connected with the character of a citizen'.[100]

Modern society was divided into countless factions and fraternities under the rule of law, whereas the system of education recommended by Aristotle and Plato could not 'fail to communicate to the citizen a powerful & earnest love of his commonwealth & of all his fellow citizens'.[101] One of the 'earliest subjects of meditation in Athens', he observed, was the purpose, form, and 'utility' of the active life, the 'rights and obligations of the citizen as such, *both towards individuals & towards his fellow citizens collectively*'.[102] Whereas Bentham had defined liberty in conventional terms as the absence of coercion – 'an idea purely negative', as he put it – Grote gestured towards a more complex form of liberty in which political virtue emerged spontaneously from the quest for self-development.[103] He used the word 'liberty' to denote the free performance of obligations, as well as the legal obligations whose performances were legitimately compelled by the state – that is, liberty in the civil Lockean sense – and he returned time and again to the idea that the Athenians voluntarily chose political participation over other private interests, and that they conceptualised the performance of civic obligations not as encroachments on their private freedom but as edifying displays of individuality.

The relationship between obligation and political virtue was thus a reflexive one which stimulated, and was itself stimulated by, democratic institutions. The performance of civic obligations became a voluntary and even pleasurable act. The 'theory of democracy', he opined, was 'eminently seductive, creating in the mass of citizens an intense *positive attachment*, and disposing them to *voluntary action* and suffering on its behalf, such as no coercion on the part of other governments could exhort'.[104] Turning orthodox doctrines of political obligation on their head, he argued that the performance of civic duties was motivated not by the coercive force of the state, but by individual spontaneity and the bonds of political unity.[105]

---

[99] Grote, 'Grote papers, 1818–1822', BL Add. MS 29529, f. 36. J. S. Mill agreed that Spartan citizens were 'creatures and instruments of the ideal being called the state': *CW*, XI, p. 301.

[100] Grote, 'Grote papers, 1818–1822', BL Add. MS 29529, f. 30.   [101] Ibid., f. 29.

[102] Ibid. My emphasis. Grote's argument in recent years has been used to challenge Isaiah Berlin's distinction between positive and negative liberty. See, for example, M. Edge, 'Athens and the spectrum of liberty', *History of Political Thought* 30 (2009), pp. 1–47.

[103] See Rosen, *Classical utilitarianism from Hume to Mill*, p. 50.

[104] Grote, *HG*, IV, p. 178. My emphasis.

[105] The widely used 'νόμος' (*nomos*) meant both law and custom.

That these duties were performed freely by individuals who cultivated democratic sentiments was a theme of Grote's unpublished as well as his published writings; as early as the 1820s, in his essay on education, he had outlined the 'essential idea of democracy' as giving 'to each of the free citizens *who choose it a chance of enjoying the pleasures of power*, & of taking his turn (to use the expression of Aristotle) in commanding & being commanded'.[106]

Political participation in Athens took the form of an obligation but the character of a voluntary act, which meant that citizens remained free to pursue the pleasures of private as well as public action.[107] The 'liberty of individual action', he asserted, 'belongs more naturally to a democracy . . . than to any other form of government', and this helped to explain the Athenians' progress in science, philosophy, literature, and aesthetics.[108] Like John, he theorised the conditions of Greek flourishing and enquired into the sentiments which 'kept alive' the 'genuine light of truth and patriotism'.[109] These sentiments were encouraged by various political, educational, and cultural institutions, thanks to which the Athenians experienced the 'largest amount' of 'imaginative pleasures ever tasted by any community known to history; pleasures essentially social and multitudinous, attaching citizens to each other, rich and poor, by the strong tie of community of enjoyment'.[110] Civic and religious rituals, including the Panathenaea and the Dionysia, provided opportunities for the social exchange of pleasure, and, through that pleasure, a willingness to perform obligations in the city's name. In a manuscript essay from the 1820s, Grote argued that worship, sacrifice, and the ancient festivals 'presented pleasures to be enjoyed in common; the sacrifices afforded feasts of which all the citizens partook . . . The co-enjoyment of these pleasures caused a great extension of sympathetic feeling among the citizens'.[111] The social expression of religion entered into 'all the enjoyments and sufferings, the hopes and fears, the affections and antipathies, of the people, not simply imposing restraints and obligations, but protecting, multiplying, and diversifying all the social pleasures and all the decorations of existence'.[112]

---

[106] Grote, 'Grote papers', BL Add. MS 29520, f. 203. My emphasis.   [107] Grote, *HG*, IV, p. 178.
[108] Ibid., VI, p. 150.
[109] Grote, 'Grote papers, 1818–1822', BL Add. MS 29529, f. 36. Grote's praise of *On liberty* took a similar line: *Companions of Socrates*, II, p. 143.
[110] Grote, *HG*, XI, p. 353.
[111] G. Grote, 'Papers of George Grote', Cambridge University Library [CUL] Additional Manuscripts [Add. MS] 1933, f. 1.
[112] Grote, *HG*, IV, p. 53.

Grote, unsurprisingly, was reluctant to bind the sentiments of democracy to the spirit of religion.[113] He placed a far greater emphasis on the secular and civic sentiments which allowed political freedom to coexist, paradox-free, with individual restraint. In the *History*, these sentiments took the form of two interdependent concepts: 'constitutional morality' and 'democratical sentiment', both of which, he asserted in volume four, conciliated not only the 'good-will' but also the 'passionate attachment' of 'the mass of citizens, insomuch that not even any considerable minority should be deliberately inclined to alter . . . [political outcomes] by force'.[114] The lawgiver Cleisthenes, for instance, had protected the fledgling democracy from demagogues and factions by instilling '*that rare and difficult sentiment which we may term a constitutional morality*'.[115] Constitutional morality was sustained not by the laws and decrees of the assembly, but by a respect *for* those laws and decrees. The *demos*, on occasion, even took measures to protect itself from itself; towards the end of the fifth century, for example, the *graphe paranomon* and the *nomothetai* were introduced as institutional bulwarks against demagogy.[116] Basic liberties, such as the liberty of the press and 'pacific criticism', were sustained by the idea that citizens were free to shoulder political responsibility, which involved both the formation of, as well as obedience to, the laws.[117] The pervading spirit of constitutional morality prevented the democracy from degenerating into anarchy; citizens, theoretically free to pursue vested interests, instead chose to obey the laws established by the city and exhibited

> a paramount reverence for the forms of the constitution, enforcing obedience to the authorities acting under and within those forms, yet combined with the habit of open speech, of action subject only to definite legal control, and unrestrained censure of those very authorities as to all their public acts, combined too with a perfect confidence in the bosom of every citizen, amidst the bitterness of party contest, that the forms of the constitution will be not less sacred in the eyes of his opponents than in his own. This [demonstrated the] coexistence of freedom and self-imposed restraint . . .[118]

---

[113] See C. Fuller, 'Bentham, Mill, Grote and An analysis of the influence of natural religion on the temporal happiness of mankind', *Journal of Bentham Studies* 10 (2008), pp. 1–15.

[114] Grote, *HG*, IV, p. 154.   [115] Ibid. My emphasis.

[116] See Grote, 'Grote papers', BL Add. MS 29520, f. 36. On the protective institutions of the democracy, see *HG*, IV, pp. 155–157.

[117] Grote, *HG*, IV, p. 155. The origins of 'constitutional morality' can be traced to the rhetoric of new and evangelical Whigs: I. Newbould, *Whiggery and reform 1830–41: the politics of government* (California: Stanford University Press, 1990), p. 316. See also J. Bord, *Science and Whig manners: science and political style in Britain, c. 1750–1850* (London: Palgrave, 2009), p. 83.

[118] Grote, *HG*, IV, p. 154.

Constitutional morality was a necessary but insufficient condition of political virtue because regimes other than democracy could, in theory, inspire a spontaneous attachment to the laws. Through the concept of 'democratical sentiment' Grote attempted to explain the success of democracy *as* a democracy, whose development he traced from its early beginnings under Solon to the Cleisthenic reforms of 508/7 and the reforms of Ephialtes. The third – but especially the fourth and fifth – volumes of the *History* charted the ways in which 'democratical sentiment' went on 'steadily increasing' until all citizens had a reasonable chance of gaining office.[119] The 'abolition of all pecuniary qualifications for magistracies' curbed the threat of oligarchy and instilled in the *demos* 'self-reliance', 'mutual sympathies', and 'ambition', all of which were indispensable to democracy's flourishing.[120] The lot was celebrated as a 'symptom of pronounced democratic spirit' because it demonstrated a willingness to maintain basic political and legal equalities – *isonomia, isegoria,* and so on – through 'direct action'.[121] Grote, like James Mill, located in the Athenian nobility an ongoing threat to democracy's vitality and the spontaneous energies of the *demos*. Given that these middle volumes were written shortly after the 1848 revolutions and the final resurgence of Chartism, it is unsurprising that they were received by the likes of Shiletto as a casual defence of republican principles.[122]

Grote saw the gradual enervation of democratic sentiment as a primary reason for the democracy's collapse. In his exegesis of Demosthenes' *Third Philippic*, he agreed that the passion for democracy developed an eventually fatal anaemia, and, like Demosthenes, he lamented the indolence and apathy of the *demos* even as the threat of Philip's Macedon drew near. Whereas the Athenians under Pericles had exhibited an 'active interest' in the constitution, 'being at once a mark of previous growth of democratical sentiment during the past, and a cause of its farther development during the future', the citizens of the late fourth-century fulfilled only basic obligations recompensed by public pay.[123] While the Athenians had retained their constitutional morality – in other words, they obeyed the laws and participated in political affairs – they merely acquiesced in the forms of institutional activity prescribed to them by the state so that the 'active sentiment of obligation' became

---

[119] Ibid., V, p. 355; III, p. 132.   [120] Ibid., V, p. 354; III, p. 127. See also III, 132; IV, p. 136.
[121] Ibid., III, p. 132.
[122] See J. Sperber, *The European revolutions, 1848–1851* (Cambridge: Cambridge University Press, 2005), p. 261.
[123] Grote, *HG*, VI, p. 1.

comparatively inoperative; the citizen, it is true . . . is willing to perform his ordinary sphere of legal duties towards it; but he looks upon it as a thing established . . . capable of maintaining itself . . . without any such personal efforts as those which his forefathers *cheerfully imposed upon themselves.* The orations of Demosthenes contain melancholy proofs of such altered tone of patriotism, of that languor, paralysis, and waiting for others to act . . .[124]

Lessons for Liberty

Athenian democracy accentuated the differences between ancient and modern society. That its operative sentiments were 'difficult to establish and diffuse, judging by the experience of history' consorted well with Grote's historicism.[125] The Greeks did not resemble Englishmen, but they did provide unrivalled insights into human nature and the sentiments through which public and private liberty might be reconciled. The vanguard of civilisation began with the Greeks and their 'spontaneous' intellect, 'sometimes aided but never borrowed from without', and they were the first to spark humanity's 'dormant intellectual capacities'.[126] Athens was a specimen of democracy not because it was practically superior to modern representative government, but because human nature in antiquity was simpler and easier to measure against the prevailing ethical sentiment. Modern society, by contrast, was ineffably the product of countless historical developments and modifying forces.[127] John in his review of Grote picked up this argument when he praised the Greeks' 'meteor-like . . . manifestation of human nature', and elsewhere, in an unpublished essay written in the 1860s, he argued that individual and collective sentiments marked 'the meeting point between judgement & feeling' and formed a 'practically important part of the constitution of human nature'.[128] The sentiments of the Athenian *demos*, however unique and unprecedented, thus provided opportunities for reflection.

Mill in reviews of the *History* and essays from the 1850s and 1860s provided many such reflections.[129] He was among the *History's* most

---

[124] Ibid., IV, p. 180. My emphasis.   [125] Ibid., p. 157.   [126] Ibid., I, p. v.
[127] '[W]hen once any special ethical antipathy has become rooted in a society, it transmits itself from generation to generation, with scarcely any chance of being ever eradicated': Grote, *Fragments on ethical subjects*, p. 76.
[128] *CW*, XI, p. 274; J. S. Mill, 'By what means may sentimentality be checked without discouraging healthy sentiment & individuality of character?', John Stuart Mill papers, Yale University Library, MS 350, f. 2. This essay, written in 1865, has not been included in the *Collected works* and will shortly feature in an article by the present author.
[129] A brief treatment of Mill's reception of Grote can be found in Nippel, *Antike oder moderne Freiheit?*, pp. 254–261. See also W. Donner, *The liberal self: John Stuart Mill's moral and political philosophy* (Ithaca: Cornell University Press, 1991), p. 160.

vocal champions, and his reviews in *The Spectator* (in 1849) and the *Edinburgh Review* (in 1846 and 1853) praised Grote's historicism whilst theoretically reflecting on Athenian democracy; like Grote, he was interested in the sentiments which reconciled public and private liberty, and in *Considerations of Representative Government* (1861) he drew explicitly on the concepts of constitutional morality and democratic sentiment. Democracy, he concluded, depended as much on citizens' feelings and sentiments as on formal limitations of power.[130]

> Where this school of public spirit does not exist, scarcely any sense is entertained that private persons, in no eminent social situation, owe any duties to society, except to obey the laws and submit to the government. There is no unselfish sentiment of identification with the public. Every thought or feeling, either of interest or of duty, is absorbed within the individual and in the family. The man never thinks of any collective interest, of any objects to be pursued jointly with others, but only in competition with them, and in some measure at their expense.[131]

Grote's *History* altered Mill's views on ancient liberty, whose disregard for individual freedom was a recurring theme in his early writings. In an article on François Guizot (1787–1874) from 1836, for example, he agreed that the 'love of liberty, in the modern sense of the phrase, was repudiated by the notions prevalent in those commonwealths respecting the duties of the citizen. The imaginary being, the *civitas*, the πόλις, demanded the annihilation of every individuality'. Every citizen, he maintained, 'was a perfect slave'.[132] Like Guizot, he traced the origins of modern liberty to the Teutonic 'conquerors' of the middle ages, rather than to the 'ancient civilisations[s]' of Greece and Rome.[133] This alternative genealogy, in common currency by the 1840s, became freshly significant in the work of John Mitchell Kemble (1807–1857) and Francis Palgrave, both of whom claimed that modern liberty was an expression of Germanic self-will as embodied in the *Wergild* and *Frankpledge* of ancient Saxon society; as Kemble argued in *The Saxons in England* (1849), the *mark* community established 'civil society at the least possible sacrifice to individual freedom'.[134] Mill's departure from this position is worth retracing.

---

[130] *CW*, XIX, pp. 377, 422.

[131] Ibid., p. 412. The 'positive political morality' of the *demos* protected it from tyranny: *CW*, XIX, p. 422.

[132] Ibid., XX, p. 384.   [133] Ibid., p. 274.

[134] J. M. Kemble, *The Saxons in England: a history of the English Commonwealth till the period of the Norman Conquest* (London: Longman, Brown, Green & Longmans, 1849), I, p. 128. See also Burrow, *A liberal descent*, pp. 97–126; Smith, *The Gothic bequest*, p. 142.

In 1837, one year after the review of Guizot and five after Grote's election to Parliament, Mill and Grote collaborated on a review of Henry Taylor's *The Statesman*, in which they argued that the English had sacrificed political virtue to 'commercial activity' and 'expertness in money-getting'.[135] They sought explanation in the pervasive neglect of 'classical studies', for if there was 'any one vocation of active life to which the classical studies belong with the most exact pertinence and speciality, it is that of a statesman'. If, they continued, 'the sense of obligation should in his [the statesman's] case be peculiarly exalted', then to study 'the best works of classical antiquity comes recommended by still higher considerations; for the public obligations stood in the foreground of all the ancient morality; the idea of the commonwealth, as the supreme object of his duty and solicitude, attracted to itself the strongest emotions in the bosom of every virtuous man'.[136] This indicated a softening of Mill's earlier position, but the idea of political virtue still sat awkwardly in his mind. Since the state remained the 'supreme object' of citizens' duty, it remained to be seen how, if at all, individuality could flourish in an onerous sphere of obligations.

Mill throughout the 1840s thought sporadically about the ways in which the sentiment of political virtue could be revived within modern representative governments, with the proviso that civic obligations benefited the individual *as* an individual. By the time he wrote the fourth of five reviews of Grote's *History* for *The Spectator* in March 1849, his position had shifted. Quoting at length Grote's analysis of Pericles' funeral oration, he set out 'to correct an assertion, often far too indiscriminately made, respecting antiquity as contrasted with modern societies – an assertion that the ancient societies sacrificed the individual to the state, and that only in modern times has individual agency been left free to the proper extent'.[137] In the passage from which Mill quoted, Grote argued that 'positive liberty' and the 'liberty of individual action' belonged 'more naturally to a democracy ... than to any other form of government'.[138] Four years later, in the *Edinburgh Review*, Mill agreed with Grote in his own words, concluding that the *History* reversed 'what we are so often told about the entire sacrifice, in the ancient republics, of the liberty of the individual to an imaginary good of the state'; 'imaginary', because it was absurd to claim that the good of the state was anything other than the aggregation of individual utilities and thus qualitatively distinct.[139]

---

[135] *CW*, XIX, p. 620. [136] Ibid., pp. 624–625. [137] *CW*, XXV, p. 1129–1130. [138] Ibid., p. 1130.
[139] Ibid., XI, p. 319. See also a letter from Mill to Grote, 10 January 1862: *CW*, XV, p. 762.

Mill's comments between 1849 and 1853 reflected a newfound belief that extensive civic duties cultivated individuality. In the 1853 review, he celebrated Pericles' funeral discourse as a 'remarkable testimony' to how 'the public interest was held of paramount obligation in all things which concerned it; but, with that part of the conduct of individuals which concerned only themselves, public opinion did not interfere; while in the ethical practice of the moderns, this is exactly reversed'.[140] It would be a stretch to argue that Grote was solely responsible for Mill's change of mind – we must factor in, for example, the influence of Alexis de Tocqueville (1805–1859), whose analysis of America pointed out to Mill new correlations, many of them negative, between individuality and representative democracy – but it is undeniably the case that the *History* gave further meaning and illustration to Mill's evolving views, and prepared the way for his attempts in the *Considerations on Representative Government* and *On Liberty* to slacken the distinction between individual liberty and the sentiments of democracy.[141]

On Liberty was conceived in 1854, shortly after the publication in the *Edinburgh Review* of Mill's final article on Grote.[142] Although the continuities between the two works are not seamless, owing to their fundamentally different aims, both tried to reconcile the performance of civic duties with the claims of individual liberty. In chapter one of *On Liberty*, however, Mill appeared to revert to a well-worn attack on the 'ancient commonwealths' for regulating 'every part of private conduct by public authority, on the ground that the state had a deep interest in the whole bodily and mental discipline of every one of its citizens'.[143] This criticism was more relevant to Sparta than Athens, but he proceeded to qualify his remark, first, by acknowledging the peculiarities of life in the ancient city-state, where war was constantly threatened by neighbouring enemies; and, second, by condemning the passivity and acquiescence of modern citizens, whose preference for 'obedience' contrasted unfavourably with the Greeks' exalted sense of obligation.[144] In an echo of his argument in the

---

[140] Ibid, XI, p. 319.

[141] Ibid., XIX, p. 390; XVIII, pp. 224–225. For Tocqueville's influence, see *CW*, XVIII, pp. 47–91, 153–205.

[142] Mill and Grote even corresponded about the subject. In a letter to Mill from 1857, Grote commended Wilhelm von Humboldt's *The sphere and duties of government*, published posthumously in German in 1850 and translated into English in 1854, for the 'frankness with which it puts forward free individual development': H. Grote, *The personal life of George Grote*, p. 237.

[143] *CW*, XVIII, 226.

[144] Ibid., pp. 226, 256. He echoed Grote's point that the *demos* of the fourth century was 'so lowered in public spirit and moral energy, that she threw away all her opportunities': *CW*, XI, p. 312. Mill even opened the *Considerations* with a vision of a passive and languid democracy: *CW*, XIX, p. 377.

Edinburgh Review, he commended the 'potency of Grecian democracy' for making 'every individual in the multitude identify his feelings and interests with those of the state, and regard its freedom and greatness as the first and principal of his own personal concerns'.[145] As in Grote's *History*, the democratic citizen did not have to choose between individual liberty and patriotic acts of self-abnegation because, in well-ordered communities, they were one and the same.

Mill, like Grote, saw in modern passivity and acquiescence the constituent elements of tyranny.[146] In *Considerations of Representative Government*, he proposed, by means of redress, what is now recognised by scholars as a ground-breaking synthesis of utilitarian liberalism and deliberative agonism, positing a course of political education which assigned to individual citizens a 'considerable' amount of 'public duty'.[147] In illustration of his point Mill referred his readers to Grote's *History* and argued that the 'social system and moral ideals of antiquity ... raised the intellectual standard of an average Athenian citizen far beyond anything of which there is yet an example in any other mass of men, ancient or modern', the 'proofs' of which 'are apparent in every page of our great historian of Greece'.[148] This course of political education – that is, the 'social system' and 'moral ideals' of the Athenian *demos* – produced natural limits to citizens' power. In another reference to Grote, he drew on the semantics of constitutional morality to disclose 'the temper of mind which the electors ought to bring to the discharge of their functions'.[149] He went as far as to claim that governments depended for their 'very existence' on 'constitutional morality', and that the 'Athenian constitution', along with other 'well-constructed democracies', relied on a set of 'unwritten rules' which limited the use of 'lawful powers'.[150] Healthy democracies were self-limiting. They guarded against the abuse of power natural to all political actors and encouraged public morality. These sentiments, they agreed, occurred

---

[145] Ibid., XI, p. 325.
[146] Urbinati, *Mill on democracy*, pp. 150–151; A. Zakaras, *Individuality and mass democracy: Mill, Emerson, and the burdens of citizenship* (Oxford: Oxford University Press, 2009), p. 127; J. R. Riley, 'Mill's Greek ideal of individuality' in Demetriou and Loizides (eds.), *Mill: A British Socrates*, pp. 97–126. See also R. Harrison, 'John Stuart Mill, mid-Victorian': G. Stedman Jones and G. Claeys (eds.), *The Cambridge history of nineteenth-century political thought* (Cambridge: Cambridge University Press, 2011), p. 303.
[147] *CW*, XIX, p. 411. On Tocqueville's influence in this respect, see *CW*, XIX, p. 167.
[148] Ibid., p. 411.
[149] Ibid., p. 504. This semantic overlap has been noted only in passing: F. M. Turner, 'Antiquity in Victorian contexts', *Browning Institute Studies* 10 (1982), p. 11; Urbinati, *Mill on democracy*, pp. 126, 146, 274.
[150] *CW*, XIX, p. 423.

within but were not reducible to democratic institutions, and it remained to be seen whether modern society could successfully refashion them.

Conclusion

Grote's historiography is usually associated more with James Mill than Bentham, and clearly there were overlaps in their use of general principles, which I have presented as broadly compatible with Niebuhr's historicism.[151] It is arguably the case, however, that his conception of philosophical history more closely resembled Bentham's *science historique* than James's scale of civilisations, and that his attraction to Niebuhr can be explained, at least partly, by his Benthamite logic; like Bentham, he stressed the past's particularity and distinctness, in pursuit of which he embraced the hermeneutic, philological, and critical strands of *Historismus*. The concord between historicism and utilitarianism is evident in his essay on ethical sentiment, in which he argued that writers 'have paid more attention to the *Matter* of this sentiment than to the *Form*, and have considered the latter as if it were something subordinate to and dependent upon the former'. This method was 'erroneous and unphilosophical' because it ignored the psychological uniformities that transcended history.[152] When, therefore,

> we consider ethical sentiment with reference, not to its Form, but to its Matter, we cannot but discern that uniformity and similarity, as between various societies, does not extend beyond a few capital points. The rest is all peculiarity and diversity: on which each age and each nation clings to tenets of its own, without recognising any basis of reference common to itself with others . . .[153]

Greece's 'peculiarity' provided opportunities for reflection without resorting to a vacuous presentism, or to the abstract philosophies of history criticised by Bentham and Burton. Grote's examination of democratical sentiment and constitutional morality illustrated modern society's comparative selfishness and the difficulty of reproducing those sentiments *ex nihilo*. John, I argued, drew explicitly on these observations in an attempt

---

[151] The historian came to know the particular by the general: Niebuhr, *The history of Rome*, III, p. 51.
[152] Grote, *Fragments on ethical subjects*, p. 18.
[153] Ibid. As he put it in an essay on John's philosophy, '[t]here has always been, and still are, many philosophers who consider the abstract and general to be prior both in nature and time to the concrete and particular: and who hold further that these two last are explained, when presented as determinate and successive manifestations of the two first . . . [but this] mode of philosophising . . . is not ours': *Minor works*, p. 297.

to reconcile individuality with extensive civic duties, with Tocqueville very much in the intellectual ether. His reviews of Grote's *History*, alongside his essays *On Liberty* and *Considerations of Representative Government*, contrasted modern societies' individualism with the Athenians' spontaneous exaltations of political virtue. As we shall see in Chapter 4, history's lessons could not be discovered by a crude analogising logic, or by making the past a mirror of the present. To study the past, John reasoned, was to profoundly enlarge one's experience by entering sympathetically into alien and irretrievable worlds.

CHAPTER 4

J. S. Mill's Historical Criticism

Interpretations and Debates

> An university is indeed the place where the student should be intro-
> duced to the philosophy of history ... [and also to] the causes and
> explanation, so far as within our reach, of the past life of mankind in
> its principal features. Historical criticism also – the tests of historical
> truth – are a subject to which his attention may well be drawn in this
> stage of his education.[1]

German *Historismus*, Forbes observed, revolutionised English historical
thinking between 1820 and 1840, before the arguably more emphatic revolution of evolutionary social science.[2] John's historicism, like its sources of
inspiration, was multifaceted and contradictory; and if Reill, Beiser, Iggers,
and others are correct, then these contradictions bring into focus a defining
paradox of late eighteenth- and early-nineteenth century historicism, whose
principles of individuality and development are not easily reconciled.[3] This,
then, was not an exclusively German ambiguity, and many of the English
historians who discovered Niebuhr – Thirlwall, Thomas Arnold (1795–
1842), Hare – also rediscovered Vico, whose *storia ideale eterna* provided
a divine framework in which to make sense of historical diversity.[4] These
predominantly liberal Anglican thinkers attempted to recover the past's
uniqueness within the laws of historical development, so that national
individualities could coexist as a providential unity.[5] John's writings,

---

[1] 'Inaugural address to the University of St. Andrews' (1867): *CW*, XXI, p. 225.
[2] Forbes, '*Historismus* in England', p. 389.
[3] See, for example, Beiser, 'Historicism', p. 159; Reill, *The German Enlightenment and the rise of historicism*, p. 214; Iggers, *The German conception of history*, p. 29.
[4] On the rediscovery of Vico in the 'age of classical historicism', see Kent Wright, 'History and historicism', pp. 117–118.
[5] See Forbes, *The liberal Anglican idea of history*, pp. 60, 66.

I contend, exhibited a different but comparable tension between a progressive and an individualising historicism, whose differences structure the following chapters.[6] I concentrate here on his Romantic, historicist, and utilitarian approaches to historical criticism, which emphasised the past's uniqueness, while the next two chapters examine his science of history as a logically unsteady commitment to historical relativism (Chapter 5) and universal history (Chapter 6).[7] This section serves as an introduction to them all.

Shortly before his death in 1873, John (hereafter Mill) confessed to the Italian historian and politician Pasquale Villari (1827–1917) that whereas Grote had dedicated his career to 'explorations of the past', his own work 'lies rather in anticipations of the future'.[8] To serious readers of Mill's work this distinction might seem misleading, given the deft historical touches with which he outlined a science of society in *A System of Logic*. Few would deny outright the significance of the past to Mill's philosophy, but it is rarely studied with the analytical vigour that his ethical and political writings generally command. The complaint made in 1965 by C. W. Bouton still rings true: 'the failure to achieve a coherent understanding of Mill's liberalism', he observed, 'has been caused by the failure to recognise the central role that a philosophy of history plays in his thought'.[9] The inclination even in recent work is to downplay Mill's interests in history and historiography and emphasise instead his views on psychology, ethology, and political economy, into which his historical interests – to the extent that they are recognised at all – are typically subsumed.[10] My aim, therefore, is to

---

[6] Christopher Macleod acknowledged this tension in an illuminating essay: 'Mill on history' in C. Macleod and D. Miller (eds.), *A companion to Mill* (Oxford: Wiley Blackwell, 2017), pp. 266–279.

[7] As Stuart Jones helpfully reminds us, 'to emphasise the systematic quality of his thought is not to suggest that he successfully resolved basic problems': 'John Stuart Mill as moralist', *Journal of the History of Ideas* 53.2 (1992), p. 308.

[8] Mill to Pasquale Villari, 28 February 1872: *CW*, XVII, p. 1873. For a similar argument, see *CW*, XXI, p. 294.

[9] Bouton, 'John Stuart Mill on liberty and history', p. 569. For similar complaints see Ryan, *J. S. Mill*, p. xi; M. Levin, *Mill on civilisation and barbarism* (London: Routledge, 2004), p. 68; R. López, 'John Stuart Mill's idea of history: a rhetoric of progress', *Res Publica: Revista de Filosofía Política*, 27 (2012), p. 64. Alan Ryan has concluded that 'Mill plainly did want . . . to attack the view [supposedly held by Bentham] that history could be no more than a narrative of past events, innocent of general implications': *The philosophy of John Stuart Mill* (London: Macmillan, 1987), p. 137. See also V. Guillin, *Auguste Comte and John Stuart Mill on sexual equality: historical, methodological and philosophical issues* (Leiden: Brill, 2009), p. 36; Y. Kawana, *Logic and society: the political thought of John Stuart Mill, 1827–1848* (London: Palgrave, 2018), pp. 107–126; J. Eisenberg, *John Stuart Mill's philosophy of history*, PhD dissertation, Drew University (2016).

[10] Frederick Rosen, for instance, sees history as insignificant compared to Mill's views on ethology and psychology: *Mill*, p. 253. Limited discussions of Mill's historical thought have taken place in the context of his philosophy of logic and theory of character formation; see, for example, J. Skorupski, *John Stuart Mill* (London: Routledge, 1989), p. 250.

recover Mill's historicism not simply as an ancillary to other intellectual interests, but as a key – if not *the* key – with which to unlock his political thought.

Mill, like Bentham, approached political questions from one of two perspectives. On the one hand, he intervened in British politics with a view to its gradual melioration, forsaking as a result appeals to ideal constitutions. As a practical reformer he understood that radical breaks with the past might worsen existing political divisions, especially in England where historical continuity was often equated with political legitimacy: it was, he asserted in his essay on Coleridge (1840), the 'native country of compromise' which clung instinctively to tradition.[11] On the other hand, the region of 'ultimate aims' brought within the purview of teleology the unfolding of universal social trends, and it was here, in history's unwritten ends, that presently controversial or impractical ideas, such as the co-operative principle, could become 'ripe' for public consumption.[12] These two perspectives required different historical parameters, with one looking to the 'immediately useful' and 'practically attainable' – to the unique organisation and structure of a given society – and the other to civilisation in its aggregate.[13] These perspectives were soldered together by an inconsistent theory of progress, whose articulation in the 1830s and 1840s marked a conscious if somewhat misleading break with Benthamism.

It might seem odd, therefore, that Mill neither published nor wrote a substantive work of history, notwithstanding his early foray into Roman constitutional history; youthful imitations of his father's *History of British India*, which he continued to regard as among 'the most instructive' histories ever written despite its obvious 'deficiencies'; and his abandoned history of the French Revolution.[14] He was more a theorist than a practitioner of historical enquiry, and aside from these largely unrevealing endeavours we must look for evidence elsewhere, in his autobiography and correspondence; in his two major political works, the *Logic* and the *Principles of Political Economy* (1848); in his reviews of other historians; and in discussions of European and world history in his celebrated essays *On Liberty, Considerations on Representative Government* (1861), and *The*

---

[11] *CW*, X, p. 131. Earlier, in 1833, he claimed that Bentham misunderstood how acquiescence in government was shored up by fears of 'a break in the line of historical duration': *CW*, X, p. 17.

[12] *CW*, I, p. 196. On the realisation of the co-operative principle, see *CW*, II, p. xciii.

[13] Ibid., I, p. 196.

[14] Ibid., p. 28. On his abandoned history of Roman government, see *CW*, I, pp. 15–17. He wrote to Thomas Carlyle in 1833 about his proposed history of the French Revolution, about which he remarked that 'it is highly probable I shall do it sometime if you do not': *CW*, XII, p. 182.

Subjection of Women (1861, but published in 1869). These works were written at different times for different audiences, but together they demonstrate an increasingly nuanced concern with the relationship between history and politics, hence my relatively lengthy treatment of them.

Mill's historicism was inseparable from his utilitarianism, and his early writings on the past's practical uses were clearly influenced by Bentham and his father. In the 1820s, before the onset of his mental crisis and during his self-proclaimed period of youthful propagandism, he took aim at those political institutions whose foundations were not rational but historical, and thus incompatible with the normative ends of utility.[15] As he threw off the shackles of his adolescent Benthamism, he began to think with increasing complexity about history's explanatory power, but even then he kept up his attack on Conservatives and Whigs, who, citing the dangers of political extremes, defaulted to positions of historical continuity. He agreed with Bentham and Hume that history conditioned human nature, and that its laws were subject to modification by external factors ranging from the environmental and physical to the moral and intellectual. While he never figured out how to reconcile his proposed science of society with the facts of historical-cultural difference – the former required laws which presumed a degree of uniformity across time and space – he did believe, like Hume, Bentham, and James, that history helped philosophy to furnish maxims beneficial to the art of government.[16] This position was relatively consistent across his writings, whose conception of history, by contrast, became increasingly eclectic.

Even in the period between James's death in 1836 and the publication in 1848 of the *Principles of Political Economy*, which is conventionally seen as one of protracted rebellion against the parochialism of his youth, Mill made characteristically utilitarian arguments about theory's role in politics.[17] In the *Logic*, a text written at the height of his Comtism, he reprimanded those who, like Macaulay, read into Bacon a method of induction that explicitly opposed theory, in the vain hope of extracting from their direct experiences of nature self-evident propositions about society. In a remark which could have belonged to his father, Mill claimed that the 'vulgar notion' of Bacon as a thinker who promoted 'specific experience' at the expense of 'general reasoning . . . will one day be quoted as among the most unequivocal marks of a low state of the speculative faculties in any age in which it is accredited'.[18] He believed, like James, that

---

[15] Ibid., XXVI, p. 392.   [16] Ibid., XXI, p. 277.
[17] On his criticisms of Macaulay, see *CW*, I, p. 165.   [18] Ibid., VII, p. 452.

Bacon's recruitment into a canon of unphilosophical empiricism hindered intellectual progress, and in the *Autobiography* he recalled his father's attack on the idea that 'something was true in theory but required correction in practice', when in fact mere practice – that is, practice without theory – led to sweeping generalisations and an intractable conservatism towards established institutions.[19]

Mill's views on history owed less, in the end, to Bentham and James than to Grote's *History of Greece*, which married German criticism with utilitarian philosophy. Both Mill and Grote absorbed German critiques of presentism but only Mill looked to France – to Saint-Simon (1760–1825), Comte, Guizot, Jules Michelet (1798–1874), and Tocqueville – for speculative philosophies of history. Furthermore, Mill saw Grote as a parochial and zealous thinker who was overly sanguine about the march of utility, while Grote worried about Mill's association with Comte, whose philosophy of history, intellectual Catholicism, and sweeping criticisms of classical society he fulsomely rejected.[20] Although Mill's relationship with Comte deteriorated sharply in December 1845, he remained more devoted than Grote to a law-giving science of history, concluding in the early 1840s that social facts were essentially 'unknowable' and intelligible only in relation to other facts by way of 'succession or similitude'.[21] The search for essences and final causes was, in effect, a remnant of metaphysical longing. Following Comte in the *Cours de philosophie positive* (1830–1842), he sharpened his emphasis on the laws of succession and, in Book VI of the *Logic*, declared that society was increasingly conditioned by its own historical consciousness and thus by 'the influence exercised over each generation by the generations which preceded it'.[22] Grote had some sympathy with this position but worried about Comte's lack of evidence and sweeping generalisations, which fell victim to the same defects of Enlightenment thinking that Mill had set out to correct.[23]

Mill was alone amongst the classical utilitarians in attempting to situate history within an all-encompassing social science. He developed in the 1840s an epistemology of social phenomena modelled on the natural sciences, and, with Comte's help, concluded that whereas human beings

[19] Ibid., I, p. 35.
[20] See M. Pickering, *Auguste Comte: an intellectual biography* (Cambridge: Cambridge University Press, 2009), II, p. 93.
[21] *CW*, VIII, p. 928.   [22] Ibid., p. 915.
[23] As Grote put it in a letter to Cornewall Lewis in 1851, 'John Mill says more in praise of Comte's speculations on history than I think they deserve': H. Grote, *The personal life of George Grote*, pp. 203–204. However, in an article for *The Westminster* in 1866, he praised Mill's 'psychological analysis sustained by abundant historical illustration': *Minor works*, p. 290.

had once followed the simple and undisturbed laws of their nature, they had since entered into progressively complex social relations shaped by their individual and collective experiences.[24] In *Auguste Comte and Positivism* (1865) he returned to the idea that individuals were not abstract but rather 'historical human beings', shaped by the historically conditioned society in which they lived.[25] This position influenced his later conceptions of ethics, society, and government, which eschewed timeless political typologies in favour of a scientific conception of progress.[26] As he put it in 1865, whoever 'disbelieves that [the] philosophy of history can be made a science, should suspend his judgement until he reads the volumes of M. Comte'.[27] That the philosophy of history was a science, not an art, was no verbal trifle. The role of art, he claimed, was to suggest an agreeable premise or axiological first principle with which to order one's actions, while science suggested precepts. On its own, therefore, history could not tell us what to do; how to think; how to live well; or how to reform our laws and institutions; but it could enrich our political understanding within a general science of society by suggesting ways in which a desired end – the province of art – might be achieved.

By examining the past and devising logical methods for its use, Mill hoped to establish the causal relations between social phenomena; to discover and invite for assessment the trajectories of modern society; and to demonstrate the interplay between human nature and circumstance. On this point Alburey Castell's astute but seldom read study, published over seventy years ago, offers an illuminating insight. Mill's philosophy of history, Castell argued, was intended to 'provide data for and point to the possibility of a "science of human nature and society"', which was itself an admission of humanity's progressiveness because 'the capacity to learn from the experience of predecessors' through the 'transmission of social customs and institutions' showed history to be a 'record of cumulative instead of cyclical change'.[28] According to Mill, human beings were not doomed to repeat the past because they could learn from its mistakes. They could see, in society's immediate and long-term trends, the direction of

---

[24] *CW*, XXI, p. 294.   [25] Ibid., X, p. 307.
[26] This aspect of Mill's logic has received some attention: A. Weinberg, *The influence of Auguste Comte on the economics of John Stuart Mill* [1949] (London: E. G. Weinberg, 1982), p. 129; I. W. Mueller, *John Stuart Mill and French thought* (Urbana: University of Illinois Press, 1956), p. 58; Collini, Winch, and Burrow, *That noble science of politics*, p. 129; Skorupski, *John Stuart Mill*, p. 13.
[27] *CW*, X, p. 318.
[28] A. Castell, *Mill's logic of the moral sciences: a study of the impact of Newtonism on early nineteenth century social thought* (Chicago: University of Chicago Libraries, 1936), pp. 8–9.

political travel; and the facts of history, instead of burdening the shoulders of the living, became indispensable to progress.

These preliminary remarks demonstrate the complexity of Mill's historical writings and the need to treat them at length. His parallel interests in history's uniqueness and the laws of development require me to separate his logic of historical explanation – that is, his developmental or progressive historicism – from what Preyer called the 'practical problems' of historical enquiry.[29] This distinction, which punctuates some recent commentary, is one that Mill himself encouraged.[30] In a speech to the University of St Andrews in 1867, he separated the 'philosophy of history' from the 'tests of historical truth', while in the *Logic* he followed Comte's distinction between social statics and social dynamics.[31] Statics enquired into the conditions of social order while dynamics enquired into the laws of progress. My interests in this chapter are largely confined to the former, although Mill, as we shall see, broke down this distinction by acknowledging the constitutive role of dynamics in societies' formation.[32] The division between the synchronic and the diachronic, statics and dynamics, failed to account for society's increasing historical consciousness, but this did not eliminate the need to study historical societies individually, subject, therefore, to the usual problems of interpretation and analysis. Indeed, Mill reflected at length on the qualities demanded of the philosophical historian, who transcended the bare facts of history as well as their own ideological preconceptions. His critique of presentism, I contend, was a prominent vein of his historicism.

Mill's historical criticism has been unjustifiably neglected. J. C. Cairns argued that he 'did not unduly prize historiography; at best, for him, it was the first step toward a proper understanding of the past'.[33] It is precisely for this reason, however, that we should take Mill's historiography seriously. If the past was to be integrated into a general science of society, then we must lay down rules for its study by contemplating what we can legitimately claim to know and how best to present our knowledge. Mill's approach to these questions was structured by his three-stage theory of historiography,

---

[29] Preyer, *Bentham, Coleridge, and the science of history*, p. 4.
[30] Macleod, 'History', p. 272; Capaldi, *John Stuart Mill*, p. 136.
[31] *CW*, XXI, p. 225. An English translation of the *Cours* would not appear until 1853: A. Comte (ed. H. Martineau), *The positive philosophy of Auguste Comte* (London: John Chapman, 1853), 2 vols.
[32] See L. S. Feuer, 'John Stuart Mill as a sociologist: the unwritten ethology' in J. M. Robson and M. Laine (eds.), *James and John Stuart Mill/Papers of the centenary conference* (Toronto: University of Toronto Press, 1976), p. 93; R. Kiliminster, *The sociological revolution: from the Enlightenment to the global age* (London: Routledge, 1998), pp. 11–13.
[33] J. C. Cairns, 'Mill and history', *CW*, XX, p. xxvii.

which appeared in a review of Jules Michelet's *Histoire de France* in 1844, and onto which I map the ensuing sections of this chapter. First, I explore Mill's critique of present-mindedness, in which the past was made to reflect the spirit and problems of the age. Second, I examine his theory of historical imagination, a poetic ideal with which he hoped to recover the past's distinctness and the inner life of its inhabitants. Finally, I anticipate the third and final stage of historical enquiry, whose imminence he predicted and hoped for, and whose logic helped to determine the 'state' of societies both contemporary and historical. As he argued in Book VI of the *Logic*, the state of society is 'the simultaneous state of all the *greater* social facts or phenomena'.[34] What were those facts and phenomena and how, if at all, did they help the interpretation of historical events?

Projections of the Present

J. H. Burns was among the first to acknowledge Mill's role in the 'radical transformation taking place in the nature and role of history in European thought' in the second quarter of the nineteenth century.[35] The institution in 1838 of the Public Record Office and the growing popularity of local history pointed to a burgeoning historical culture and an increased concern with the administration and analysis of historical sources.[36] Political events also stoked an enthusiasm for history, especially when they promised to shed light on contemporary predicaments.[37] Henry Hallam's *A Constitutional History of England* (1827) made historical cases for Catholic emancipation, the abolition of slavery, and limited electoral reform, while the July Revolution of 1830 renewed debates in Britain about the legacy of the French Revolution and its implications for domestic reform.[38] The Swing Riots of 1830 and the fall in November 1830 of Wellington's Tory government suggested urgent parallels between Britain and France, especially to Tories and Whigs who remained hostile to France's revolutionary legacy. Archibald Alison (1792–1867), later Lord Rector at the University of Glasgow, contributed a series of essays to

---

[34] *CW*, VIII, pp. 911–912. My emphasis.

[35] J. H. Burns, 'The light of reason: philosophical history in the two Mills' in G. W. Smith (ed.), *John Stuart Mill's social and political thought: critical assessments* (London: Routledge, 1998), p. 76.

[36] See P. J. A. Levine, *The amateur and the professional: antiquarians, historians, and archaeologists in Victorian England 1838–1886* (Cambridge: Cambridge University Press, 1986), p. 101.

[37] See B. Fontana, *Rethinking the politics of commercial society: The Edinburgh Review 1802–1832* (Cambridge: Cambridge University Press, 1985), pp. 11–46, 183.

[38] K. O'Brien, 'English Enlightenment histories, 1750–c. 1815' in Rabasa and Woolf (eds.), *The Oxford history of historical writing*, III, p. 532.

Blackwood's Magazine in which he used French history to alert Britain's landed élite. Along with other Tories such as John Croker (1780–1857), Alison used history to discourage further widenings of the franchise, presenting the French Revolution as a forerunner of democratic excess and a rip in Britain's 'splendid fabric'.[39] Mill, ever alive to an impoverished analogy, reviewed Alison's *History of Europe* in 1833 and complained to Carlyle of its 'twaddling' narrative and want of 'research'.[40]

Given these virulent abuses of history it is unsurprising that Mill contemplated, but soon abandoned, a political history of France from Louis IV to the French Revolution.[41] Quite how far he went with the project is unclear, but he did collect vast materials for its production and repurposed those materials in later essays. He also commented feverishly on contemporary histories of Europe, publishing throughout the 1830s and 1840s an entire volume's worth of reviews.[42] I want to focus here on one such review: his article on Jules Michelet's *Histoire de France* from 1844, which appeared in the *Edinburgh Review* shortly after the publication of *A System of Logic* in 1843. That the article came hot on the heels of the *Logic* explains the distinctly Comtean nature of its approach. Even though Mill's relationship with Comte was in disrepair, the article used the law of three stages to demarcate, in an ascending order of merit, the defining characteristics of modern historical enquiry. This led Mill to reaffirm the position that he had set out in Book VI of the *Logic*, namely, that the 'tendencies of the age [were] set strongly in the direction' and 'improvement' of 'historical enquiry'.[43]

Mill was optimistic about the progress of historical knowledge, at least in France where it was seen increasingly as a science. England's universities, by contrast, cared little for the study of modern history and could not lay claim, as the French did, to a distinguished tradition of *érudits* and *philosophes*. In a letter to Villari from 1854, Mill lamented that 'le public anglais est tellement en arrière du mouvement intellectuel Européen, que les hautes spéculations historico-sociales ne sont ni goûtées ni comprises'.[44] Likewise, in the review of Michelet, he worried that England exhibited 'no signs of a new [historical] school' and instead hearkened back to Gibbon, Hume, and the Scottish historians of the eighteenth century. While a select

---

[39] A. Alison, *A history of Europe from the commencement of the French Revolution to the restoration of the Bourbons* (Edinburgh: William Blackwood, 1839), VII, p. 214.

[40] Mill to Carlyle, 18 May 1833: *CW*, XII, p. 155.

[41] He became 'sick' of studying the French Revolution shortly after penning the review of Alison. Mill to W. J. Fox, 18 May 1833: *CW*, XII, p. 157.

[42] *CW*, XX. See also *CW*, I, p. 135; letter from Mill to Carlyle, 17 September 1832: *CW*, XII, p. 120.

[43] *CW*, VIII, p. 914; XX, p. 219.   [44] Mill to Villari, 1 November 1854: *CW*, XIV, p. 243.

few, such as Thomas Arnold and Thomas Carlyle, had opened themselves to Continental influences – the former to Niebuhrian historicism, the latter to Fichtean idealism – it was still the case that England lagged behind 'Germany and France'. It was, Mill claimed, to the likes of Niebuhr, Leopold von Ranke (1795–1886), Augustin Thierry (1795–1856), Guizot, and Michelet (1798–1874) that England must look for inspiration because the higher forms of historical explanation aspired to more than the narration of events, and they could be realised only by 'those who have narrated as well as philosophised; who have written history, as well as written *about* history'.[45]

Mill's three stages of historical enquiry emphasised the discipline's gradual maturity as a science, beginning with simple forms of historical reconstruction based on everyday experience and ending with the attainment of genuine explanatory power. The first stage, therefore, was one in which historians transferred 'present feelings and notions back into the past, and refer[red] all ages and forms of human life to the standard of that in which the writer himself lives'.[46] This gave rise to all sorts of historical absurdities, not least to the assumption that the historian might understand the past without seriously engaging it. The *Logic* expressed similar concerns about empirical generalisations 'from past to present times', which, until 'a very recent period', used their own age as a framework in which to interpret 'the events of history'.[47] Mill believed that the historian's role was to exhibit human nature in its changing material and social circumstances, rather than to level out historical differences through *sciences de l'homme*. The first stage, by contrast, was wilfully assimilative, flattening out human experiences across time and space in the vain hope of using the past to illustrate the present. Historians of this kind lacked the imagination to bring their readers level with the past: whatever 'cannot be translated into the language of their own time, whatever they cannot represent to themselves by some fancied modern equivalent, is nothing to them, calls up no ideas in their minds at all'. They were, Mill concluded, incapable of imagining 'anything different from their own everyday experience'.[48]

---

[45] Ibid, XX, pp. 219, 221. Mill's emphasis. The irony was that Comte said the same about England, where the writing of history was given an 'explanatory or scientific character'. Quoted in Palmeri, *State of nature, stages of society*, p. 101.

[46] *CW*, XX, p. 223. See O. Anderson, 'The political uses of history in mid nineteenth-century England', *Past and Present* 36 (1967), pp. 87–105.

[47] *CW*, VIII, p. 791.   [48] Ibid., XX, p. 223.

The failure, however, was only partly one of intellectual and moral parochialism.[49] Prejudice also played its part, which was why Michelet in a letter to Mill insisted that he was 'dominé par la passion de la vérité' in Niebuhr's image and not 'un homme d'imagination'.[50] A cultivated imagination might avoid parochialism but it did not necessarily respect the evidence. If 'an historian of this stamp takes a side in controversy', Mill argued, 'and passes judgement upon actions or personages that have figured in history, he applies to them in the crudest form to the canons of some modern party or creed. If he is a Tory, and his subject is Greece, everything Athenian must be cried down'.[51] Like Grote, he believed that the historian must refrain from imposing onto the past the standards of the society 'in which the writer himself lives'.[52] This was not to assert, in the fashion of an ontological realist, that history occupied an Archimedean standpoint outside experience, or that we might fully escape our biases. Rather, it was to call for an imaginative leap into the historical unknown, conferring on the living an increased awareness of human nature as modified by various social, intellectual, and physical conditions. As he put it in *Definition of Political Economy* (1836), those who 'never look backwards seldom look far forwards: their notions of human affairs, and of human nature itself are circumscribed within . . . their own times'.[53] This idea recurred throughout Mill's writings, not least in *On Liberty*, which made truth, progress, and liberty contingent on the individual's ability to transcend the preconceptions of his or her age.

Mill's first stage of historical enquiry invoked familiar enemies. Throughout the 1830s, 40s, and 50s, he attacked William Mitford as a historian whose interests were anything but historical, and who, like his friend Edward Gibbon, read into the French and Greek experiments in democracy an imminent threat to private property and social stability. Mitford's *History of Greece* was effusive in its praise of the Homeric monarchies and fulsome in its criticism of republics, soliciting throughout the 1820s and 1830s a range of responses in the *Westminster Review*, *Knight's Quarterly*, and *Blackwood's Edinburgh Magazine*.[54] According to Mill, Mitford's *History of Greece* made a historically undifferentiated argument about the endemic weaknesses of democracy and pure forms of government,

---

[49] See Collini, Winch, and Burrow, *That noble science of politics*, p. 144.
[50] Michelet to Mill, 24 September 1841: J. Michelet (ed. and trans. P. Villaneix and C. Digeon), *Journal* (Paris: Gallimard, 1959), I, p. 814.
[51] *CW*, XX, p. 224.   [52] Ibid., p. 223.   [53] Ibid., IV, p. 333.
[54] By the late 1830s criticism of Mitford was rife: Roberts, *Athens on trial*, p. 231. See, for instance, E. Bulwer-Lytton (ed. O. Murray), *Athens: its rise and fall* [1837] (London: Routledge, 2004). See also E. Hadley, *Living liberalism* (Chicago: University of Chicago Press, 2010), pp. 188–190.

premised on an unshakable faith in Britain's (theoretically) mixed constitution.[55] In the *Autobiography*, he recalled reading Mitford 'continually' in his youth while his father cautioned against the 'Tory prejudices of this writer, and his perversions of facts for the whitewashing of despots, and blackening of popular institutions ... [but] my sympathies were always on the contrary side to those of the author'.[56] In an earlier article from 1849, he suggested that Mitford's 'narrative' illustrated the 'wildest ... Antijacobin frenzy ... vitiated by an intensity of prejudice against whatever bears the name or semblance of popular institutions'.[57]

The first stage of historical enquiry was overcome by critically reading the evidence, even when it contradicted the historian's personal beliefs. In a review of Grote's *History* from 1846, Mill acknowledged the growing number of counter-histories which had emerged in the 1830s and 1840s in response to Mitford, including Connop Thirlwall's *History of Greece* (1835–1847). Thirlwall, he argued, had effectively destroyed Mitford 'as an historical authority' by drawing on Niebuhr's philology and critical approach to partial, incomplete, and fantastical evidence.[58] Elsewhere, in an earlier article on Friedrich Schleiermacher (1768–1834) and Gustav Friedrich Wiggers (1777–1860), he acknowledged the debts of the 'English public' to 'Bishop Thirlwall, whose *History of Greece* is throughout conceived as a kindred spirit [to Niebuhr]'.[59] Mill was no less wedded than Grote and Thirlwall to a science of historical criticism, especially in the field of ancient history where conjecture often took the place of written evidence; and while his sympathies for historicism have been noted in passing by Irwin, Cairns, Preyer, and others, we do not yet understand its place in the three stages of historical enquiry, or how it helped Mill to develop a speculative philosophy of history.[60]

---

[55] As Mill put it, the 'moral of the history, as related by most modern historians, is that democracy is a detestable kind of government, and that the case of Athens strikingly exemplifies its detestable qualities': *CW*, XXV, p. 1161.

[56] Ibid., I, p. 14. Mill admitted to reading 'Greek books' for the 'principles of legislation and government which they often illustrated': *CW*, I, p. 23. Those principles were, he confessed, shaped by James's 'unbounded confidence in ... representative government and complete freedom of discussion': *CW*, I, p. 108.

[57] Ibid., XXIV, p. 867. It was as Alexander Bain later reflected: 'the persistent denunciations of Grecian democracy, of which Mitford's book is a notable sample, were kept up for the sake of their application to modern instances [regarding] ... the growth of popular government in the present day': 'Introduction' in Grote (ed. Bain), *Minor works*, p. 16. See also W. Thomas, *The Philosophic Radicals*, pp. 129, 196.

[58] Ibid., XI, p. 275; C. Thirlwall (ed. P. Liddel), *History of Greece* [1835] (Exeter: Bristol Phoenix Press, 2007), p. 39.

[59] *CW*, XI, p. 242.

[60] Irwin, 'Mill and the classical world'; Cairns, 'Mill and history'; Preyer, 'Mill and the utility of classical Greece'.

It is likely that Mill first became aware of Niebuhr in the early 1820s. He admitted in the *Autobiography* that he was 'ignorant of Niebuhr's researches' when he attempted 'in his eleventh and twelfth year' to write a constitutional history of Roman government down to the Licinian laws, based on close readings of Livy, Dionysius, and Nathaniel Hooke's *The Roman History* (1745).[61] Niebuhr had published the first part of his lectures in Berlin in 1811 and soon developed a following in Britain, especially at Cambridge where he found acolytes in Thirlwall and Hare. Mill's poor German suggests that his exposure to Niebuhr was second-hand, at least until the publication between 1828 and 1832 of Thirlwall and Hare's English edition of the *Lectures*. His library at Somerville shows that he read the first volume of Niebuhr's *The History of Rome* in 1855, even though it originally appeared in 1844. Thus, his exposure to German historicism was channelled, at least initially, through the historicist counter-histories of the 1830s and 1840s. He commended Thomas Arnold's *History of Rome* (1838) for closely following Niebuhr's method and championed Grote as a leading light of historicism's vast 'school'.[62] Grote's *History*, Mill claimed, had effected in the scholarship of archaic and classical Greece a 'radical revolution' comparable to that of early Roman historiography.[63] The writing of classical history, he suggested, was a new 'art' which broke with the 'uncritical histories' of the preceding two millennia.[64] What was it, however, that made historicism different to other forms of historical criticism, and why did Mill enthusiastically endorse it?

Mill disagreed with Carlyle's withering attack on Niebuhr's 'vain jargon of *cognoscente* scholarcraft'.[65] He celebrated Niebuhr's application of hermeneutical and philological techniques to the study of ancient myths, which had previously been judged according to their credibility as historical evidence, rather than as artefacts whose claim to historical significance lay in their social and cultural assumptions; the manner of their expression; and the broader historical contexts in which they were enmeshed and which they, in turn, helped to shape.[66] By making use of even the most

---

[61] *CW*, I, p. 16. Collini has argued that Mill formed his basic ideas before 'the fashion of looking to Germany for cultural nourishment had become at all widespread': *English pasts*, p. 138.

[62] *CW*, XXIV, p. 869.   [63] Ibid., XI, p. 328.   [64] Ibid.

[65] Carlyle to Mill, 4 April 1838: T. Carlyle (ed. C. R. Sanders), *The collected letters of Thomas and Jane Welsh Carlyle* (Durham: Duke University Press, 1976), X, pp. 57–58. On Niebuhr's impact in England, see Heinrich Ritter von Srbik, *Geist und Geschichte vom deutschen Humanismus bis zur Gegenwart* (Salzberg: Otto Muller Verlag, 1960), I, pp. 210–220; K. Dockhorn, *Der Deutsche Historismus in England: Ein Beitrag zur Englischen Geistesgeschichte des 19. Jahrhunderts* (Göttingen: Vandenhoeck & Ruprecht, 1950); Forbes, '*Historismus* in England', pp. 387–400.

[66] Mill praised Coleridge for realising, unlike Bentham, that 'the long duration of a belief', however erroneous, 'is at least proof of an adaption in it to some portion or other of the human mind': *CW*, X, p. 120.

unreliable of sources, historicism was able to offer an alternative to conjectural anthropological accounts of early historical societies for which there was scant or unreliable evidence.[67] Niebuhr, Mill argued, was able to construct an 'imperishable model' of imagination based on 'scattered evidences' and a critical reading of Livy, recovering in the process a coherent account of pre-classical Roman society before the expulsion of the Tarquins.[68] Indeed, the historicists went further than the *érudits* in seeking to establish not only the meaning of a text as disclosed by its linguistic contexts, but also the intentions with which a text was written. Their goal was to form a complete picture of past societies by approaching them as unique and inimitable wholes and by recognising what Karl Friedrich Schlegel (1772–1829) had called *den unermeßlichen Unterschied* – the immeasurable distinctness – of the past.[69] As Niebuhr himself put it in 1812 in a letter to Count Adam Moltke (1710–1792), philology would be 'cherished' if only 'people knew the magical delight of living and moving amidst the most beautiful scenes of the past', of feeling 'familiar with Greece and Rome'.[70]

Historicism as Mill understood it opposed all forms of presentism, not just those with which the author personally disagreed. Historical criticism was the 'test of historical truth', the foundations on which speculative philosophies of history were built.[71] 'We do not say', he argued in 1846, 'that an author is to write history with a purpose of bringing out illustrations of his own moral and political doctrines, however correct they may be. He cannot too carefully guard himself against any such temptation. If he yield [sic] to it, he becomes an unfaithful historian'.[72] Thus, when Macaulay attacked Mitford in 1824, some two years before Grote's article appeared in the *Westminster Review*, Mill remained silent. While Macaulay's aims were not entirely dissimilar to Grote's – both drew attention to Mitford's 'ignorance of the most obvious phenomena of human nature', as well as democracy's role in making 'the interests of the governors and the governed . . . the same' – he conceded that as far as the ancient Greeks were concerned he could not 'speak with fairness. It is a subject on which I love to forget the accuracy of a judge, in the veneration of a worshipper, and the gratitude of a child'.[73] Mill opposed presentism even when it was politically beneficial. Like James and Bentham, he

---

[67] Preyer, *Bentham, Coleridge, and the science of history*, p. 29.   [68] *CW*, XX, p. 225.
[69] Iggers, 'Historicism: the history and meaning of the term', p. 130; Beiser, *The German historicist tradition*, p. 184.
[70] Quoted in Turner, *Philology*, p. 169.   [71] *CW*, XXI, pp. 420–421.   [72] Ibid., XXIV, p. 868.
[73] T. B. Macaulay, *Miscellaneous writings*, I, pp. 156, 160, 178.

attributed to the 'consummate *judge*' of history the 'difficult art of weighing evidence' as objectively as possible.[74] In 1845, he complained that the
'latest school of German metaphysicians, the Hegelians, are well known to
treat of it [historical enquiry] as a science which might even be constructed
à priori'.[75] Their mistake, he argued in a letter to Theodor Gomperz
(1832–1912) from 1854, was to use their own 'opinions' and 'feeling[s]' as
'proof', much like intuitionists whom he derided in *Logic*.[76] Historical
criticism was a science of truth, not a framework of belief, and the
significance of this remark is often lost on Mill's modern readers.

Poetries of the Past

> From the data afforded by a person's conversation and life, to frame
> a connected outline of the inward structure of that person's mind, so
> as to know and feel what the man is, and how life and the world paint
> themselves to his conceptions: still more to decipher in that same
> manner the mind of an age or a nation, and gain from history or
> travelling a vivid conception of the mind of a Greek or Roman ... is
> an effort of genius ...[77]

If the first stage of historiography was fundamentally inward-looking, then
the second stage embraced the subjectivities, consciousness, and inner life
of past peoples in a sympathetic act of reconstruction. As Mill argued in the
review of Michelet, 'humble as our estimate must be of this kind of writers
[in the first stage], it would be unjust to forget that even *their* mode of
treating history is an improvement upon the uninquiring credulity which
contented itself with copying or translating the ancient authorities, without ever bringing the writer's own mind in contact with the subject' as
a '*living being*'.[78] According to this scheme, 'Mitford, so far, is a better
historian than Rollin [Charles Rollin, 1661–1741]' because he 'does give
a sort of reality to historical personages: he ascribes to them passions and
purposes which, though not those of their age or position, are still human'.
This was 'a first step; and, that step made, the reader, once in motion, is not
likely to stop there'.[79] On this account, Rollin's *Histoire ancienne*

---

[74] *CW*, XX, p. 56. Mill's emphasis. See L. J. Snyder, *Reforming philosophy: a Victorian debate on science and society* (Chicago: University of Chicago Press, 2010), pp. 99–104.

[75] *CW*, XX, p. 261.

[76] Ibid., XIV, 239. In a letter to Bain on 4 November 1867, Mill argued that 'conversancy with him [Hegel] tends to deprave one's intellect': *CW*, XVI, p. 1324.

[77] 'On genius' (1832), *CW*, I, p. 333.   [78] Ibid., XX, p. 224. My emphasis.   [79] Ibid.

(1730–1738) belonged to the stage of 'mere literature or of erudition' in which the past was 'studied for the facts, not for the explanation of facts'.[80] Likewise, Connop Thirlwall's *History of Greece*, while 'candid and impartial', offered 'mere facts' without the 'causes and agencies which gave birth to them', taking no notice of the 'opinions and feelings' of historical agents.[81] This tallies with Forbes's depiction of historicism as an 'emancipation from storytelling' and the pursuit of underlying causes.[82]

Historians of the 'second stage of historical study', Mill argued, attempted 'to regard former ages not with the eye of a modern, but, as far as possible, with that of a contemporary; to realise a true and living picture of the past time, clothed in its circumstances and peculiarities'.[83] The aim of Romantic historians and historicists was to see beyond 'dry generalities' into the 'consistent whole to which they once belonged ... Such gifts of imagination he [the historian] must possess; and, what is rarer still, he must forbear to abuse them'.[84] In reconstructing the past as a distinct whole, the 'Romantic' historian must 'have the conscience and self-command to affirm no more than can be vouched for, or deduced by legitimate inference from what is vouched for'.[85] Mill's qualification spoke to an enduring unease about the relationship between imagination and historical criticism. There was no easy way to protect facts from the historian's sprawling imagination, other than to invoke basic moral principles. While imagination could bring out the inner consciousness of human life, reaching, like the poet, to subjective truths beyond the surface of events, it was also vulnerable to abuse. That was why Mill censured Walter Scott's *The Life of Napoleon* (1827) for displaying imagination but not 'industry, candour, and impartiality'.[86] The goal was not to perform transcendental acts of the imagination in defiance of the evidence, but rather to relate that evidence to the past as a whole.

Mill developed his theory of imagination in the 1830s, partly as a reaction to Bentham's philosophy, which, he believed, overlooked the importance of affective states in the motivation of other-regarding action.[87] It is well known that his mental crisis and friendship with John Sterling precipitated a turn to Romantic poetry, specifically to Coleridge, Wordsworth, and the German Idealists. He later remarked of his upbringing that from the 'neglect both in theory and practice of the cultivation of

[80] Ibid., p. 260. [81] From Mill's review of Grote: *CW*, XXIV, pp. 868–869. See also XI, p. 275.
[82] Forbes, '*Historismus* in England', p. 387. [83] *CW*, XX, p. 224. [84] Ibid. [85] Ibid., p. 225.
[86] Ibid., p. 56.
[87] See R. S. Stewart, 'Utilitarianism meets Romanticism: J. S. Mill's theory of imagination', *History of Philosophy* 10.4 (1993), pp. 369–388.

feeling' resulted 'an undervaluing of poetry, and of imagination generally'.[88] His liberation from Benthamism was secured only by his father's death in 1836, shortly after which he criticised Bentham for failing to see that imagination was 'the power by which one human being enters into the mind and circumstances of another', so as to enlarge one's knowledge of human nature and the 'distinctive characters of the different races and nations of mankind from the facts of their history'. The true 'historian' understood this, and so too did the dramatist and poet.[89] Imagination resisted narrowness by promoting the kind of 'self-consciousness' that Mill considered typical of geniuses like Wordsworth, Byron, Goethe, and Chateaubriand. Bentham, by contrast, offered a 'slender stock of premises' with which to account for the general propensities of human nature, leading him, inevitably, to a narrow view of utility based on universal precepts.[90]

Thomas Carlyle crystallised Mill's burgeoning interests in the relationship between history and imagination.[91] He reviewed Carlyle's history of the French Revolution in 1837, which, he claimed, was 'not so much a history, as an epic poem' and thus 'the truest of histories'.[92] Following in the footsteps of Fichte and Schelling, Carlyle surpassed 'the histories of Hume, Robertson, and Gibbon' by making vivid 'the lives and deeds' of his 'fellow-creatures', feeling them to be 'real beings, who once were alive'.[93] Whereas the 'ordinary historian' merely conveyed 'his opinions of things', the true historian conveyed 'the things themselves' and brought into 'ever greater distinctness and impressiveness the poetic aspect of realities'.[94] The past was made to *feel* present and many-sided, as in Goethe's notion of many-sidedness (*Vielseitigkeit*), which for a time 'possessed' Mill's thoughts.[95] The break with the Enlightenment historians, at least as Mill construed them, was deliberate. He rejected the idea that the past was best viewed from a distance, even though this was by no means a staple of eighteenth-century historiography but rather a bastardisation of it, a foil for early-nineteenth-century Romantics who laid claim to a new form of historical inwardness.[96]

---

[88] *CW*, I, p. 115.   [89] Ibid., X, p. 92.   [90] Ibid., p. 93.

[91] Donner, *The liberal self*, p. 100; N. Capaldi, *John Stuart Mill: a biography* (Cambridge: Cambridge University Press, 2004), pp. 89–96.

[92] *CW*, XX, p. 133.   [93] Ibid., p. 134.

[94] Ibid., p. 137. This reinforced Carlyle's relativism: the 'inward condition of life', he argued, 'is the same in no two ages': T. Carlyle, 'On history' [1830] in A. Shelston (ed.), *Thomas Carlyle: selected writings* (London: Penguin, 1971), p. 53.

[95] Mill to Carlyle, 12 January, 1834: *CW*, XII, p. 205.

[96] See M. S. Phillips, 'Relocating inwardness: historical distance and the transition from Enlightenment to Romantic historiography', *Modern Language Association* 118.3 (2003), pp. 436–449.

Hume on this account scarcely counted as a historian, and neither did Robertson and Gibbon.[97] Carlyle, by contrast, had managed to 'imaginatively' realise the 'persons, things, and events' of the French Revolution, making it vivid and immediate.[98] He wrote in the dramatic present tense and concerned himself less with chronology and mundane facts – that is, with dispassionate historical analysis – than with the Revolution's eternal spirit.

Mill's praise of Carlyle was not unqualified. He felt personally responsible for the destruction of Carlyle's original manuscript – his maid had accidentally burned it – and perhaps made amends in his review.[99] Beneath the surface of his laudatory language, however, Mill doubted Carlyle's method, and the first sign of dissent came when he called the poetic imagination the tool 'of the artist, not of the man of science'. Carlyle, he argued, had figured things to himself 'as wholes' and had gone 'too far in his distrust of analysis and generalisation, as others (the Constitutional party, for instance, in the French Revolution)' had gone 'too far in their reliance upon it'.[100] His failure to employ general principles left the past adrift on a 'boundless ocean of *mere conjecture*'.[101] Even though truth could only ever be approximated, it was far better, Mill insisted, to approximate it through general principles than by diving head-first into historical events, or into what Bentham had called the unintelligible 'maze' of particular facts.[102] Mill had expressed these doubts to Carlyle as early as 1833. His review from 1837 confirmed them publicly.[103] 'Thus far', Mill argued, 'we and Mr. Carlyle travel harmoniously together; but here we apparently diverge'. How, if not by 'general principles', 'do we bring the light of past experience to bear upon the new case? The essence of past experience lies embodied in those logical, abstract propositions, which our author makes so light of: – there, and no where else'.[104]

Mill and Carlyle were always an awkward fit. Mill's father had drilled into him the importance of applying general principles to particular cases, a stipulation which John retained, in one form or another, for the rest of his life. It was a characteristically Scottish commitment. Adam Smith, John Millar, and John Logan (1748–1788) had all distinguished between

[97] *CW*, XX, p. 134.   [98] Ibid., p. 158.
[99] See J. E. Jacobs, *The voice of Harriet Taylor Mill* (Indiana: Indiana University Press, 2002), p. 69.
[100] *CW*, XX, p. 161.   [101] Ibid. See Ryan, *Philosophy of John Stuart Mill*, p. 154.
[102] 'Bentham papers', University College London Library, box 27, f. 95.
[103] Mill to Carlyle, 5 July 1833: *CW*, XII, p. 161.
[104] Ibid., XX, p. 161. Even Mitford, Mill contended, had navigated his evidence with mid-level propositions, without which we can never know 'what end to begin at, what points to enquire into': *CW*, XX, p. 162.

common observation and philosophical insight, a distinction they traced to Bacon.[105] Carlyle in Mill's eyes favoured feeling above explanation and sentiment above understanding, thus depriving the past of its practical and scientific uses. Some years earlier, in a review of Adam Sedgwick's *Discourse on the Studies of the University of Cambridge* (1833), Mill had argued that history could not be classified as an experimental science because it is 'susceptible of as many different explanations as there are possible theories of human affairs'.[106] The same logic applied to his critique of Carlyle. History, he reasoned, could only serve as the verification, as opposed to the foundation, of social-scientific knowledge, and Carlyle's mistake had been to undervalue the 'general principles' which steered the hand of the truly philosophical historian.[107]

Mill's ambivalence towards Carlyle reflected a wider problem in his thinking: what did imagination *do* to historical facts? Were they compatible or did one always take precedence over the other? These uncertainties had something to do, perhaps, with imagination's awkward place in his philosophy.[108] While Mill placed a high value on the imagination as a tool of sympathy, he was at least nominally aware of its ambiguity within empiricism.[109] James in the *Analysis* subsumed it into the laws of association, stripping it of mystery, while in the *History* he denounced 'wild and ungoverned' imagination as the hallmark of 'rude' and credulous minds.[110] Governed imaginations, James argued, formed from individuals' experiences and memories of the world aesthetically pleasing trains of thought, to which we often ascribe poetic status, even though there is nothing distinct about them: they conformed, like all forms of mental activity, to the laws of contiguity and association. Ungoverned imaginations, by contrast, were prone to flights of fancy, confined, usually, to less civilised minds.[111] In lieu of a scientific understanding of the world we appeal to imagined entities and agencies, deriving from them a cultural identity that becomes

---

[105] Phillips, 'Relocating inwardness', pp. 436–449.

[106] 'Not only is history not the source of political philosophy, but the profoundest political philosophy is requisite to explain history': *CW*, X, p. 44.

[107] Ibid., X, p. 45; XX, p. 162.

[108] This conventional review has been recently challenged: G. Budge (ed.), *Romantic empiricism: poetics and the philosophy of common sense 1780–1830* (New Jersey: Associated University Press, 2007).

[109] In the essay on Michelet, for example, he argued that the 'spirit of the age' was something that 'cannot be extracted literally from ancient records, but must be distilled from those arid materials by the chemistry of the writer's own mind': *CW*, XX, p. 233.

[110] [James] Mill, *Analysis*, I, p. 239; *HBI*, I, p. 143.

[111] In the *Elements*, Dugald Stewart had made a similar distinction, calling the poetic imagination but 'the association of ideas': *Works*, I p. 209.

solidified in history and resistant to change.[112] Imagination, on this latter account, was the natural ally of conservatism.[113]

James's attack on imagination was directed at a range of opponents, the Kantians chief among them. Kant in his *Critique of Pure Reason* (1781) had raised the point, echoed by Schelling and Fichte, that we introduce into nature regularities produced by the transcendental synthesis of imagination (*Einbildung*).[114] Against this tradition, or so James argued in the *History* and the *Analysis*, stood Hartley's belief that imagination belonged to 'the infancy of knowledge, in the early ages of the world'.[115] This fault line became more pronounced in the 1810s and early 1820s as the Kantian position found a champion in Coleridge.[116] In a letter to Lord Liverpool, then Prime Minister, Coleridge hit out against the 'mechanic philosophy' of Epicurean physics, citing the importance of organic historical unities constituted by the imagination.[117] Likewise, William Hazlitt in his essay *The Plain Speaker* (1826) defended the imagination and, elsewhere, attacked James for writing a history of India without seeing the country for himself, much like a painter who sketched from memory as opposed to the 'living man'.[118] These animadversions of utilitarianism would become all too familiar: mechanical philosophy, Coleridge claimed, could not account for the presence of organic harmonies in the noumenal realm. He chastised the empiricists for looking lazily on the world with their 'irreligious metaphysics', unaware that imagination was 'the living power and prime agent of human perception'.[119]

The presence of imagination in John's historicism, puzzling as it is, requires further explanation. It is not altogether clear what he meant by the term or how exactly he intended its use. On the one hand, it guarded against the first stage of historiography in which the historian, ignorant of the past's distinctiveness, searched mindlessly for the present; on the other,

---

[112] See, for example, Mill, *HBI*, II, p. 84.
[113] In the essay on Bentham, John drew attention to the 'effect of mere habit and imagination' in the 'acquiescence of mankind in government': *CW*, X, p. 17.
[114] See A. Schultz, *Mind's world: imagination and subjectivity from Descartes to Romanticism* (Seattle: Washington University Press, 2009), p. 85.
[115] D. Hartley, *Observations on man, his fame, his duty, and his expectations* [1749] (London: Thomas Tegg, 1834), p. 271.
[116] See M. Class, *Coleridge and Kantian ideas in England, 1796–1817: Coleridge's responses to German philosophy* (London: Bloomsbury, 2012), pp. 191–195.
[117] S. T. Coleridge (ed. E. L. Griggs), *Collected letters* (Oxford: Clarendon Press, 1971), IV, p. 761.
[118] See W. Hazlitt, *The plain speaker: opinions on books, men, and things* (London: Henry Burlington, 1826), p. 101; W. Hazlitt (eds. A. R. Waller and A. Glover), *The collected works of William Hazlitt* (London: Dent & Co., 1904), XII, p. 51.
[119] Quoted in Stewart, 'Utilitarianism meets Romanticism', p. 376.

Mill's conception of imagination was more complex and problematic than that, extending to the ways in which we express the inner domain of consciousness and the coming to terms with cultures, historical or otherwise, that are alien to our own. Its epistemic status was unclear. If imagination afforded truths beyond experience and reflection, then this would leave problematically open the question of whether knowledge is derived exclusively from experience, a position that he evidently wished to defend. Conversely, if imagination was presented as a branch of general reasoning, then it is difficult to understand why Mill made special claims on its behalf. In other words, we need to understand what, if anything, was distinct about the historical imagination as Mill saw it, and for this we can turn to an article on America from 1836, in which he suggested that experience, not imagination, offered the clearest route into distant historical realities. Nobody, he argued,

> learns any thing very valuable either from history or from travelling, who does not come prepared ... No one can know ... other ages and countries so well as he may know his own age and country: and the wisdom acquired by the study of ourselves, and of the circumstances which surround us, can alone teach us to interpret the comparatively little which we know of other persons and other modes of existence .... [120]

There is little in this passage with which James or the eighteenth-century Scots would have disagreed, especially when John argued that the only way to interpret 'other modes of existence' was to draw on experience, into which we deposit our direct impressions of the world and our reflections on them. On other occasions, however, he seemed to suggest that the imagination granted access to a higher plane of subjective truth, that it allowed the historian to reach beyond the parameters of their social world by reflecting internally on their experiences and feelings, coming to subjective truth by a process of self-observation. As he put it in 1832 in an essay on genius, the 'capacity of extracting the knowledge of general truth from our own consciousness', he argued, 'whether it be by simple *observation*, by that kind of self-observation which is called *imagination*, or by a more complicated process of analysis and induction, is *originality*'.[121] Quite how the imagination was supposed to extract truths from the individual's consciousness was left open-ended, perhaps hopelessly so.[122]

---

[120] *CW*, XVIII, p. 93. Mill had made a similar argument in 1827, when he looked towards 'the book of human nature' as opposed to the 'book of history' for political instruction: *CW*, XXVI, p. 393.
[121] Ibid., I, 332.
[122] This point has been raised critically by Jay Eisenberg: *John Stuart Mill's philosophy of history*, p. 79.

Mill continued to think about the historical imagination well into the 1840s. In the review of Michelet from 1844, he concluded that the 'French historians of the present day', skilled as they were at bringing the past to life, suffered from 'superficiality and want of research'.[123] Shortly afterwards he levelled the same criticism at the Germans, using Grote's *History* to do so: 'those Germans', he observed, 'have seldom possessed the quality which eminently characterises Mr. Grote, of keeping their historical imagination severely under the restraints of evidence'. Niebuhr and Karl Müller were 'skilful in conjecture, but they often pass off upon themselves and upon us their guesses for facts: Mr. Grote never does. His deep respect for truth ... and historical scepticism enable the reader ... to place great reliance on him'.[124] From the late 1840s onwards, Grote's *History* became a crutch for Mill's historical reflections, allowing him to ruminate on the relationship between imagination and historicism. Indeed, he reviewed Grote's *History* on several occasions, twice for the *Edinburgh Review* and once, in serialised form, for *The Spectator*. Throughout those reviews ran a rich vein of praise, celebrating in equal measure Grote's powers of imagination, generalisation, and historical criticism.

Mill claimed that Grote possessed a uniquely 'modern imagination', so much so that he became 'himself a Greek' and took the reader 'along with him'.[125] He attributed to the *History* all the qualities demanded of a Romantic imagination and committed historicist: inwardness, sympathy, immediacy, and an eye for the particular. What made the *History* exceptional, however, was its demarcation between speculation and proof, imagination and fact. All histories of Greece relied to an extent on guesswork and conjecture, especially when they sought to establish from limited evidence a coherent narrative of its archaic origins. Grote did rely on 'speculations', but he did so without selling them 'for more than they are worth'.[126] He was so 'cautious and sober' in the 'estimation of evidence', so 'constantly on his guard against letting his conclusions outrun his proofs', that he was able to arrive at 'positive and certifiable' conclusions.[127] 'Anybody', Mill continued,

---

[123] *CW*, XX, pp. 275, 220.
[124] Ibid., XXIV, p. 1086. That Niebuhr argued with 'insufficient *warrant* from the evidence' made him 'not at all comparable to Mr. Grote': *CW*, XXIV, p. 331.
[125] Ibid., XI, pp. 290, 332.   [126] Ibid., p. 298.
[127] Ibid., p. 330. One obvious example was the vindication of democracy, which provided the 'moral of the history': *CW*, XXV, p. 1161.

can scrawl over the canvas with the commonplaces of rhetoric or the catchwords of party politics; and many, especially in Germany, can paint-in a picture from the more or less ingenious suggestions of a learned imagination. But Mr. Grote commands the confidence of the reader by his sobriety in hypothesis, by never attempting to pass off an inference as a fact . . . [or expecting] that anything will be taken upon trust. He has felt that a history of Greece, to be of any value, must be also a running commentary on the evidence . . .[128]

Mill was not alone. As the lexicographer William Smith (1813–1893) put it in 1842, the 'earlier writers on this subject [classical antiquity] display little historical [i.e., philological] criticism, and give no comprehensive view or living idea of the public and private life of the ancients'.[129] Smith had studied at University College London, Grote's 'cherished institution', and in June 1856 penned a laudatory review of the *History* for the *Quarterly Review*.[130] Mill, meanwhile, used the *History* to ventriloquise his theory of imagination, which accommodated historical difference without losing sight of general principles. Grote, he suggested, 'never so far adopts Hellenic ideas and sentiments as to lose sight of his own standard. He enters into the feelings and opinions of the actors, not to supersede but to assist his applications of the general principles of justice and political experience'.[131] Mill appeared to have at least one eye on Grote's detractors. The symmetry between imagination and criticism, specu-lation and philosophy, justified Grote's 'triumphant vindication of Athenian democracy', which he achieved not through a 'formal dissertation', but as an obvious inference from the narrative, coming out 'with ever-increasing clear-ness from the facts of the history'.[132] Mill suggested that criticism helped to tame the imagination and, when applied correctly, governed its use. With these two qualities Grote acquired a 'searching character' that extended beyond 'matters in which his own political opinions may be supposed to be interested', allowing him to imagine Greek life in all its complexity.[133]

Finally, Mill believed that the ability to read sources in their original language was integral, first, to the imagination of historical otherness and, second, to the cultivation of active characters in society.[134] These

---

[128] Ibid., XI, p. 330.
[129] W. Smith, *A dictionary of Greek and Roman antiquities* (London: John Murray, 1842), p. vii.
[130] H. Grote, *The personal life of George Grote*, p. 231.   [131] *CW*, XXIV, p. 1087.
[132] Ibid., p. 1088. Grote, Mill argued, did not arrive at his conclusions 'by divination or conjecture', but by an acute cross-examination of the authorities', and by 'the possession of broader, deeper, and more many-sided views of human affairs': *CW*, XXV, p. 1159.
[133] Ibid., XI, p. 328.
[134] On the relationship in Mill's thought between self-cultivation and the learning of foreign lan-guages, see P. Kitcher, 'Mill, education, and the good life' in B. Eggleston, D. Miller, and

points recurred throughout his writings, from his essay on civilisation in 1836 to his rectorial address at the University of St Andrews in 1867. In the essay on civilisation, he argued that the 'intrinsic greatness' of the Greeks stemmed from their 'opinions, habits, and institutions *most remote from ours*', leading us to a 'catholic toleration' of other cultures. 'Were but the languages and literature of antiquity so taught', he continued, then 'the glorious images they present might stand before the student's eyes as living and glowing realities' and not as some 'foreign substance' lying at 'the bottom of his mind'.[135] Aside from a few scholars and clergymen, for whom *koine* Greek was essential, the neglect of classical languages was troublingly widespread. As he put it in his rector's address from 1867, 'part of the great worth to us of our Greek and Latin studies, [is] that in them we read history in the original sources. We are in actual contact with contemporary minds; we are not dependent on hearsay; we have something by which we can test and check the representations and theories of modern historians ... we are not only learning to understand the ancient mind, but laying in a stock of wise thought and observation'.[136]

Mill in his rectorial address from 1867 argued that a knowledge of foreign languages helped to develop active characters, whose importance to representative government he emphasised throughout his later political essays. Without knowing 'the language of a people', he reasoned, 'we never really know their thoughts, their feelings, and their type of character; and unless we do possess this knowledge, of some other people than ourselves ... our intellects [remain] only half expanded'.[137] Classical literature held a double value in this respect. Not only did it presuppose the historical skills mentioned above, but it also demanded a familiarity with Greek and Latin. When we turn to foreign languages and pasts, Mill argued, we become more fully educated, bringing us ever nearer to the 'perfection of our nature'.[138] By looking sympathetically at others we come to better know ourselves, developing in the process a set of critical skills with which to scrutinise established authorities and beliefs. He had offered a similar argument in *On Liberty*, which held that all 'languages and literatures are full of general observations on life, both as to what it is, and how to conduct oneself in it'.[139] By encountering distant social realities, one became a fuller individual and better citizen.

D. Weinstein (eds.), *John Stuart Mill and the art of life* (Oxford: Oxford University Press, 2011), p. 194.

[135] *CW*, XVIII, p. 145.   [136] Ibid., XXI, p. 228.   [137] Ibid., p. 226.
[138] Ibid., p. 217. See H. S. Jones, *Intellect and character in Victorian England: Mark Pattinson and the invention of the Don* (Cambridge: Cambridge University Press, 2007), p. 211.
[139] *CW*, XVIII, p. 250.

States of Society

Much has been made in recent years of Mill's projected science of society.[140] In the late 1830s and early 1840s, as the influence of Comte's *Cours* reached its peak, he became acutely interested in the laws of social statics and social dynamics.[141] This is evident not only in the *Logic*, which defined statics as the 'theory of the mutual actions and reactions of contemporaneous social phenomena', and dynamics as the observation and explanation of 'sequences of social conditions', but also in the *Principles*, which turned to statics for 'a collective view of the economical phenomena of society, considered as existing simultaneously'.[142] The goal of statics, then, was to explain social phenomena holistically, positing between their composite elements laws of coexistence and consensus. Unlike dynamics, statics was overwhelmingly concerned with social stability, and thus with explaining society in synchronic rather than diachronic terms. Mill generally referred to this as the 'state of society', a term which he employed frequently from the 1830s onwards and owed, perhaps, to his father's writings.[143] The laws of historical development, fundamental as they were to positive sociology, were seen by Comte and Mill as the purview of dynamics. Here, I examine Mill's historiography as a constituent branch of social statics, paving the way in the next chapter for a discussion of social dynamics and his developmental or progressive historicism.

Mill in a letter to Comte from October 1843 appeared to downplay the relationship between social statics and history. History, he argued, occupied 'first place' only in dynamics, which concerned itself with scientific explanations of social change, and he stressed instead the importance of ethology, a prospective 'secondary science' with which he hoped to explain character formation at both the individual and social level.[144] In the *Logic* and various other writings, however, he argued that the laws of statics applied to historical societies, too, and that the historian should draw on them to explain historical phenomena. Writing for *The Spectator* in 1846, he commended Grote for delineating the Athenian 'state of society', and in the *Logic* he argued that

[140] See, for example, Kawana, *Logic and society*.
[141] See Robson, *The improvement of mankind*, p. 117.   [142] *CW*, VIII, pp. 918, 924; II, p. 705.
[143] For an early formulation of his science of society, see 'The state of society in America' from 1836: *CW*, XVIII, p. 105.
[144] Haac (ed.), *Correspondence*, pp. 197–198.

what is called a state of society, is the simultaneous state of all the greater social facts or phenomena. Such are, the degree of knowledge, and of intellectual and moral culture, existing in the community, and in every class of it; the state of industry, of wealth and its distribution; the habitual occupations of the community; their division into classes, and the relations of those classes to one another; the common beliefs which they entertain on all the subjects most important to mankind, and the degree of assurance with which those beliefs are held; their tastes, and the character and degree of their aesthetic development; their form of government, and the more important of their laws and customs. The condition of all these things, and of many more which will spontaneously suggest themselves, constitute the state of society or the state of civilisation *at any given time.*[145]

Following Comte, Mill claimed that 'states of society are like different constitutions or different ages in the physical frame; they are conditions not of one or a few organs or functions, but of the whole organism. Accordingly, the information that we possess respecting past ages, and respecting the various states of society now existing in different regions of the earth, does, when duly analysed, exhibit uniformities'.[146] He called these the 'Uniformities of Coexistence'.[147] As in physiology, the social world observed a consensus that pointed to the interrelation of its composite elements by simultaneity or succession. Each element in this account was both a cause and an effect of the others, or, as Mill put it, of 'any other of the contemporaneous social phenomena'. This was a clear repudiation of geometric reasoning, an attempt on Mill's part to correct the abstract method of Bentham and Hobbes.[148] His point was that the state of society could not be determined by any one of its constitutive elements, but only by a range of elements considered functionally as a whole. While some elements were more significant than others, such as the state of knowledge and the *pouvoir spirituel*, Mill sought in statics a fuller explanation of social phenomena than Bentham had been willing or able to provide.[149]

Mill in the *Logic* claimed that the state of any given society is the product of phenomena either coexistent with or prior to itself. This tallied with the two types of relational activity between phenomena: that of simultaneity and that of succession. Together they provided materials for a 'General Science of Society' that examined 'the laws of succession and the coexistence of the great facts constituting the state of society'.[150] Although Mill

[145] *CW*, XXIV, p. 871; VIII, pp. 911–912. My emphasis.   [146] Ibid., VIII, p. 912.   [147] Ibid.
[148] Mill nevertheless agreed with his father that the philosopher must aspire to 'build' the 'universal principles of human nature' on a small 'number of propositions': *CW*, VIII, p. 906.
[149] Ibid., p. 926. See also Mueller, *Mill and French thought*, p. 123.   [150] *CW*, VIII, p. 908.

and Comte disagreed on a variety of issues pertaining to social statics –
including psychology, phrenology, ethology, and the status of women –
they agreed that history explained the transition from one state of society to
another, and that history itself was a determining factor in those
transitions.[151] The laws of coexistence and succession were inextricably
linked because, as Mill put it, the 'proximate cause of every state of society
is the state of society immediately preceding it'.[152] In *Auguste Comte and
Positivism*, we find the idea that human beings, 'on the laws of whose
nature the facts of history depend', were 'not abstract or universal but
historical human beings, already shaped, and made what they are, by
human society'.[153]

It is not hard to imagine why Mill was drawn to this idea. In his more
prominent writings, including his commentaries on Bentham and
Coleridge; the *Logic*; the *Principles*; and his essays *On Liberty* and
Considerations of Representative Government, he attempted to reconcile
order with progress. As a self-appointed mediator of political extremes,
he looked to combine the laws of dynamics (progress) with those of statics
(order).[154] He wanted to observe regularities in the laws of development
before measuring them against 'the psychological and ethological laws on
which they must really depend'.[155] This was, as we shall see, the basis of the
historical or inverse deductive method as outlined in Book VI of the *Logic*;
but his deep thought, like Comte's, was that the distinction between statics
and dynamics broke down at a certain level of analysis, because the
character of any given society was determined by the laws of succession
and consensus. Society, in other words, contained a mixture of stable and
progressive elements, hence his attempt in the *Logic* to 'combine the
statical [sic] view of social phenomena with the dynamical, considering
not only the progressive changes of the different elements, but the contemporaneous condition of each'.[156] Onto this idea he fastened several
hopes: first, that it might weaken the arguments of anti-reformers, since the
relationship between order and progress was no longer seen as mutually
exclusive; and, second, that it might consolidate history's role in social
science.

---

[151] See L. C. Raeder, *John Stuart Mill and the religion of humanity* (Columbia: University of Missouri
Press, 2002), pp. 48–49. However, David Lewisohn argued that 'the greater part of ... [Mill's]
theory was formulated by 1830–31, ten years before Comte's influence': 'Mill and Comte on the
methods of social science', *Journal of the History of Ideas* 33 (1972), p. 315.
[152] *CW*, VIII, p. 912.   [153] Ibid., X, p. 307.   [154] Skorupski, *John Stuart Mill*, p. 271.
[155] *CW*, VIII, p. 908.   [156] Ibid., p. 925.

This brings us back to our original line of enquiry. 'There is', Mill argued in the review of Michelet, 'yet a third, and the highest stage of historical investigation, in which the aim is not simply to compose histories, but to construct a science of history'. In the order of nature this must 'follow, not precede, that last described; for before we can trace the filiation of states of society one from another, we must rightly understand and clearly conceive them, each apart from the rest'.[157] He appeared to contradict himself a few pages later when he argued that the order of filiation must be established *before* we can 'explain the facts of any age or nation', but I suggest in the next chapter that this has something to do with what Mill took to be the natural order of progress and its correspondence to actual historical events.[158] My point here is that, for Mill, historical criticism was logically prior to the science or philosophy of history. Without that criticism, the laws of history could be made to reflect almost anything: the writer's politics, for instance, or a view of human nature that reflected the present above the past. In his address to St Andrews in 1867, he reminded his audience that 'historical criticism', or the 'tests of historical truth', must be studied alongside the philosophy of history and its search for the 'causes' of past life 'in its principal features'.[159] The two enterprises were inextricably linked, but political science stood to benefit especially from the latter – from a 'theory of human progress' or 'philosophy of history', which, he argued in the *Autobiography*, necessarily underpinned any 'general theory or philosophy of politics'.[160]

Conclusion

Mill in the 1830s and early 1840s thought extensively about the practical problems of historical enquiry, bringing to a head many of the themes which I have been discussing. His progressive theory of historiography, sketched in the article on Michelet, rejected presentism and the resort to 'everyday experience'.[161] Niebuhr's historicism explicitly opposed it, while Romantic and 'Continental' philosophers set out to de-familiarise and imaginatively reconstruct the past. The best modern historians were more attentive than their eighteenth-century predecessors to the past's animating uniqueness, and it is significant that Hume, Gibbon, and other eighteenth-century luminaries barely featured in his canon: the 'historians in Germany' – Niebuhr, Friedrich Schlosser (1776–1861), and

[157] Ibid., XX, p. 225. [158] Ibid., p. 228. [159] Ibid., XXI, pp. 420–421. [160] Ibid., I, p. 169.
[161] Ibid., XX, p. 223.

Ranke – had enabled the 'renovation of historical studies' while French historians surpassed them 'in historical speculations'.[162] At the same time, his defence of general principles provided continuities with Scottish philosophical history and the utilitarian tradition in which he was raised. Carlyle's account of the French Revolution, while innocent of presentism, was ultimately conjectural and uncritical, whereas Grote's *History of Greece* combined criticism with philosophical insight, placing it somewhere between the second and third stages of historical enquiry.

The final stage, however, was neither assimilative nor poetic. It was scientific. Its touchstones were Comte's *Cours de philosophie positive* and Book VI of the *Logic*, which presented history as an independent science whose laws were uniquely its own, but also as ancillary to a general science of society whose ambitions he never fully realised. This, *pace* Cairns, is why we must carefully situate Mill's historiography within his philosophy of history. The historian, he reasoned, must establish the 'facts of each generation' before arranging them, in the intellectual spirit of positivism, as 'one complex phenomenon, caused by those of the generation preceding, and causing, in its turn, those of the next in order'.[163] It followed that these sequences must abide by 'some law' and how 'to read that law' is 'the fundamental problem of the science of history'.[164] Mill's search for answer in Comtean positivism sat uneasily with Grote, who, as we have seen, defended the '*facts* of history' from Comte's abstract divinations.[165] However, the failure to mediate between historical facts and their scientific laws – which could be framed, in the contexts which I have outlined, as a failure to reconcile an individualising with a progressive historicism – was not uniquely Mill's or Comte's. As the next two chapters demonstrate, its roots can be traced to other intellectual traditions in England and France.

---

[162] Ibid., pp. 219–220.   [163] Ibid., p. 225.   [164] Ibid.
[165] Grote, *The personal life of George Grote*, p. 203.

PART III

Sciences of History

CHAPTER 5

J. S. Mill and Historical Relativism

Practical Eclecticism

Mill's science or philosophy of history tends to confuse the few readers who seriously engage it. John Gibbins was left puzzled by its relationship to utilitarianism, while Collini, Winch, and Burrow stressed the ambivalence with which Mill historicised Bentham's philosophy and the scientific study of politics.[1] Mill himself extolled the virtues of a 'practical eclecticism' to intellectually bridge the eighteenth and nineteenth centuries.[2] His indebtedness in the 1830s and 1840s to 'Continental' philosophy – to Coleridge, Goethe (1749–1832), Carlyle, and Comte – has been amply discussed.[3] The eighteenth century, he declared, had gone too far in prescribing 'model institutions' for all times and places, whereas the nineteenth century sought principles 'from which the institutions suitable to any given circumstances might be deduced'.[4] Mill's distinction was more autobiographical than historical, and his mature view that any 'general theory or philosophy of politics' must repose on a 'philosophy of history' counts among his most significant but equivocal shifts.[5] His sketch in the *Logic* of an 'Inverse Deductive, or Historical Method' is widely regarded as an act of rebellion

---

[1] Gibbins, 'J. S. Mill, liberalism, and progress', p. 91; Collini, Winch, and Burrow, *That noble science of politics*, p. 145.

[2] See Mill to Gustave d'Eichthal (1804–1886), 7 November 1829: *CW*, XII, p. 42. As Mill put it in his autobiography, he never 'undervalued that great century' but 'kept as firm hold of one side of the truth as I took of the other': *CW*, I, p. 169. He was not alone in making the distinction, which persisted throughout the nineteenth century: S. Hodgson, *The philosophy of reflection* (London: Longmans, Green, and Co., 1878), I, p. 19.

[3] Mill considered his ideas as largely fixed from the 1840s onwards: *CW*, I, p. 229.   [4] Ibid., p. 169.

[5] Ibid. Weinberg concluded that it 'may be assumed that he [Mill] imbibed the spirit' of 'historical relativism' from Comte: *The influence of Auguste Comte on the economics of John Stuart Mill*, pp. 31, 37. In a letter to John Sterling from 20 October 1831, Mill observed that his purpose was to work out 'principles: which are of use for all times, though to be applied cautiously & circumspectly to any': *CW*, XII, p. 38.

against Bentham and his father, but scholars have failed to treat the subject 'in its own right' by playing close attention to the intellectual contexts in which it developed.[6]

Mill in 1840 argued that the English were an 'ancient people' whose 'political notions rest on an historical basis'.[7] It followed that any theory of politics must account not just for the optimum conditions of human happiness, in which consideration is given to society's ideal laws and institutions, but also for history's cumulative effect on social phenomena.[8] Coleridge in his *Second Lay Sermon* (1817) likewise tried to reconcile the principles of permanence and progress, which he framed as a settlement between the interests of property and commerce.[9] Mill was similarly accommodating.[10] The *Considerations*, published in 1861, intervened in debates on parliamentary reform not simply to agitate for particular measures, but to reconcile order with progress in the pursuit of a 'better doctrine'.[11] Neither the Conservatives nor the Liberals, Mill claimed, had managed to preserve 'all kinds and amounts of good which currently exist' whilst promoting the 'increase' of those same goods.[12] This task aspired, first, to the reconciliation of two conventionally opposed principles – permanence and progress – and, second, to the reformation of political science as a branch of sociology. 'I understand by Sociology', he argued to John Chapman (1821–1894) in 1851, 'not a particular *class* of subjects included *within* Politics, but a vast field *including* it'.[13]

The Regius Professor of Modern History at Cambridge, Sir James Fitzjames Stephen (1829–1894), denounced sociology as farrago. All social phenomena, Mill claimed, were 'subject to fixed laws', but those laws were said to operate in an 'endless variety of circumstances'. The sociologists – Comte, Mill, and Grote – wanted to have their cake and eat it: to establish invariable causal laws whilst obscuring their operation in 'particular cases', in a doomed effort to reconcile the clarity of theory with the complexities of practice.[14] Years later, in 1873, Stephen resumed his attack by contrasting Mill's writings on logic and political economy, whose conception of human nature was unequivocally historical, with his essays *On Liberty*,

---

[6] Ryan, *J. S. Mill*, p. xi.   [7] *CW*, XVIII, p. 195.   [8] Ibid., VIII, p. 915.
[9] See S. T. Coleridge (ed. J. Morrow), *Coleridge's writings on politics and society* (London: Macmillan, 1990), p. 147.
[10] See J. N. Gray, 'John Stuart Mill: traditional and revisionist interpretations', *Literature of Liberty* 2.2 (1979), pp. 7–38.
[11] *CW*, XIX, p. 373.   [12] Ibid., p. 385.   [13] Mill to Chapman, 9 June 1851: *CW*, XIV, p. 68.
[14] J. Stephen, *Lectures on the history of France* [1852] (London: Longman, Brown, Green, Longmans, and Roberts, 1857), I, p. 15. See also B. W. Young, *The Victorian eighteenth century: an intellectual history* (Oxford: Oxford University Press, 2007), p. 127.

Utilitarianism, Considerations of Representative Government, and *The Subjection of Women.* The latter, he observed, set aside 'facts and experience' by presenting human nature in hypothetical rather than actual historical circumstances, returning full circle to the deductive simplicities of Benthamism.[15] Mill's utilitarianism, on this account, trumped his commitments to historicism and positive sociology.[16]

Sidgwick in his *Elements of Politics* (1891) agreed that the *Considerations* reverted to deductions from 'general characteristics of man', notwithstanding 'the views expressed [by Mill] in his *Logic of the Moral Sciences*'.[17] Despite Mill's intention to strengthen the 'relation of Politics to History', the *Considerations* used the past strategically 'either to confirm practical conclusions otherwise arrived at, or to suggest the limits of their applicability'.[18] Sidgwick, unlike Stephen, welcomed Mill's reversion to a more innocuous position, citing history's 'secondary' role 'in framing the precepts or maxims of Practical Politics'.[19] Both, however, agreed that Mill employed two conflicting and possibly irreconcilable logics, the first of which was relative and historical, and the second of which was universal and abstract.[20] John Gray had something like this in mind when he suggested that Mill's utilitarianism jarred with his 'historicist' emphasis on 'the cultural and historical contexts in which human nature occurs'.[21] Logical tensions between the science of human nature (theory), the laws of progress, and actual historical events (practice) can be traced, I have argued, via the utilitarians to Stewart, Smith, Hume, and Bacon, and more variedly to Montesquieu and the German historicists. One admiring French reader, the positivist and historian Hippolyte Taine (1828–1893), felt the need to argue that the problem was not uniquely Mill's, and that all social sciences struggled to mediate between the 'accidentelle et locale' and 'lois primitives'.[22] Mill even argued in a letter to Taine that the *Considerations* did

[15] J. Stephen, *Liberty, equality, fraternity* (New York: Holt and Williams, 1873) p. 22.
[16] The contradiction was possibly inevitable. Historicism, according to Robert D'Amico, abandoned 'efforts to prove the validity or "rightness" of concepts' by rejecting a 'purely psychological or ethical account of social forces': *Historicism and knowledge* (London: Routledge, 1989), pp. xi, 6.
[17] Sidgwick, *Elements of politics*, p. 8n. *The logic of the moral sciences* was drawn from Book VI of the *Logic* and published in 1872 as a standalone text.
[18] Sidgwick, *Elements of politics*, p. 8. See also H. Sidgwick, 'The historical method', *Mind* 11.42 (1886), p. 212.
[19] Sidgwick, *Elements of politics*, pp. 8, 8n. See R. Crisp, *The cosmos of duty: Henry Sidgwick's method of ethics* (Oxford: Oxford University Press, 2015), p. 223; A. Loizides, 'Mill on the method of politics' in A. Loizides (ed.), *Mill's A system of logic: critical appraisals* (London: Routledge, 2014), p. 228.
[20] This tension has been acknowledged in Macleod, 'History', p. 272; Capaldi, *John Stuart Mill*, p. 136. Zakaras, *Individuality and mass democracy*, p. 143; Robson, *The improvement of mankind*, p. 174.
[21] Gray, 'John Stuart Mill: traditional and revisionist interpretations', p. 31.
[22] H.A. Taine, 'Philosophie anglais: John Stuart Mill', *Revue des deux mondes* 32 (1861), p. 80. See also H.A. Taine, *Le positivisme anglaise: étude sur Stuart Mill* (Paris: Ballière, 1864), p. 143.

not offer 'en thèse générale' of representative government because it was above all 'une question de temps et de lieu'.[23]

Mill was more deeply immersed than other utilitarians in French political economy, historiography, and *science sociale*; and these influences further underlined the difficulty of reconciling actual historical events with a law-giving science of history, let alone the laws of human nature on which they ultimately reposed.[24] If we consider that Mary Pickering identified two contradictory strains in Comte's historical thought, one 'relativist' and another 'absolutist', and that Ceri Crossley pointed to a similar contradiction in Saint-Simonianism, then it is perhaps unsurprising that Mill's historicism was similarly double-edged.[25] His science of history, to qualify as such, cancelled out historical accidents with empirical laws, which meant – as with Comte and the Saint-Simonians – that it conceptualised history in both relative and universal terms: relative, because it related political truth to the 'given state or situation of society'; universal, because that state or situation was relative to the general laws of progress.[26] His claim in the *Autobiography* that he wrote either within the 'region of ultimate aims' or the region of the 'immediately useful and practically attainable' can be understood in broadly these terms.[27] So, too, can the following chapters. This chapter examines Mill's science of history as a logical framework in which to think circumstantially about politics, while the final chapter explores his writings on universal history and the 'ultimate aims' of civilisation.

Before we can parse Mill's science of history, we must first reconstruct his growing faith in history's capacity to explain and predict social phenomena, about which he was initially sceptical. This requires me to retrace our steps. His writings in the 1820s, under Bentham's influence, doubted that the past could be examined with the same methods and precision as the natural world, which, unlike historical events, could be studied directly

[23] Mill to Taine, 15 March 1861: *CW*, XV, p. 722.
[24] On the emergence in France of *sciences sociale*, see M. S. Staum, *Minerva's message: stabilising the French Revolution* (Montreal: McGill-Queen's University Press, 1996), pp. 3–19; M. Sonenscher, 'Ideology, social science and general facts in late eighteenth-century French political thought', *History of European Ideas* 35 (2009), pp. 24–37.
[25] M. Pickering, *Auguste Comte: an intellectual biography* (Cambridge: Cambridge University Press, 1993), I, pp. 113, 283; C. Crossley, *French historians and romanticism: Thierry, Guizot, the Saint-Simonians, Quinet, Michelet* (London: Routledge, 1993), p. 119.
[26] *CW*, I, p. 323.
[27] Ibid., p. 139. Shortly after the appearance in 1829 of Macaulay's broadside, Mill had urged his father to respond by saying, 'I was not writing a scientific treatise on politics, I was writing an argument for parliamentary reform': I, p. 184. Helen McCabe in a recent article also drew attention to Mill's distinction between the 'ideal' and the practically attainable: 'Navigating by the North Star: the role of the "ideal" in John Stuart Mill's view of "utopian" schemes and the possibilities of social transformation', *Utilitas* 31 (2019), pp. 291–309.

and experimentally.[28] His exposure to 'Continental' philosophy – shorthand for a range of sometimes conflicting influences – convinced him otherwise. He came to believe that the science of history was foundational to the study of politics and social phenomena, and that Bentham had overlooked their interdependence. His reception in the 1830s of Germano-Coleridgianism, liberal Anglicanism, Saint-Simonianism, and Comtean positivism persuaded him that political institutions were not universal but relative to society's progress. The goal of any well-ordered society, therefore, was to establish principles which reflected the current stage of progress whilst facilitating the emergence of the next.

Early Scepticism

Mill in the 1820s was a diligent propagandist of Bentham's and his father's ideas. He contributed regularly to the *Westminster Review* and the Utilitarian and London Debating societies, all of which he helped to establish.[29] One such debate enquired into 'the use of history', details of which are limited to Mill's written report. We do not know who provided the 'luminous' opening speech that preceded his own, or how his arguments were received by a predominantly Radical and Whig audience.[30] It is also difficult to precisely determine the date on which he delivered the address. Some manuscript sources point to 1823, which would make it a product of the Utilitarian Society, although it is more likely that the speech was delivered to the London Society at some point in the first half of 1827.[31] 'I come here', he began, 'with my mind not fully made up on this interesting question [on whether history had a use, and if so, what]'.[32] He was nevertheless convinced that 'the importance of history as a source of political knowledge has been greatly overrated', an argument which he regarded as 'greatly at variance with the received opinions of the world'.[33] By this he did not mean, as 'several of the defenders of history' alleged, that we ought to refrain from the judging 'of the future from the past', or that we should ignore the lessons of experience.[34] His point was that 'there is a right way of consulting experience, and there is a wrong way – and the question now is, which is the right way, and which is the wrong'?[35]

Mill had addressed this question before. In 1823, he replied in the *Morning Chronicle* to a speech given by the Whig MP Colonel William Lewis Hughes

---

[28] R. Harré, 'Positivist thought in the nineteenth-century' in T. Baldwin (ed.), *The Cambridge history of philosophy 1870–1945* (Cambridge: Cambridge University Press, 2003), I, p. 11.
[29] *CW*, I, p. 131. [30] Ibid., XXVI, p. 392.
[31] The speech was edited by Harold J. Laski. See Robson's textual introduction: *CW*, XXVI, p. 392.
[32] Ibid. [33] Ibid. [34] Ibid., pp. 392–393. [35] Ibid., p. 393.

(1767–1852), who had staunchly defended Whig principles from the encroachments of modern Radicalism; the former, Hughes claimed, sought only the inalienable rights bestowed by the constitutional settlement of 1689, while Francis Burdett (1770–1844), John Hobhouse (1786–1869), and William Cobbett (1763–1835) championed extensive reforms for which there was no historical basis. Mill, possibly at his father's or even Bentham's behest, responded to Hughes by defending progress from the claims of a 'venerable antiquity', an 'abuse of terms' which spoke not to the wisdom of ages but to the 'nonage of the world'.[36] Like Bentham in *The Book of Fallacies*, he argued that appeals to ancestral wisdom were antithetical to progress, and that he was among the 'friends' of innovation who wished 'to see the human race well governed'.[37] The doctrine of inalienable rights, with which Hughes justified the settlement of 1689, emerged in now defunct circumstances; as Mill put it five years later, we must discourage those who 'ridiculously invoke the wisdom of our ancestors as authority for institutions which in substance are now totally different'.[38]

Mill's speech from 1827 pursued a similar line of argument. When we use history as a guide for politics, he observed, we tend to make misguided assumptions about the nature of historical knowledge, which is too complex and varied to produce valid inductions and analogies. If our goal is to improve social institutions, then what we require, much more than historical precedents, is a knowledge of man's essential nature: 'I mean, a knowledge of the causes, rules or influences which govern the actions of mankind ... and of those other principles of human nature upon which depends the influence of the social arrangements over their happiness'.[39] The appeal to human nature, he added, was not diametrically opposed to practice because 'human affairs' were approached even by the most ardent theorist as a matter of direct individual and indirect collective experiences, however so conceptualised.[40] The question was whether an inductive approach to history added anything to the principles of human nature beyond those afforded by 'a diligent study of our own minds, together with a careful observation of a few others'.[41] This kind of induction, he reflected in the *Autobiography*, made politics 'a science of specific experience'.[42]

---

[36] Ibid., XXII, p. 72.   [37] Ibid., p. 71.   [38] Ibid., p. 258.   [39] See also Bentham, *Works*, I, p. 22.
[40] *CW*, XXVI, p. 392.
[41] Ibid., p. 393. See a letter from Bain to Mill in which he discussed their views on 'past experiences' as an 'object for the mind to think on': Bain to Mill, 18 January 1863, 'Hutzler collection', Johns Hopkins University Special Collections, HUT. 004, ff. 13–14.
[42] *CW*, I, p. 164.

Inductive political theories failed to understand that in history one instance could never 'be a rule for another', unless, by some inconceivable accident, 'all the circumstances were the same: but they are never the same'.[43] Even if society's material circumstances were more or less consistent, in contrast to incidental or local circumstances, it would be impossible even then to account for hidden causes, or to extract from one or two putative similarities a general law of causation. While we might observe empirical correlations between social phenomena – that under this or that political system a country seems to prosper, stagnate, or decline – this does not, however, amount to a scientific causal relationship.[44] Mill in the *Logic* repeated this point by arguing that inductions of this kind would reveal 'as much of the facts of history as mere erudition can teach', at least without 'the assistance of theory'.[45] The speech also foreshadowed his criticism in the *Logic* of 'chemical' political methods which privileged comparison and experimentation. It was not the case, he argued, that human beings in society were converted into a new kind of substance, as when hydrogen combined with oxygen.[46] It was impossible to conduct political experiments with the same precision as natural experiments, because of the practically infinite number of variables whose effects could not be individually observed.

Mill's hostility to the chemical method fuelled his subsequent attack on Macaulay, but his target in the speech on history was natural theology and other doctrines which took things 'in the gross as the hand of nature had left them'.[47] His point was that by taking history at face value, independent of general laws, we run the risk of 'fancy' and 'airy hypothesis'.[48] There was, he continued, only 'one branch of physical science now in which from the impossibility of experiment we have nothing better than history to go upon, I mean geology'.[49] The reference to geology was brief and unclear, so we can only guess at its meaning based on what Mill said later about the concrete sciences, which, unlike the abstract sciences of physiology and chemistry, took combinations 'actually realised in nature, as distinguished from the general laws which would equally govern any other combinations of the same elements'.[50] Since abstract sciences dealt in the elementary facts of nature, it was up to the concrete sciences to explain the interaction of phenomena actually 'in existence' and 'which really take place'.[51] If history generated a knowledge of special cases only, that is, of things as they

[43] Ibid., XXVI, pp. 393–394.   [44] Ibid., p. 394.   [45] Ibid., VIII, p. 880.   [46] Ibid., p. 879.
[47] Ibid., XXVI, p. 394.   [48] Ibid.   [49] Ibid.
[50] Mill's essay on Hamilton is one source, his essay on Comte another: *CW*, IX, p. 472; *CW*, X, pp. 279–280.
[51] *CW*, X, p. 280.

actually occurred, then it must be seen as a function of theory and not a theory in its own right.[52] It could illustrate general laws only in complex circumstances, thereby reaffirming its status as a concrete rather than an abstract, law-giving science.[53]

This argument, as we have seen, had links to Hume and Scottish philosophical history, and beyond that to Bacon's contested intellectual legacy. Mill, like Bentham and James, was sceptical that history could independently explain and evaluate social phenomena, or that it could be used experimentally to furnish comparisons across historical time. While the political dangers of doing so were obvious, the past did have its uses: 'however much the political importance of history has been overrated', he argued, 'it appears to me utterly impossible to overrate its moral importance'.[54] The switch from political to moral instruction changed the rules of the game.[55] In cases of moral instruction, Mill reasoned, we are concerned less with generalisations, analogies, and laws, than with effecting through great historical deeds 'an incentive to virtue and a source of happiness'.[56] History could thus provide the intellectual and affective stimuli to learn from the exalted moralities of others.[57] The reward for doing so was 'prospective'. It was sufficient 'for them [the moral agents] to know that one day they would be appreciated'.[58] If, however, history 'were to be annihilated', we might lose sight of humanity's higher capabilities amidst our more limited own.[59] As Bentham in *IPML* put it, the 'pains of an ill-name', the 'pains of ill-repute', and the 'pains of dishonour' acted as social sanctions which applied no less to a historical than to an immediate social context.[60] In other words, we want to be remembered fondly not only by our peers but by the dead whom we remember and revere, a point to which Mill returned some years later when discussing the religion of humanity. The 'thought that our dead parents or friends would have approved our conduct' was, he maintained, 'a scarcely less powerful motive than the knowledge that our living ones do approve it'.[61]

Mill in the 1820s, I have argued, remained committed to Bentham's science of man, which subjected institutions to a rigorous litmus test based on individuals' known appetites, aversions, and mental laws. His speech on the use of history, however, was not intended as definitive. Its primary objective was to illustrate history's shortcomings as a political method, with

---

[52] Ibid., p. 281.   [53] Ibid., XX, pp. 117–118.   [54] Ibid., XXVI, p. 395.
[55] Mill in the *Principles* went on to argue that history was integral to the formation of moral character: *CW*, II, p. 137. See Robson, *The improvement of mankind*, p. 141.
[56] *CW*, XXVI, p. 397.   [57] Ibid., p. 396.   [58] Ibid.   [59] Ibid.   [60] Bentham, *Works*, I, p. 20.
[61] From Mill's posthumous *Utility of religion*: *CW*, X, pp. 421–422.

at least one eye on Tories and Whigs whose appropriation of inductive logic I have lengthily explored. His other writings from the 1820s complicate the picture further. In a review of François Mignet's *Histoire de la Révolution française* from 1826, for example, he followed Hume in making history subservient to the 'laws of human nature and human society', which, he acknowledged, necessitated the use of 'generalisations'. Without them, history's 'endless' details would 'be of no use' to the practical philosopher, and since a generalisation showed 'that something which has happened once or twice will always happen', it is difficult to understand why Mill in the speech on history argued in the way that he did.[62] His review of Mignet seemed less worried about the logical possibility of generalisations than with their practical formation. Mignet's generalisations, while generally 'acute', were made 'upon first impressions' and led him to affirm 'that [sic] to be true in all cases which is only true in some'.[63] Likewise, in a review of Scott's *Life of Napoleon* from 1828, Mill suggested that if it be 'any part of the duty of an historian to turn the facts of history to any use', then 'the historian who is fit for his office must be well disciplined in the art of connecting facts into principles, and applying principles to the explanation of facts: he must be a man familiar with generalisation and general views ... in short, a *philosopher*'.[64]

How should we account for this discrepancy? One option is to conclude that Mill was simply inconsistent, an answer made more plausible by the intellectual uncertainty to which he openly admitted in 1827. Another is to examine the intentions with which these works were written, based less on their political than their philosophical themes. The speech from 1827 examined history's value as an independent branch of knowledge, while the review of Mignet addressed its value to philosophy. The distinction, which mimicked Bentham's, resurfaced in some of his later writings. In a review of John Todd's *The Book of Analysis* from 1832, he resisted 'those clamorous appeals we hear daily ... to history and statistics, by men, the sum total of whose knowledge of facts in history and statistics ... is like an insect's knowledge of the great earth; and their inductions, very like an oyster's conjectures of the laws which govern the universe'.[65] Later, in *The Subjection of Women* (1869), he argued that history, while 'so much better understood than formerly', disclosed little to those 'who do not bring much with them to its study'.[66] The more pressing question, therefore, is

---

[62] Ibid., XX, pp. 4, 13.   [63] Ibid., p. 13.   [64] Ibid, p. 56.
[65] Ibid., XXIII, p. 412. In the same year he dismissed the French *Doctrinaires* as 'speculators ... for whom history has no lessons, because they bring to its study no real knowledge of the human mind, or of the character of their own age': *CW*, XXIII, p. 513.
[66] Ibid., XXI, p. 277.

how did Mill come to see history as foundational to politics and how did he construct that foundation? His writings from the 1830s and 1840s on Coleridge, the Saint-Simonians, and Comte suggest that the transformation was significant and swift. The 1859 reprint of his essay on 'Civilisation' (1836) retracted his earlier attack on 'the puerile notion' that political wisdom can be 'founded' on history, and his 'early blindness' to history evidently transformed into a rich historical consciousness.[67]

Germano-Coleridgianism

Mill in a letter to John Pringle Nichol from 1834 confessed that 'few persons have exercised more influence over my thoughts and character than Coleridge has ... [both] by his works, and by the fact that several persons with whom I have been very intimate were completely trained in his school'.[68] I have neither the space nor need to lengthily explore Coleridge's influence, but it is important to address the intellectual contexts in which Mill placed him. Coleridge in his major works – *The Lay Sermons* (1817); *Aids to Reflection* (1825); and *On the Constitution of Church and State* (1830) – attacked the 'mechano' corpuscularism of the eighteenth century, whose origins he traced to Aristotle.[69] Even though Mill sided with Locke and Newton on metaphysical questions, he paid close attention to Coleridge's attack on radical empiricism as a framework in which to think about social and ethical questions. Society, Coleridge argued, could not be reduced like a machine to its different functions or parts; it better resembled an organism with dynamic rather than static laws. Purely nominal forms of empiricism, such as those espoused by Locke and Hartley, reduced human life to a physics of necessity, and Mill in his essay on Coleridge took up both themes without clearly endorsing either. First, he repeated Coleridge's point that the mechanical philosophers had succeeded only in describing and categorising the world, whereas the goal was to understand it; and, second, that the same philosophers undermined individual agency by asserting that 'motives act on the will, as bodies act on bodies'.[70]

---

[67] Ibid., XVIII, p. 145; C. Turk, *Coleridge and Mill: a study of influence* (Aldershot: Avery, 1988), p. 139.

[68] *CW*, XII, p. 221. F. D. Maurice and John Sterling (1806–1844) were perhaps the two most significant figures in this respect. Sterling prior to his death relayed to Mill the many areas on which they agreed: Sterling to Mill, 8 September 1844: 'John Stuart Mill papers', Yale University Library, MS. 350, f. 3. See also *CW*, I, p. 133.

[69] Edwards, *The statesman's science*, p. 147.

[70] Ibid., p. 137; S. T. Coleridge, *Aids to reflection in the form of a manly character* (London: Taylor and Hessey, 1825), p. 136.

While Mill considered these questions independently of Coleridge – the doctrine of necessity, for example, weighed on him like an 'incubus' – he drew enthusiastically on his account of civil society, which, unlike Bentham's, was consciously historical.[71] This was why he presented the two schools as dialectical opposites, with each serving as the other's completing counterpart. The essays on Bentham (1838) and Coleridge (1840), inspired by Goethe's ideal of many-sidedness, brought together the dominant philosophies of the age, if not as a *via media*, then as a richer understanding of what was good and bad in each. The connective tissue, for Coleridge as for Mill, was to be found in Bacon's *Novum Organum*; and his attempts from 1816 onwards to combine Bacon's experimentalism with Platonic science, based on the concept of *lumen siccum*, reflected his enduring concern with 'Ideas' and the moral mission of science.[72] This intellectual eclecticism was especially pronounced in his essay *On the Constitution of Church and State* (1829), which made history the witness of what Pamela Edwards has called an 'empirically grounded idealist account of institutional governance', a combination, in other words, of Bacon's logic and neo-Platonic idealism.[73]

Mill dismissed attempts to reconcile empiricism with Kantian or neo-Platonic metaphysics, on the grounds that it strayed dangerously close to intuitionism.[74] When in 1831 Carlyle called him a 'new mystic', in the hope of converting him to the cause of transcendentalism, he played down the compliment 'for the sake of my own integrity'.[75] What Mill saw in Coleridge, then, had less to do with the metaphysical poverties of empiricism than with the narrowness of eighteenth-century philosophy, and, in particular, its disregard for the historical contexts in which institutions emerged and acquired legitimacy. The fractured politics of the early 1830s made this an especially urgent task. Coleridge's value to Mill, as with Carlyle's and Comte's, lay in the attempt to restore equipoise in the wake of Enlightenment. The previous century, for all its welcome attacks on prejudice and custom, had too readily dismissed the enduring principles of political society whose discovery was quintessentially historical.[76] Its leading thinkers extended from their own experiences a virulent contempt for history, and, with it, 'the truth which is in the traditional opinions'.[77]

[71] *CW*, I, p. 175. [72] Edwards, *The statesmen's science*, p. 149.
[73] P. Edwards, 'Coleridge on politics and religion' in F. Burwick (ed.), *The Oxford handbook of Samuel Taylor Coleridge* (Oxford: Oxford University Press, 2009), p. 236.
[74] On the Kantian dimension of Coleridge's thought, see: M. Class, *Coleridge and Kantian ideas in England, 1796–1817: Coleridge's responses to German philosophy* (London: Bloomsbury Academic, 2012), pp. 129, 132.
[75] *CW*, I, p. 182. [76] Ibid., X, pp. 80, 112. [77] Ibid., p. 120.

Coleridge, on the other hand, had built on the intellectual rubble of Enlightenment a philosophical conservatism that combined historical development with the enduring features of civil society. He was not, in Mill's reading of him, a defender of authority for authority's sake, or of 'the mere practical man' who appealed to the 'rule-of-thumb school of political craftsmanship'.[78] The kind of conservatism with which Mill associated Coleridge – specifically his ideas regarding political obedience and the clerisy – was seen as compatible with the eighteenth-century's critical spirit.[79] If Bentham had identified pathologies in the body politic, then Coleridge had analysed it systematically with the intention of establishing a new political science. Whereas Bentham and the *philosophes* had been contemptuous of 'ancestorial [sic] wisdom' and the ideational and affective structures which kept alive not just this or that social order, but the very *fact* of social order, Coleridge paid attention to the historical origins of laws, customs, and institutions.[80] The 'inductive laws of the existence and growth of human society', Mill argued, revealed three requisites of permanent political society, which were, first, an established system of education; second, a spirit of allegiance; and, third, an 'active principle of cohesion'.[81] The equilibrium between order and change made history a dynamic and not a cyclical process by presenting society in the abstract, as an 'Idea', rather than as a set of timeless institutions.[82]

The permanent features of political society were not 'accidental' to the 'particular polity or religion' which the Coleridgians 'happened to patronise'.[83] They had produced, 'in the spirit of Baconian investigation ... not a piece of party advocacy, but a philosophy of society, in the only form in which it is yet possible, that of a philosophy of history'.[84] Bentham's mistake had been to tether civil society to an institutional 'vesture' that presumed an empirically consistent human nature.[85] They had failed to see 'the historical value of much of which had ceased to be useful', to realise, in other words, that even corrupt and ineffective institutions 'still filled a place in the human mind' and the 'arrangements of society'.[86] They had thrown the baby

---

[78] Ibid., p. 121.
[79] D. A. Habibi, *John Stuart Mill and the ethic of human growth* (Dordrecht: Springer Science & Business Media, 2001), p. 36.
[80] *CW*, X, p. 79.   [81] Ibid., pp. 138–139; 133–5. See Turk, *Coleridge and Mill*, p. 139.
[82] Alexander, 'The principles of permanence and progression', p. 133. Mill in the *Logic* set out the conditions in which order could be reconciled with progress: *CW*, VIII, pp. 917–925.
[83] Ibid., X, p. 139.   [84] Ibid.   [85] Ibid., p. 138.   [86] Ibid.

out with the bath water, seeing in 'the weakening of all government' only 'the weakening of bad government'.[87] Whereas d'Alembert had proposed to blot out 'all record whatever of past events', the Coleridgians, much like Herder and Michelet, saw history as a 'science of causes and effects' that helped to liberate politics from the confines of its age.[88] This is why Mill presented Bentham as 'abstract and metaphysical' and Coleridge as ontological, conservative, concrete, and historical, even though those attributions were, as several scholars have observed, inconsistent with previous remarks.[89]

Mill did not share the Coleridgians' belief that historical consciousness was essentially palingenetic, an aesthetic process of retrieval and rebirth, because it could not be verified empirically. The idea that the historian's job was to perform subjective acts of recreation, simultaneously calling into being and interpreting the past, waded once more into the murky waters of intuitionism.[90] As philosophers of history, however, the Coleridgians mitigated the aporetic effects of Enlightenment: its disregard for historical and cultural factors; its 'mistaking [of] the state of things with which they had always been familiar, for the universal and natural condition of mankind'; its inability to see, in even the most corrupt and inutile of institutions, enduring ideational and aesthetic elements 'of the social union'; and, perhaps most importantly of all, its consequent attack on civil society.[91] He singled out d'Alembert and the *philosophes* for criticism, all of whom had failed to uncover in 'the facts and events of the past' even the slightest 'meaning', established not by the loyalties of party politics but by philosophical 'speculations'.[92]

The Coleridgians made no such error. Seen as 'the gradual evolution of humanity', their philosophy of history represented 'the only means of predicting and guiding the future, by unfolding the agencies which have produced and still maintain the present'.[93] They were the first English thinkers to stress the importance of national character, whose scientific laws Bentham had overlooked.[94] Mill agreed that by studying a nation's

---

[87] Ibid., p. 137.   [88] Ibid., p. 139.

[89] Ibid., p. 125. See R. P. Anschutz, 'The logic of J. S. Mill', p. 53.

[90] M. J. Kooy, 'Romanticism and Coleridge's idea of history', *Journal of the History of Ideas* 60.4 (1999), pp. 717–718.

[91] *CW*, X, p. 132, 134.   [92] Ibid., p. 139; XX, p. 261.

[93] Ibid., X, pp. 139–140. As in Comte's positivism, this unfolding made allowances for ideas and emotions, if not for what Thirlwall termed 'moral forces': C. Thirlwall (ed. J. J. Stewart Perowne), *Remains literary and theological of Connop Thirlwall* (London: Daldy, Isbister & Co., 1878), III, p. 280.

[94] See G. Varouxakis, 'National character in John Stuart Mill's thought', *History of European Ideas* 24.6 (1998), pp. 375–391.

character and education, one might reveal both the 'principal causes of its [society's] permanence as a society' and also 'the chief source of its progressiveness', or how, from that very same education, it 'called forth and invigorated the active faculties' to produce change.[95] The *Considerations* went even further by arguing that progress was not opposed to because it actually implied order (a testament, perhaps, to Coleridge's enduring influence).[96] Any proposal for reform, Mill argued, must take into account the variability of social conditions as illustrated by history. Seen as the 'gradual evolution' of humanity, the historical record showed not just that institutions changed, but that those changes both shaped and reflected a nation's character.[97]

While this idea was not uniquely the Coleridgians', it demonstrated to a sceptical English audience that history could be interpreted scientifically. In France, by contrast, there was an established tradition of social science that began with Montesquieu and Rousseau; found modern champions in Tocqueville, Comte, and the *Doctrinaires*; and which foregrounded the laws of social development and the contexts in which political institutions emerged. The Coleridgians' principal achievement had been to rescue England from its 'Cimmerian darkness' regarding the 'views of general history, which have been received throughout the Continent of Europe for the last twenty or thirty years'.[98] They were not as original, perhaps, as the German or French – Comte was just as insistent that social questions implied both static and dynamic elements, and Saint-Simon was arguably the first to punctuate Mill's thought with a grammar of historical relativism – but they played an important role in Mill's intellectual separation of the eighteenth and nineteenth centuries. Like Guizot and Niebuhr, they questioned the extent to which a belief in progress precluded what Coleridge called a 'lively sympathy' with 'the generous actions recorded in history', so that past institutions retained their value as ideas if not as timeless forms.[99] Bentham, by contrast, had failed to see in history anything beyond the universal principle of self-interest, the hyperbolic simplicity of which was a frequent source of disagreement between a young Mill and Sterling, and which informed the *Logic's* critique of Bentham.[100]

---

[95] *CW*, X, p. 140.   [96] Ibid., XIX, p. 373.
[97] See Robson, *The improvement of mankind*, p. 71.   [98] *CW*, X, p. 140n.
[99] S. T. Coleridge, *The friend* (London: Gale and Curtis, 1812), pp. 306–307.
[100] *CW*, VIII, p. 891. See F. Rosen, *Mill* (Oxford: Oxford University Press, 2013), pp. 57–58.

Two things emerge from this analysis. The first is that Mill saw the Coleridgians as representatives of a continental aliveness to history. The second is that, for precisely this reason, he praised other English thinkers who popularised German and French historians. His reception of the liberal Anglicans illustrates this well. Like Mill and Grote, the liberal Anglicans drew heavily on Niebuhr and German *Historismus*, in addition to Coleridge, Kant, and the Cambridge Platonists.[101] Thomas Arnold, Arthur Stanley (1815–1881), Connop Thirlwall, and H. H. Milman (1791–1868) broke with eighteenth-century empiricism by outlining a cyclical philosophy of history, which allowed them to think analogously and chart humanity's divine unfolding.[102] Since all societies underwent similar stages of transcendental development, expressed anthropomorphically as the phases of birth, life, and death, it was possible, they contended, to compare two societies regardless of their outward differences.[103] This naturalised conception of progress, which they traced to Niebuhr and Niebuhr's reading of Vico, challenged the materialist theory of historical development posited by the Scottish political economists. Whereas they had focused on the outer dynamics of improvement, Niebuhr proposed to study the 'inner dynamic of a nation's life' – its moral, emotional, and aesthetic transformations – and thus to restore history's ethical and affective contents.[104]

The avowed Hellenist Arthur Stanley claimed that it was the historian's duty to 'judge whether a nation is in an early or an advanced stage . . . [and that one could therefore] discover a *modern history* in the ages of Greece and Rome'.[105] This allowed Stanley and other liberal Anglicans to make political moves that Mill could not. Their cyclical understanding of progress made it easier to learn lessons by way of analogy. Classical antiquity, for example, exhibited a complete cycle of development in which civilisation's birth, life, and death was represented in microcosm, to the benefit of civilisations entering the same stage of development. Thirlwall put it like this: 'a clear exhibition of the course of events' is provided not merely by 'chronological sequence' but by their 'outward aspect', 'real nature', and 'intrinsic relations'.[106] Carlyle in *Past and Present* (1843) also questioned the linearity of historical time by presenting it as 'an

---

[101] Coleridge met Niebuhr in 1828: C. J. Murray (ed.), *Encyclopedia of the Romantic era* (London: Routledge, 2004), I, pp. 807–808.
[102] See Forbes, *Liberal Anglican idea of history*, p. 16.   [103] Ibid., pp. 16–28.
[104] Murray, *Encyclopedia of the Romantic era*, p. 807.
[105] Forbes, *Liberal Anglican idea of history*, p. 47. My emphasis.
[106] Thirlwall, *Remains*, III, p. 280.

ever-living, ever-working chaos of being'.[107] The future, otherwise unbounded and uncertain, became suddenly explicable, hence Arnold's famous assertion that 'the largest portion of that history which we commonly call ancient is practically modern, as it describes society in a stage analogous to that in which it now is'.[108]

While Arnold 'showed few and faint symptoms' of moving beyond the second stage of historical enquiry, Mill considered his *Lectures on Modern History* (1842) to be 'instructive' and his personality 'enlightened and liberal'.[109] The attempt to realise a science of history was certainly welcome, but there were reasons why Arnold and presumably Coleridge, too, belonged to the second and not the third stage of historical enquiry. It had something to do with what, in Mill's eyes, a science of history should look like. The liberal Anglicans expressed in abstract metaphysical terms the divine forces of natural order, while the third stage of historical enquiry searched for causes of a non-divine or metaphysical origin, in accordance with Comtean positivism; furthermore, Mill in the *Logic* rejected their Vichian view of history as *corsi e ricorsi* – as revolving 'in an orbit' – because it sacrificed 'the idea of a trajectory of progress'.[110] After all, the analogy between history and human life, when pursued to its logical extent, suggested that society was destined to become senile and over-civilised.[111]

Mill was less dyspeptic, but he did share Coleridge's and Arnold's doubts about the march of mind and the infinite potential of commercial society.[112] Beyond that, however, he was unconvinced that 'bodies politic', like 'bodies natural', tend 'spontaneously to decay'.[113] The decay of natural bodies could be 'distinctly traced to the natural progress of those very changes of structure which, in their earlier stages, constitute its growth to maturity: while in the body politic the progress of those changes cannot, generally speaking, have any effect but the still further continuance of growth'. 'Bodies politic die', he concluded, 'but it is of disease, or violent death: they have no old age'.[114] The Vichians had overegged the analogy between living organisms and the figurative organism of the state, prompting Mill to scrutinise their theory of human nature. While the liberal Anglicans testified to the uniformity of man, drawing their proof from

---

[107] See T. Carlyle (ed. C. R. Vanden Bossche), *Historical essays* (Berkeley: University of California Press, 2002), p. 7; F. L. van Holthoon, *The road to utopia: a study of John Stuart Mill's social thought* (Assen: Van Gorcum, 1971), p. 40.
[108] T. Arnold, *The history of the Peloponnesian War by Thucydides: with notes, chiefly historical and geographical* [1830] (London: John Henry and James Parker, 1861), I, p. 522.
[109] *CW*, XX, p. 226; Mill to d'Eichthal, 20 November 1831: *CW*, XII, p. 92.
[110] Ibid., VIII, p. 913.   [111] Preyer, *Bentham, Coleridge and the science of history*, p. 37.
[112] Ibid., p. 39.   [113] *CW*, VIII, p. 796.   [114] Ibid.

the unvarying laws of human agency, Mill pointed to a dynamic relationship between human actions and the material, social, and intellectual
circumstances in which they were performed: 'mankind', he argued,
'have [sic] not one universal character, but there exist universal laws of
the formation of character'.[115] He praised Vico for tying 'the succession of
historical events' to 'fixed laws' – this, after all, was precisely what a science
of history should do – but he denied that those laws told a providential
story about civilisation's growth and decay.[116]

Mill, then, used the Germano-Coleridgians to reassess the intellectual
legacies of Benthamism and the eighteenth century, and to underscore to an
English audience the importance of studying history scientifically, to show,
as Coleridge put it, that 'general principles are to the facts' as 'the root and
sap of a tree [are] to its leaves'.[117] Mill's openness to speculative historical
enquiry was a far cry from his earlier position, but Coleridge only consolidated an already deepening commitment. The essay on Coleridge was
written primarily for an English audience whose aversion to speculative
historical enquiry Mill had noted in reviews of Tocqueville from 1835 and
1840.[118] The Coleridgians were nineteenth-century balms for eighteenth-
century wounds. They restored history to the forefront of political science,
but Mill was clear that the origins of this new history – scientific, sociological, and positive – as against the old history – antiquarian, enumerative,
and metaphysical – belonged not to England and the Coleridgians but to
France and its philosophical school: to Saint-Simon, Comte, Guizot,
Michelet, and Tocqueville.

Spirits of the Age

Saint-Simon in his *Mémoire sur la science de l'homme* (1813) conjured the
ghost of Francis Bacon, who appeared to the emperor Napoleon as
a paradigm of *l'historien politique. L'historien politique* treated politics as
a science of observation and history as a chain of causes and effects, and
not, as Napoleon had believed, as objects of national pride.[119] The ghost
whispered that the past, when studied scientifically, disclosed the secrets of
the future.

---

[115] Ibid., p. 864.   [116] Ibid., p. 913.
[117] From *The statesman's manual* (1816): S. T. Coleridge, *The complete works* (New York: Harper and
Brothers, 1854), I, p. 426.
[118] *CW*, XVIII, p. 159.
[119] On the idea of *l'historien politique*, see *Le producteur* (Paris: Chez Sautelet, 1826), III, p. 442.

L'histoire, en effet, sous son rapport scientifique, n'est pas encore sortie des langes de l'enfance. Cette importante branche de nos connaissances n'a encore d'autre existence quelle celle d'une collection de faits plus ou moins bien constatés. Ces faits ne son liés par aucune théorie, ils ne sont point enchaînés dans l'ordre des conséquences; ainsi l'histoire est encore un guide insuffisant pur les Rois ainsi que pour leurs sujets; elle ne donne ni aux uns ni aux autres les moyens de conclure *ce qui arrivera,* de *ce qui est arrivé.* Il n'existe encore que des histoires nationales dont les auteurs se sont proposé pour principal objet de faire valoir les qualités de leurs compatriotes . . . Aucun historien ne s'est encore placé au point du vue général; aucun n'a fait encore l'histoire de l'espèce . . .[120]

It was appropriate that Saint-Simon should be heard through another's voice. In the years following his death in 1825, his disciples split into two factions, one of which was led by Barthélemy Enfantin (1796–1864) and another by Olinde Rodrigues (1795–1851) and Gustave d'Eichthal.[121] Collectively they were known as the Saint-Simonians, whose writings influenced much of Mill's political thinking in the late 1820s and early 1830s, culminating in the publication between 1830 and 1831 of his articles on 'The Spirit of the Age'. D'Eichthal sent him editions of *Le producteur* (1825–1826) and *Le globe* (1824–1832), the literary organs of Saint-Simonianism which disseminated to a reading public its programme for a new humanist mysticism.[122] The Saint-Simonians attacked more fulsomely than their mentor the liberal economics of Smith, Jean-Baptiste Say (1767–1832), and Thomas Malthus (1766–1834), to whom they traced the ideological origins of a selfishness now writ large on the economies of Western Europe. They looked forward to a time when the universal brotherhood of love would displace the scourges of nationalism, Catholicism, irrationalism, obscurantism, and idleness.[123] While Mill shared the need for a new terrestrial ethics tailored to the problems of the age, he limited their influence in the *Autobiography* 'solely' to their 'philosophy of history'.[124] He agreed more with the form and substance of their

[120] H. Saint-Simon, *Œuvres de Saint-Simon* (Bruxelles: Van Meenen, 1859), II, pp. 195–196.
[121] For an account of the Saint-Simonian movement, see F. Manuel, *The prophets of Paris: Turgot, Condorcet, Saint-Simon, Fourier, and Comte* (New York: Harper, 1962), pp. 149–195; G. G. Iggers, *The cult of authority: the political philosophy of the Saint-Simonians* (Leiden: Martinus Nijhoff, 1970); P. Pilbeam, *Saint-Simonians in nineteenth-century France: from free love to Algeria* (London: Palgrave Macmillan, 2014).
[122] The phrase 'humanist mysticism' belongs to Frank Manuel: *Prophets of Paris*, pp. 172, 193.
[123] See J. Tresch, *The romantic machine: utopian science and technology after Napoleon* (Chicago: University of Chicago Press, 2012), p. 198.
[124] This comment appeared in an early draft of the *Autobiography* but was subsequently omitted: *CW,* I, p. 174.

critiques than with their normative proposals, a distinction which also applies to his reception of Comte. What resonated with him, rather, was the Saint-Simonians' innovative use of history as a tool of social criticism; their rejection of theological and metaphysical doctrines; and their ambition to restore society's moral and intellectual unity, which, as a discourse of post-Enlightenment, chimed with Romantic disillusionments with the eighteenth century.

Mill's reception of the Saint-Simonians took place against a changing political backdrop, and the fall of Charles X in August 1830 spurred him excitedly into action. He went immediately to France where he met Say and the Marquis de Lafayette (1757–1834), and after returning he commented feverishly on French affairs for *The Examiner* and *Monthly Repository*. The domestic political situation was never far from his mind.[125] The connections between the Polignac ministry and Wellington's Tory government undoubtedly hastened the latter's fall, with public opinion shifting rapidly in the direction of reform.[126] However, Mill's interest in the Saint-Simonians went further than immediate political events. The belief that Europe had outgrown its old social and political institutions had already led him to contemplate, *inter alia*, how a new intellectual leadership might emerge from the wreckage of the old.[127] This aspect of Mill's thought has been well served.[128] Here, however, I want to focus on the Saint-Simonians' historical relativism, with the hope of placing Mill's own relativism in its intellectual context.

Of all the Saint-Simonians Mill was closest to d'Eichthal.[129] Their correspondence suggests a reticence on Mill's part to unreservedly embrace their project of social reform, although he confessed in a letter from 1829 that there was much 'to approve and admire' in their 'school'. First, he accepted the 'necessity of a *pouvoir spirituel*' or, as Saint-Simon put it, the

---

[125] See G. Varouxakis, 'French radicalism through the eyes of John Stuart Mill', *History of European Ideas* 30.4 (2004), pp. 433–461.

[126] R. Quinalt, 'The French Revolution of 1830 and parliamentary reform', *History* 79 (1994), pp. 377–393.

[127] Mill found it ironic that 'this particular time, in which there are fewer great intellects . . . should be the precise time at which everybody is cackling about the progress of intelligence'. Mill to Carlyle, 17 July 1832: *CW*, XII, p. 112. See B. Knights, *The idea of the clerisy in nineteenth-century Britain* (Cambridge: Cambridge University Press, 1978), p. 7.

[128] See, for example, Mueller, *Mill and French thought*, pp. 48–92; Robson, *The improvement of mankind*, p. 76; Pickering, *Auguste Comte: an intellectual biography*, I, p. 514; Levin, *Mill on civilisation and barbarism*, p. 5; H. Saint-Simon (trans. G. G. Iggers), *The doctrine of Saint-Simon: an exposition, first year, 1828–9* (Boston: Beacon Press, 1958), p. xlvi.

[129] For further details see *CW*, I, p. 172.

necessity of reorganising 'le pouvoir spirituel sur de nouvelles bases'.[130] History for Saint-Simon was driven by intellectual, national, class, and interpersonal antagonisms. Progress, therefore, implied the decline of these antagonisms and the concomitant rise of natural productive functions, much in the same way that Aristotle in *Nicomachean Ethics* (1.7) made rational activity the defining function of human beings.[131] This optimism was counterbalanced by a perceived lack of spiritual and intellectual leadership. Saint-Simon railed against the entropies of modern industrial society – its acquisitiveness, disregard for the poor, and undermining of true science – and the dissolution of common goals, a sentiment which Mill expressed to Sterling as the breakdown of 'individual sympathy'.[132] Saint-Simon's final work, *Le noveau christianisme* (1825), placed *le pouvoir spirituel* at the centre of a new social equipoise, freed from unfettered capital, false science, and idleness.[133]

The Saint-Simonians' political thought was at least superficially compatible with Bentham's and the Philosophic Radicals', but while Mill saw the need for a new *pouvoir spirituel*, he rejected the messianic language with which they declared a new Christianity, mindful of England's conservative attitudes towards religion.[134] He also rejected the Saint-Simonians' vision for a reconstructed industrialism in which society was to be divided into three classes of scientists, artists, and workers.[135] The Saint-Simonian future seemed to him neither inevitable nor particularly desirable, but he embraced their philosophy of history as a tool with which to historicise and critique the present. The events of 1830, when placed in this context, accentuated the liminal quality of the age and the importance of developing new ideas to replace the embattled old. This was the historical vantage point from which the Saint-Simonians rationalised their programme for reform, and Mill in a letter to d'Eichthal commended their distinction between *la partie critique* and *la partie organique* because it anticipated

[130] Mill to d'Eichthal, 7 November 1829: *CW*, XII, p. 40; H. Saint-Simon (ed. O. Rodrigues), *Œuvres de Saint-Simon* (Paris: Capelle, libraire-éditeur, 1841), p. 182.

[131] See F. Manuel, *The new world of Henri Saint-Simon* (Cambridge: Harvard University Press, 1956), p. 317.

[132] Mill to Sterling, 15 April 1829: *CW*, XII, p. 30.

[133] See H. Saint-Simon, *Noveau chrstianisme, dialogues entre un conservateur et un novateur* (Paris: Bossange Père, 1825), p. 56.

[134] See Saint-Simon, *Noveau christianisme*, p. 3. On Mill's reservations about the Saint-Simonians' *noveau christianisme*, see Raeder, *John Stuart Mill and the religion of humanity*, p. 240.

[135] Before any such reorganisation could take place, one had to remove all 'sinister interests' from the political class: Mill to d'Eichthal, 7 November 1829: *CW*, XII, p. 40.

a new social order.[136] His *Autobiography* recalled the influence of their 'connected view' of 'human progress' and

> their division of all history into organic periods and critical periods. During the organic periods (they said) mankind accept with firm conviction some positive creed, claiming jurisdiction over all their actions ... Under its influence they make all the progress compatible with the creed, and finally outgrow it; when a period follows of criticism and negation, in which mankind lose their old convictions without acquiring any new ones, of a general or authoritative character, except the conviction that the old are false.[137]

The distinction between *époques critiques* and *époques organiques* was increasingly prevalent in French and German thought. Charles Fourier (1772–1837) in his *Théorie des quatres mouvements* (1808) had made a striking case for the ephemeral nature of commercial society, whose displacement by a new industrialism he saw as both inevitable and imminent.[138] Mill himself conceded that the periodical alternation between organic unity and critical disunity could be traced along a different path, to Fichte's *Die Grundzüge des gegenwärtigen Zeitalters* (1806), which he had not then read.[139] It was the Saint-Simonians, however, who consolidated their historical relativism as a political position, and to which they 'paid more attention & attached more importance than other philosophers'.[140] Comte and the Saint-Simonians proved that political truth was 'strictly relative, implying as its correlative a given state or situation of society', and Mill in letters to Sterling relayed the intensity with which he came to share this view, pointing out its uses in the fight against 'practical Toryism'.[141] The Saint-Simonians guarded against the appeal to historical authority, first, by approaching the past on its own terms, and, second, by challenging the ways in which politicians turned for guidance to the 'inanimate corpses of dead political & religious systems'.[142]

The Saint-Simonians were the perfect foil for Mill's eclecticism. Their historical relativism allowed him to argue, as he did in a letter to Sterling, that the *pouvoir spirituel* should reflect the 'wants & tendencies' of the age,

---

[136] Ibid., p. 42.   [137] Ibid., I, p. 171.

[138] On the connections between Saint-Simon and Fourier, see J. Beecher, *Charles Fourier: the visionary and his world* (Berkeley: University of California Press, 1986), p. 413.

[139] *CW*, I, p. 171. See J. G. Fichte (trans. W. R. Smith), *Characteristics of the present age* (London: John Chapman, 1847), pp. 2, 131.

[140] *CW*, I, p. 171. Mill mentioned Herder and von Humboldt as early theorists of historical relativism. See S. Sikka, *Herder on humanity and cultural difference: enlightened relativism* (Cambridge: Cambridge University Press, 2011), pp. 126–127.

[141] *CW*, I, p. 323; Mill to Sterling, 20 October 1831, *CW*, XII, pp. 84–85.   [142] Ibid., p. 84.

even if it fell short of an ideal standard. He was adamant that the 'national *clerisy*' ought to shake 'firm convictions & feelings of duty' only when they could furnish 'an effectual substitute'. In France, therefore, where 'Christianity has lost a hold on men's minds', a Christian 'would be positively less fit than a St. Simonian' to 'form part of a national church', whereas in England the opposite was true.[143] As he put it to d'Eichthal, the Saint-Simonians had showed that even institutions like the Catholic church 'may yet, at a particular stage in the progress of the human mind, have not only been highly useful but absolutely indispensable' to its 'ulterior stage of improvement'.[144] Without these 'enlarged views of the history of mankind' there could be

> no possibility of viewing or judging past times with candour, or trying them by any standard but that of the present. And yet, he who does not do this, will judge the present as ill as the past. For surely at every present epoch there are many things which would be good for that epoch, though not good for the being man, at every epoch, nor perhaps at any other than that one . . . . Every age contains countries, every country contains men, who are in every possible state of civilisation, from the lowest of all, to the highest which mankind have reached in that age, or in that country. Yet one hardly meets with a single man who does not habitually think & talk as if whatever was good or bad for one portion of these countries or of these individuals was good or bad for all the other portions. It is very unlikely that any person who is imbued with the spirit of the St. Simon school, should fall into this error.[145]

Mill's foray into Saint-Simonianism complemented his reading of Coleridge.[146] Together they convinced him that 'political institutions' were 'relative, not absolute', and that 'different stages of human progress not only will have, but ought to have, different institutions'.[147] Whereas once he had regarded representative democracy as an absolute ideal, as had his father and the later Bentham, he now considered it to be 'a question of time, place, and circumstance'.[148] Nowhere was this more evident than in his essays *On Liberty* and *Considerations*, which made sharp distinctions between European civility and non-European barbarism, premised ostensibly on consultations of history. As he put it in the *Considerations*, the doctrine of relativism justified a benevolent colonial despotism to set in motion the liberty of the colonised. 'The last age', by contrast, routinely

---

[143] Mill to Sterling, 20 October 1831, *CW*, XII, p. 76.
[144] Mill to d'Eichthal, 7 November 1829: *CW*, XII, p. 41.   [145] Ibid.
[146] B. Kinzer, 'British critics of utilitarianism' in Macleod and Miller, *A companion to Mill*, pp. 95–96.
[147] Mill, *CW*, I, p. 169.   [148] Ibid., p. 176.

claimed 'representative democracy for England and France by arguments which would equally have proved it the only fit form of government for Bedouins or Malays'.[149]

Evidence for Mill's relativism is spread throughout his writings, not least in his Saint-Simonian articles on 'The Spirit of the Age' and *A System of Logic*.[150] Less clear is whether this relativism solved, or even addressed, the limits of induction which he had outlined in 1827. It is difficult to arrive at an answer, not least because the Saint-Simonians showed scant interest in logic. But it is possible to make some tentative points. In their *Doctrine de Saint-Simon* (1830), the Saint-Simonians decried the use of historical analogies and 'les leçons' which they were called upon to produce, since 'les mêmes faits pouvaient toujours se reproduire identiquement à toutes les époques'.[151] Comparative approaches to history were illusory because they approached the past as 'un arsenal en désordre' which could support any number of political opinions. Citing Saint-Simon's *memoire* to Napoleon from 1815, they argued that true philosophers of history took as their subject 'la vie de l'espèce humain', which necessitated an enlarged, even cosmic view of progress. To contemplate the decline into barbarism of once civilised nations – of Egypt, Athens, and Rome – was to see progress as the product of accidental causes: of world-historical figures, scientific discoveries, and so on. This chaotic picture of history could not meet the conditions for a scientific theory, whose goal was to understand how and to what extent 'l'état de société' precipitated these political and intellectual transformations, or how accidental causes could be distinguished scientifically from the trends of natural progress.[152]

The Saint-Simonians anticipated Comte by emphasising the totality of the historical process, conceiving it, like the Coleridgians, as an evolving organism. Just as Mill in 1827 rejected the logic of historical experiments, the Saint-Simonians considered it impossible to recreate states of society once they had given way to new ones. When Mill in 1865 assessed the legacy of Comte's positivism, he argued that the 'vulgar mode of using history', which looked for 'parallel cases, as if any cases were parallel', had been 'irrevocably discredited'.[153] There could be no return to a golden past. Institutions and beliefs were endogenous to the needs of the age, which was why the Saint-Simonians defended the ecclesiastical regimes of the Middle Ages. Their idea of history as holistic and progressive led to a parting of

---

[149] Ibid., XIX, p. 394.   [150] Ibid., XXII, p. 257; VIII, p. 938.
[151] A. Bazard et al., *Doctrine de Saint-Simon. Exposition.* (Paris: Bureau de l'organisateur, 1831), p. 50.
[152] Ibid., p. 52.   [153] *CW*, X, p. 308.

ways with Condorcet, whose emphasis on reason had neglected the affective, devotional, and irrational aspects of human life.[154] Although the Saint-
Simonians imagined a universal mind working itself out historically, they
rejected the attempt to measure and evaluate this process according to
a universal standard of reason. Progress was an intricate choreography of
the rational and the irrational, the organic and the critical.

I have touched already on Mill's misgivings about the analogy between
organic entities and progress. Social phenomena, he maintained, were not
subject to the natural laws of growth and decay, even though the methods
of physiology helped the social scientist to appreciate the laws of consensus,
that is, why the appearance of one social element usually implied the
presence or absence of others. The elision between natural and organic
bodies encouraged a fatalism according to which societies at similar stages
of development would be expected to exhibit similar or even identical
characteristics; as he put it to d'Eichthal in 1829, however, 'nations, & men
nearly in an equally advanced stage of civilisation, may yet be very different
in character'. Although changes 'may take place in a man or a nation,
which are neither steps forward nor backward, but steps to one side', the
Saint-Simonians seemed to think 'that the mind of man, by a sort of
fatality or necessity, grows & unfolds its different faculties always in one
particular order, like the body: & that therefore we must be always either
standing still, or advancing, or retrograding'.[155]

Mill in his articles on 'The Spirit of the Age' questioned the extent to
which progress took on necessary forms, but he also guarded against
inductive philosophies of history that failed to acknowledge similarities
between individual nations' progress:

> I say, those who have endeavoured to erect an inductive philosophy of
> history, may be charged with having taken insufficient account of the
> qualities in which mankind in all ages and nations are alike, their attention
> being unduly engrossed by the differences; but there is an error on the other
> side, to which those are peculiarly liable, who build their philosophy of
> politics upon what they term the universal principles of human nature. Such
> persons often form their judgments, *in particular cases*, as if, because there
> are universal principles of human nature, they imagined that all are such
> which they find to be true universally of the people of their own age and

[154] See D. Williams, *Condorcet and modernity* (Cambridge: Cambridge University Press, 2004), pp. 4,
49, 70–79.
[155] Mill to d'Eichthal, 7 November 1829: *CW*, XII, p. 43. In his essay on America from 1836, he argued
that '[e]ach nation, and the same nation in every different age, exhibits a portion of mankind, under
a set of influences . . . more or less peculiar': *CW*, XVIII, p. 94.

country . . . [even though] each [age] possesses, along with those invariable tendencies, others which are changeable, and peculiarly its own; and in no age, as civilisation advances, are the prevailing tendencies exactly the same as in the preceding age, nor do those tendencies act under precisely the same combination of external circumstances.[156]

Mill's third way was to argue that the historical process was driven by both 'general' and 'changeable' tendencies, and that the 'progress of civilisation' was at once 'necessary' and varied.[157] This, to put it mildly, was constructively ambiguous. He confessed to d'Eichthal, who pressed him regularly on his commitment to Saint-Simonianism, that the English distrusted 'general views' even when they expressed 'the most obvious truths', a problem which he framed to Tocqueville in 1840 as a contrast between England's 'microscopic' and France's 'telescopic' view of social phenomena.[158] Given these strategic pressures, Mill urged the Saint-Simonians to emphasise the development of the 'nation in question' and play down the effects of a universal historical process, further illustrating the tensions between his individualising and progressive historicism.[159] The first 'step in the investigation of practical political truths', he argued, was 'to ascertain what is the state into which, in the natural order of the advancement of civilisation *the nation in question* will next come' and then 'to facilitate the transition to this state'.[160]

These reservations aside, Mill's encounter with the Saint-Simonians marked a departure from his earlier views. The philosophy of history now occupied a role, however vague, in his architecture of social science. While his scepticism regarding historical analogies persisted, he began to relax the boundaries between historical and political science. It was precisely this scepticism that drew him to the Saint-Simonians, whose philosophy of history stressed the totality of the historical process and the poverty of historical analogies. We find Mill in 'The Spirit of the Age' engaging in historical analysis to anticipate future states of society, which, in the context of the early 1830s, involved lifting England from its 'crisis of transition' and returning once again 'to a natural state of society'.[161] More than that, he hoped to combine the 'best qualities of the critical with the best of the organic periods' so that the accumulative wisdom of past ages

---

[156] Ibid., XXII, pp. 256–257. My emphasis.   [157] Ibid., p. 233.
[158] Mill to d'Eichthal, 9 February 1830: *CW*, XII, p. 48; Mill to Tocqueville, 30 December 1840: *CW*, XIII, p. 458.
[159] As he put it to Comte in February 1842, 'l'existence des véritables conditions du progrès continu a été prouvée a posteriori par l'ensemble de leur [the nations'] histoire': *CW*, XIII, p. 502.
[160] Mill to d'Eichthal, 7 November 1829: *CW*, XII, p. 43. My emphasis.   [161] Ibid., XXII, p. 316.

was not 'periodically thrown off and replaced by others'. By combining the incredulity of the critical age with the harmoniousness of the organic, he looked to end the historical undulations which plunged societies intermittently into crisis.[162]

Towards a Logic of Progress

Mill never became the committed Saint-Simonian that d'Eichthal had hoped for, confessing in a letter from 1831 that he was 'not a Saint-Simonist nor at all likely to become one'.[163] The movement effectively ended in 1832. Enfantin, Charles Duveyrier (1803–1866), and Michel Chevalier (1806–1879) were brought before a court in Ménilmontant on a litany of charges, after which they turned their attention away from the French metropole and towards the colonial civilising mission. Mill at any rate was sceptical of their increasing sentimentalism and the monastic intensity with which they pursued the revolutionary cause.[164] As he put it in a letter to Carlyle from 1834, the 'intermediate state' of his character, which lasted approximately from 1827 to 1832, had given way to a new 'sincerity' that looked more favourably on the utilitarian tradition in which he was raised.[165] Mill preserved the Saint-Simonian distinction between critical and organic epochs and their conception of *pouvoir spirituel*, but even then he stressed the limits of their approach. He wrote to d'Eichthal and Duveyrier in May 1832 to clarify his objections to their social doctrines, which had 'much to learn, in political economy from the English . . . and in the philosophy of history, literature, and the arts, from the Germans'.[166] Whereas the Germans had preserved the sanctity of historical facts, theirs was a speculative rather than a scientific philosophy of history, the theoretical realisation of which Mill attributed to Saint-Simon's former student, Auguste Comte.[167]

Mill first became aware of Comte in the late 1820s and obtained through d'Eichthal some of his earliest writings.[168] He wrote to Comte for the first

---

[162] Ibid., I, p. 172. Central to this balance of the organic and the critical was Guizot's idea of systematic antagonism, which he considered the 'only condition under which stability and progressiveness can be permanently reconciled to one another': *CW*, XX, p. 269.

[163] Ibid., XII, p. 70.   [164] Mueller, *John Stuart Mill and French thought*, p. 89.

[165] Mill to Carlyle, 12 January 1834: *CW*, XII, pp. 204–208.   [166] Ibid., p. 109.

[167] 'Historical facts', he argued in the review of Michelet from 1844, 'are hardly yet felt to be, like other natural phenomena, amenable to scientific laws': *CW*, XX, p. 260.

[168] On Comte's influence in England, see T. R. Wright, *The religion of humanity: the impact of Comtean positivism on Victorian England* (Cambridge: Cambridge University Press, 1986); C. Kent, *Brains and numbers: elitism, Comtism, and democracy in mid-Victorian England*

time in November 1841 and even delayed the publication of the *Logic* to accommodate the final volumes of the *Cours de philosophie positive* (1830–1842), whose influence on Book VI has been widely acknowledged.[169] In the heady years of their correspondence Mill and Comte revelled in each other's contempt for *apriorism* and their mutual desire to scientifically transform the study of social phenomena.[170] Whereas the likes of Whewell and John Herschel (1792–1871) had only hinted at the idea, Comte in the *Traité de politique positive* (1824) had given Mill 'une forte secousse', rousing him from the dogmatism of 'la section Benthamiste'.[171] He recalled in the *Autobiography* that Comte's ideas 'harmonised well' with his 'existing notions' and gave them a 'scientific shape', although questions linger as to whether Mill downplayed Comte's influence after disavowing his politics.[172] His influence can be traced nonetheless. To the 'general idea' of Saint-Simonianism Comte added 'something much more definitive and instructive': an account of positivism's emergence from the dead intellectual forms of theology and metaphysics.[173] Comte, in turn, hoped that the *Logic* would facilitate the transition to positivism by placing the study of society on a scientific footing.[174]

Their relationship soured in December 1845 and ended for good in 1847. Comte had repeatedly pestered Mill, Grote, and William Molesworth (1810–1855) for money – he lived off a modest stipend as an entrance examiner at the Polytechnique – and expressed increasingly dogmatic views, turning eventually to Richard Congreve (1818–1899), Frederic Harrison (1831–1923), and Edward Spencer Beesly (1831–1915) to spread positive philosophy abroad.[175] While Mill and Comte's early correspondence gestured at significant intellectual differences, they remained

---

(Toronto: University of Toronto Press, 1978); L. Krieger, *Time's reasons: philosophies of history old and new* (Chicago: Chicago University Press, 1989), pp. 84–85.

[169] *CW*, XIII, p. 567.

[170] Mill continued to wage war on the *a priori* school well into the 1860s: Bain to Mill, 18 January 1863 in 'Hutzler collection', HUT. 004, ff. 13–14. Grote did likewise: Grote to Mill, 6 November 1866 in 'Hutzler', HUT. 004, f. 87.

[171] Mill to Comte, 8 November 1841: *CW*, XIII, p. 489.

[172] In subsequent editions of the *Logic*, Mill downplayed Comte's influence by excising several references to the *Cours*. Stuart Jones, meanwhile, has observed that Tocqueville may have been a more significant influence on Mill's historical method: H. S. Jones, '"The true Baconian and Newtonian method": Tocqueville's place in the formation of Mill's System of logic', *History of European Ideas* 25.3 (1999), pp. 153–161.

[173] *CW*, I, p. 173. D'Eichthal in 1863 remembered 'la politique positive d'Auguste Comte, que je vous apportais en 1828': 'Hutzler collection', HUT. 004, f. 56.

[174] Comte to Mill, 16 May 1843 in Haac (ed.), *Correspondence*, p. 154.

[175] *CW*, X, p. 329. On the financial fallout with Comte, see a letter from Molesworth to Mill, 17 September 1845, 'Hutzler collection', HUT. 004, f. 126.

confident of reconciliation in the spirit of positive science.[176] As their
relationship deteriorated, however, these differences became increasingly
pronounced.[177] While they agreed on the laws of social dynamics, where
history held 'first place', they disagreed on the place in social statics of
phrenology, political economy, psychology, sexual equality, and individual
liberty.[178] The cleavages between an intellectual and a social positivism
grew ever wider, with Mill – and Émile Littré (1801–1881) in France –
becoming increasingly concerned by Comte's attempt in the aftermath of
1848 to establish an Occidental Positivist Republic.[179] Mill went as far as to
denounce Comte's *Système de politique positive* (1851–1854) as the 'complet-
est system of spiritual and temporal despotism, which ever yet emanated
from a human brain'.[180] Comte's republicanism became increasingly sacri-
ficial and despotic, and Mill could only watch on in horror as Comte
committed 'liberticide' against the freedom of thought and conscience.[181]
By the time *Auguste Comte and Positivism* was published in 1865, his
admiration for Comte extended only to his early work on the classification
of the sciences; the laws of social dynamics; and the outline of a new
epistemic organon.[182] While there were no

> fundamental errors in M. Comte's general conception of history ... [there was
> no] scientific connexion between his theoretical explanation of the past progress
> of society, and his proposals for future improvement. The proposals are not, as
> we might expect, recommended as that towards which human society has been
> tending and working through the whole of history. It is thus that thinkers have
> usually proceeded, who formed theories for the future, grounded on historical
> analysis of the past ... We do not find M. Comte supporting his recommenda-
> tions by a similar line of argument. They rest as completely, each on its separate
> reasons of supposed utility, as with philosophers who, like Bentham, theorise
> on politics without any historical basis at all.[183]

Mill dismissed Comte's later speculations as 'false and misleading' but
continued to commend the *Cours* for its 'essentially sound view of

---

[176] On their differences, see a letter from Comte to Mill, 4 March 1842: Haac (ed.),
Correspondence, p. 55.
[177] Pickering, *Auguste Comte*, II, p. 62.
[178] See Mill to Comte, 30 October 1843: Haac (ed.), *Correspondence*, pp. 197–198. Their underlying
disagreements reached a crescendo in a debate over the psychology and social status of women:
Guillin, *Auguste Comte and John Stuart Mill on sexual equality*, pp. 149–157.
[179] See Pickering, *Auguste Comte*, I, pp. 101, 288, 322; II, p. 332. See also R. C. Scharff, *Comte after
positivism* (Cambridge: Cambridge University Press, 1995), p. 6.
[180] *CW*, I, p. 221.   [181] Mill to Harriet Taylor, 15 January 1855: *CW*, XIV, p. 294.
[182] As Frederick Rosen pointed out, *Auguste Comte and positivism* provided Mill with an opportunity to
subtly revise his relationship with Comte, playing down his earlier admiration: *Mill*, p. 118.
[183] *CW*, X, pp. 322, 324–325.

philosophy'.[184] Its fourth, fifth, and sixth volumes, published between 1839 and 1842, were especially pertinent to Mill's discussion in the *Logic* of the epistemology and methods of social science. The problem was that Comte, unlike Tocqueville, had failed to scientifically connect his analyses of past, present, and future, despite the 'theoretical explanation' of progress presented in the *Cours*. The *Système* was not a work of political sociology. Rather than using history to suggest or verify political truths, it prescribed a social order whose despotism was matched only by the 'rigid' disciplinarians of antiquity.[185] The *Cours*, by contrast, ordered historical time according to the development of scientific knowledge, which Comte divided into six branches: mathematics, astronomy, physics, chemistry, biology, and sociology.[186] Each branch progressed through a theological, metaphysical, and positive stage; mathematics was the first to become fully positive, whereas sociology, because of its complexity and dependence on the others, was last. From these transformations history acquired its progressive shape. Over time, Comte hoped, the subjective worlds of theology and metaphysics would give way to positive knowledge, just as the military way of life would give way to the industrial. The process was already underway. Shifts in intellectual consciousness had made possible a new form of society, whose levers were to be pulled by a new spiritual power, the secular priesthood, which Thomas Huxley (1825–1895) famously called 'Catholicism minus God'.[187] The feudal order was dead, and so too were the revolutionary dreams of the previous century. Positive knowledge required positive politics.

Mill agreed with Comte that intellectual development was 'the predominant agency in the evolution of our species'. Animals were governed by instinct and human beings by the capacity to develop intellectual 'attributes, comparatively to ... [their] animal and purely organic ones'.[188] Other agencies – religious, moral, and political – were preceded *a posteriori* by 'an advance in knowledge', a point that Mill raised in the *Logic* and again in *Comte and Positivism*.[189] The latter work presented the state of knowledge as 'the guiding part [of our nature], and [which] acts not

[184] Ibid., p. 265. Some scholars have since cast doubt on whether we can effectively separate the Comte of the *Cours* from the Comte of the *Système*: A. Wernick, *Auguste Comte and the religion of humanity: the post-theistic program of French social theory* (Cambridge: Cambridge University Press, 2003), p. 25. Other excellent recent studies of Comte's philosophy include A. Petit, *Le système d'Auguste Comte: de la science à la religion par la philosophie* (Paris: Vrin, 2016) and A. Wernick (ed.), *The Anthem companion to Auguste Comte* (London: Anthem, 2017).
[185] 'On liberty': *CW*, XVIII, p. 227.
[186] Wernick, *Auguste Comte and the religion of humanity*, pp. 27, 56.
[187] Quoted in Scharff, *Comte after positivism*, p. 120.   [188] *CW*, X, p. 315.   [189] Ibid., VIII, p. 927.

with its own strength alone, but with the united force of all parts of our nature which can draw after it'.[190] If this was true of society then it was true of individuals as well. Comte was no *Idéologue* but he welcomed Pierre Cabanis's (1757–1808) attempt to build a science of society on the laws of human nature.[191] His own theory of progress thus attempted to replicate at a collective social level the intellectual transformations which delimited the epochs of human life. Childhood represented the theological age; youth the metaphysical; and adulthood the positive. Mill's methodological individualism likewise set out to prove that the laws of development were consistent with the laws of psychology. Progress on this account was not an operation performed on the social world by agencies beyond it. Its laws were neither divine nor metaphysical in origin, but resolvable, rather, into the cognitive and epistemic frameworks in which individuals made sense of the world.[192]

Mill in the *Logic* argued that the great belief systems of Western history – polytheism, Judaism, Christianity, Protestantism, critical philosophy, and positive science – were instrumental in 'making society what it was at each successive period'. When one considered 'the whole of past time', these transformations began to arrange themselves in a 'general order of sequence', and because history never repeated itself, progress was shown to be linear, not cyclical.[193] This was a methodological rather than a normative claim because social phenomena could change for the worse as well as the better.[194] It is no surprise, therefore, that the *Logic* defined progress in relatively neutral terms. Setting to one side the meliorism of other historical vocabularies, including Comte's, Mill attempted to show that progress was not synonymous with improvement. That things were always improving was a theorem but not a method of social science, a summary of effects, not causes. 'For our purpose', Mill argued, 'it is sufficient that . . . in each successive age the principal phenomena of society are different from what they were in the age preceding, and still more different from any previous age'.[195] This resulted, on the one hand, in a form of cumulative epochal dissonance. The present state of society was the furthest removed from the laws of human nature, whose effects were increasingly combined with other agencies. Societies were increasingly

---

[190] Ibid., X, p. 316.   [191] Pickering, *Auguste Comte*, I, p. 217.   [192] *CW*, VIII, p. 914.
[193] Ibid., p. 927.
[194] Civilisation, he argued, had advanced 'in some things' but gone back 'in others': Mill to d'Eichthal, 8 October 1829: *CW*, XII, p. 37. This was also a central lesson of Grote's *History of Greece*: *CW*, XI, p. 314.
[195] *CW*, VIII, p. 914.

products of their history, shaped not by the elementary laws of psychology but by the 'accumulated influence of past generations over the present'.[196]

On the other hand, this meant that the present was intelligible only as a link in the historical chain, hence Mill's remark in *Comte and Positivism* that history has 'taught us the intimacy of the connexion of every age of humanity with every other ... [so that] all the generations of mankind become indissolubly united into a single image'.[197] This intimacy is well summarised by what Jennifer Pitts has called Mill's 'vanguard' conception of progress, which, she argued, shared more than a passing resemblance to Hegel's and Comte's. Its defining characteristic was the 'designation of a society as progressive and advanced (at least at a given stage in its history, until it passed on the spirit of progress to its spiritual heir), or stagnant and backward'.[198] The thrust of Pitts's argument is correct. Mill in 1865 commended Comte for confining himself 'to the main stream of human progress, looking only at the races and nations that led the van, and regarding as the successors of a people not their actual descendants, but those who took up the thread of progress after them'.[199] Likewise, in his posthumous chapters on socialism, he observed that causes 'which go deep down into the roots of future events produce the most serious parts of their effect only slowly'.[200] Practical examples permeate Mill's writings. In his review of Grote's *History*, for instance, he argued that the 'true ancestors of the European nations ... are not those from whose blood they are sprung, but those from whom they derive the richest portion of their inheritance', prompting him to conclude that 'the Battle of Marathon, even as an event in English history, is more important than the Battle of Hastings'.[201]

These connections were not analogous but causal. To say that *x* resembled *y* was not to argue that *x* caused or affected *y*. Mill's definition of progress thus provided him with a logical platform from which to reject the 'vulgar' conjectures of analogy whilst acknowledging the 'intimacy' of

---

[196] Ibid., X, p. 307.   [197] Ibid., p. 334.

[198] Pitts, *A turn to empire*, p. 141. James had seconded Bacon's argument in the *Advancement of learning* that 'it happeneth, sometimes, that the grand-child, or other descendant, resembleth the ancestor more than the son': *CPB*, I, ch. 8.

[199] *CW*, X, p. 318. Cornewall Lewis countered that '[p]articular nations may be taken as representatives of the most advanced and civilised portions of mankind, as the Greeks and Romans in antiquity; but their history has much that is peculiar' that we cannot use them to delineate 'the necessary development of civilisation': *A treatise on the methods of observation and reasoning in politics*, I, p. 302.

[200] *CW*, V, p. 707.

[201] Ibid., XI, p. 273. Elsewhere he argued that 'Greece had left a "still richer inheritance"' that 'did not come much into play until a later period': *CW*, XX, p. 271.

different ages.[202] This science of cause and effect, he argued in 1840, saved the past from the historian's Macbeth, for whom history was 'a tale told by an idiot, full of sound of fury, signifying nothing'.[203] Positivism, by contrast, called on the social physician to identify clear patterns and tendencies, with the aim of developing a prognostic science of history. Mill agreed that the 'derivative laws of social order and of social progress' allowed us to look 'far forward into the future history' and determine 'what artificial means may be used, and to what extent, to accelerate the natural progress in so far as it is beneficial'.[204] But how did Comte propose to study the past scientifically? His answer in the *Cours* was to turn, like Saint-Simon, to Francis Bacon.[205] In volume four, he argued

> que les observations sociales quelconques, soit statiques, soit dynamiques, relatives au plus haut degré de complication possible des phénomènes naturels, doi vent exiger, plus nécessairement encore que toutes les autres, l'emploi continu de théories fondamentales destinées à lier constamment les faits qui s'accomplissent aux faits accomplis . . .[206]

Comte's defence of *théories fondamentales* was a rebuke to the kind of simplistic induction with which he associated pre-positive thought.[207] Throughout the *Cours* he distinguished between an authentic Bacon who foreshadowed positivism's intellectual triumph, and a false Bacon who defended a sterile empiricism. It was not the case, Comte argued, that scientific theories materialised as if by magic from a maze of facts.[208] Positivism, by contrast, held that facts and theory were interdependent, a point also raised by Whewell and Herschel in their respective studies of inductive logic.[209] As science moved closer to its perfection, the crude

---

[202] As he put it in the *Logic*, 'unless two societies could be alike in all the circumstances which surround and influence them . . . no portion whatever of the phenomena will, unless by accident, precisely correspond': *CW*, VIII, p. 899.

[203] From 'Coleridge' (1840): *CW*, X, p. 139.   [204] Ibid., VIII, p. 929–30.

[205] See S. Turner (eds. R. S. Cohen and M. W. Wartowsky), *The search for a methodology of social science: Durkheim, Weber, and the nineteenth-century problem of cause, probability, and action* (Dordrecht: Springer, 1986), pp. 11–12.

[206] A. Comte, *Cours de philosophie positive* (Paris: Bachelier, Imprimeur-Libraire, 1830–1842), IV, pp. 419–420.

[207] See J. Smith, *Fact and feeling: Baconian science and the nineteenth-century literary imagination* (Wisconsin: University of Wisconsin Press, 1994), p. 18; J. Grange, *Auguste Comte: la politique et la science* (Paris: Odile Jacob, 2000), pp. 37–42.

[208] Mill had acknowledged this long before his association with Comte. In a review of Todd's *The book of analysis* from 1832, he struck out against those misguided Baconians who believed that truths could be discovered 'by collating an immense variety of very complicated instances, until, in the midst of the apparently inextricable confusion, there manifested itself something like an invariable order, or law': *CW*, XXIII, pp. 413–414.

[209] Smith, *Fact and feeling*, pp. 23–27.

instruments of induction would give way to deductions from general principles; induction, then, was only the first step on the long road to scientific discovery. The implication of this was not lost on Comte's and Mill's readers. George Henry Lewes (1817–1878) observed that as social science progressed, its laws would decreasingly resemble the 'real' observable world, that is, the world as it was ordinarily experienced. Science, he argued, 'is essentially an ideal construction very far removed from a real transcript of facts. Its most absolute conclusions are formed from abstractions expressing modes of existence which never were, and never could be, real; and are very often at variance with sensible experience'.[210]

Comte's science of history produced a similar dissonance between historical events and their theoretical construction. The law of three stages, for example, did not faithfully restage historical events. The abstractions of science, to borrow Lewes's phrase, were categorically distinct from the everyday world, and Mill in *Comte and Positivism* agreed that the science of history was made up of the 'vulgarest' acts because they were 'the most important'.

> A movement common to all mankind ... must depend on causes affecting them all; and these, from the scale on which they operate, cannot require abstruse research to bring them to light: they are not only seen, but best seen, in the most obvious, most universal, and most undisputed phenomena. Accordingly M. Comte lays no claim to new views respecting the mere facts of history; he takes them as he finds them, builds almost exclusively on those concerning which there is no dispute, and only tries what positive results can be obtained by combining them ... When local or temporary disturbing causes have to be taken into the account as modifying the general movement, criticism has more to say. But *this will only become important when the attempt is made to write the history or delineate the character of some given society on M. Comte's principles.*[211]

The science of history was not a science of specific historical experience. It surveyed the 'most universal' and 'undisputed phenomena' on a scale large enough to eliminate 'disturbing causes'. This led to occasional errors of detail, hence Comte's 'insufficient understanding of the peculiar phenomena of English development', namely, Protestantism's effect on the 'intelligence and conscience of the individual believer'.[212] I will address shortly Mill's struggle to reconcile an individualising with a progressive historicism, but it is worth mentioning here that neither Mill nor Comte

---

[210] G. H. Lewes, *Problems of life and mind* (Boston: Osgood, 1874), I, p. 265.
[211] *CW*, X, p. 319. My emphasis. [212] Ibid., pp. 321–322.

expected local phenomena to illustrate general laws, or for general laws to explain local phenomena. Outliers could not disprove general tendencies, while general tendencies could not account for the causes that produced the outliers.[213] Again, however, it was not clear where the emphasis should fall, and Pickering is surely right to question the seriousness with which Comte declared an allegiance to historical relativism. 'Tout est relative', he exclaimed in 1817, 'voilà la seule chose absolue'.[214] How, Pickering asks, are we supposed to reconcile his faith in the historical necessity of progress, which took the form of 'la loi fondamentale de succession des trois états généraux', with his rejection of intellectual absolutism?[215] The charge is that Comte failed to account for the ways in which historical accidents may irrevocably alter the tendencies of universal history, and that he dismissed contradicting evidence as anomalous. At the heart of Comte's argument, Pickering argued, lies an irresolvable tension between his zealous 'faith in progress' and a commitment to 'relativism and historicism'.[216]

Mill, however, saw no contradiction between Comte's 'comprehensive view of universal history' and the rejection of 'universal' and 'absolute' ideas.[217] Like Coleridge and Saint-Simon, Comte correlated 'political truth' to the 'given state or situation of society'.[218] As we have seen in Chapter 4, the state of society could not be established without understanding its emergence from previous states, or what kind of society could be reasonably assumed from present trends. The laws of progress were not facsimiles of historical events but Mill was adamant that those laws, once 'ascertained', would 'enable us to predict future events'.[219] This argument from the *Logic* found its way into the review of Michelet, in which Mill

---

[213] Comtean positivism, according to Frederic Harrison, opposed historicism's emphasis on the irreducibly particular over the general: Young, 'History', pp. 163–164.

[214] A. Comte (eds. P. E. de Berredo Carneiro and P. Arnaud), *Écrits de jeunesse, 1816–1828: suivis du memoire sur la cosmogonie de Laplace, 1835* (Paris: Ecole Pratique des Hautes Etudes, 1970), p. 71. One explanation can be found in Comte's reception of Herder, who attempted to write universal history whilst insisting on the past's uniqueness. D'Eichthal fed him only those parts of Herder that accorded with his idea of progress as a 'linear growth of scientific knowledge and material improvement': Pickering, *Auguste Comte*, I, p. 283.

[215] Comte, *Cours*, IV, p. viii. For Mill's agreement, see *CW*, I, p. 173.

[216] Pickering, *Auguste Comte*, I, pp. 113, 282–283.

[217] Mill in an exchange of letters with Richard Congreve pressed home the importance of situating the ancient Greeks in their historical context. Congreve denied that Comte had 'travestied' the Greeks by judging them by his own modern standards: Congreve to Mill, 3 August 1865, 'Hutzler collection', HUT. 004, f. 22. As Mill put it earlier in a letter to Harriet Taylor, his own praise of Greece was '*relative* to the then state & not the *now* state of knowledge': *CW*, XIV, p. 18.

[218] *CW*, X, pp. 322, 323. As with Saint-Simon, the present state of society helped to determine our obligations to the next: A. Comte, *Discours sur l'espirit positif* (Paris: Carilian-Goeury and Dalmont, 1844), p. 25.

[219] *CW*, VIII, p. 914.

claimed that social prognosis was the true purpose of scientific history. Comte's great achievement had been to conceptualise the past as 'a gradually unfolding web, in which every fresh part that comes to view is a prolongation of the part previously unrolled, whether we can trace the separate threads from the one into the other, or not'.[220] Note the order in which this was to be done: the 'facts of any age or nation' depended 'first' on a 'connected view of the main outline of history' and the silhouettes of progress.[221]

Mill agreed with Comte that any 'political thinker who fancies himself able to dispense with a connected view of the great facts of history, as a chain of causes and effects, must be regarded as below the level of the age'.[222] But even if we could establish the laws of succession within a reasonable range of error, they would not amount to a law of progress *per se*; not a scientific law, in other words, but an empirical one. Mill in Book VI of the *Logic* claimed that, in order to make the empirical laws of progress scientific, we must demonstrate their consilience with the known laws of human nature, a necessity which Comte alone had understood among 'the new historical school'.[223] This worked both ways. Deductions from the laws of human nature worked only for the earliest stages of social life in which communities existed in relative simplicity. The laws of so-called Being Man, however, could not predict what would happen in societies where the laws of nature had been modified by progressively complex interactions between 'Circumstances' and 'Man'.[224] Most societies fell into this category, which meant that direct deductions from the laws of human nature were inadequate. One solution would be to measure history's cumulative effect on the laws of human nature, but this, Mill conceded, required prohibitively long computations.[225] Another would be to employ empirical generalisations as an index of historical development, assuming that such generalisations were readily apparent. 'By good fortune', he remarked in *Comte and Positivism*, 'the history of our species, looked at as a comprehensive whole, does exhibit a determinate course, a certain order of [intellectual] development: though history alone cannot

---

[220] Ibid., XX p. 225.
[221] Ibid., p. 228. Isaiah Berlin was mistaken, therefore, to assert that Mill did not concern himself with the '*grandes lignes*' of development': 'John Stuart Mill and the ends of life', p. 193.
[222] *CW*, X, p. 308.   [223] Ibid., VIII, p. 915.
[224] Ibid., p. 916. The phrase 'Being Man' appears in *Comte and positivism* but not in the *Logic*: *CW*, X, p. 307. As Mill put it in *The subjection of women* (1869), history demonstrated 'the extraordinary susceptibility of human nature to external influences, and the extreme variableness of those of its manifestations which are supposed to be most universal and uniform': *CW*, XXI, p. 277.
[225] *CW*, VIII, p. 916.

prove this to be a necessary law, as distinguished from a temporary accident'.[226]

The problem was that the laws of human nature were too general to explain social phenomena in the context of society, while history's empirical regularities were insusceptible to proof *a priori*.[227] This, he tells us in the *Autobiography*, is why the *Logic* proposed a method of inverse as opposed to direct deduction. Instead of arriving at conclusions by general reasoning and then verifying them by specific experience, as deductive methods usually did, inverse deduction (which he also called the 'Historical Method') generalised from a 'collation of specific experience' before seeking verification in 'known general principles'.[228] Whereas direct deduction descended immediately from the highest to the lowest generalisations, that is, from the laws of human nature to the empirical laws which resulted 'from simple observation', the historical method used *axiomata media* – a term popularised by Bacon – to establish an indirect connection. The aim of this method was to bridge the gap between the universal laws of psychology and the actual course of events. Comte was overly optimistic in thinking that 'les principes de la théorie biologique de l'homme' could navigate the 'compilation de faits déjà improprement qualifiée d'histoire' without the help of mid-level propositions, which Mill proposed to draw from political economy and his prospective science of ethology.[229]

Mill's attempt to combine a deductive science of human nature with historical analysis continued to attract criticism into the twentieth and twenty-first centuries. The angle of that criticism should now be clear. History, Mill claimed, proves nothing on its own because it provides anecdotal evidence instead of causal necessities. If we are to claim that history's empirical generalisations are more than mere accidents, or reflections of whatever view of human nature the practitioner happens to possess, then we must demonstrate their consilience with the laws of human nature.[230] But Mill called into question the universality of such laws, partly in response to Macaulay and partly as a result of his conservations with Austin, who took aim at the 'principles of human nature of the political economists'.[231] The *Logic* put it this way: what 'we now are and do' is only in a 'very small degree the result of universal circumstances of the human race', and in a very large degree 'the qualities produced in us by the whole previous history of humanity'.[232] Even so, it is hard to see how Mill

[226] Ibid., X, p. 307. Mill offered the same argument in the *Logic*: *CW*, VIII, p. 925.
[227] See Ryan, *J. S. Mill*, p. 92.   [228] *CW*, I, p. 219.   [229] Comte, *Cours*, V, p. 18.
[230] See Mill on the fallacies of generalisation: *CW*, VIII, p. 791.   [231] Ibid., I, p. 187.
[232] Ibid., VIII, pp. 915–916.

proposed to connect the laws of human nature to actual events, and harder still to see how his predictions met the criteria for a scientific law.

The problem may be insoluble, but that should not undermine its political significance. Too often, Mill argued, inductive theories of politics made unwarranted generalisations 'from times past to times still to come' and from 'present times to time past'.[233] His move in 1827 was to deny this kind of reasoning the status of a law-giving science. This, he hoped, would undermine conservative arguments in which institutional continuity was equated with political legitimacy. In the *Logic*, for instance, he questioned the conclusion that an institution must be good simply because 'the country has prospered under it'.[234] The check to this kind of argument was a rigorous science of human nature, from which one could deduce whether or not such an institution was likely to have the ascribed effect. But Mill became increasingly concerned that deductions of this sort were narrow and unhistorical. Macaulay's stinging criticisms of his father's 'On Government' had brought these concerns to a head. His exposure in the 1820s and 1830s to Saint-Simon, Coleridge, and Comte variously confirmed, expedited, and shaped his newfound faith in the philosophy of history, whose place in a general science of society was enshrined in the *Logic*. There we find him proclaiming that 'one of the requisites of a general system of social doctrine' is to 'connect by theories the facts of universal history'.[235] From this, he argued in 1845, we can gain insight into the 'progressive unfolding of the capabilities of humanity – of a tendency of man and society towards some distant result – of a destination, as it were, of humanity'.[236]

Conclusion

Mill's utilitarian protest at 'vulgar' uses of the past gave way in the 1830s to an eclectic science of history which drew on Coleridge, the Saint-Simonians, and Comte. These influences, to repurpose Alan Ryan's phrase, helped to modify 'the utilitarianism he had inherited by the historicism he had acquired'.[237] Book VI of the *Logic* thus sketched a theoretical outline of progress whose scientific conversion came about when it was connected, indirectly, to the ultimate laws of psychology. The triumph of sociology reflected Mill's settled view that society was increasingly a historical phenomenon, shaped less and less by the psychological laws from which

[233] Ibid., p. 791.   [234] Ibid., VII, p. 452.   [235] Ibid., VIII, p. 930.   [236] Ibid., XX, p. 260.
[237] Ryan, *J. S. Mill*, p. 197.

Hobbes, Bentham, and the 'geometric' reasoners had deduced their polit-ical ideas.[238] This realisation pulled in two directions. While it provided a logic and vocabulary of historical relativism, its theoretical sketch of progress – the subject of the final chapter – was neither relative nor concretely historical because it encompassed the 'whole previous history of humanity' as a progressive chain of causes and effects.[239] This double consciousness, I have argued, can be profitably situated within German historicism, French *science sociale*, and utilitarianism itself, all of which acknowledged the logical dissonance between historical facts and their theoretical reconstruction.

Grote made passing allusions to the sequences of progress, as did Bentham, but only James and John thought seriously about them as political propositions. Their missteps in doing so, while important in other ways, are tangential to their intellectual history. It is worth noting, however, that both Mills relaxed Bentham's distinction between criticism and exposition whilst rhetorically upholding it, and that through their own ideas and intellectual influences – from Dugald Stewart in James's case to Auguste Comte in John's – they blurred the boundaries between politics and history. This can be read as evidence either that Benthamism lacked a sense of history, or that it was theoretically receptive to historical analysis. The former helps to explain John's substitution of direct for inverse deduction, while the latter accounts, partly, for the outward similarities between Bentham's logic and Mill's method in the *Considerations*. If Benthamism wasn't as systematically unhistorical as previously thought, then Mill's science of history becomes both less and more of a puzzle.

---

[238] *CW*, VIII, p. 895.   [239] Ibid., p. 916.

CHAPTER 6

J. S. Mill on Universal History

Necessities and Relics

Political thinkers, who at one time may have been over-confident in their power of deducing systems of social truth from abstract human nature, have now for some time shown a tendency to the far worse extreme, of postponing the universal exigencies of man as man, to the beliefs and tendencies of particular portions of mankind as manifested in their history ... [we must therefore ask] which of them are grounded in *permanent necessities of humanity*, and which are but *relics of facts and ideas of the past*, not applicable to the present.[1]

In a review of Henry Maine's *Village Communities in the East and West* (1871), an ageing Mill expressed ambivalence about the historical method with which the nineteenth century was now associated.[2] Whereas once he had lamented the Cimmerian darkness that shrouded the past and its study, he turned now to the 'far worse extreme' in which the 'exigencies of man' were as much occluded as revealed by history. One year later, he complained to John Elliot Cairnes (1823–1875) that Freeman's *The Growth of the English Constitution* (1872) had 'perverted' the 'historical school' into 'an attack on the use of reason in matters of politics and social arrangements'.[3] It is ironic, therefore, that shortly after Mill's death the political economist Thomas Leslie (1825–1882) associated him with a strand

---

[1] 'Maine on village communities' (1871): *CW*, XXX, p. 215. My emphasis. Sidgwick in the same year argued to Alfred Marshall (1842–1924) that Benthamism could be supplemented by 'historical sociology' but that it was unlikely to become 'over-historical': Sidgwick to Marshall, August 1871 in A. Marshall (ed. J. K. Whitaker), *The correspondence of Alfred Marshall* (Cambridge: Cambridge University Press, 1996), I, p. 13.

[2] For a contemporary account, see F. Harrison, *The meaning of history* (London: Trübner & Co., 1862).

[3] Mill to Cairnes, 2 August 1872: *CW*, XVII, p. 1903. The discussion was of E. A. Freeman's *The growth of the English constitution from the earliest times* (London: Macmillan, 1872).

of historicism that he had seemingly come to reject.[4] This undoubtedly said more about the intellectual mood of the 1870s than Mill's intentions in the *Logic*, whose audience he took to be almost wholly ignorant of history. By 1855, however, F. D. Maurice could proclaim 'a cry for history in our day such as there has not been in any other', while John Seeley (1834–1895) looked back on history's 'new importance' as 'the possible basis of a science'.[5] But the fashion for historical-mindedness was not embraced by all. Sidgwick and A. V. Dicey (1835–1922) were late-century sceptics, while Mill after his death was invoked as both a champion and foe of this new historical mood.[6]

Mill's views on history did not change significantly beyond the 1840s but the contexts in which he expressed them did. His remarks in 1871 addressed a new enthusiasm for history whose growth in the 1850s and 1860s had reduced political science to a quest for institutional beginnings. Its proponents, he argued, were unable to separate accidental factors from universal tendencies because they studied only 'particular portions of mankind as manifested in their history'.[7] The science of history, as an accessory of political science and the science of society, was possible only as universal history, stripped of national accidents and particularities. In his address to St Andrews four years earlier, he argued that all 'true political science is, in one sense of the phrase, *a priori*, being deduced from the tendencies of things, tendencies known either through our general experience of human nature, or as the result of an analysis of the course of history, considered as a progressive evolution'.[8] The 'worse extreme' of political science, he argued in 1871, was a Trojan horse for Tory cant. It insulated a 'large class of conservative prejudices, by pointing out the historical origin not only of institutions, but of ideas'.[9]

It is tempting to read this 'worse extreme' as a softening of Mill's historicism, but continuities between his arguments in the 1840s and early 1870s should not be overlooked. He never held, even at the height of his eclecticism, that the foundations of political science resided in 'particular portions of mankind', or that societies should accommodate national characteristics which slowed or counteracted progress. We have

[4] T. E. C. Leslie, *Essays in political and moral philosophy* (London: Longmans, Green, & Co, 1879), p. vi.
[5] Maurice to Charles Kingsley, 26 December 1855: F. D. Maurice (ed. F. Maurice), *The life of Frederick Denison Maurice chiefly told in his own letters* (London: Macmillan, 1885), II, p. 276; J. R. Seeley, *Classical studies as an introduction to the moral sciences* (London: Bell and Daldy, 1864), p. 19.
[6] See A. V. Dicey, *Introduction to the study of the law of the constitution* [1885] (London: Macmillan, 1931), p. 14.
[7] *CW*, XXX, p. 215.   [8] Ibid., XXI, p. 237.   [9] Ibid., XXX, p. 215.

already seen that the intellectual boundaries between utilitarianism and historicism were slacker than previously supposed, and that many historicists commended the use of historically informed principles to navigate their evidence. These connections also help to explain certain continuities within utilitarianism. In a letter to Ricardo from 1817, Mill's father, James, lauded Millar's *Historical View of the English Government* (1787) for demonstrating on a 'great scale' the fundamental developments of 'human affairs', just as Stewart in his commentary on Smith emphasised 'simple' over accidental progress.[10] John's historical method was closer to James's 'real business of philosophy' than perhaps he was willing to admit, and his indebtedness to Bacon, Hume, and the eighteenth-century Scots was not entirely superseded by contemporary French and German influences.[11]

Mill's distinction between the eighteenth and nineteenth centuries tended to mask these continuities, in the same way that Romantic, historicist, and positivist writers inveighed against their own constructions of Enlightenment.[12] Despite sympathising with his father's 'philosophic' method of induction, he reserved his praise for modern French historians who showed that 'the human mind has a certain order of possible progress, in which some things must precede, others, an order which governments and public instructors can modify to some, but not to an unlimited extent'.[13] Longer sequences revealed more effectively than shorter ones the trends of natural progress, hence his attempt in the review of Michelet to separate 'disturbing causes' from 'universal tendencies'.[14] If history was to have even a limited prognostic use, it could not be as Freeman and others had conceived it: an exposition of national characteristics within a relatively short period. Social dynamics assumed a level of abstraction in which the

---

[10] James Mill as quoted in Collini, Winch, and Burrow, *That noble science of politics*, p. 116; Smith (ed. Stewart), *Essays on philosophical subjects*, p. lviii. On the idea of natural progress in the Scottish Enlightenment, see S. Sebastiani, *The Scottish Enlightenment: race, gender, and the limits of progress* (London: Palgrave, 2013), pp. 45–73. Vico's idea of natural progress had a profound effect on the French historians whom Mill admired: L. Pompa, *Vico: a study of the 'new science'* (Cambridge: Cambridge University Press, 1990), p. 86.

[11] By 1869 he seemed to regard Scottish philosophical history as tentative first steps in the discipline's scientific transformation: Collini, Winch, and Burrow, *That noble science of politics*, p. 144.

[12] Leslie Stephen in a biography of Alexander Pope documented the 'tyrannising' of eighteenth-century 'common sense' over the 'romantic' imagination that succeeded it: *Alexander Pope* (London: Macmillan, 1880), p. 28.

[13] *CW*, I, p. 169.

[14] From the review of Michelet's *Histoire de France*: *CW*, XX, p. 230. This is one crucial difference between Mill and the eighteenth-century Scots, whose fascination with historical accidents is well known: C. Smith, 'The Scottish Enlightenment, unintended consequences, and the science of man', *The Journal of Scottish Philosophy* 7.1 (2009), pp. 9–28. Comteans in England and France were more concerned with 'successions' and 'a long series of events': Harrison, *The meaning of history*, p. 17.

arbitrary actions of individuals and nations dissolved into the theoretical unities of universal history, and it was precisely those unities to which Grote objected in the letter to Cornewall Lewis.

Mill in 1871 placed the rhetorical weight of his argument on 'permanent necessities', but this had more to do with perversions of the historical method than with history *per se*. Four years earlier, in *Comte and Positivism* (1865), he had argued that the 'vulgar mistake of supposing that the course of history has no tendencies of its own, and that great events usually proceed from small causes, or that kings, or conquerors, or the founders of philosophies and religions, can do with society what they please' had been 'tellingly exposed' by Comte.[15] The 'worse extreme' of political science privileged special over general causes: general causes laid bare the great facts of progress minus their local particularities, while special causes showed that societies developed in different ways and at different rates, and why, therefore, progress was neither uniform nor steady but prone to stagnation and decline. One of Mill's self-appointed tasks, therefore, was to ascertain general causes without raising the spectre of necessity, to show, in other words, that many 'of those effects which it is of most importance to render amenable to human foresight' are determined 'in an incomparably greater degree by general causes, than by all partial causes taken together'.[16] As he put it in 1862, the science of history proved that 'regularity *en masse*' was compatible with 'extreme irregularity in the cases composing the mass', and that the past could be both irreducibly distinct and uniform in its development.[17]

The publication of Henry Buckle's *History of Civilisation in England* (1857–1861) brought to a head the conceptual tensions between free will and a law-giving science of history. Goldwin Smith (1823–1910), Charles Kingsley (1819–1875), J. A. Froude (1818–1894), and others criticised Buckle for abrogating individual agency within a 'scheme of universal order'.[18] Mill defended Buckle in 1862 but conceded in 1865 that he had ascribed too much to 'general causes'.[19] However, the genie of necessity was not easily put back and Mill's readers have periodically accused him of determinism. From Popper's *The Poverty of Historicism* (1957) to Kurer's *The Politics of Progress*

---

[15] *CW*, X, p. 322.   [16] Ibid., VIII, p. 847.   [17] Ibid., p. 932.
[18] H. Buckle, *History of civilisation in England* (London: Parker, Son, and Bourn, 1861), I, p. 28. For a contemporary summary of the debate that Mill himself endorsed, see J. Stephen, 'The study of history', *The Cornhill Magazine* 4 (1861), pp. 25–43. See also R. Smith, *Free will and the human sciences in Britain, 1870–1910* (London: Routledge, 2013), pp. 133–159; R. Jann, *The art and science of Victorian history* (Columbus: Ohio State University Press, 1985), p. 212.
[19] *CW*, X, p. 322.

(1993), there are many who see Mill as engaged in a liberal civilising mission, behind which lay a normative account of natural progress that resembled, in form if not in substance, Smith's four stages of historical development.[20] Mill, according to Kurer, saw the progress of backwards societies as footsteps on the pre-established path to civility.[21] Political agents in this scenario could not meaningfully alter the laws of progress that governed which kind of regime was appropriate to which kind of society, even though Mill denied that civilisations shared out of historical or metaphysical necessity a common destination arrived at by universal means.[22]

Alan Ryan has argued persuasively for a different Mill, one whose predictions were not absolute but approximate and provisional.[23] The universal tendencies on which he relied for prediction, Ryan claimed, were not the divinations of an absolute science. They were statements of probability which approximated but never achieved certainty, because 'we cannot say how people *will* behave in certain circumstances, only how they *would* behave in the absence of (unforeseen) modifying factors'.[24] Mill in Book VI of the *Logic* was clear that predictions 'of phenomena in the concrete are for the most part only approximately true'.[25] The sociologist furnished from the historical data a set of trends with which to predict what *might* happen in the future, assuming those trends continued without major interference. In his reviews of Tocqueville, for instance, Mill presented the increasing equality of conditions as something that resembled – but was not in fact – a law of nature, precisely so that we might make 'the best of it when it does come'. We cannot halt 'a progress which has continued with interrupted steadiness for so many centuries' but we can mitigate its weaknesses and cultivate its benefits.[26] Democracy may be inevitable but our responses to it are not.[27] As he put it in his article on 'Civilisation' from 1836:

---

[20] Popper, *The poverty of historicism*, p. 111; O. Kurer, *John Stuart Mill: the politics of progress* (London: Garland, 1991), pp. 11, 27–31.

[21] Kurer, *The politics of progress*, p. 31. See also Zakaras, *Individuality and mass democracy*, p. 125.

[22] See *CW*, VIII, p. 836.

[23] Much of the confusion, Ryan argued, stems from Mill's definition of a causal law, the proof of which derived not from the consistency of its deductions but from its consilience with the laws of human nature: *J. S. Mill*, p. 93.

[24] Ryan then reproached Mill for mistaking 'rational explanation' for causal laws: *Philosophy of John Stuart Mill*, pp. 152, 163.

[25] *CW*, VIII, p. 848. He remarked in his review of Tocqueville that we 'must guard ... against attaching to these conclusions ... a character of scientific certainty that can never belong to them': *CW*, XVIII, p. 190.

[26] Ibid., pp. 50, 51.

[27] See H. Mitchell, *Individual choice and the structures of history: Alex de Tocqueville as historian reappraised* (Cambridge: Cambridge University Press, 1996), pp. 43–46.

Those advantages which civilisation cannot give – which in its uncorrected influence it has even a tendency to destroy – may yet coexist with civilisation; and it is only when joined to civilisation that they can produce their fairest fruits. All that we are in danger of losing we may preserve, all that we have lost we may regain, and bring to a perfection hitherto unknown; but not by slumbering, and leaving things to themselves, no more than by ridiculously trying our strength against their irresistible tendencies: only by establishing counter-tendencies, which may combine with those tendencies, and modify them . . .[28]

Years later, in 1856, Mill praised Tocqueville's *L'Ancien régime et la Révolution* as 'un chapitre d'histoire universelle' whose lessons were not France's but humanity's.[29] This demonstrative use of the nation underpinned Mill's science of history, whose indeptedness to universal history I address below. I begin with his writings on French history from the 1830s and 1840s before examining a neglected chapter of the *Logic*, 'Additional Elucidations of the Science of History', which he added in 1862 to defend Buckle from predominantly religious detractors. Mill in that chapter absolved Buckle from charges of historical determinism, first, by articulating a science of history in which universal tendencies prevailed over special causes without downplaying them, and, second, by demonstrating a consilience between universal history and the actual course of events. This can be read as an attempt to logically bridge historical events and their theoretical expression, or to reconcile an individualising with a progressive historicism whose laws were not national but universal. I end by asking whether Mill's conception of universal history sheds light on what he called 'the region of ultimate aims', that is, on what kind of society might plausibly emerge from the trends of Europe's past. I call this Mill's timely politics.

Universalising France's Past

Ranke in 1859 argued that the waning decades of the eighteenth century had witnessed a rise in the historiography of nationality, whose ambitions ran contrary to those of a cosmopolitan or universalising Enlightenment.[30] Scholars are generally agreed that political developments in Prussia and the dissolution in France of the *ancien régime*

---

[28] *CW*, XVIII, pp. 135–136.   [29] Mill to Tocqueville, 15 December 1856: *CW*, XV, p. 518.
[30] See U. Muhlack, 'Universal history and national history: eighteenth- and nineteenth-century German historians and the scholarly community' in Stuchtey and Wende (eds.), *British and German historiography 1750–1950*, p. 26.

encouraged historians to conceptualise the past in national as opposed to universal terms.[31] Stuart Macintyre, Juan Maiguashca, and Attila Pók have argued 'the universal history associated with the eighteenth century European Enlightenment gave way to restricted, state-oriented histories that served national objectives', while Michael Bentley has pointed to its displacement by a Hegelian *Weltgeschichte* and the late-century historicisms which blossomed in universities across Western Europe.[32] However, the definitions of – and thus the distinctions between – universal and national history were more varied than one might think. Cornewall Lewis, for example, contrasted the synthetic unities of *Weltgeschichte* with universal history proper, which arranged national histories into 'a series of parallel lines'.[33] Others conferred on universal history the scientific credibility it previously lacked. Victor Cousin (1792–1867) in his *Histoire de philosophie* (1828) acknowledged 'toutes les difficultés d'une histoire universelle' and the failures of Jacques-Bénigne Bossuet (1627–1704), Vico, Voltaire, Herder, Ferguson, Condorcet, and Turgot to scientifically connect the various 'élémens fondamentaux de l'humanité'; the task of the nineteenth century, therefore, was to look beyond national pasts and elevate to 'la hauteur d'une science positive' the general laws 'qui les engendrent et qui les dominent'.[34]

Mill's writings on French history deliberately blurred the boundaries between national and universal history. His striking thought, which he borrowed from the Romantic historiographies of François Mignet (1796–1884), Jacques-Antoine Dulaure (1755–1835), Augustin Thierry, Jules

---

[31] Ibid., pp. 35–36.

[32] S. Macintyre, J. Maiguashca, and A. Pók (eds.), *The Oxford history of historical writing* (Oxford: Oxford University Press, 2011), IV, p. 2; M. Bentley, 'Theories of world history since the Enlightenment' in J. H. Bentley (ed.), *The Oxford handbook of world history* (Oxford: Oxford University Press, 2012), pp. 19–36. See also J. Walch, *Les maîtres de l'histoire 1815–1850: Augustin Thierry, Mignet, Guizot, Thiers, Michelet, Edgar Quinet* (Paris: Champion-Slatkine, 1986), p. 13. C. Crossley, 'History as a principle of legitimation in France (1820–48)' in S. Berger, M. Donovan and K. Passmore (eds.), *Writing national histories: Western Europe since 1800* (London: Routledge, 1999), p.49.

[33] Cornewall Lewis, *A treatise on the methods of observation and reasoning in politics*, II, p. 438. Cornewall Lewis, as a devotee of Niebuhr, fiercely criticised Karl von Rotteck's (1775–1840) *Weltgeschichte* in *Allgemeine Geschichte* (1813–1827) for transcending national history: *A treatise on the methods of observation and reasoning in politics*, I, p. 303n.

[34] V. Cousin, *Cours de philosophie* (Paris: Pichon et Didier, 1828), leçon II, pp. 5–6. Mill was familiar with Cousin's work and they exchanged letters: *CW*, XII, pp. 198–199, 232–234. On universal history in this period, see T. Griggs, 'Universal history from the Counter-Reformation to Enlightenment', *Modern Intellectual History* 4.2 (2007), pp. 219–247; J. Pitts, 'The global in Enlightenment historical thought' in P. Duara, V. Murthy, and A. Sartori (eds.), *A companion to global historical thought* (Sussex: Wiley Blackwell, 2014), pp. 184–197.

Michelet, and François Guizot, was that some national histories illustrated better than others the natural course of European progress.[35] Here the shadow of 1789 loomed large as an event not just in French but in global or even cosmic history.[36] According to Ceri Crossley, these Romantic historians located the Revolution within a vast historical topography whose central feature was the decline of arbitrary rule and the rise of liberty. This allowed them to preserve the integrity of 1789 – or at least the underlying forces which gave rise to it – whilst setting to one side the violent republicanisms of the Terror.[37] History would have its momentary lapses, but it tended overall towards the liberation of the species from various forms of constraint, that is, from the political constraints of despotism and the physical constraints of nature. 'Je suis convaincu', Guizot remarked in 1828, 'qu'il y a, en effet, une destinée générale de l'humanité, une transmission du dépôt de la civilisation, et, par conséquent, une histoire universelle de la civilisation à écrire'.[38]

Mill's conception of universal history was shaped by French encounters with its ancient feudal and recent revolutionary pasts. He spoke often of a French philosophy or school whose ideas were 'scattered' among 'many minds'.[39] What this philosophy was, exactly, is difficult to describe in anything other than general terms because its construction was as polemical as it was descriptive; his conception of French 'Liberalism', for instance, served as a baton with which to beat the parochial English, who tended to judge 'universal questions' by a 'merely English standard'.[40] But there are clues. In a letter to Comte from May 1842, for example, he praised Guizot's *Cours d'histoire* as a groundwork of positive sociology whose 'capacité speculative plus générale' mirrored Comte's in its ambition to connect general facts to general laws, and to sustain a spirit of 'speculation historique' which had entered only fitfully into the minds of Mill's compatriots.[41] Likewise, Mill saw Tocqueville as Guizot's natural successor because he situated American democracy within the broader conditions of

---

[35] As Varouxakis, Kawana, and Marion Filipiuk have argued, Mill believed that France was a site of intellectual experimentation that resonated if not universally, then at least within the progressive societies of Western Europe: Varouxakis, *Mill on nationality*, p. 95; Kawana, *Logic and society*, p. 107; M. Filipiuk, 'John Stuart Mill and France' in M. Laine (ed.), *A cultivated mind: essays on J. S. Mill presented to John M. Robson* (Toronto: Toronto University Press, 1991), p. 96.

[36] Mill in 1828 claimed that 1789 was a moment that belonged to the entire world: *CW*, XX, pp. 58–60.

[37] Crossley, *French historians and romanticism*, pp. 4–7.

[38] F. Guizot, *Histoire générale de la civilisation en Europe, depuis la chute de l'empire romain jusqu'a la Révolution Français* [1828] (Bruxelles: J. Jamar, 1839), p. 9.

[39] From 'Armand Carrel' (1837): *CW*, XX, p. 184.   [40] *CW*, I, p. 63.

[41] Comte to Mill, 6 May 1842: *CW*, XIII, p. 510.

progress, thus opening up its experiences to a global theatre.[42] The French were more alive to history's general tendencies, hence his hope in 1840 that Guizot's residence in London would encourage 'our stupid incurious people' to finally 'read his books'.[43]

Mill in the 1830s and 1840s wrote essays and reviews in praise of the school that he constructed.[44] His essay on 'Civilisation' (1836), for example, drew reverently on 'the tendencies of civilisation' with which Guizot and Tocqueville had rationalised the sweep of European history.[45] But he feared that these tendencies would read to an English audience as dangerously speculative. As he put it in his second review of Tocqueville from 1840,

> [t]he opinion that there is this irresistible tendency to equality of conditions, is, perhaps, of all the leading doctrines of the book, that which most stands in need of confirmation to English readers. M. de Tocqueville devotes but little space to the elucidation of it. To French readers, the historical retrospect upon which it rests is familiar: and facts known to every one establish its truth, so far as relates to that country. But to the English public, who have less faith in irresistible tendencies, and who, while they require for every political theory an historical basis, are far less accustomed to link together the events of history in a connected chain, the proposition will hardly seem to be sufficiently made out. Our author's historical argument is, however, deserving of their attention.[46]

Mill, like Tocqueville, mobilised the philosophy of history against a politics of specific experience. Universal history provided a narrative framework in which to 'link' the disparate 'events of history', and to defend a timely politics in which institutional regimes were made to reflect and progressively transform *l'état social*. If America provided Tocqueville with a specimen of democratic society, then France provided Mill and the Romantic historians with a specimen of European society whose progress encapsulated humanity's. As Michelet remarked in his *Introduction à l'histoire universelle* (1831), '[c]e petit livre pourrait aussi bien être intitulé: *Introduction à l'histoire de France*; c'est à la France qu'il aboutit'.[47] But these

---

[42] On Tocqueville's relationship with Guizot, see A. Kahan, *Tocqueville, democracy, and religion: checks and balances for democratic souls* (Oxford: Oxford University Press, 2015), pp. 40–43.

[43] Mill to d'Eichthal, 17 June 1840: *CW*, XIII, pp. 438–439. According to Kent Wright, Guizot was an heir to various historicist inheritances, from Scottish philosophical history to Montesquieu and Herder: 'Historicism and history', p. 123.

[44] In a letter to R. B. Fox from 1840, he claimed, rather immodestly, that 'but for me' nobody in England would have read Guizot: *CW*, XIII, p. 427. See G. Varouxakis, 'Guizot's historical works and J. S. Mill's reception of Tocqueville', *History of Political Thought* 20.2 (1999), pp. 292–312.

[45] *CW*, XVIII, p. 126.   [46] Ibid., p. 159.

[47] J. Michelet, *Introduction à l'histoire universelle* [1831] (Paris: Libraire Classique de L. Hachette, 1834), p. v.

conflations – between France and Europe, and between Europe and the world – require further unpacking. Why did Mill see France as a laboratory and crucible of progress, and how, if at all, did these universal histories of France shape his political views and rhetoric?

Mill in 1826 took stock of 'modern French historical works' and France's exemplary status, declaring in a review of Jacques-Antoine Dulaure's (1755–1835) *Histoire physique, civile et morale de Paris* (1825–1827) that 'the history of civilisation in France' was, 'to a great degree, the history of civilisation in Europe'.[48] This assimilative logic was prevalent in Doctrinaire, liberal, and Romantic histories from the 1830s, but its roots can be traced to the Restoration and revolutionary periods.[49] While Mill's analysis lacked the sophistication of later essays, he praised Dulaure for taking an interest in human nature as history revealed it. The 'vulgar histories' of English *littérateurs*, by contrast, showed scant interest in the life of man *as man*.[50] When they told the story of English feudalism, for instance, they did so without referring to the natural course of progress, whereas Dulaure showed that France up to the 1790s told the story of Europe's ascent from feudalism into a post-feudal modernity, and which brought together the composite elements of a distinctly European progress.[51] Feudalism in England had 'never existed in its original purity'. Its kings had exercised an unprecedented level of discretionary power, while continental monarchs had remained in thrall to the nobility and other municipal powers, leaving France as the only 'theatre on which to exhibit feudality and its train of effects'.[52]

It was Guizot, however, who provided Mill with a definitive version of the argument.[53] Despite his involvement with the Orléanists and the 'profoundly immoral, as well as despotic *régime* which France is now enduring', Mill shared Guizot's interest in the lineaments of European

[48] *CW*, XX, p. 18.
[49] The Revolution, according to Matthias Middell, set out to 'universalise' its ideas: 'The French Revolution in the global world of the eighteenth century' in A. Forest and M. Middell (eds.), *The Routledge companion to the French Revolution in world history* (London: Routledge, 2016), p. 23.
[50] *CW*, XX, p. 18.
[51] Guizot in 1828 proposed to focus on the nation that was 'la plus complète, la plus vraie, la plus civilisée': *Histoire générale de la civilisation en Europe*, p. 133. There is evidence that Mill occasionally saw the need to refer to non-European history. In his review of Guizot from 1845, he remarked that ideally (but unrealistically) universal histories looked beyond 'modern' and 'European experience', 'so far as possible': *CW*, XX, p. 262.
[52] Ibid., p. 26. France after 1791 was a different matter. Napoleon's capricious rule afforded 'little or nothing' to the historian except 'ordinary characters and ordinary events': 'Scott's Life of Napoleon' (1828), *CW*, XX, pp. 57–58.
[53] Scholars are increasingly mindful of their relationship, whereas traditionally Tocqueville and Comte are seen as dominant authorities behind Mill's turn in the 1830s and 1840s to a science of society. See Varouxakis, 'Guizot's historical works and J. S. Mill's reception of Tocqueville', pp. 292–312.

progress.[54] His appointment in 1812 to the Chair of Modern History at the Sorbonne; his lectures on European history; and his institution in 1833 of the *Société de l'histoire de France* gave him the authority of a professional historian who grounded his 'speculations' in the 'true sources of history', combining two putatively conflicting aims: a rigorous criticism of the evidence and the discovery of 'natural laws'.[55] As Mill put it in 1845, his *Histoire générale de la civilisation en Europe* was among 'the most valuable contributions yet made to universal history' and, by implication, to the third stage of historical enquiry.[56] While Guizot drew 'his details and exemplifications from France', his principles were 'universal' because the 'social conditions and changes' he described 'were not French, but European'.[57] Besides holding a normative interest in European history, Guizot acknowledged its practical benefits. The historian, he argued, 'doit limiter son ambition; tout en ayant conscience que l'Europe n'est qu'une partie, la civilisation européenne qu'un fragment d'un tout ... [et] à propos de laquelle les documents abondent'.[58]

Mill reviewed Guizot on two occasions, first in 1836 – in a collaboration with Joseph Blanco White (1755–1841) – and again in 1845.[59] Both dates are significant. The first was written after his initial review of Tocqueville and shortly before the publication in April 1836 of his essay on civilisation. James died in June.[60] The second was published approximately two years after the *Logic* and one year after the review of Michelet, in which he sketched the three stages of historical enquiry. In the article from 1836, he returned to the idea that France was a model of European progress. Since 'the sources of civilisation' – Roman, Christian, and Barbarian – were 'the same among the whole European family, the philosophical historian may choose any of the nations where the growth of civilisation has been continuous and vigorous, as an example, applicable to all the rest, under certain modifications which must be learnt from the detailed history of each'. It was 'natural', he continued, 'that M. Guizot should prefer France', not because of his 'national predilections', but because he 'considers the general progress of European civilisation to be more faithfully imaged in

[54] *CW*, XX, p. 370. On the relationship between Guizot's idiosyncratic liberalism and his use of history, see A. Craiutu, *Liberalism under siege: the political thought of the French Doctrinaires* (Oxford: Lexington, 2003), pp. 101–102, 172–185.
[55] *CW*, XX, p. 264.   [56] Ibid., pp. 259, 228.   [57] Ibid., p. 231.
[58] Guizot, *Histoire générale de la civilisation en Europe*, p. 133.
[59] Mill was initially unhappy with Blanco's contributions, which he amended to reflect his own position. See a letter from Mill to H. S. Chapman, November 1835: *CW*, XII, p. 284.
[60] James, according to John, read and 'approved' of the essay on civilisation shortly before his death: *CW*, I, p. 211.

the history of France than in that of any other country'.[61] It was, simply, the country 'best suited to illustrate the general character and growth of European civilisation'.[62] 'Il est évident', Guizot remarked, 'qu'une certaine unité éclate dans la civilisation des divers États de l'Europe; que, malgré de grandes diversités de temps, de lieux, de circonstances, partout cette civilisation découle de faits à peu près semblables, se rattache aux mêmes principes et tend à amener à peu près partout des résultats analogues'.[63]

The systematic antagonisms under which Europe had steadily progressed – which combined elements of theocracy, monarchy, aristocracy, and democracy – were better exemplified in France than anywhere else. Whereas China had stagnated under the dominance of a single political principle, Europe over time had combined pagan self-assertion with Christian self-denial, encouraging a progressive conflict of ideas, institutions, and classes.[64] France was the most progressive nation in Europe, while Europe was the only civilisation in which these fragile coexistences had been successfully maintained. In the review of Michelet from 1844, Mill claimed that the 'stream of civilisation' was 'identical in all the western nations' until the Reformation, which meant that 'any one country, therefore, may, in some measure, stand for all the rest. But France is the best type, as representing best the average circumstances of Europe'.[65] The English had suffered a double conquest at the hands of the Romans and Normans, while 'secondary and modifying agencies' had complicated the histories of Scandinavia, Germany, Italy, and Spain. In France, by contrast, 'no disturbing forces, of anything like equal potency, can be traced; and the universal tendencies, having prevailed more completely, are more obviously discernible'. It was only when the 'subordination of the Church to the State' was 'fully established', and the 'struggles between the king and the barons' intensified, that France ceased to represent 'the history of Europe and of civilisation'.[66]

Universal history provided a framework in which to connect progress with politics. Michelet in his *Introduction à l'histoire universelle* (1831), for example, narrated a tragic conflict between freedom and necessity, in which he distinguished between an emancipated *être collectif* and an unfree

[61] Ibid., XX, pp. 373–374. [62] Ibid., p. 378.

[63] Guizot, *Histoire générale de la civilisation en Europe*, p. 8.

[64] This argument is forcefully presented in *On liberty*: CW, XVIII, p. 266. For analysis see V. Guillin, 'The French influence' in Macleod and Miller (eds.), *A companion to Mill*, pp. 136–137.

[65] CW, XX, p. 230. On Guizot's influential definition of civilisation, see P. Rosanvallon, *Le moment Guizot* (Paris: Bibliotheque des Sciences Humaines, 1985), pp. 191–193.

[66] CW, XX, p. 254.

world of disaggregated individuals. The local fatalisms of language, climate, and geography were to be overcome by a heroic struggle stretching across time and space.[67] Once again France's history was key. Whereas the English pursued a 'politique égoïste et matérielle', the 'assimilation universelle à laquelle tend la France ... [est] l'assimilation des intelligences, la conquête des volontés: qui jusqu'ici y a mieux réussi que nous?'[68] The argument hit home. Mill regarded Michelet as 'a pupil of M. Guizot, or at least an admiring auditor', and commended the way in which he combined Romantic subjectivities with speculative insight; brought to the forefront of his account a 'consideration of races'; and forensically revised the histories of Rome and the Middle Ages.[69] One of his greatest strengths, however, was to examine individuals only as 'specimens, on a larger scale, of what was in the general heart of their age. His chief interest is for the collective mind ... as if mankind or Christendom were one being, the single and indivisible hero of a tale.[70] Humanity was its own Prometheus whose struggle for liberty would unlock the gates to 'la cité de la Providence'.[71]

The theme of heroic universalism ran through Vico's *Scienza Nuova*, which Michelet translated in 1827.[72] Indeed, it was Vico who taught Michelet to separate universal from accidental tendencies and providentially reveal the *storia ideale eterna*:

> Dégager les phénomènes réguliers des accidentels, et déterminer les lois générales qui régissent les premiers; tracer l'histoire universelle, éternelle, qui se produit dans le temps sous la forme des histoires particulières, décrire le cercle idéal dans lequel tourne le monde réel, voilà l'objet de la nouvelle science. Elle est tout à-la-fois la philosophie et l'histoire de l'humanité.[73]

Mill in his article on Michelet agreed that universal history related society's natural tendencies in conformity with the laws of human nature. This, he argued, was the real purpose of historical enquiry in its final form: to discriminate scientifically between universal and special causes, and to make possible a new kind of politics in which humanity's progressive tendencies trumped the accidents of wars, policies, and individuals. Its leading practitioners were Guizot and, of course, Comte:

---

[67] S. Kippur, *Jules Michelet: a study of mind and sensibility* (Albany: State University of New York Press, 1981), p. 64.
[68] Michelet, *Introduction à l'histoire universelle*, p. 79.   [69] *CW*, XX, pp. 231, 235.
[70] Ibid., pp. 231–232.
[71] J. Michelet, *Oeuvres de M. Michelet* (Bruxelles: Meline, Cans et Compagnie, 1840), III, p. 201.
[72] See McCalla, 'Romantic Vicos', pp. 389–408.   [73] Michelet, *Oeuvres*, I p. 71.

The great universal results must be first accounted for, not only because they are the most important, but because they depend on the simplest laws. Taking place on so large a scale as to neutralise the operation of local and partial agents, it is in them alone that we see in undisguised action the inherent tendencies of the human race ... while it would be impossible to give a full analysis of the innumerable causes which influenced the local or temporary development of some section of mankind; and even a distant approximation to it supposes a previous understanding of the general laws, to which these local causes stand in the relation of modifying circumstances.[74]

Mill went further in his review of Guizot in 1845 by claiming that 'the time must come' when all doctrines which aspired 'to direct the consciences of mankind, or their political and social arrangements, will be required to show not only that they are consistent with universal history, but that they afford a more reasonable explanation of it than any other system'. An attempt must be made, he continued, 'to disentangle the complications of those [historical] phenomena, to detect the order of their causation, and exhibit any portion of them in an unbroken series, each link cemented by natural laws with those which precede and follow it'.[75] This inevitably raised questions about free will, a matter made more complex by that 'ordinary artifice of modern French composition', namely, the 'personification of abstractions'.[76] Guizot, in particular, offered metaphysical rather than scientific or positive explanations of history, and he wrote privately about 'l'empreinte de la fatalité' and the ontological limits to freedom, a Calvinist tick that became increasingly pronounced in his later years.[77] Mill had no time for these views, but he did address – in 1843 and again in 1862 – the relationship between free will and a law-giving science of history. If the 'order of causation' could be modified only to a limited extent, and even then in the most exceptional of circumstances, then how should we account for the 'local and partial agents' which co-existed with 'great universal results'?

---

[74] *CW*, XX, p. 228.   [75] Ibid., pp. 261–262.   [76] Ibid., p. 255.

[77] F. Guizot (ed. H. de Witt), *Lettres de m. Guizot à sa famille et à ses amis, recueillies par Mme de Witt* (Paris: Hachette, 1884), p. 47. See also F. Guizot, *L'histoire de France: depuis les temps les plus reculés jusqu'en 1789* (Paris: Hachette, 1870), I, p. i. On Michelet and providence, see Kippur, *Jules Michelet: a study of mind and sensibility*, p. 77; J. R. Williams, *Jules Michelet: historian as critic of French literature* (Alabama: Summa, 1987), p. 20; C. Crossley, *Edgar Quinet: a study in romantic thought* (Lexington: French Forum, 1983), p. 120.

The Collective Experiment

> It is dishonest in Mr. Buckle, because he must be aware that he is using the words *law* and *necessity* in a sense quite different from that intended by ordinary mortals.[78]

Mill revised the *Logic* periodically until his death in 1873. One edition, published in 1862, added a new chapter entitled 'Additional Elucidations on the Science of History'. In it he challenged the assumption that the law of universal causation implied a form of philosophical necessity, and that the science of history undermined individual agency precisely because it was a science, a tool with which to generalise and predict social behaviour. The puzzle is that he had addressed the subject before, in Book VI, Chapter 2 of the *Logic*. He even confessed in the added chapter from 1862 that he intended to 'repeat' his earlier position, and to sketch broad equivalences between the laws of human nature and history.[79] His reasoning was that individual freedom translated into collective freedom: if human beings were not ruled by necessity, then neither was history. The pressing question, then, is why did Mill feel the need to revisit a problem to which he had already provided an answer, especially one that he regarded as clear and authoritative? Since the secondary literature provides little guidance in this respect, I propose, first, to reconstitute the intellectual contexts in which Mill spelled out his original position, and, second, to identify his intended audience in 1862.

Any discussion of liberty and necessity must begin with Hume's *Enquiry Concerning Human Understanding* (1748) because Mill in the *Logic* retraced its steps.[80] In that work, Hume offered the notorious and frequently misunderstood claim that mankind is 'so much the same, in all times and places, that history informs us of nothing new or strange in this particular', except to point out the 'varieties of circumstances and situations' in which human beings find themselves.[81] The uniformity to which he referred was psychological. His evidence was historical: '[a]mbition, avarice, self-love, vanity, friendship, generosity, public spirit: these passions, mixed in various degrees, and distributed through society, have been, from the beginning of the world, and still are, the source of all the actions

---

[78] J. D. Acton, 'Mr Buckle's thesis and method', *The Rambler* 10 (1858), p. 36.
[79] *CW*, VIII, p. 932.
[80] See T. W. Merrill, *Hume and the politics of Enlightenment* (Cambridge: Cambridge University Press, 2015), pp. 45, 84–89.
[81] Hume, *An enquiry concerning human understanding*, p. 55.

and enterprises, which have ever been observed among mankind'.[82] The Enlightenment project of a *science de l'homme* – as *the* social science from which others were derived – was seen by many of its detractors as *fatalisme historique*, a problem compounded by the dissemination in Germany, and then in England and France, of histories which emphasised the past's distinctness over its underlying structures and uniformities.[83] Duncan Forbes in *Hume's Philosophical Politics* stated the problem thus: 'on the one hand, there is the principle of the uniformity of human nature' based on a reading of history as 'a psychological monochrome', and, on the other, a 'sociological relativism' with which it cannot be reconciled.[84]

Forbes attempted to clear up the issue by showing that, for Hume at least, the law of invariable causation did not imply that human beings were in any sense predetermined, only that their actions had causes, and, moreover, that those causes could be explained without contradiction at both the general and local level. The problem was purely verbal. Any account of freedom must imply or at least take into account the fact of causation, because it would be absurd to claim that true freedom is freedom from causality, or that our liberty is somehow threatened if we cannot deny the effects of causal or antecedent forces.[85] Hume's point, therefore, was that social phenomena could be explained at different levels of uniformity, ranging from the general and universal to the accidental and local, with no expectation that one would explain or cause the other. The 'local patterns of expected and predictable behaviour', Forbes concluded, sat alongside 'the general principle of the uniformity of human behaviour'.[86] On the one hand, there is universal man, whose actions can be deduced from the laws of human nature; on the other, there is social man, who, in addition to those psychological laws, acts within the uniformities of custom.

Mill in the first edition of *Logic* followed on explicitly from Hume. He argued that the 'word [necessity], in its other acceptations, involves much more than mere uniformity of sequence: it implies irresistibleness'.[87] The culprit here was the utopian socialist Robert Owen (1771–1858), who had attacked the Christian doctrine of free will because it made the poor responsible for their poverty, the implication being that character was

---

[82] Ibid.

[83] See Frazer, *The enlightenment of sympathy*, pp. 142–150. The debates in the 1780s surrounding Diderot's *Jacques le fataliste et son maître* are a case in point: A. Vartanian, *Science and humanism in the French Enlightenment* (Charlottesville: Rockwood, 1999), pp. 153–157.

[84] D. Forbes, *Hume's philosophical politics*, p. 115. Popper accused Mill of a similar confusion: *The poverty of historicism*, p. 111.

[85] Forbes, *Hume's philosophical politics*, p. 112.   [86] Ibid., p. 116.   [87] *CW*, VIII, p. 839.

formed *by* society *for* the individual, and that we must consequently rethink our notions of accountability. For instance, Malthus in *An Essay on the Principle of Population* (1798) had identified sexual promiscuity as a cause of the poor's distress, whereas Owen pointed to factors beyond their control.[88] The 'doctrines which have been taught to every known sect, combined with the external circumstances by which they have been surrounded ... could not fail', Owen argued, 'to produce the characters which have existed'.[89] Mill in the *Logic* compressively rejected this position. The issue, he explained, boiled down to 'the application of so improper a term as necessity to the doctrine of cause and effect in the matter of human character'.[90] The solution was to abandon the language of necessity. Whereas Hume had insisted that necessity was inseparable from the idea of cause and effect – a view reinforced by Owen – Mill believed that the connection was psychological, a product of the mind's associations.

> The causes, therefore, on which action depends, are never uncontrollable; and any given effect is only necessary provided that the causes tending to produce it are not controlled. That whatever happens, could not have happened otherwise unless something had taken place which was capable of preventing it, no one surely needs hesitate to admit. But to call this by the name necessity is to use the term in a sense so different from its primitive and familiar meaning, from that which it bears in the common occasions of life, as to amount almost to a play upon words.[91]

Shortly after completing the *Logic* in 1843, Mill argued to Robert Barclay Fox (1817–1855) that the 'sixth book on Liberty & Necessity' is 'in short & in my judgement the best chapter in the two volumes'.[92] Why, then, did he revisit the theme in the 1862 edition of the *Logic*, to which he made further emendations in 1865 and 1868? The problem becomes even more complex when we consider, first, that Mill's argument was essentially the same as before, and, second, that the chapter appeared in the same book in which he responded to Hume, which rules out the possibility that he intended to restate or popularise his position. The answer must be historical, a reflection of changed circumstances rather than serious intellectual revision. His new chapter on the science of history was, first and foremost, an intervention into a series of debates which had become increasingly fraught

---

[88] See G. Claeys, *Citizens and saints: politics and anti-politics in early British socialism* (Cambridge: Cambridge University Press, 1989), pp. 115–119.
[89] R. Owen, *A new view of society* [1813] (London: Longman, Hurts, Rees, & Co, 1817), p. 106.
[90] *CW*, VIII, p. 841.   [91] Ibid., p. 839.
[92] Mill to R. B. Fox, 14 February 1843: *CW*, XIII, p. 569.

after the publication in 1857 of Buckle's *History of Civilisation in England*. One of Buckle's more contentious points, or so his detractors claimed, was that 'to those who have a steady conception of the regularity of events', it is clear that 'the actions of men, being guided by their antecedents, are in reality never inconsistent'.[93] Here Buckle was fleshing out in tangible historical terms Comte's theory of social dynamics, and Mill, as someone who was more than passingly sympathetic to Comte's science of history, saw the need to unpack and defend Buckle's position.[94]

The backlash against Buckle exposed existing anxieties about the reduction of moral agency to scientific laws. In the decades after the publication of the *Logic*, a statistical revolution had taken place in municipal, national, and academic societies, bringing ever closer into view a predictive science of society and, with it, new concerns about the regularity and predictability of social phenomena.[95] Immediately after the publication of Buckle's *History*, the likes of R. B. Drummond (1833–1920), Goldwin Smith, Stubbs, Kingsley, Froude, Acton (1834–1902), and James Fitzjames Stephen argued that Buckle's statistical method pointed to invariable causal laws, the consequences of which were roughly threefold: first, that human history was fatalistic; second, that this fatalism undermined individuals' moral responsibility; and, finally, that individuals and acts of government had little to no influence on the course of history.[96] Stephen pithily summed up Buckle's hostile reception: 'Englishmen, in general, are startled and offended by speculations which appear to deny individual freedom'.[97] Drummond, meanwhile, captured the spirit of the Christian response: '[it] is possible', he argued, 'for men to yield themselves indolently to the disposal of forces outside them, to resign that freedom which God has committed to them ... But such is not the part of the Christian

---

[93] Buckle, *History of civilisation in England*, I, p. 28.

[94] Mill in a letter lamented Buckle's premature death and praised him for 'stimulating the desire to apply general principles to the explanation and prediction of social facts', notwithstanding 'the undue breadth of many of his conclusions'. Mill to Samuel Henry Chapman (1803–1881), 24 February 1863: *CW*, XV, p. 845.

[95] Mill in the 1862 edition of the *Logic* observed that the 'facts of statistics, since they have been made a subject of careful recordation and study, have yielded conclusions, some of which have been very startling to persons not accustomed to regard moral actions as subject to uniform laws': *CW*, VIII, p. 932. On the statistical revolution, see L. Goldman, 'Victorian social science: from singular to plural' in M. Daunton (ed.), *The organisation of knowledge in Victorian Britain* (Oxford: Oxford University Press, 2005), pp. 87–115; T. M. Porter, *The rise of statistical thinking 1820–1900* (New Jersey: Princeton University Press, 1986), pp. 160–177.

[96] See Hesketh, *The science of history in Victorian Britain*, p. 36; Smith, *Free will and the human sciences in Britain, 1870–1910* (London: Routledge, 2013), pp. 133–159; C. Parker, 'English historians and the opposition to positivism', *History and theory* 22.2 (1983), pp. 120–145.

[97] J. Stephen, 'Buckle's History of civilisation in England', *The Edinburgh Review* 107 (1858), p. 241.

who knows himself the servant of God, and feels that it is given to him to choose, if he will, the right before the pleasant'.[98]

The debate about necessity had changed significantly between 1843 and 1862, but Mill's views had not. The differences were of degree rather than kind, and, in a way, his methodological individualism allowed him to resolve the problem in the same way as before. Working upwards from individuals to society, Mill suggested that 'if this principle [the denial of fatalism] is true of individual man, it must be true of collective man. If it is the law of human life, the law must be realised in history' – a fact brought out 'triumphantly . . . by Mr Buckle'. While Mill was aware that some 'defenders of the theory' had overemphasised 'the influence of general causes at the expense of special', he welcomed Buckle's emphasis on the universal laws of causation because the influences 'special to the individual' – character, custom, physical environment, the state of civilisation, and so on – could not form the basis of a scientific theory.[99] It was only by studying history on a vast scale, so vast, in fact, that the influence of anomalies was reduced effectively to nil, that we might establish propositions about humanity's progressive tendencies.

> [If] we now take the whole of the instances which occur within a sufficiently large field to exhaust all the combinations of these special influences, or, in other words, to eliminate chance . . . [then] we may be certain that if human actions are governed by invariable laws, the aggregate result will be something like a constant quantity.[100]

These special influences were not to be trifled with because they accounted for differences in national character and the historical conditions of progress. Mill in chapter sixteen of the *Considerations* listed race, descent, language, religion, geography, 'political antecedents', and, above all, 'the possession of a national history and consequent community of recollections' as the materials of national character, and which determined the likelihood of its progress, stagnation, or decline.[101] These variables, moreover, explained why history rarely followed its natural course, and why some nations were more civilised than others. By winnowing out as many special influences as possible, a story began to emerge about the progress

---

[98] R. B. Drummond, *Free will in relation to statistics. A lecture containing some suggestions in way of reply to certain objections advanced to the doctrine of free will, by Mr Buckle, in his History of civilisation in England* (London: E. T. Whitefield, 1860), p. 20.

[99] *CW*, VIII, p. 934.   [100] Ibid., p. 933.

[101] Ibid., XIX, p. 546. See Vaoruxakis, *Mill on nationality*, p. 14.

not just of this or that society, but of civilisation in the aggregate. Mill in his chapter on the science of history called this 'the collective experiment'.

> [The] collective experiment, as it may be termed exactly separates the effect of the general from that of the special causes, and shows the net result of the former; but it declares nothing at all respecting the amount of influence of the special causes, be it greater or smaller, since the scale of the experiment extends to the number of cases within which the effects of the special causes balance one another, and disappear in that of the general causes.[102]

Mill's point was that human actions are conjointly the result of general laws, the circumstances in which they are performed, and the performer's character, that character again being a consequence of the circumstances of their education, amongst which he included their own conscious efforts. Although the laws of progress were regular and invariable, they were not in themselves a power in history.[103] The mistake was to assume that historical laws were similar in kind to mechanical or chemical laws, which, for obvious reasons, could not account for our ability to form ideas and act on them. While human beings were shaped by the laws of social development and the 'physical agencies of nature', they distinguished themselves from animals by converting them into 'instruments' of their design, and 'the extent to which ... [they do so] makes the chief difference between savages and the most highly civilised people.[104] The law of invariable causation, he concluded, does not require us to surrender blithely to our fate, but only to acknowledge the subjection of 'historical facts to historical laws' and to reduce to a 'canon of regularity' the 'human volitions' on which they depend.[105] The 'doctrine of the causation of human actions' thus affirmed 'no mysterious *nexus* or overruling fatality: it asserts only that men's actions are the joint result of the general laws and circumstances of human nature'.[106]

In a further attempt to pre-empt objections to a science of history based on the doctrine of free will, Mill claimed that while 'the results of progress, except as to the celerity of their production, can be, *to a certain extent,* reduced to regularity and law', the 'belief that they can be so is equally consistent with assigning very great, or very little efficacy, to the influence of exceptional men, or of the acts of governments. And the same may be

---

[102] *CW*, VIII, p. 934.
[103] In an article on Tocqueville from 1840, he suggested that 'economic and social changes', though among the greatest, were 'not the only forces which shape the course of our species; ideas are not always the mere signs and effects of social circumstances, they are themselves a power in history': *CW*, XVIII, p. 197–8.
[104] Ibid., VIII, pp. 936–937.   [105] Ibid., pp. 931–932.   [106] Ibid., p. 932.

said of all other accidents and disturbing causes'.[107] Individuals' place in history had long been the subject of debate.[108] Carlyle in 1840 began his lecture on hero-worship with the salvo that 'Universal History . . . [is] the History of the Great Men who have worked here', while Archibald Alison, whose history of the French Revolution Mill had derided in 1833, criticised Guizot for viewing human affairs 'not from year to year but from century to century; and when considered in that view, it is astonishing how much the importance of individual agency disappears'. History's 'tide' was pulled 'to and fro' by the genius of world-historical figures.[109] Kingsley in *The Limits of Exact Science as Applied to History* (1860) provided a more sober analysis, declaring to his Cambridge audience that the 'history of mankind' was not the 'history of its masses' but rather the 'history of its great men'.[110] A 'true philosophy of history', he concluded, 'ought to declare the laws . . . by which great minds have been produced into the world'.[111]

That, ironically, was precisely what Mill and Buckle were attempting to do.[112] Kingsley's argument became snarled when he insisted that individuals' actions were both irreducibly theirs and subject to uniform laws. Mill and Buckle freely admitted to the role of eminent individuals, but they refused to see them as the underlying cause of historical change.[113] If we can reduce to a sufficient level of regularity the conditions in which great individuals are produced, then history assumes a regularity that Kingsley was otherwise keen to deny. That history threw up the occasional Caesar was significant only to the extent that it demonstrated society's transformative effect on character. Herbert Spencer (1820–1903) in his essay *The Social Organism* (1860) agreed that '[t]hose who regard the histories of societies as the histories of their great men . . . overlook the truth that such great men are the products of their societies', a theme which he resumed in 1873 in his canonical *The Study of Sociology*.[114] In it, Spencer defended Buckle from

[107] Ibid., p. 939. My emphasis.   [108] Mill said so himself: *CW*, VIII, p. 937.
[109] T. Carlyle (ed. H. D. Traill), *The works of Thomas Carlyle* [1896] (Cambridge: Cambridge University Press, 2010), V, p. 1; A. Alison, 'Guizot and the philosophy of history', *The Eclectic Magazine* 4 (1845), p.184.
[110] C. Kingsley, *The limits of exact science as applied to history* (Cambridge: Macmillan & Co., 1860), p. 44.
[111] Ibid.
[112] Mill offered precisely this argument in the chapter on the science of history: *CW*, VIII, p. 939.
[113] Of the Greeks' victory at Salamis, Mill remarked that had 'there had been no Themistocles there would have been no victory of Salamis; and had there not, where would have been all our civilisation?': *CW*, VIII, p. 941.
[114] H. Spencer, *Essays: scientific, political, speculative* (London: Williams and Norgate, 1863), p. 146. See J. Offer, *Herbert Spencer and social theory* (London: Palgrave, 2010), p. 69. On Spencer's relationship with Mill, Grote, and Buckle, see H. Spencer, *An autobiography* (New York: Appleton, 1905), II, pp. 4, 22.

Kingsley, Froude, and others who denied 'the doctrine of averages' without understanding what, exactly, that doctrine tried to explain.[115]

Another way of thinking about the problem is to pursue Alison's analogy between history and the tide. Mill in the *Logic* made a similar comparison between the science of human nature and 'tidology', a term he attributed to Whewell in the *Novum Organon Renovatum* (1858). His purpose in doing so was to model social prediction on an inexact science, and to strike a balance, therefore, between the general causes we can account for and the special causes we cannot.

> Inasmuch, however, as many of those which it is of most importance to render amenable to human foresight and control are determined like the tides, in an incomparably greater degree by general causes, than by all partial causes taken together; depending in the main on those circumstances and qualities which are common to all mankind, or at least to large bodies of them, and only in a small degree on the idiosyncrasies of organisation or the peculiar history of individuals; it is evidently possible with regard to all such effects, to make predictions which will *almost* always be verified, and general propositions which are almost always true.[116]

These approximations were causal in a requisite rather than literal sense.[117] When it came to predicting what will happen in the future, Mill acknowledged the practical difficulties of knowing what will happen in each individual case, especially when special causes were likely to affect the outcome. Even if human nature could be made as plain as the road from Charing Cross to St Pauls, as his father had hoped, it would still struggle to neutralise the impact of special factors. We can only make our observations 'in a rough way, and *en masse*', and by examining the circumstances which '*oftenest*' exist.[118] It may well be impossible, as Stephen Turner has argued, to resolve into a deductive compositional analysis the effects of both general and special causes, but for Mill this did not mean that we ought to abandon the task, however difficult, of inferring the future from past events.[119] He was optimistic that the task would become easier as time wore on. In the early stages of civilisation, when political communities were relatively small and isolated, events were often determined by special causes, but as civilisation progressed events were determined increasingly by 'the collective agency of the species'.

[115] H. Spencer, *The study of sociology* [1873] (New York: Appleton & Co., 1874), pp. 45–46.
[116] *CW*, VIII, p. 847.   [117] Turner, *The search for a methodology of social science*, p. 47.
[118] *CW*, VIII, p. 866. Mill's emphasis.
[119] Turner, *The search for a methodology of social science*, p. 49.

The longer our species lasts, and the more civilised it becomes, the more, as Comte remarks, does the influence of past generations over the present, and of mankind *en masse* over every individual in it, predominate over other forces: and though the course of affairs never ceases to be susceptible of alteration both by accidents and by personal qualities, the increasing preponderance of the collective agency of the species over all minor causes, is constantly bringing the general evolution of the race into something which deviates less from a certain and preappointed track. Historical science, therefore, is always becoming more possible: not solely because it is better studied, but because, in every generation, it becomes better adapted for study.[120]

What, exactly, did Mill mean by the course of affairs? I have discussed at length the logical apparatuses with which he examined historical change, but I have said comparatively little about their substantive political contents.[121] My purpose in the final section, therefore, is to delve more deeply into the trends with which he anticipated the future, and to examine their influence on (what I call) his timely politics. I focus on Mill's writings on the empowerment of masses, a social, economic, and political theme that became increasingly prominent after the passing of the Reform Act in 1832 and his introduction in 1835 to Tocqueville's *Democracy in America*. His journalism from this period was fevered and historical. As he put it in 1832, the people stood before a new 'epoch in English history' and it was 'time to mount and journey onward'. The 'machine' was now in 'the people's hands, but how to work it skilfully is the question'.[122]

Timely Politics

[G]overnment is always either in the hands, or passing into the hands, of whatever is the strongest power in society, and that what this power is, does not depend on institutions, but institutions on it: [so] that any general theory or philosophy of politics supposes a previous theory of human progress, and that this is the same thing with a philosophy of history.[123]

Isaiah Berlin once likened Mill to Hegel's owl of Minerva, who could not see past the 'circumstances of his age'.[124] In this and the preceding two chapters, I have argued for the opposite view. Spurred on by Saint-Simon, Comte, Coleridge, Guizot, and Tocqueville, timeliness became the fulcrum on

---

[120] *CW*, VIII, p. 942.   [121] Ibid., p. 791.   [122] Ibid., XXIII, p. 489.
[123] 'Autobiography', *CW*, I, p. 169.   [124] Berlin, 'John Stuart Mill and the ends of life', p. 198.

which Mill levered a new philosophical politics. His commitment to representative democracy transformed into a historically dynamic account of 'political institutions' whose capacity for 'further progress' was made a condition of their utility.[125] If Mill is to be believed, this new progressiveness did not alter his 'practical political creed as to the requirements' of his 'own time and country'.[126] It would be easy, then, to see this transformation as one of form over substance – a position that has attracted many – but this would require us to gloss over his conception of political timeliness, which sought to either slow down or speed up inexorable social change, and to determine accordingly the strategy and pace of reform. In the *Autobiography*, for instance, he distinguished between the 'region of ultimate aims' and the region of the 'immediately useful and practically attainable'; the latter strove gradually for achievable reforms, while the former looked beyond the present age to possible futures beyond, to a time when human beings had increased their moral and intellectual capacities.[127] His own strength, he asserted, 'lay wholly in the uncertain and slippery intermediate region [between the two], that of theory ... whether as political economy, analytic psychology, logic, [or the] philosophy of history'.[128]

Mill, as ever, saw himself as an umpire of extremes. He argued to Tocqueville in 1840 that political science must reconcile the 'microscopic' philosophy of the English – that is, the 'stricter & closer deductions' of political economy – with the 'telescopic' philosophy of the French.[129] He stated the case more polemically in 1833, observing in an open letter to Duveyrier that the English were 'unmoved by Utopian schemes'. Reformers must 'tell them only of the next step they have to take, keeping back all mention of any subsequent step'. But 'progressive science' held that 'none of the great questions of social organisation can receive their true answer, except by being considered in connexion with views which ascend high into the past, and stretch far into the future'.[130] The English evinced less faith in irresistible trends, but that did not prevent Mill from telling political time by the 'clock of history'.[131] The point of doing so, he reasoned, was to manage the effects of universal tendencies, either by slowing down or speeding up political time, and to decide whether or

---

[125] *CW*, I, p. 177.   [126] Ibid.   [127] Ibid., p. 197.   [128] Ibid.
[129] Mill to Tocqueville, 30 December 1840: *CW*, XIII, p. 458.
[130] Ibid., XXIII, pp. 445–446. Likewise, he reasoned in 1831 that even if the Saint-Simonians' 'social organisation' was to become 'the final and permanent condition of the human race', it would 'require many, or at least several, ages, to bring mankind into a state in which they will be capable of it': Mill to d'Eichthal, 30 November 1831, *CW*, XII, pp. 88–89.
[131] This phrase belongs to Collini, Winch, and Burrow: *That noble science of politics*, p. 119.

not society was sufficiently prepared for the change to come.[132] In his essay on 'Civilisation', for instance, he argued that if a 'rational person' thinks the masses 'unprepared for complete control over their government . . . he will exert his utmost efforts in contributing to prepare them . . . [and] might think that, in order to give more time for the performance of them, it were well if the current of democracy, which can in no sort be stayed, could be prevailed upon for a time to flow less impetuously'.[133]

John Robson, Dennis Thompson, and Oscar Kurer are among the few to have appreciated Mill's use of historical trends, the purpose of which, Robson argued, was to enable 'prediction and control through understanding'.[134] This is especially evident in his newspaper writings from the 1830s, which drew on historical analysis to guide reform and guard against potential dangers.[135] His political intent was twofold; first, to reprimand Mackintosh and other philosophic Whigs for confounding 'the authority of time' with the timeliness or untimeliness of political reform, and, second, to show that reform was at once inevitable and undetermined; inevitable, because the spirit of the age demanded it; undetermined, because we must decide on the nature and intensity of the reform, as well as the moment at which to propose and enact it.[136] In some states of society, he argued, sweeping reform would do more harm than good, in which case the reformer must take into account the limits of the age, approaching their task piece-by-piece, until such a time when society is able to overcome those endogenous limits and sustain new forms of political community. As he put it in 1833, the present required the kind of politician

> who, taking the reins of office in a period of transition, a period which is called, according to the opinions of the speaker, an age of reform, of destruction, or of renovation, should deem it his chief duty and his chief wisdom to moderate the shock: to mediate between adverse interests; to make no compromise of *opinions,* except by avoiding any ill-timed declaration of them . . . to reform bit-by-bit, when more rapid progress is impracticable, but always with

---

[132] James Mill in the *Fragment on Mackintosh* had alluded to the timely 'spirit of law reform' and the harvest 'ripe for the sickle': p. 153.

[133] *CW*, XVIII, p. 127. There are some who see these years as Mill's conservative moment: Capaldi, *John Stuart Mill*, pp. 120, 156.

[134] Robson, *The improvement of mankind*, pp. 160, 106–107. See Thompson, *John Stuart Mill and representative government*, pp. 158–170; Kurer, *The politics of progress*, p. 10.

[135] Mill in 1831 argued that the concern with the spirit of the age was scarcely 'fifty years in antiquity': *CW*, XXII, p. 228. See R. A. Vieira, *Time and politics: parliament and the culture of modernity in Britain and the British world* (Oxford: Oxford University Press, 2015), pp. 47–84.

[136] From 'Rationale of representation' (1835): *CW*, XVIII, p. 42. James Mill had attacked Mackintosh on precisely these grounds: *Fragment on Mackintosh*, p. 147.

a comprehensive and well-digested plan of thorough reform placed before him as a guide.[137]

One year earlier, in an article on pledges, he reproached John Black (1783–1855) for suggesting 'that our [Radical] doctrine is untimely', while in 1831 he argued that extensive reform would take place only after the 'idlest fears' have been given 'time . . . to wear off'.[138] This was especially the case in newly established democracies and free governments, whose survival depended on the salutary effects of 'time and habit'.[139] This did not mean, *contra* Mackintosh, that time's palliative effects provided the grounds on which to moderate or suspend reform, the logic being that the longer an institution lasts, the more evidence we have of its pliancy and progressiveness.[140] It simply meant that the 'wrongful partialities' of class, which shored up aristocratic privilege, would give way only gradually to 'the feelings proper to a free government'.[141] This was not in itself a reason to moderate or postpone reform.[142] As he put it in May 1832, shortly before the passage of the first Reform Act, France showed that the present age was one of uncertainty and transition, a period in which the new regime of public opinion will gradually replace aristocratic privilege, because 'she [France] has . . . got forward into another phasis of the change which all Europe is passing through, and of which we ourselves are in the earlier stages'. But the process in any case could not be rushed. For reform to take root 'time is required; and it must be given'.[143]

Mill's timely politics were emboldened by the publication in 1835 and 1840 of Tocqueville's *Democracy in America*.[144] He credited Tocqueville for inaugurating a new era of political science, combining 'deduction with induction' and the principles of 'human nature' with the examples of America and France.[145] Collini, Winch, and Burrow have dismissed these comments as 'generous puff', while Stuart Jones has argued persuasively for the opposite case.[146]

---

[137] *CW*, XXIII, pp. 598–599. He praised Guizot in 1840 for letting 'some of his maxims go to sleep while the time is unpropitious for asserting them': Mill to Robert Barclay Fox, 23 December 1840: *CW*, XIII, p. 455.

[138] *CW*, XXIII, pp. 503, 340. See Black's critique in *The Morning Chronicle*, 10 July 1832, pp. 2–3.

[139] *CW*, XXIII, p. 498.

[140] Mackintosh was fond of Montesquieu's conception of time as 'the great innovator': J. Mackintosh, *The miscellaneous works of the Right Honourable Sir James Mackintosh* (London: Longman, Brown, Green, and Longmans, 1851), p. 178.

[141] *CW*, XXIII, p. 498.

[142] 'Timely reform' was a catchphrase of those who, like Lord Grey, believed it 'prevents Revolution': *The Shrewsbury Chronicle*, 16 November 1832, p. 1; *The Morning Chronicle*, 6 April 1832, p. 2.

[143] *CW*, XXIII, pp. 457–458.

[144] See H. O. Pappé, 'Mill and Tocqueville', *Journal of the History of Ideas* 25.2 (1964), pp. 217–234.

[145] *CW*, XVIII, p. 157.

[146] Collini, Winch, and Burrow, *That noble science of politics*, p. 132. Mill, according to Jones, commended Tocqueville's use of 'the Baconian and Newtonian' method in the study of 'society and government': Jones, '"The true Baconian and Newtonian method"', pp. 154–155.

Tocqueville's absence from the *Logic* is certainly conspicuous, but it is also true that Mill in the *Autobiography* praised him for pursuing a method 'wholly inductive and analytical' rather than 'purely ratiocinative'.[147] As he put it in 1840, Tocqueville employed the true 'Baconian and Newtonian method' by examining the effects of democracy as they existed 'in those countries in which the state of society is democratic', connecting them 'with democracy by deductions *à priori*, tending to show that such would naturally be its influences upon beings constituted as mankind are'.[148] The equalisation of conditions was given its freest scope in America, whose citizens were free to exercise their private judgement without the burden of 'traditions' and the 'wisdom of ancestors'.[149] Their contempt for historical 'form', Mill argued, provided the optimum conditions in which to observe democracy's natural progress, which referred not only to the development of democratic institutions and laws, but to the emergence of a democratic society. In Britain, however, the 'equalisation of conditions' had made the 'least progress'.[150]

Without this process of double verification – the first inductive and empirical and the second deductive and *a priori* – it is unlikely that Mill would have praised Tocqueville so effusively. We know from his marginalia that he found fault with Tocqueville's method – 'on what induction', he asked, 'rests any proposition beginning with "les nations democratique"?' – but he agreed that the best place 'in which to study democracy, must be that where its natural tendencies have the freest scope; where all its peculiarities are most fully developed and most visible'.[151] The absence in America of an established landed élite; its high wages and high profits; and the strength of its municipal institutions were instrumental in developing an egalitarian commercial society.[152] The presence of these special causes, together with the absence of modifying forces, was not, however, enough to make the induction valid. The American experiment in democracy was shown to be consistent, first, with the general course of history, and, second, with the known laws of human nature.[153]

As with Mill in the *Logic*, Tocqueville strove to balance general with special causes, and to find 'le fait générateur dont chaque fait particulier

---

[147] *CW*, I, p. 211.   [148] Ibid., XVIIII, p. 157.   [149] Ibid., p. 179.

[150] Ibid., p. 193. However, Mill's definition of equality was not entirely consistent: M. Morales, *Perfect equality: John Stuart Mill on well-constituted communities* (Maryland: Rowman and Littlefield, 1996), p. 21.

[151] Mill, 'Verbal marginalia in Alexis de Tocqueville's De la démocratie en Amérique', *MMO*, IV, p. 116; *CW*, XVIII, p. 56.

[152] *CW*, XVIII, p. 63.

[153] One example is Tocqueville's discussion of the democratic courtier-spirit, which Mill considered 'inherent in human nature': *CW*, XVIII, p. 83.

semblait descender'.[154] In the introduction to the first volume, he argued
that this 'generating event' was the increasing equality of conditions, which
assumed the character of a natural law: '[l]e développement graduel de
l'égalité des conditions est donc un fait providentiel, il en a les principaux
caractères: il est universel, il est durable, il échappe chaque jour à la
puissance humaine; tous les événements, comme tous les hommes, servent
à son développement'.[155] Despite the providential language in which he
couched Europe's past – drawing, like Guizot, on a chronologically protracted and comparative history – Tocqueville did not believe that democracy was divinely ordained, or that its effects were immediately apparent.[156]
He even wrote to Mill in 1843 to praise the *Logic's* solution to the problem
of necessity, which, as we have seen, attempted to reconcile free will with
invariable causation.[157] Tocqueville in his analysis of America likewise
insisted that, while democracy was an inevitable fact of social relations,
its spirit or form was not; it could align itself either with the spirit of
freedom or with despotism, depending on whether we take the necessary
precautions. The point once again was that democracy's effects will depend
largely on our responses to it, and that we must endeavour to counteract its
negative tendencies, chief amongst which were mass conformity, stagnation, and the tyranny of masses.[158]

Mill in his review from 1840 argued that Tocqueville 'has bound up in
one abstract idea the whole of the tendencies of modern commercial
society, and given them one name – Democracy', which meant that he
had ascribed to democracy 'several of the effects naturally arising from the
mere progress of national prosperity'.[159] Mill then turned to Canada for an

---

[154] A. de Tocqueville, *De la démocratie en Amérique* [1835–1840] (Paris: M. Lévy, 1864), I, p. 2. See
J. Elster, *Alexis de Tocqueville, the first social scientist* (Cambridge: Cambridge University Press,
2009), pp. 32–33. As H. C. Mansfield and Delba Winthrop put it, Tocqueville's political science
'does not seek to determine exactly what will happen … but it does say what one can expect to
happen, unless someone intervenes or something interferes': 'Tocqueville's new political science' in
C. B. Welch (ed.), *The Cambridge companion to Tocqueville* (Cambridge: Cambridge University
Press, 2006), p. 101.
[155] Tocqueville, *De la démocratie en Amérique*, I, p. 7. The 'movement towards democracy', Mill
agreed, 'dates from the dawn of modern civilisation': *CW*, XVIII, p. 50.
[156] 'The universal aim', Mill agreed, 'should be, so to prepare the way for democracy, that when it
comes, it may come in this beneficial shape': *CW*, XVIII, p. 57. On Tocqueville's use of history, see
S. Henary, 'Tocqueville and the challenge of historicism', *The Review of Politics* 76 (2014), pp.
469–494.
[157] As Mill put it in his reply from 3 November 1843, '[v]otre approbation du point de vue d'où j'ai
envisagé la question de la liberté humaine m'est aussi très précieuse': *CW*, XIII, p. 612. Tocqueville's
embrace of general causes and his rejection of fatalism had their roots in Montesquieu. See
D. W. Carrithers, 'Montesquieu and Tocqueville as philosophical historians' in R. E. Kingston
(ed.), *Montesquieu and his legacy* (Albany: State University of New York Press, 2009), pp.149–179.
[158] See Mitchell, *Individual choice and the structures of history*, p. 109.   [159] *CW*, XVIII, p. 191.

example of an egalitarian or democratic but not a commercial or industrious society, which, for all its equalities, lacked the 'restless, impatient eagerness for improvement' which characterised the American middle class. Their rigorous assertion of private judgement and indifference to authority were features of a commercial society acting in tandem with democracy, whereas Tocqueville conflated them with democracy itself.[160] Mill wanted to parse the effects of democracy and commerce whilst acknowledging the connections between them. In his essay on civilisation, for instance, he combined a political economy of progress – or how the 'natural laws of the progress of wealth' had facilitated social 'intercourse' – with a corresponding account of the ways in which political power had passed 'from individuals to masses'.[161] The inevitability of that empowerment made even more urgent the political, social, and economic reforms which could effectively temper or counteract its negative effects.[162]

Mill in the *Principles of Political Economy* (1848) restated his belief that the idea of equality was 'spreading daily' and could 'no longer be checked'.[163] By the mid-1840s, however, he was convinced that existing political economies had failed to manage industrial progress, to the detriment of labourers and society at large. When reformers of various camps – radical, conservative, liberal, and socialist – addressed the social question, they tended to give little thought to workers' intellectual and moral improvement, leaving intact the basic structures of industrialism. The philanthropic movements of the 1840s, many of which had Tractarian or Young England connections, failed to combine the spirit of independence – a hallmark of progressive industrial society – with the 'spirit of equality'.[164] Mill was clear that humanity's ultimate prospects depended on the cultivation of workers' moral, intellectual, and aesthetic faculties, whereas a majority of reformers, including the Saint-Simonians and Comte, wanted to preserve the social structures of industrialism and reconstruct on its basis a new kind of society in which the masses were excluded from spiritual and temporal power.[165] In the case of the Irish famine, Mill proposed to combine 'relief to immediate destitution' with the 'permanent

---

[160] Ibid., p. 192.   [161] Ibid., p. 126.   [162] Ibid., p. 131.   [163] Ibid., III, p. 767.

[164] For an analysis of the contexts in which the *Principles* was written, see J. Betts 'John Stuart Mill, Victorian liberalism, and the failure of cooperative production', *The Historical Journal* 59.1 (2016), pp. 153–174.

[165] As Mill put it in 1865, Comte's division of political leadership into 'positive thinkers' and 'leaders of industry' was a poor 'historical forecast ... for are there not the masses as well as the leaders of industry? and is not theirs also a growing power?': *CW*, X, p. 325.

improvement of the social and economic condition of the Irish people', an idea that he regarded as 'new and strange'.[166]

Mill's advocacy for peasant proprietorship in Ireland made sense for a pre-industrial society whose progress depended on the cultivation of a 'new moral atmosphere' and 'national character'.[167] He hoped that in Britain a 'qualified socialism' would have a similar effect on the condition of industrial labourers and employers.[168] As he put it in the *Autobiography*, both he and Harriet Taylor (1807–1858) came to see the 'ideal of ultimate human improvement' as something which 'went far beyond democracy [in the political sense], and would class us decidedly under the general designation of socialists'.[169] Much ink has been spent debating Mill's preferred brand of socialism and whether or not it can be reconciled with his defence of laissez-faire capitalism and Ricardian economics.[170] The difficulty in doing so can be ascribed, partly, to the diachronic nature of his argument, which posited that certain forms of social organisation were more suited than others to Britain's current stage of progress.[171] He was in little doubt that society tended in the long run towards the equitable distribution of capital and power, whereas in a 'rude and violent state of society' the ownership of capital was usually determined by force.[172] But this did not mean that the time was now ripe for an accelerated socialism; in 1869, for instance, he wrote to the socialist Andrew Reid, then secretary of the Land Tenure Reform Association, to argue that it was not 'timely' to propose 'taking possession of all the land & managing it by the State', since 'we have

---

[166] *CW*, I, p. 243. Mill suspended the writing of the *Principles* to engage with the Irish question: *CW*, I, p. 243. See L. Zastoupil, 'Moral government: J. S. Mill on Ireland', *The Historical Journal* 26.3 (1983), pp. 707–717.

[167] *CW*, XXIV, p. 955.   [168] Ibid., I, p. 199.

[169] Ibid., p. 238. Mill in the *Principles* defined socialism as 'any system which requires that the land and instruments of production should be the property, not of individuals, but of communities or associations, or of the government': *CW*, II, p. 203.

[170] Some, such as the Fabian Sydney Webb (1859–1947), have argued that Mill in the 1840s and 1850s became a 'convinced socialist', whereas others have emphasised his critical attitudes towards the utopian socialism of Louis Blanc (1811–1882) and Robert Owen, as well as the centralised socialism of Saint-Simon. He has also been portrayed as a liberal democratic socialist; a sympathiser of Fourierism and other decentralised forms of economic co-operation; a syndicalist; and a liberal economist whose defence of market capitalism amounted to a modified form of Ricardianism. See H. McCabe, 'Navigating by the North Star', pp. 291–309; B. Baum, 'J. S. Mill and liberal socialism' in Urbinati and Zakaras (eds.), *J. S. Mill's political thought*, p. 99; J. R. Riley, 'J. S. Mill's liberal utilitarian assessment of capitalism versus socialism', *Utilitas* 8.1 (1996), pp. 39–71.

[171] According to McCabe, 'Mill felt socialism ought to guide our current efforts at reform, however incremental, and however far we would still remain from an "ultimate" standard which might, in itself, never be reached': 'Navigating by the North Star', p. 292.

[172] *CW*, II, p. 69. Mill learnt from Tocqueville and Guizot that the decline of force as a principle of legitimation was a defining feature of progressive civilisation: *CW*, X, p. 315.

[not] yet reached such a degree of improvement as would enable' it. The 'general mind of the country', he concluded, 'is as yet totally unprepared to entertain the question'.[173]

Mill presented a similar argument in the third edition of the *Principles* (1852). While socialism was indeed 'an ultimate result of human progress', it was a question which 'must be left . . . to the people of that [future time] to decide' since those 'of the present' were 'not competent to decide it'.[174] His hope was that education would raise workers' intellectual capacities to make them fit for cooperative production, and less suited, therefore, to the kind of labour that enervated individuality, deadened the mind, and preserved the artificial inequalities of the unfettered market. As Joseph Pesky notes, the transition to a cooperative economy 'would take time and effort' and come about only through intermediary stages, such as profit-sharing and the gradual introduction of cooperative associations.[175] After the revolutions of 1848, however, and the rise in France of worker-owned cooperatives, Mill came to believe that the 'public mind' was slowly being opened to 'novelties in opinion, especially those of a socialist character'.[176] This prompted him to revise his arguments in the *Principles* regarding private property and the 'probable futurity' of the labouring classes.[177] In that third edition from 1852, he declared that the time was now 'ripe' for 'a larger and more rapid extension of association among labourers', whereas before he had accepted the utility of private property and the industrial wage economy (but not primogeniture and entails).[178] The difference, he argued, was between those who wanted labour to be regulated *for* rather than *by* the poor; the latter had never been 'historically realised' because the time had not been ripe.[179]

Mill in the same edition made a distinction between the 'ideal of human society' and the 'practical purposes of [the] present times'.[180] He even argued in the first volume that the 'object to be principally aimed at *in the present stage of human improvement*, is not the subversion of the system

---

[173] Mill to Andrew Reid, 5 October 1869: *CW*, XVII, p. 1644. Likewise, in his posthumous *Chapters on socialism* (1879), he argued that 'when the time shall be ripe, whatever is right in them [these popular political creeds] may be adopted, and what is wrong rejected by general consent': *CW*, V, p. 707.

[174] *CW*, II, p. xciii. He offered a similar argument in the first volume, suggesting that '[m]ankind are capable of a far greater amount of public spirit than the present age is accustomed to suppose possible': *CW*, II, p. 205.

[175] J. Persky, *The political economy of progress: John Stuart Mill and modern radicalism* (Oxford: Oxford University Press, 2016), p. 133. On the role of socialism in Mill's vision of the future, see S. Hollander, *The economics of John Stuart Mill* (Toronto: Toronto University Press, 1985), II, p. 817; G. Claeys, *Mill and paternalism* (Cambridge: Cambridge University Press, 2013), p. 127.

[176] *CW*, I, pp. 239–240.   [177] Ibid., II, p. xciii.   [178] Ibid., III, p. 794; I, p. 23.

[179] Ibid., III, p. 760.   [180] Ibid., p. 758.

of individual property, but the improvement of it'.[181] His argument for the
perfection of capitalism and private property rested on a historically situated account of 'industrial progress', the exhaustion of which, he hoped,
would lead to a new rationalised mode of labour.[182] As 'mankind improve',
joint enterprises of 'many kinds, which would now be impracticable, will
be successively numbered among possibilities, thus augmenting, to an
indefinite extent, the powers of the species'.[183] If, however, the system of
private property was destined to last for the foreseeable future, as Mill
thought it would, then we must perfect its institutions and more evenly
distribute its 'benefits', which included the security of person and property;
the establishment of an effective 'power of nature'; and, finally, the 'great
increase both of production and of accumulation'.[184] The end of industrial
progress, Mill concluded, will be marked by the 'irresistible necessity' of
the stationary state, a phase of economic progress at which the population
stagnates and the rate of accumulation drops effectively to zero.[185]

Mill rejected the classical view, held by Smith and John McCulloch
(1789–1864), that the stationary state implied a corresponding stagnation of
'human improvement'.[186] 'The mind', he argued, would be discontented
'with merely tracing the laws of the movement; it cannot but ask the
further question, to what goal? Towards what ultimate point is society
tending by its industrial progress?'[187] As with the arrival of democracy, the
task was to effectively manage the change to come, which in this case
involved promoting workers' self-control (that is, slowing the rate of
population and establishing worker-owned cooperatives) and cultivating
their moral, intellectual, and social faculties. If the requisite improvements
were made, the stationary state would allow individuals to practise the 'art
of living' above the 'art of getting on'.[188] Mill's hope was that, as our
intellectual and moral capacities advanced, the pursuit of material needs
would give way to higher social ones, namely, the extension of individual
freedom and public spirit. Progress in this society would be maintained by
the clash of antithetical forces, even though economic progress had effectively stagnated; we would seek the maximum amount of liberty that was
compatible with the necessity of government, although Mill was reluctant

[181] Ibid, II, p. 214.
[182] Ibid., III, p. 719. Of the historical increase in production and population, he observed that 'there is
no reason to doubt, that not only these [civilised] nations will for some time continue so to increase,
but that most of the other nations of the world, including some not yet founded, will successively
enter upon the same career': CW, III, p. 706.
[183] Ibid., p. 987n.   [184] Ibid., pp. 706–707.   [185] Ibid., p. 752.   [186] Ibid., p. 756.
[187] Ibid., p. 752.   [188] Ibid., pp. 756, 754.

to hazard a guess as to how or when this might be achieved. As he put it in the *Autobiography*, he looked forward

> to a time when society will no longer be divided into the idle and the industrious ... when the division of the produce of labour, instead of depending, as in so great a degree it now does, on the accident of birth, will be made by concert, on an acknowledged principle of justice; and when it will no longer either be, or be thought to be, impossible for human beings to exert themselves strenuously in procuring benefits which are not to be exclusively their own, but to be shared with the society they belong to. The social problem of the future we considered to be, how to unite the greatest individual liberty of action, with a common ownership in the raw material of the globe, and an equal participation of all in the benefits of combined labour. We had not the presumption to suppose that we could already foresee, by what precise form of institutions these objects could most effectually be attained, or at how near or how distant a period they would become practicable. We saw clearly that to render any such social transformation either possible or desirable, an equivalent change of character must take place both in the uncultivated herd who now compose the labouring masses, and in the immense majority of their employers.[189]

Mill elsewhere argued that an enlargement of sympathy would irrevocably transform society.[190] He claimed in *Utilitarianism* that the salutary effects of education and co-operation would help individuals to adjudicate more fairly between their own and others' interests, even though 'a long succession of generations will perish in the breach before the conquest is completed, and this world becomes all that, if will and knowledge were not wanting, it might easily be made'.[191] In March 1849, as he prepared the second edition of the *Principles*, he argued to Harriet Taylor that while 'the best people now are necessarily so much cut off from sympathy with the multitudes', a time will soon come when 'the more obvious & coarser obstacles & objections to the community system will have ceased or greatly diminished'. As for the transformation required for such a system, 'I think it quite fair to say to common readers that the present race of mankind (speaking of them collectively) are not competent to it. I cannot persuade myself that you do not greatly overrate the ease of making people unselfish'.[192] Mill's blend of sanguinity and caution characterised many of his writings, leading him in 1863 to argue that

---

[189] Ibid., I, p. 239.
[190] See Robson, *The improvement of mankind*, pp. 126, 133–134. Smith had earlier addressed the enlargement of sympathy: D. Winch, *Adam's Smith's politics* (Cambridge: Cambridge University Press, 1978), pp. 96, 114, 180, 187.
[191] *CW*, X, p. 217.   [192] Ibid., III, p. 1030.

I do not ... take a gloomy view of human prospects. Few persons look forward to the future career of humanity with more brilliant hopes than I do. I see, however, many perils ahead, which unless successfully avoided could blast these prospects, & I am more specially in a position to give warning of them since being in strong sympathy with the general tendencies of which we are all feeling the effects, I am more likely to be listened to than those who may be suspected of disliking them.[193]

Conclusion

This chapter has examined Mill's writings on universal history, beginning with his reviews of Michelet, Guizot, and Buckle, and ending with Tocqueville's prophetic account of democracy and the timely socialism of the *Principles*. Building on the work of Robson, McCabe, and others, I have argued that we must take seriously the two historical perspectives from which Mill theorised politics: the first looked to the special causes which determined the timeliness or untimeliness of a given doctrine, reform, or phenomenon, while the latter looked to general causes and the region of ultimate aims.[194] The first depended logically on the second. Any attempt to historicise the study and practice of politics – by making laws relative to time and place, for example – must reckon with civilisation's provisional trends. The debate surrounding Mill's universalism and relativism can be helpfully understood in these terms. Alex Zakaras, for example, has argued that Mill employed 'narratives of progress and decline' only when they suited his argumentative purposes, and that his universalism ultimately trumped his historicism.[195] Mill denied the contradiction, and the historicists, as we have seen, held equally bipolar interests in 'large-scale historical development' and 'the particular nature of historical phenomena'.[196]

Mill in the *Logic* argued that the discovery of historical trends helped to shape circumstances 'to the ends we desire', and that those trends were categorically distinct from scientific facts; they 'must not assert that something will always, or certainly, happen', but only that 'such and such will be the effect of a given cause, so far as it operates uncounteracted [sic]'. These

---

[193] Mill to Charles Cummings, 23 February 1863: *CW*, XV, p. 843.
[194] As he put it in an essay on religion, '[while] individual life is short, the life of the human species is not short; its indefinite duration ... [suggests] indefinite capability of improvement': 'The utility of religion' (1874, but written between 1850 and 1858): *CW*, X, p. 420.
[195] Zakaras, *Individuality and mass democracy*, p. 143. See also Robson, *The improvement of mankind*, p. 174; Macleod, 'History', p. 272; Capaldi, *John Stuart Mill*, p. 136.
[196] Kent Wright, 'History and historicism', p. 129.

propositions, 'being assertive only of tendencies, are not the less universally true because the tendencies may be frustrated'.[197] Mill's argument is difficult to credulously follow, but his intentions were clear: general and special circumstances always coexisted, and because they coexisted the past was both irreducibly distinct and uniform in its development. This position developed out of Saint-Simonianism and Comtean positivism; Germano-Coleridgianism; a variety of German and French historicisms; utilitarian logic; and eighteenth-century Scottish conceptions of natural progress. One additional consequence of this intellectual remapping might be to re-establish continuities between the eighteenth and nineteenth centuries, and to consolidate Lorraine Daston's view that the nineteenth-century social sciences were 'continuous but by no means identical' with the eighteenth-century moral sciences.[198] This is certainly in keeping with Mill's self-professed eclecticism and his enduring regard for that 'great century' in which this irreducibly philosophical problem became significant once again.[199]

---

[197] *CW*, VIII, pp. 869–870.
[198] L. Daston, *Classical probability in the Enlightenment* (Princeton: Princeton University Press, 1988), p. 298. Palmeri has echoed this view: *State of nature, stages of society*, p. 12.
[199] *CW*, I, p. 169.

Conclusion

> Niebuhr has justly remarked . . . [that] we can neither apprehend nor
> verify anything beyond progress, or development, or decay – change
> from one set of circumstances to another, operated by some definite
> combination of physical or moral laws.[1]

One advantage of intellectual history is that it can alert us to the occasionally vast gap between intentions and receptions. The utilitarians' conscrip-
tion into an ahistorical Enlightenment is doubly misconceived, first,
because they opposed only the crudest forms of historical enquiry,
and, second, because the eighteenth-century Enlightenments were neither
systematically ahistorical nor neatly superseded by Romantic, organic, and
historicist ideas. Frank Palmeri, for example, has identified continuities
between eighteenth-century conjectural history and nineteenth-century
social science, while Bevir, Knudsen, Reill, Kent Wright, and others have
situated Romanticism and historicism within their formative eighteenth-
century contexts.[2] If, therefore, these new historical perspectives were both
products and unruly offshoots of Enlightenment, then the utilitarians'
intellectual history assumes a more fluid shape. This reshaping, I have
argued, cannot take place solely at the level of historiography, whose
commentators are typically unconcerned with history's informal political,
moral, and legal uses, or with its rhetorical deployments.

When historians of historiography do address the utilitarians, it is
usually to equate their historical with their political endeavours, and to
reassert well-worn arguments about the past's role in legitimating and

---

[1] Grote, *HG*, II, p. 59.

[2] Palmeri, *State of nature, stages of society*, p. 12; Knudsen, 'The historicist Enlightenment', p. 45.
According to Mark Bevir, a 'variety of linguistic turns' has helped to recover 'powerful continuities
between the eighteenth and nineteenth centuries': 'The long nineteenth century in intellectual
history', *Journal of Victorian Culture* 6.2 (2001), p. 313; Reill, *The German Enlightenment and the
rise of historicism*, p. 191; Kent Wright, 'History and historicism', p. 114.

contesting political ideas. The purpose of historical enquiry, they argue, was to stage and restage the present at a time of unusually rapid change; to invent political languages, traditions, and bequests; and, perhaps, to myth-ologise the nation. Frank Turner has argued that the Victorians wrote about the past 'to write about themselves', while Grote is often seen as a methodologically presentist historian who monumentalised liberalism and representative democracy.[3] This reading, however critically perceptive, inadequately situates the utilitarians within contemporary reflections on the methods and purpose of historical enquiry, and even less adequately to that troubled signifier 'historicism'. That they rejected vulgar uses of history; posited analogies between the historian and the judge; and attempted to logically relate theory to practice, matter to form, exposition to criticism, and universals to particulars demonstrates the seriousness with which they thought about the past, not simply as an envoy for their beliefs, but as a site of philosophical and political reflection.

Intellectual historians have more profitably examined the utilitarians' use of history in political science, political economy, jurisprudence, and ethics.[4] The still prevalent view, however, is that they theorised politics abstractly and without historical finesse, a reputation that originated in the early-nineteenth century and persisted well into the twentieth, with only occasional notes of dissent. The publication in 1817 of Bentham's *Plan of Parliamentary Reform*, followed by the publication in 1820 of James Mill's essay 'On Government', revived longstanding debates about the dangers of theoretical abstraction and general views in politics. Those debates can be traced to the French Revolution and its intellectual aftershocks, but it was the establishment in 1823 of *The Westminster Review* and the reprints in 1823, 1825, and 1828 of James's essay 'On Government' which prompted a series of ideological contests whose repercussions can be felt even today.[5] These contests, they acknowledged, were inextricably linked to the reform movements of the 1820s and 1830s.[6]

Bacon's *Novum Organum* was a recurring peg on which both sides hung their arguments, and whose battle, James opined, 'I have often to fight'.[7] The utilitarians contrasted the shallowness of Whig empiricism with Bacon's vigilant consultations of experience; the first led to Bentham's 'maze of history' and the second to enlightened historical analysis, based on general principles which were themselves historical. The philosophic

---

[3] Turner, *Greek heritage*, p. 8.   [4] Forbes, Ryan, Collini, Winch, and Burrow are notable examples.
[5] See J. E. Crimmins, 'Bentham and utilitarianism in the early nineteenth century' in Eggleston and Miller (eds.), *The Cambridge companion to utilitarianism*, pp. 38–61.
[6] Mill, 'The state of the nation', pp. 1, 18.   [7] Bain, *James Mill*, p. 168.

Whigs, along with their Romantic and Tory counterparts, pursued an effective rhetorical strategy in which the fabrications of theory were set against the certainties of practice, even though the utilitarians denied on logical grounds the opposition between the two. Their vehement rebukes of tradition made it easier to place them on the wrong side of history. Bentham famously saw himself as Bacon's anointed heir in moral science who would clear away the rubbish of antiquity, while John in 1838 posited a familiar dichotomy between Tories' 'love of the past' and Liberals' 'faith in the future'.[8] As I argued in Chapter 1, however, it is misleading even in Bentham's case to conflate his contempt for historical authority with a contempt for history *per se*, or to see him as intellectually cocooned from the enlightened historicisms of the eighteenth century: Montesquieu, Barrington, Kames, and others.

The utilitarians did not see themselves as ignorant of time and place; it was their opponents, they claimed, who peddled abstract theories and ignored the facts – and, worse, the laws – of historical change. John put it clearest when he agreed with Tocqueville that the 'face of society' since the French Revolution had been totally 'reversed ... and [yet] there are people who talk of standing up for ancient constitutions, and the duty of sticking to the British Constitution settled in 1688! What is still more extraordinary, these are the people who accuse others of disregarding variety [sic] of circumstances, and imposing their abstract theories upon all states of society without qualification'.[9] Bentham's inversion of old and early times exposed a similar fallacy of political debate. These admonitions, then, should not be mistaken for an indifference to history and the variety of approaches which fall under historicism's ever-growing umbrella. While the utilitarians embodied a 'more rationalistic strand of Enlightenment thinking' than their Whig and Romantic critics, they opposed history only when it attempted to answer the quintessentially philosophical question: is it good?[10]

The utilitarians and philosophic Whigs disagreed less about history's importance than its relationship to general principles, which is why the vexed relationship between universals and particulars continually reared its head. James in *A Fragment on Mackintosh* attempted to settle the dispute by substituting a universal for a probable method, whilst continuing his defence of 'general laws' against 'exceptions'.[11] John's concessions in the

[8] Bentham, *Works*, IV, p. 577; *CW*, I, p. 467.
[9] From 'Civilisation' (1836): *CW*, XVIII, p. 126. See also his first review of Tocqueville: *CW*, XVIII, p. 51.
[10] Bevir, 'Historicism and the human sciences in Victorian Britain', p. 17.
[11] Mill, *A fragment on Mackintosh*, p. 279.

Logic were greater but demonstrably more confused, and commentators have questioned whether he succeeded in making utilitarianism more substantively historical. The more pertinent observation, however, is that the utilitarians' struggle to mediate between general principles and historical phenomena connects rather than separates them to nineteenth-century historicism, which, as John Burrow noted, occupied a spectrum of generality from the 'individual to the universal'.[12] Many of the utilitarians' German, French, Scottish, and English influences inhabited a similar spectrum, which reposed on even older dichotomies, traceable to the late-seventeenth and early-eighteenth centuries, between Christian universal history and *res gestae*.[13]

These continuities further complicate what Knudsen has called the 'predominantly aesthetic divide between historicism and the Enlightenment'.[14] Silvia Sebastiani, for example, has examined the blurred lines in the Scottish and French Enlightenments between 'the history of natural man' and 'the natural history of man in society', both of which occupied a broad spectrum and reconstructed the past philosophically.[15] James's mentor at Edinburgh, Dugald Stewart, looked back on conjectural history as invariably at odds with 'genuine history', while Alexander Tytler (1747–1813) observed similarities between Scottish philosophical history and Montesquieu's hypothetical reasoning, both of which stressed 'general laws' over 'accidental circumstances' and 'authentic facts'.[16] James also attacked the imprecision with which Scottish historians had adumbrated society's natural progress, while Grote in a letter to Cornewall Lewis (and Cornewall Lewis in his reply) levelled similar charges at Comte, whose stages of development bore little resemblance to actual events.[17] Even John acknowledged a difference between Comte's ethereal philosophy of history and the Romantic historiographies of Thierry, Guizot, and Michelet.[18]

The gap between 'general laws' and 'authentic facts' allowed the utilitarians to flexibly position themselves within the currents of debate. John in 1862 defended Buckle for emphasising general over special causes, a position that was broadly compatible with Scottish conceptions of natural progress, but he conceded in 1865 that Buckle had probably gone

[12] Burrow, 'Historicism and social evolution', p. 253.
[13] Reill, *The German Enlightenment and the rise of historicism*, p. 29.
[14] Knudsen, 'The historicist Enlightenment', p. 45.
[15] Sebastiani, *The Scottish Enlightenment*, p. 7.
[16] A. F. Tytler, *Memoirs of the life and writings of the Honourable Henry Home of Kames* [1807] (Edinburgh: T. Cadell and W. Davies, 1814), I, pp. 279–280.
[17] H. Grote, *The personal life of George Grote*, p. 203.   [18] *CW*, XX, p. 221.

too far in ascribing 'all to general causes', as if 'neither casual circumstances, nor governments by their acts, nor individuals of genius by their thoughts, materially accelerate or retard human progress'.[19] John contended that general causes did not necessarily eliminate or obscure historical facts, as Buckle's myriad critics had alleged. They could illuminate 'the laws of evolution common to all mankind', as in Comte's positivism, or their 'diversities', as in Buckle's *History of Civilisation in England*.[20] The utilitarians agreed that even national histories required general principles to navigate and explain the evidence, and that enlightened reconstructions of the past were impossible without an accompanying *science de l'homme*. Niebuhr made the same point in his *History of Rome*.[21]

The relationship between historical events and their theoretical construction; between general and special causes; and between the matter and form of institutions, laws, and sentiments can be situated more broadly within the history of the philosophy of science. The purpose of theory, the utilitarians agreed, was to simplify and causally explain the social world, rather than to faithfully reproduce it.[22] The past could not independently explain why things did or did not happen; why they happened in this instead of that way; or at this instead of that time. Only theory could provide explanations of this sort. As Bentham put it in a manuscript,

> they [enemies of theory] think they have found a sure way to escape error by laying down none but particular positions – and yet if they were to take the pains to examine the construction of their arguments they would find that all the foundation their particular positions have lies in their being necessary consequences from some general principles which they [implicitly] recognise . . .[23]

Theories, however, could overreach themselves. Bentham in *The Book of Fallacies* criticised the propensity 'by those who adopt this or that theory, to push it too far: meaning, to set up a general proposition which is not conformable to reason and utility and until certain exceptions have been taken out of it', while John proposed to rebrand James's essay 'On Government' as an argument for parliamentary reform and not, as James had intended, a scientific treatise.[24] The question of universality appeared elsewhere in their writings. In his *Unsettled Questions of Political Economy* (1844), John explained that political economy isolated one element of

[19] Ibid., X, p. 322.   [20] Ibid., p. 287n.   [21] Niebuhr, *The history of Rome*, III, p. 51.
[22] 'Theory', James argued, 'is essentially something more perfect than practice': *CPB*, I, ch. 8.
[23] 'Bentham papers', University College London Library, box 97, f. 5.
[24] Bentham, *Book of fallacies*, p. 204; *CW*, I, p. 184.

society – the pursuit of wealth – to trace its natural effects, without mistaking it for society itself.[25] It 'does not treat of the whole of man's nature as modified by the social state, nor of the whole conduct of man in society ... It predicts only such of the phenomena of the social state as take place in consequence of the pursuit of wealth ... Not that any political economist was ever so absurd as to suppose that mankind are really thus constituted, but because this is the mode in which science must necessarily proceed'.[26] The science of history, like all other sciences, prioritised certain phenomena over others, from ideas and institutions to economic and material forces. This partly explains the utilitarians' assimilative conceptions of progress and often condescending attitudes towards historical and cultural difference: the science of history, by definition, could not faithfully reproduce the world in its diversity.[27] The result was a profound politicisation of human time and a conception of history that rationalised European experiences and beliefs.

These leitmotifs demonstrate the need to study the utilitarians collectively, but I have stopped short of advancing a utilitarian idea of history. There are three reasons for this. The first is that any such reification sacrifices authorial intent for clarity, and context for accessibility. The second is that the utilitarians did not unanimously agree on history's methodology, form, or purpose. Grote conspicuously abandoned James's scale of civilisations for Niebuhr's critical *Historismus*, and elsewhere he criticised Comte – and, implicitly, John – for privileging abstract laws over historical facts, and for muddying the distinction between exposition and criticism.[28] The final reason is that, by studying the utilitarians individually within their respective contexts, their arguments retain their naturally jagged lines. The mythologies of doctrine and coherence are easier to resist if we abandon the search for analytically stable ideas, and the utilitarians, arguably more than other nineteenth-century thinkers, stand to profit from that resistance.

[25] *CW*, IV, p. 321. Palmeri has observed that conjectural political economy exhibited 'a generalising and universalising tendency that can also at times be combined with more local, particular histories': *State of nature, stages of society*, p. 16.
[26] *CW*, IV, p. 322. See B. Fontana, 'Democracy and civilisation: John Stuart Mill and the critique of political economy', *Economies et sociétés* 20.3 (1986), pp. 3–24.
[27] See Marwah, *Liberalism, diversity, and domination*, p. 3.
[28] Grote, *The personal life of George Grote*, pp. 203–204.

Bibliography

Primary Manuscripts

Bentham, J., 'Bentham papers', University College London Library, 161.

Grote, G., 'Bodleian Library Oxford Additional Manuscript', Eng.Let.d.122.

Grote, G., 'Fragments of Mr. Grote's handwriting', Bodleian Library Oxford Additional Manuscript, c. 208.9.

Grote, G., 'George Grote. Four notebooks', Senate House Library, MS429, III.

Grote, G., 'Grote papers, 1818–1822', British Library Additional Manuscript, 29514–29529.

Grote, G., 'Grote papers. Essays and notes', Bodleian Library Oxford Additional Manuscript, MS. d. 85.

Grote, G., 'Grote papers', University College London Additional Manuscripts, A2.

Grote, G., 'Papers of George Grote', Cambridge University Library Additional Manuscripts, 1933.

Grote, G., 'Papers of the Mayor and related families', Trinity College, Cambridge, Additional Manuscript, C12/53.

Mill, J. S., 'Hutzler collection', Johns Hopkins University Special Collections, HUT. 004.

Mill, J. S., 'By what means may sentimentality be checked without discouraging healthy sentiment & individuality of character?', John Stuart Mill papers, Yale University Library, MS 350.

Walker, A., 'Walker papers', National Library of Scotland, MSS. 13724.

Primary Printed

Acton, J. D., 'Mr Buckle's thesis and method', *The Rambler* 10 (1858), pp. 27–42.

Alison, A., *A history of Europe from the commencement of the French Revolution to the restoration of the Bourbons* (Edinburgh: William Blackwood, 1833–1843), 10 vols.

Alison, A., 'Guizot and the philosophy of history', *The Eclectic Magazine* 4 (1845), pp. 177–192.

Arnold, T., *The history of the Peloponnesian War by Thucydides: with notes, chiefly historical and geographical* [1830] (London: John Henry and James Parker, 1861), 3 vols.

226

Bacon, F. (eds. Jardine, L. and Silverthorne, M.), *The new organon* [1620] (Cambridge: Cambridge University Press, 2008).

Bacon, F. (ed. Wright, W. A.), *The advancement of learning* [1605] (Oxford: Clarendon Press, 1876).

Bain, A., *James Mill: a biography* (London: Longmans, Green, and Co., 1882).

Bain, A., *John Stuart Mill: a criticism* (London: Longmans, Green, and Co., 1882).

Bazard, A. and others, *Doctrine de Saint-Simon. Exposition* (Paris: Bureau de l'organisateur, 1831).

Bentham, J. (ed. and trans. Bentham, G.), *Essai sur la nomenclature et la classification des principles branches d'art-et-science* (Paris: Bossange, 1823).

Bentham, J. (ed. Bowring, J.), *The works of Jeremy Bentham* (Edinburgh: William Tait, 1838–1843), 11 vols.

Bentham, J. (eds. Burns, J. H. and Hart, H. L. A.), *A comment on the Commentaries and A fragment on government* (Oxford: Oxford University Press, 1997).

Bentham, J. (eds. Christie, I. R., Milne, A. T., Sprigge, T. L. S.), *The correspondence of Jeremy Bentham* (London: UCL Press, 2017), 5 vols.

Bentham, J. (ed. Dumont, E., trans. Neal, J.), *Principles of legislation* (Boston: Wells and Lilly, 1830).

Bentham, J. (ed. Engelmann, S. G.), *Selected writings* (New Haven: Yale University Press, 2011).

Bentham, J. (ed. Larrabee, H. A.), *Handbook of political fallacies* (Baltimore: The Johns Hopkins Press, 1952).

Bentham, J. (ed. Place, F.), *Not Paul, but Jesus* (London: John Hunt, 1823).

Bentham, J. (ed. Schofield, P. and Harris, J.), *Legislator of the world: writings on codification, law, and education* (Oxford: Oxford University Press, 1998).

Bentham, J. (ed. Schofield, P.), *Official aptitude maximized; expense minimized* (Oxford: Clarendon Press, 1993).

Bentham, J. (ed. Schofield, P.), *Of the limits of the penal branch of jurisprudence* (Oxford: Oxford University Press, 2010).

Bentham, J. (ed. Schofield, P.), *The book of fallacies* (Oxford: Oxford University Press, 2015).

Bentham, J. (ed. Smith, M. J. and Burston, W. H.), *Chrestomathia* (Oxford: Oxford University Press, 1983).

Bentham, J. (eds. Burns, J. H. and Hart, H. L. A.), *An introduction to the principles and morals of legislation* (Oxford: Oxford University Press, 2005).

Bentham, J. (eds. Schofield, P., Pease-Watkin, C., and Blamires, C.), *Rights, representation, and reform: nonsense upon stilts and other writings on the French Revolution* (Oxford: Oxford University Press, 2002).

Bentham, J. (ed. Goldworth, A.), *Deontology together with A table of the springs of action and Article on utilitarianism* (Oxford: Oxford University Press, 1983).

Bentham, J., *A plan for parliamentary reform in the form of a catechism, with reasons for each article, with an introduction, shewing the necessity of radical, and the inadequacy of moderate, reform* (London: R. Hunter, 1817).

Bentham, J. (eds. Long, D. G. and Schofield, P.), *Preparatory principles* (Oxford: Oxford University Press, 2016).

Berkeley, G. (eds. Stock, J. and Wright, G. N.), *The works of George Berkeley* (London: Thomas Tegg, 1843), 4 vols.

Blackstone, W., *Commentaries on the laws of England* (London: W. Strahan and T. Cadell, 1783), 4 vols.

Blair, H., *Lectures on rhetoric and belles lettres* (Philadelphia: Robert Aitken, 1784).

Blakely, R., *History of moral science* [1833] (Edinburgh: James Duncan, 1836), 2 vols.

Bolingbroke, H., *Letters on the study and use of history* (Basil: J. J. Tourneisen, 1791).

Bolingbroke, H., *The patriot king; and, an essay on the spirit of patriotism* [1738] (London: John Brooks, 1831).

Buchez, P. (ed.), *Le producteur* (Paris: Chez Sautelet, 1825–1826), 5 vols.

Buckle, H., *History of civilisation in England* (London: Parker, Son, and Bourn, 1861), 3 vols.

Bulwer-Lytton, E. (ed. Murray, O.), *Athens: its rise and fall* [1837] (London: Routledge, 2004).

Bulwer-Lytton, E., *England and the English* (London: Richard Bentley, 1833), 2 vols.

Burke, E., *Reflections on the revolution in France* (London: J. Dodsely, 1790).

Burke, E., *The works of the Right Honourable Edmund Burke* (London: Henry G. Bohn, 1856), 6 vols.

Burton, J. H., *The history of Scotland from Agricola's invasion to the Revolution of 1688* (Edinburgh: William Blackwood and Sons, 1867), 7 vols.

Carlyle, T. (ed. Sanders, C. R.) *The collected letters of Thomas and Jane Welsh Carlyle* (Durham: Duke University Press, 1976), 15 vols.

Carlyle, T. (ed. Shelston, A.), *Thomas Carlyle: selected writings* (London: Penguin, 1971).

Carlyle, T. (ed. Tennyson, G. B.), *A Carlyle reader: selections from the writings of Thomas Carlyle* (Cambridge: Cambridge University Press, 1984).

Carlyle, T. (ed. Traill, H. D.), *The works of Thomas Carlyle* [1896] (Cambridge: Cambridge University Press, 2010), 30 vols.

Carlyle, T. (ed. Vanden Bossche, C. R.), *Historical essays* (Berkeley: University of California Press, 2002).

Carlyle, T., 'The signs of the times' in Himmelfarb, G. (ed.), *The spirit of the age: Victorian essays* (Yale: Yale University Press, 2007), pp. 31–50.

Coleridge, S. T., *Aids to reflection in the form of a manly character* (London: Taylor and Hessey, 1825).

Coleridge, S. T. (ed. Griggs, E. L.), *Collected letters* (Oxford: Clarendon Press, 1956–1971), 6 vols.

Coleridge, S. T. (eds. Coleridge, S., Coleridge, H. N., and Shedd, W. G. T.), *The complete works* (New York: Harper and Brothers, 1854), 7 vols.

Coleridge, S. T. (eds. McFarland, T. and Halmi, N.), *Opus maximum* (Princeton: Princeton University Press, 2002).

Coleridge, S. T. (eds. Morrow, J., Taylor, A., Goodson, A., Beer, J., Vallins, D.), *Coleridge's writings* (London: Macmillan, 1990–2003), 5 vols.

Coleridge, S. T., *The friend* (London: Gale and Curtis, 1812).

Comte, A., *Cours de philosophie positive* (Paris: Bachelier, Imprimeur-Libraire, 1841), 6 vols.

Comte, A., *Discours sur l'espirit positif* (Paris: Carilian-Goeury and Dalmont, 1844).

Comte, A. (ed. Lenzer, G.), *Auguste Comte and positivism* (New Brunswick: Transaction Publishers, 1998).

Comte, A. (ed. Martineau, H.), *The positive philosophy of Auguste Comte* (London: John Chapman, 1853), 2 vols.

Comte, A. (eds. de Berredo Carneiro, P. E. and Arnaud, P.), *Écrits de jeunesse, 1816–1828: suivis du memoire sur la cosmogonie de Laplace, 1835* (Paris: Ecole Pratique des Hautes Etudes, 1970).

Constant, B., *De la liberté chez les modernes: écrits politiques* (Paris: Pluriel, 1980).

Conway, M. D., *A memorial discourse in honour of John Stuart Mill* (Finsbury, 1873).

Conway, S. (ed.), *The correspondence of Jeremy Bentham. Volume 8* (Oxford: Clarendon Press, 1988).

Cornewall Lewis, G., *A treatise on the methods of observation and reasoning in politics* (London: John W. Parker and Son, 1852), 2 vols.

Coulson, W., 'Mill's British India', *Edinburgh Review* 41 (1818), pp. 1–44.

Cousin, V., *Cours de philosophie* (Paris: Pichon et Didier, 1828).

Dicey, A. V., *Introduction to the study of the law of the constitution* [1885] (London: Macmillan, 1931).

Drummond, R. B., *Free will in relation to statistics. A lecture containing some suggestions in way of reply to certain objections advanced to the doctrine of free will, by Mr Buckle, in his History of civilisation in England* (London: E. T. Whitefield, 1860).

Dumont, E., *Traités de législation civile et pénale* (Paris: Bossange, Masson et Besson, 1802), 3 vols.

Ferguson, A., *An essay on the history of civil society* (Philadelphia: A. Finley, 1819).

Fichte, J. G. (trans. Smith, W. R.), *Characteristics of the present age* (London: John Chapman, 1847).

Freeman, E. A., 'A history of Greece by George Grote', *The North British Review* 25 (1856), pp. 141–173.

Freeman, E. A., *Historical essays* (London: Macmillan and Co, 1873), 4 vols.

Freeman, E. A., *The growth of the English constitution from the earliest times* (London: Macmillan, 1872).

Gibbon, E. (ed. Smith, W.), *The history of the decline and fall of the Roman Empire* (London: John Murray, 1855), 8 vols.

Gillies, J., *The history of ancient Greece, its colonies, and conquests, from the earliest accounts to the division of the Macedonian Empire in the East* [1786] (London: T. Cadell and W. Davies, 1801), 2 vols.

Goldsmith, O., *The history of Greece from the earliest state, to the death of Alexander the Great* [1774] (London: Rivington, 1823), 2 vols.

Grote, G. (ed. Bain, A.), *Aristotle* (London: John Murray, 1872), 2 vols.

Grote, G. (ed. Bain, A.), *Fragments on ethical subjects* (London: John Murray, 1876).

Grote, G. (ed. Bain, A.), *The minor works of George Grote. With critical remarks on his intellectual character, writings and speeches* (London: John Murray, 1873).

Grote, G., 'Clinton's Fasti Hellenici. The civil and literary chronology of Greece', *Westminster Review* 5 (1826), pp. 269–331.

Grote, G., 'Early Roman history', *Eclectic Review* 10 (1855), pp. 172–190.

Grote, G., *Essentials of parliamentary reform* (London: Baldwin, Craddock, 1831).

Grote, G., *History of Greece; from the earliest period to the close of the generation contemporary with Alexander the Great* [1846–1856] (New York: Harper and Brothers, 1880), 12 vols.

Grote, G., *Plato and other companions of Socrates* (London: John Murray, 1867), 3 vols.

Grote, G., *Poems by George Grote 1815–1823* (London: Savill, Edwards and Co., 1872).

Grote, G., *Seven letters concerning the politics of Switzerland, pending the outbreak of the civil war in 1847* (London: John Murray, 1876).

Grote, G., *Statement on the question of parliamentary reform* (London: Baldwin, Cradock, and Joy, 1821).

Grote, H. (ed.), *The personal life of George Grote. Compiled from family documents, private memoranda, and original letters to and from various friends* (London: John Murray, 1873).

Grote, H., *The philosophic radicals of 1832* (London: Savill and Edwards, 1866).

Grote, J., *A few remarks on a pamphlet by Mr. Shilleto, entitled "Thucydides or Grote?"* (Cambridge: John Deighton, 1851).

Guizot, F. (ed. De Witt, H.), *Lettres de m. Guizot à sa famille et à ses amis, recueillies par Mme de Witt* (Paris: Hachette, 1884).

Guizot, F., *Histoire générale de la civilisation en Europe, depuis la chute de l'empire romain jusqu'a la Révolution Français* [1828] (Bruxelles : J. Jamar, 1839).

Guizot, F., *L'histoire de France: depuis les temps les plus reculés jusqu'en 1789* (Paris: Hachette, 1870–1876), 5 vols.

Haac, O. A. (ed.), *The correspondence of John Stuart Mill and Auguste Comte* (London: Transaction, 1995).

Hallam, H., *Introduction to the history of Europe in the fifteenth, sixteenth, and seventeenth centuries* [1837] (New York: Harper, 1848), 8 vols.

Harrison, F., *The meaning of history* (London: Trübner & Co., 1862).

Hartley, D., *Observations on man, his fame, his duty, and his expectations* [1749] (London: Thomas Tegg, 1834).

Hazlitt, W., 'Bentham, Principes de legislation, par Dumont', *The Edinburgh Review* 4 (1804), pp. 1–26.

Hazlitt, W., 'The new school of reform: a dialogue between a rationalist and a sentimentalist' [1826] in Hazlitt, W. (ed. Hazlitt, W. C.), *The plain speaker: opinions on books, men, and things* (London: Bell and Daldy, 1870), pp. 250–273.

Hazlitt, W. (eds. Waller, A. R. and Glover, A.), *The collected works of William Hazlitt* (London: Dent & Co., 1904), 12 vols.

Helvétius, C. (trans. Hooper, W.), *A treatise on man: his intellectual faculties and his education* (London: Albion Press, 1810), 2 vols.

Hobbes, T. (ed. Tuck, R.), *Leviathan* [1651] (Cambridge: Cambridge University Press, 1996).

Hodgson, S., *The philosophy of reflection* (London: Longmans, Green, and Co., 1878), 3 vols.

Howard, R., 'The Westminster Review', *Edinburgh Literary Journal* 2 (1829), pp. 262–266.

Humboldt, W. (trans. Coulthard, J.), *The sphere and duties of government* (London: John Chapman, 1854).

Hume, D. (ed. Greig, J. Y. T.) *The letters of David Hume* [1932] (Oxford: Oxford University Press, 2011), 2 vols.

Hume, D. (ed. Steinberg, E.), *An enquiry concerning human understanding* (Indianapolis: Hackett, 1993).

Hume, D., *A treatise of human nature* [1738–40] (London: Thomas and Joseph Allman, 1817), 2 vols.

Hume, D. (eds. Warner, S. D. and Livingston, D. W.), *Political writings* (Indiana: Hackett, 1994).

Hume, D., *Essays and treatises on several subjects: essays, moral, political and literary* (Edinburgh: Bell and Bradfute, 1825), 2 vols.

Hume, D., *The life of David Hume* (London: Hunt and Clarke, 1826).

Jeffrey, F., *Contributions to the Edinburgh Review* (London: Longman, Brown, Green, and Longmans, 1844).

Kames, H. H., *Historical law-tracts* (Edinburgh: A. Kincaid and J. Bell, 1861).

Kemble, J. M., *The Saxons in England: a history of the English Commonwealth till the period of the Norman Conquest* (London: Longman, Brown, Green & Longmans, 1849), 2 vols.

Kingsley, C., *The limits of exact science as applied to history* (Cambridge: Macmillan & Co., 1860).

Leslie, T. E. C., *Essays in political and moral philosophy* (London: Longmans, Green, & Co, 1879).

Lewes, G. H., *Problems of life and mind* (Boston: Osgood, 1874), 2 vols.

Macaulay, T. B. (ed. Burrow, J.), *Lord Macaulay's History of England* (London: Continuum, 2009).

Macaulay, T. B., *Miscellaneous writings of Lord Macaulay* (London: Longman, Green, Longman, and Roberts, 1869), 2 vols.

Macaulay, T. B., *The works of Lord Macaulay* (London: Spottinswoode and Co., 1871), 8 vols.

Mackintosh, J., *Dissertation on the progress of ethical philosophy, chiefly during the seventeenth and eighteenth centuries* [1830] (Edinburgh: Adam and Charles Black, 1862).

Mackintosh, J. (ed. Mackintosh, R. J.), *Memoirs of the life of the Right Honourable Sir James Mackintosh* (London: Edward Moxon, 1835), 2 vols.

Mackintosh, J., *The miscellaneous works of the Right Honourable Sir James Mackintosh* (London: Longman, Brown, Green, and Longmans, 1851).

Marshall, A. (ed. Whitaker, J. K.), *The correspondence of Alfred Marshall* (Cambridge: Cambridge University Press, 1996), 3 vols.

Marx, K. (ed. Engels, F. and trans. Moore, S. and Aveling, E.), *Capital* [1867] (New York: International, 1967), 3 vols.

Maurice, F. D. (ed. Maurice, F.), *The life of Frederick Denison Maurice chiefly told in his own letters* (London: Macmillan, 1885), 2 vols.

McIlwraith, W., *The life and writings of George Grote. An essay.* (Wolverhampton: Barford & Newitt, 1885).

Michelet, J. (ed. and trans. Villaneix, P. and Digeon, C.), *Journal* (Paris: Gallimard, 1959), 2 vols.

Michelet, J., *Introduction à l'histoire universelle* [1831] (Paris: Libraire Classique de L. Hachette, 1834).

Michelet, J., *Oeuvres de M. Michelet* (Bruxelles: Meline, Cans et Compagnie, 1840), 8 vols.

Mill, J. (ed. Ball, T.), 'Education', *Political writings* (Cambridge: Cambridge University Press, 1992).

Mill, J. (ed. Fenn, R. A.), *James Mill's common place books* (2010), http://intellec tualhistory.net/mill/cpb3ch5.html, accessed on 10 March 2014.

Mill, J. (eds. Mill, J. S., Bain, A., Findlater, A., and Grote, G.), *Analysis of the phenomena of the human mind* (London: Longman, Green, Reader, and Dyer, 1878), 2 vols.

Mill, J., 'Voyages à Peking, Manille et l'île de France. Par M. de Guignes', *The Edinburgh Review; or Critical Journal* 28 (1809), pp. 407–429.

Mill, J., 'Affairs of India', *The Edinburgh Review* 16 (1810), pp. 127–157.

Mill, J., 'An historical view of the English government by J. Millar', *The Literary Journal* 2.6 (1803), pp. 325–333.

Mill, J., 'Elements of the philosophy of mind, by Dugald Stewart', *British Review and London Critical Journal* 6 (1815), pp. 170–200.

Mill, J., 'Theory and practice: a dialogue', *The London and Westminster Review* 25 (1836), pp. 223–234.

Mill, J., *A fragment on Mackintosh: being strictures on some passages in the dissertation by Sir James Mackintosh prefixed to the Encyclopædia Britannica* (London: Longman, Green, Reader, and Dyer, 1870).

Mill, J., *An essay of the impolicy of a bounty on the exportation of grain* (London: C. and R. Baldwin, 1804).

Mill, J., *Colony* (London: J. Innes, 1825).

Mill, J., *The history of British India* [1817] (London: Baldwin, Cradock, and Joy, 1826), 6 vols.

Mill, J., 'The state of the nation', *The London and Westminster Review* 25 (1835), pp. 1–24.

Mill, J., 'Whether political economy is useful?', *The London and Westminster Review* 30 (1836), pp. 553–572.

Mill, J., 'William Dawson's thoughts on public trusts', *Literary Journal* 5.12 (1805), pp. 1297–1311.

Mill, J. S. (ed. Robson, J. M. and others), *The collected works of John Stuart Mill*, (Toronto: University of Toronto Press, 1963–1991), 33 vols.

Mitford, W., *The history of Greece* (London: T. Caddell, 1838), 10 vols.

Montesquieu, C. (ed. Cohler, A. M.), *The spirit of the laws* (Cambridge: Cambridge University Press, 1989).

Niebuhr, B. G. (trans. Smith, W. and Schmitz, L.), *The history of Rome* (Philadelphia: Lea & Blanchard, 1844), 5 vols.

Owen, R., *A new view of society* [1813] (London: Longman, Hurts, Rees, & Co, 1817).

Pope, A., *An essay on man, and other poems* (London: John Sharpe, 1829).

Ricardo, D., *Reply to Mr. Bosanquet's observations on the report of the bullion committee* (London: John Murray, 1811).

Ricardo, D. (ed. Sraffa, P.), *The works and correspondence of David Ricardo* (Cambridge: Cambridge University Press, 1951), 11 vols.

Robertson, W., *The history of Scotland during the reigns of Queen Mary and of King James VI* [1759] (London: T. Cadell, 1794), 2 vols.

Saint-Simon, H., *Noveau chrstianisme, dialogues entre un conservateur et un novateur* (Paris: Bossange Père, 1825).

Saint-Simon, H. (ed. Rodrigues, O.), *Œuvres de Saint-Simon* (Paris: Capelle, libraire-éditeur, 1841).

Saint-Simon, H., *Œuvres de Saint-Simon* (Bruxelles: Van Meenen, 1859), 3 vols.

Saint-Simon, H. (trans. Iggers, G. G.), *The doctrine of Saint-Simon: an exposition, first year, 1828–9* (Boston: Beacon Press, 1958).

Seeley, J. R., *Classical studies as an introduction to the moral sciences* (London: Bell and Daldy, 1864).

Shilleto, R., *Thucydides or Grote?* (Cambridge: John Deighton, 1851).

Sidgwick, H., *The elements of politics* [1891] (Cambridge: Cambridge University Press, 2012).

Sidgwick, H., 'The historical method', *Mind* 11.42 (1886), pp. 203–219.

Smith, W., *A dictionary of Greek and Roman antiquities* (London: John Murray, 1842).

Smith, A. (ed. Stewart, D.), *Essays on philosophical subjects* (Dublin: Wogan, Byrne, Moore, Colbert, Rice, Jones, Porter, and Folingsby, 1795).

Smith, A. (eds. Campbell, R. H. and Skinner, A. S.), *An enquiry into the nature and causes of the wealth of nations* [1776] (Oxford: Oxford University Press, 1981).

Sortain, J., 'Bentham's Science of morality', *The Edinburgh Review* 61 (1835), pp. 365–379.

Spencer, H., *An autobiography* (New York: Appleton, 1905), 2 vols.

Spencer, H., *Essays: scientific, political, speculative* (London: Williams and Norgate, 1863).

Spencer, H., *The study of sociology* [1873] (New York: Appleton & Co., 1874).

Stephen, J., 'Buckle's History of civilisation in England', *The Edinburgh Review* 107 (1858), pp. 238–262.

Stephen, J., *Lectures on the history of France* [1852] (London: Longman, Brown, Green, Longmans, and Roberts, 1857), 2 vols.

Stephen, J., *Liberty, equality, fraternity* (New York: Holt and Williams, 1873).

Stephen, J., 'The study of history', *The Cornhill Magazine* 4 (1861), pp. 25–43.

Stewart, D., *The works of Dugald Stewart* (Cambridge: Hilliard and Brown, 1829), 7 vols.

Taine, H. A., 'Philosophie anglaise: John Stuart Mill', *Revue des deux mondes* 32 (1861), pp. 44–83.

Taine, H. A., *Le positivisme anglaise: étude sur Stuart Mill* (Paris: Ballière, 1864).

Thirlwall, C. (ed. Liddel, P.), *History of Greece* [1835] (Exeter: Bristol Phoenix Press, 2007).

Thirlwall, C., *A history of Greece* (London: Longman, Brown, Green, and Longmans, 1835–1844), 8 vols.

Thirlwall, C. (ed. Stewart Perowne, J. J.), *Remains literary and theological of Connop Thirlwall* (London: Daldy, Isbister & Co., 1878), 3 vols.

Thucydides (trans. Lattimore, S.), *The Peloponnesian War* (Indianapolis: Hackett, 1998).

Tocqueville, A., *De la démocratie en Amérique [1835–1840]* (Paris: M. Lévy, 1864), 3 vols.

Tytler, A. F., *Memoirs of the life and writings of the Honourable Henry Home of Kames* [1807] (Edinburgh: T. Cadell and W. Davies, 1814), 2 vols.

Villers, C. (trans. and ed. Mill, J.), *An essay on the spirit and influence of the Reformation of Luther* (London: Baldwin, 1805).

Wells, D. B., *St. Paul vindicated: being part one of a reply to a late publication by Gamaliel Smith* (T. Sevenson: Cambridge, 1824).

Whewell, W. (ed. Yeo, R. R.), *Collected works of William Whewell* (Bristol: Thoemmes, 2001), 16 vols.

Wilson, H. H., 'Preface' in Mill, J., *The history of British India* (London: James Madden, 1840), I, pp. i–xxxvi.

Winkworth, S. (ed.), *The life and letters of Barthold Georg Niebuhr: with essays on his character and influence* (New York: Harper and Brothers, 1852).

Wordsworth, W. (eds. Wordsworth, J., Abrams, M. H. and Gill, S.), *The Prelude: 1799, 1805, 1850* (New York and London: Norton, 1979).

Secondary Works

Abbatista, G., 'The historical thought of the French philosophes' in Rabasa, J. and Woolf, D. R. (eds.), *The Oxford history of historical writing* (Oxford: Oxford University Press, 2012), III, pp. 406–428.

Abi-Marshed, O. W., *Apostles of modernity: Saint-Simonians and the colonial civilising mission in Algeria* (Stanford: Stanford University Press, 2010).

Alexander, E., 'The principles of permanence and progression in the thought of J. S. Mill' in Robson, J. M. and Laine, M. (eds.), *James and John Stuart Mill/ Papers of the centenary conference* (Toronto: University of Toronto Press, 1976), pp. 126–142.

Allen, P., 'S. T. Coleridge's church and state and the idea of an intellectual establishment', *Journal of the History of Ideas* 46 (1985), pp. 89–106.

Anderson, O., 'The political uses of history in mid nineteenth-century England', *Past and Present* 36 (1967), pp. 87–105.

Anschutz, R. P., 'The logic of J. S. Mill' in Schneewind, J. B. (ed.), *Mill: a collection of critical essays* (London: Macmillan, 1968), pp. 46–83.

Armenteros, C., *The French idea of history: Joseph de Maistre and his heirs, 1794–1854* (Ithaca: Cornell University Press, 2011).

Armitage, D., 'A patriot for whom? The afterlives of Bolingbroke's Patriot King', *The Journal of British Studies* 36.4 (1997), pp. 397–418.

Armitage, D., 'Globalising Jeremy Bentham', *History of Political Thought* 32.1 (2011), pp. 63–82.

Baker, T. N., 'National history in the age of Michelet, Macaulay, and Bancroft' in Kramer, L. and Maza, S. (eds.), *A companion to Western historical thought* (London: Blackwell, 2002), pp. 185–204.

Ball, T., 'The formation of character: Mill's "ethology" reconsidered', *Polity* 33 (2000), pp. 25–48.

Barrow, R., *Utilitarianism: a contemporary statement* (London: Routledge, 1991).

Baum, B., 'J. S. Mill and liberal socialism' in Urbinati, N. and Zakaras, A. (eds.), *J. S. Mill's political thought: a bicentennial reassessment* (Cambridge: Cambridge University Press, 2007), pp. 98–124.

Baum, B. D., *Rereading freedom and power in J. S. Mill* (Toronto: University of Toronto Press, 2000).

Baumgarten, M., 'The ideas of history of Thomas Carlyle and John Stuart Mill: a summary statement', *The Mill Newsletter* 3.1 (1967), pp. 8–9.

Bayles, M. D. (ed.), *Contemporary utilitarianism* (New York: Anchor Books, 1968).

Bayly, C., *Recovering liberties: Indian thought in the age of liberalism and empire* (Cambridge: Cambridge University Press, 2011).

Bebbington, D. W., *Evangelicalism in modern Britain: a history from the 1730s to the 1980s* (London: Routledge, 2003).

Beebee, H., *Hume on causation* (London: Routledge, 2006).

Beecher, J., *Charles Fourier: the visionary and his world* (Berkeley: University of California Press, 1986).

Beiser, F. C., 'Historicism' in Rosen, M. and Leiter, B. (eds.), *The Oxford handbook of continental philosophy* (Oxford: Oxford University Press, 2009), pp. 155–180.

Beiser, F. C., *The German historicist tradition* (Oxford: Oxford University Press, 2011).

Ben-Israel, H., *English historians on the French Revolution* (Cambridge: Cambridge University Press, 1968).

Benn, A. W., *The history of English rationalism in the nineteenth century* (London: Longmans and Green, 1906), 2 vols.

Bentley, M., *Modernising England's past: English historiography in the age of modernism, 1870–1970* (Cambridge: Cambridge University Press, 2005).

Bentley, M., 'Theories of world history since the Enlightenment' in Bentley, J. H. (ed.), *The Oxford handbook of world history* (Oxford: Oxford University Press, 2012), pp. 19–36.

Berlin, I., 'Corsi e ricorsi', *Journal of Modern History* 50 (1978), pp. 480–489.

Berlin, I., *Four essays on liberty* (Oxford: Oxford University Press, 1969).

Bernstein, S., *French political and intellectual history* (New Brunswick: Transaction, 1955).

Betts, J., 'John Stuart Mill, Victorian liberalism, and the failure of cooperative production', *The Historical Journal* 59.1 (2016), pp. 153–174.

Bevir, M. (ed.), *Historicism and the human sciences in Victorian Britain* (Cambridge: Cambridge University Press, 2017).

Bevir, M., 'The long nineteenth century in intellectual history', *Journal of Victorian Culture* 6.2 (2001), pp. 313–336.

Biagini, E., 'Liberalism and direct democracy: John Stuart Mill and the model of ancient Athens' in Biagini, E. (ed.), *Citizenship and community: liberals, radicals and collective identities in the British Isles, 1865–1931* (Cambridge: Cambridge University Press, 1996), pp. 21–44.

Blaas, P. B. M., *Continuity and anachronism: parliamentary and constitutional development in Whig historiography and in the anti-Whig reaction between 1890 and 1930* (Amsterdam: Martinus Nijhoff, 1978).

Blakemore, S., *Intertextual war: Edmund Burke and the French Revolution in the writings of Mary Wollstonecraft, Thomas Paine, and James Mackintosh* (London: Associated University Presses, 1997).

Blamires, C., *The French Revolution and the creation of Benthamism* (London: Palgrave, 2008).

Bolgar, R. R. (ed.), *Classical influences on western thought, A.D. 1650–1870* (Cambridge: Cambridge University Press, 1979).

Bord, J., *Science and Whig manners: science and political style in Britain, c. 1750–1850* (London: Palgrave, 2009).

Bourke, R., *Empire and revolution: the political life of Edmund Burke* (Princeton: Princeton University Press, 2015).

Bouton, C. W., 'John Stuart Mill on liberty and history', *Western Political Quarterly* 18 (1965), pp. 569–578.

Bowden, B., *The strange persistence of universal history in political thought* (New York: Springer, 2017).

Bowles, P., 'Adam Smith and the "natural progress of opulence"', *Economica* 53 (1986), pp. 109–118.

Breisach, E., *Historiography: ancient, medieval, and modern* (Chicago: University of Chicago Press, 2008).

Brimnes, N., 'Globalisation and Indian civilisation: questionable continuities' in Mozaffari, M. (ed.), *Globalisation and civilisations* (London: Routledge, 2002), pp. 242–263.

Brink, D. O., *Mill's progressive principles* (Oxford: Oxford University Press, 2013).

Britton, K. and Robson, J. M., 'Mill's debating speeches', *The Mill Newsletter* 1 (1965), pp. 1–7.

Broadie, A., *The Scottish Enlightenment: the historical age of the historical nation* (Edinburgh: Birlinn, 2001).

Brundage, A. and Cosgrove, R. A., *British historians and national identity* (London: Routledge, 2014).

Bruno, G., 'A note on the "is/ought" problem in Hume's ethical writings', *Journal of Value Enquiry* 19 (1985), pp. 311–318.

Budge, G. (ed.), *Romantic empiricism: poetics and the philosophy of common sense 1780–1830* (New Jersey: Associated University Press, 2007).

Burns, J. H., 'Bentham and the French Revolution', *Transactions of the Royal Historical Society* 16 (1966), pp. 95–114.

Burns, J. H., 'Bentham and the Scots', *Journal of Bentham Studies* 7 (2004), pp. 1–12.

Burns, J. H., 'The light of reason: philosophical history in the two Mills' in Smith, G. W. (ed.), *John Stuart Mill's social and political thought: critical assessments* (London: Routledge, 1998), pp. 3–20.

Burrow, J., *A liberal descent: Victorian historians and the English past* (Cambridge: Cambridge University Press, 1981).

Burrow, J., 'Historicism and social evolution' in Stuchtey, B. and Wende, P. (eds.), *British and German historiography 1750–1950: traditions, perceptions, and transfers* (Oxford: Oxford University Press, 2000), pp. 251–265.

Burrow, J., 'Introduction' in Macaulay, T. B. (Burrow, J.), *Lord Macaulay's History of England* (London: Continuum, 2009), pp. 1–23.

Burrow, J., *Evolution and society: a study in Victorian social theory* (Cambridge: Cambridge University Press, 1966).

Burston, W. H., *James Mill on philosophy and education* (London: Athlone Press, 1973).

Butterfield, H., *The Englishman and his history* (Cambridge: Cambridge University Press, 1944).

Butterfield, H., *The Whig interpretation of history* [1931] (London: W. W. Norton, 1961).

Cairns, J. C., 'Mill and history', *CW*, XX, pp. viii–xciii.

Capaldi, N., *John Stuart Mill: a biography* (Cambridge: Cambridge University Press, 2004).

Carli, S., 'Poetry is more philosophical than history: Aristotle on *mimêsis* and form', *The Review of Metaphysics* 64.2 (2010), pp. 303–326.

Carrithers, D. W., 'Montesquieu and Tocqueville as philosophical historians' in Kingston, R. E. (ed.), *Montesquieu and his legacy* (Albany: State University of New York Press, 2009), pp. 149–179.

Cartledge, P., 'Grote's Sparta/Sparta's Grote' in Demetriou, K. N. (ed.), *Brill's companion to George Grote and the classical tradition* (Leiden: Brill, 2014), pp. 255–273.

Castell, A., *Mill's logic of the moral sciences: a study of the impact of Newtonism on early nineteenth century social thought* (Chicago: University of Chicago Libraries, 1936).

Ceserani, G., 'Antiquarian transformations in eighteenth-century Europe' in Schnapp, A. (ed.), *World antiquarianism: comparative perspectives* (Los Angeles: Getty, 2013), pp. 317–343.

Ceserani, G., 'Modern histories of ancient Greece: genealogies, contexts, and eighteenth-century narrative historiography' in Lianeri, A. (ed.), *The western time of ancient history: historiographical encounters with the Greek and Roman pasts* (Cambridge: Cambridge University Press, 2011), pp. 138–156.

Chabert, G., *Un nouveau pouvoir spirituel. Auguste Comte et la religion scientifique au XIXe siècle* (Presses universitaires de Caen, 2004).

Chattopadhyaya, D. P., *Sociology, ideology and utopia: socio-political philosophy of east and west* (Leiden: Brill, 1997).

Chen, J. S., *James Mill's History of British India in its intellectual context*, PhD dissertation, University of Edinburgh (2000).

Chen, J. S., 'Providence and progress: the religious dimension in Ferguson's discussion of civil society' in Heath, E. and Merolle, V. (eds.), *Adam Ferguson: history, progress and human nature* (London: Pickering and Chatto, 2008), pp. 171–187.

Claeys, G., *Citizens and saints: politics and anti-politics in early British socialism* (Cambridge: Cambridge University Press, 1989).

Claeys, G., *Mill and paternalism* (Cambridge: Cambridge University Press, 2013).

Clark, E. A., *History, theory, text: historians and the linguistic turn* (Cambridge: Harvard University Press, 2004).

Clarke, M. L., *George Grote: a biography* (London: Athlone Press, 1962).

Class, M., *Coleridge and Kantian ideas in England, 1796–1817: Coleridge's responses to German philosophy* (London: Bloomsbury Academic, 2012).

Cléro, J. P., 'Bentham et Montesquieu', *Revue Française d'histoire des idées politiques* 35 (2012), pp. 171–182.

Clive, J., 'The use of the past in Victorian England', *Salmagundi* 68/69 (1986), pp. 48–65.

Collingwood, R. G., *Speculum mentis* (Oxford: Clarendon Press, 1924).

Collingwood, R. G., *The idea of history* (Oxford: Oxford University Press, 1994).

Collini, S., *English pasts: essays in history and culture* (Oxford: Oxford University Press, 1999).

Collini, S., *Liberalism and sociology: L. T. Hobhouse and political argument in England 1880–1914* (Cambridge: Cambridge University Press, 1979).

Collini, S., *Public moralists: political thought and intellectual life in Britain, 1850–1930* (Oxford: Oxford University Press, 1993).

Collini, S., Winch, D., and Burrow, J., *That noble science of politics: a study in nineteenth-century intellectual culture* (Cambridge: Cambridge University Press, 1983).

Compton, J. W., 'The emancipation of the American mind: J. S. Mill on the Civil War', *Review of Politics* 70 (2008), pp. 221–244.

Conti, G., 'James Fitzjames Stephen, John Stuart Mill, and the Victorian theory of toleration', *History of European Ideas* 42.3 (2016), pp. 364–398.

Coward, H. G., *The perfectibility of human nature in Eastern and Western thought* (Albany: State University of New York Press, 2008).

Craiutu, A., *Liberalism under siege: the political thought of the French Doctrinaires* (Oxford: Lexington, 2003).

Crimmins, J. E., 'Bentham and utilitarianism in the early nineteenth century' in Eggleston, B. and Miller, D. (eds.), *The Cambridge companion to utilitarianism* (Cambridge: Cambridge University Press, 2014), pp. 38–61.

Crimmins, J. E., 'Bentham on religion: atheism and the secular society', *Journal of the History of Ideas* 47.1 (1986), pp. 95–110.

Crimmins, J. E., 'Bentham's philosophical politics', *The Harvard Review of Philosophy* 3.1 (1993), pp. 18–22.

Crimmins, J. E., *Secular utilitarianism: social science and the critique of religion in the thought of Jeremy Bentham* (Oxford: Oxford University Press, 1990).

Crimmins, J. E., *Utilitarian philosophy and politics. Bentham's later years* (London: Continuum, 2011).

Crisp, R., *The cosmos of duty: Henry Sidgwick's method of ethics* (Oxford: Oxford University Press, 2015).

Croce, B. (trans. Ainslie, D.), *Theory and history of historiography* (London: G. G. Harrap & Co, 1921).

Crossley, C., 'History as a principle of legitimation in France (1820–48)' in Berger, S., Donovan, M., and Passmore, K. (eds.), *Writing national histories: Western Europe since 1800* (London: Routledge, 1999), pp. 49–57.

Crossley, C., *Edgar Quinet: a study in romantic thought* (Lexington: French Forum, 1983).

Crossley, C., *French historians and romanticism: Thierry, Guizot, the Saint-Simonians, Quinet, Michelet* (London: Routledge, 1993).

Culler, A. D., *The Victorian mirror of history* (New Haven: Yale University Press, 1985).

Cumming, I., *Helvétius: his life and place in the history of educational thought* (London: Routledge, 1955).

D'Amico, R., *Historicism and knowledge* (London: Routledge, 1989).

D'Amico, R., 'Historicism' in Tucker, A. (ed.), *A companion to the philosophy of history and historiography* (London: Wiley-Blackwell, 2009), pp. 243–253.

Daston, L., *Classical probability in the Enlightenment* (Princeton: Princeton University Press, 1988).

De Champs, E., *Enlightenment and utility: Bentham in French, Bentham in France* (Cambridge: Cambridge University Press, 2015).

De Champs, E., 'The place of Jeremy Bentham's theory of fictions in eighteenth-century linguistic thought', *Journal of Bentham Studies* 2 (1999), pp. 1–28.

Demetriou, K. N., 'Bishop Thirlwall: historian of Ancient Greece', *Quaderni di Storia* 56 (2002), pp. 49–91.

Demetriou, K. N., 'In defence of the British constitution: theoretical implications of the debate over Athenian democracy in Britain, 1770–1850', *History of Political Thought* 27.2 (1996), pp. 280–297.

Demetriou, K. N., 'The sophists, democracy, and modern interpretation', *Polis* 14 (1995), pp. 1–29.

Demetriou, K. N., 'The spirit of Athens: George Grote and John Stuart Mill on classical republicanism' in Demetriou, K. N. and Loizides, A. (eds.), *John Stuart Mill: a British Socrates* (London: Palgrave, 2013), pp. 176–207.

Demetriou, K. N., *George Grote on Plato and Athenian democracy: a study in classical reception* (Berne: Peter Lang, 1999).

Demetriou, K. N., *Studies in the reception of Plato and Greek political thought in Britain* (Surrey: Ashgate, 2011).

Den Otter, S. M., 'The origins of a historical political science in Late Victorian and Edwardian Britain' in Adcock, R., Bevir, M., and Stimson, S. C. (eds.), *Modern political science: Anglo-American exchanges since 1880* (Princeton, New Jersey: Princeton University Press, 2007), pp. 37–66.

Devigne, R., *Reforming liberalism: J. S. Mill's use of ancient, liberal, and romantic moralities* (New Haven: Yale University Press, 2006).

Dinwiddy, J. R. (ed. Twining, W.), *Bentham. Selected writings of John Dinwiddy* (Stanford: Stanford University Press, 2004).

Dinwiddy, J. R, 'Early-nineteenth-century reactions to Benthamism', *Transactions of the Royal Historical Society* 34 (1984), pp. 47–69.

Dinwiddy, J. R., 'Bentham's transition to political radicalism, 1809–10', *Journal of the History of Ideas* 36.4 (1975), pp. 683–700.

Dinwiddy, J. R., 'Sir Frances Burdett and Burdette radicalism', *Journal of the Historical Association* 65 (1980), pp. 17–31.

Dinwiddy, J. R., *Radicalism and reform in Britain, 1780–1850* (London: Hambledon, 1992).

Distad, N. M., 'The Philological Museum of 1831–1833', *Victorian Periodicals Newsletter* 18 (1972), pp. 27–30.

Dockhorn, K., *Der Deutsche Historismus in England: Ein Beitrag zur Englischen Geistesgeschichte des 19. Jahrhunderts* (Göttingen: Vandenhoeck & Ruprecht, 1950).

Donatelli, P., 'Mill's perfectionism', *Prolegomena* 5.2 (2006), pp. 149–164.

Donner, W., 'Mill's utilitarianism' in Skorupski, J. (ed.), *The Cambridge companion to Mill* (Cambridge: Cambridge University Press, 1998), pp. 255–292.

Donner, W., 'Morality, virtue, and aesthetics in Mill's art of life' in Eggleston, B., Miller, D., and Weinstein, D. (eds.), *John Stuart Mill and the art of life* (Oxford: Oxford University Press, 2011), pp. 146–165.

Donner, W., *The liberal self: John Stuart Mill's moral and political philosophy* (Ithaca: Cornell University Press, 1991).

Dray, W. H., *On history and philosophers of history* (Amsterdam: Brill, 1989).

Dreyer, F. A., *Burke's politics: a study in Whig orthodoxy* (Ontario: Wilfrid Laurier University Press, 1979).

Dube, A., 'The tree of utility in India' in Moir, M. I., Peers, D. M., and Zastoupil, L. (eds.), *J. S. Mill's encounter with India* (Toronto: Toronto University Press, 1999), pp. 34–52.

Ebery, D., 'Introduction', in Ebery, D. (ed.), *Theory and practice in Aristotle's natural science* (Cambridge: Cambridge University Press, 2015), pp. 1–11.

Edge, M., 'Athens and the spectrum of liberty', *History of Political Thought* 30 (2009), pp. 1–47.

Edwards, P., 'Coleridge on politics and religion' in Burwick, F. (ed.), *The Oxford handbook of Samuel Taylor Coleridge* (Oxford: Oxford University Press, 2009), pp. 235–254.

Edwards, P., *The statesman's science: history, nature, and law in the political thought of Samuel Taylor Coleridge* (New York: Columbia University Press, 2004).

Ehrenberg, V., *Man, state, and deity: essays in ancient history* [1974] (London: Routledge, 2011).

Eisenach, E. J., 'Mill and liberal Christianity' in Eisenach, E. J. (ed.), *Mill and the moral character of liberalism* (Pennsylvania: Penn State Press, 1998).

Eisenach, E. J., 'The dimension of history in Bentham's theory of law' in Parekh, B. C. (ed.), *Jeremy Bentham: critical assessments* (London: Routledge, 1993), III, pp. 139–163.

Eisenberg, J., *John Stuart Mill's philosophy of history*, PhD dissertation, Drew University (2016).

Elster, J., *Alexis de Tocqueville, the first social scientist* (Cambridge: Cambridge University Press, 2009).

Engelmann, S. G. and Pitts, J., 'Bentham's "place and time"', *La revue Tocqueville* 32.1 (2011), pp. 43–66.

Ergang, R. R., *Herder and German nationalism* (New York: Octagon, 1976).

Evnine, S., 'Hume, conjectural history, and the uniformity of human nature', *Journal of the History of Philosophy* 31.4 (1993), pp. 589–606.

Fenn, R. A., *James Mill's political thought* (London: Garland, 1987).

Feuer, L. S., 'John Stuart Mill as a sociologist: the unwritten ethology' in Robson, J. M. and Laine, M. (eds.), *James and John Stuart Mill/Papers of the centenary conference* (Toronto: University of Toronto Press, 1976), pp. 97–110.

Filipiuk, M., 'John Stuart Mill and France', in Laine, M. (ed.), *A cultivated mind: essays on J. S. Mill presented to John M. Robson* (Toronto: University of Toronto Press, 1991), pp. 80–120.

Fink, Z. S., *The classical republicans: an essay in the recovery of a pattern of thought in seventeenth-century England* [1945] (Illinois; Northwestern University Press, 1962).

Finley, M. I. (ed.), *The legacy of Greece* (Oxford: Clarendon Press, 1981).

Finley, M. I., *Ancient slavery and modern ideology* (New Jersey: Viking Penguin, 1989).

Fischer, D. H., *Historians' fallacies: toward a logic of historical thought* (London: Routledge, 1970).

Fitzgerald, C. W. R. (ed.), *Human needs and politics* (Oxford: Pergamon Press, 1977).

Fontana, B., *Benjamin Constant and the post-revolutionary mind* (New Haven : Yale University Press, 1991).

Fontana, B., 'Democracy and civilisation: John Stuart Mill and the critique of political economy', *Economies et sociétés* 20.3 (1986), pp. 3–24.

Fontana, B., *Rethinking the politics of commercial society: The Edinburgh Review 1802–1832* (Cambridge: Cambridge University Press, 1985).

Forbes, D., 'Historismus in England', *The Cambridge Journal* 14 (1951), pp. 387–400.

Forbes, D., 'James Mill and India', *The Cambridge Journal* 5.1 (1951), pp. 19–33.

Forbes, D., *Hume's philosophical politics* (Cambridge: Cambridge University Press, 1985).

Forbes, D., *The liberal Anglican idea of history* (Cambridge: Cambridge University Press, 1952).

Franklin, M. J., *'Orientalist Jones': Sir William Jones, poet, lawyer, and linguist, 1746–1794* (Oxford: Oxford University Press, 2011).

Frazer, M., *The enlightenment of sympathy: justice and the moral sentiments in the eighteenth century and today* (Oxford: Oxford University Press, 2010).

Fredman, L. E. and Gordin, B. L. J., 'John Stuart Mill and socialism', *The Mill Newsletter* 3.1 (1967), pp. 3–7.

Frye, L. T., 'Temporality and spatial relations in Past and present: new insights into Carlyle's philosophy of history' in Kerry, E. and Judd, L. (eds.), *Thomas Carlyle resartus: reappraising Carlyle's contribution to the philosophy of history, political theory, and cultural criticism* (New Jersey: Associated University Press, 2010), pp. 148–170.

Fuchs, E., 'Conceptions of scientific history in the nineteenth-century west' in Wang, E. and Iggers, G. G. (eds.), *Turning points in historiography: a cross-cultural perspective* (Rochester: University of Rochester Press, 2002), pp. 147–163.

Fuller, C., 'Bentham, Mill, Grote, and An analysis of the influence of natural religion on the temporal happiness of mankind', *Journal of Bentham Studies* 10 (2008), pp. 1–15.

Garforth, F. W., *John Stuart Mill's theory of education* (Oxford: Martin Robertson, 1979).

Garver, E., *Aristotle's Politics: living well and living together* (Chicago: University of Chicago Press, 2011).

Gibbins, J., 'J. S. Mill, liberalism, and progress' in Bellamy, R. (ed.), *Victorian liberalism. Nineteenth-century political thought and practice* (London: Routledge, 1990), pp. 91–110.

Gibbins, J. R., *John Grote, Cambridge University and the development of Victorian ideas, 1830–1870*, PhD dissertation, University of Newcastle (1987).

Gilmour, R., *The Victorian period: the intellectual and cultural context of English literature, 1830–1890* (London: Routledge, 1993).

Ginzburg, C., 'Checking the evidence: the judge and the historian', *Critical Enquiry* 1 (1991), pp. 79–92.

Giorgini, G., 'Three visions of liberty: John Stuart Mill, Isaiah Berlin, Quentin Skinner' in Demetriou, K. N. and Loizides, A. (eds.), *John Stuart Mill: a British Socrates* (London: Palgrave, 2013), pp. 207–230.

Glover, J. (ed.), *Utilitarianism and its critics* (London: Collier Macmillan, 1990).

Goldman, L., 'Victorian social science: from singular to plural' in Daunton, M. (ed.), *The organisation of knowledge in Victorian Britain* (Oxford: Oxford University Press, 2005), pp. 87–115.

Goodin, R., *Utilitarianism as a public philosophy* (Cambridge: Cambridge University Press, 1993).

Grange, J., *Auguste Comte: la politique et la science* (Paris: Odile Jacob, 2000).

Gray, J. N., 'John Stuart Mill: traditional and revisionist interpretations', *Literature of Liberty* 11.2 (1979), pp. 7–37.

Griggs, T., 'Universal history from the Counter-Reformation to Enlightenment', *Modern Intellectual History* 4.2 (2007), pp. 219–247.

Grint, K., *James Mill's common place books and their intellectual context, 1773–1836*, PhD dissertation, University of Sussex (2013).

Guillin, V., *Auguste Comte and John Stuart Mill on sexual equality: historical, methodological and philosophical issues* (Leiden: Brill, 2009).

Habibi, D. A., *John Stuart Mill and the ethic of human growth* (Dordrecht: Springer Science & Business Media, 2001).

Hadley, E., *Living liberalism* (Chicago: University of Chicago Press, 2010).

Halévy, E. (trans. Morris, M.), *The growth of Philosophic Radicalism* (London: Faber and Faber, 1972).

Halliday, R. J., *John Stuart Mill* (London: Routledge, 2003).

Hamilton, P., *Historicism* (London: Routledge, 2003).

Harré, R., 'Positivist thought in the nineteenth-century' in Baldwin, T., (ed.), *The Cambridge history of philosophy 1870–1945* (Cambridge: Cambridge University Press, 2003), pp. 11–26.

Harris, A. L., 'John Stuart Mill's theory of progress', *Ethics* 66 (1956), pp. 157–175.

Harrison, R., 'John Stuart Mill, mid-Victorian' in Stedman Jones, G. and Claeys, G. (eds.), *The Cambridge history of nineteenth-century political thought* (Cambridge: Cambridge University Press, 2011), pp. 295–319.

Harrison, R., *Bentham: the arguments of the philosophers* (London: Routledge, 1983).

Hart, H. L. A., *Essays on Bentham. Studies in jurisprudence and political theory* (Oxford: Clarendon Press, 1982).

Hawkins, A., *Victorian political culture: 'habits of heart and mind'* (Oxford: Oxford University Press, 2015).

Henary, S., 'Tocqueville and the challenge of historicism', *The Review of Politics* 76 (2014), pp. 469–494.

Herbert, C., *Victorian relativity: radical thought and scientific discovery* (Chicago: University of Chicago Press, 2001).

Hesketh, I., *The science of history in Victorian Britain: making the past speak* (Oxford: Routledge, 2016).

Heyck, T. W., *The transformation of intellectual life in Victorian England* (London: Cromo Helm, 1982).

Heydt, C. , 'Narrative, imagination, and the religion of humanity in Mill's ethics', *Journal of the History of Philosophy* 44.1 (2006), pp. 99–115.

Highet, G., *The classical tradition* (Oxford: Clarendon Press, 1949).

Hilton, B., *A mad, bad, and dangerous people? England 1783–1846* (Oxford: Oxford University Press, 2006).

Himmelfarb, G., 'Bentham scholarship and the Bentham problem' in Parekh, B. C. (ed.), *Jeremy Bentham: critical assessments* (London: Routledge, 1993), I, pp. 423–443.

Hoesch, M., 'From theory to practice: Bentham's reception of Helvétius', *Utilitas* 30.3 (2018), pp. 294–317.

Hollander, S., *The economics of John Stuart Mill* (Toronto: Toronto University Press, 1985), 2 vols.

Holmes, G., *British politics in the age of Anne* (London: Hambledon, 1987).

Holmes, S., 'The liberty to denounce: ancient and modern' in Rosenblatt, H. (ed.), *The Cambridge companion to Constant* (Cambridge: Cambridge University Press, 2009), pp. 47–69.

Hont, I., 'Adam Smith's history of law and government as political theory' in Bourke, R. and Geuss, R. (eds.), *Political judgement: essays for John Dunn* (Cambridge: Cambridge University Press, 2009), pp. 131–172.

Hont, I., 'The language of sociability and commerce: Samuel Pufendorf and the theoretical foundations of the four stages theory' in Pagden, A. (ed.), *The languages of political theory in early modern Europe* (Cambridge: Cambridge University Press, 1987), pp. 227–99.

Hont, I., *Jealousy of trade: international competition and the nation-state in historical perspective* (Harvard: Harvard University Press, 2005).

Hoogensen, G., *International relations, security and Jeremy Bentham* (London: Routledge, 2005).

Höpfl, H. M., 'From savage to Scotsman: conjectural history in the Scottish Enlightenment', *Journal of British Studies* 17.2 (1978), pp. 19–40.

Houghton, W., *The Victorian frame of mind 1830–1870* (New Haven: Yale University Press, 1957).

Hulliung, M., 'Rousseau, Voltaire, and the revenge of Pascal' in Riley, P. (ed.), *The Cambridge companion to Rousseau* (Cambridge: Cambridge University Press, 2001), pp. 57–77.

Iggers, G. G., 'Historicism: the history and meaning of the term', *Journal of the History of Ideas* 56.1 (1995), pp. 129–152.

Iggers, G. G., *The cult of authority: the political philosophy of the Saint-Simonians* (Leiden: Martinus Nijhoff, 1970).

Iggers, G. G., *The German conception of history: the national tradition of historical thought from Herder to the present* (Connecticut: Wesleyan University Press, 1968).

Irwin, T. H., 'Mill and the classical world' in Skorupski, J. (ed.), *The Cambridge companion to Mill* (Cambridge: Cambridge University Press, 1998), pp. 423–463.

Jacobs, J. E., *The voice of Harriet Taylor Mill* (Indiana: Indiana University Press, 2002).

Jann, R., *The art and science of Victorian history* (Columbus: Ohio State University Press, 1985).

Jaume, L., *Tocqueville: the aristocratic sources of liberty* (Princeton: Princeton University Press, 2013).

Jenkyns, R., *The Victorians and ancient Greece* (Oxford: Blackwell, 1980).

Jennings, J., 'Constant's idea of modern liberty' in Rosenblatt, H. (ed.), *The Cambridge companion to Constant* (Cambridge: Cambridge University Press, 2009), pp. 69–92.

Jones, H. S., *Intellect and character in Victorian England: Mark Pattinson and the invention of the Don* (Cambridge: Cambridge University Press, 2007).

Jones, H. S., 'John Stuart Mill as moralist', *Journal of the History of Ideas* 53.2 (1992), pp. 287–308.

Jones, H. S., '"The true Baconian and Newtonian method": Tocqueville's place in the formation of Mill's System of logic', *History of European Ideas* 25.3 (1999), pp. 153–161.

Jones, H. S., 'The early utilitarians, race, and empire: the state of the argument' in Schultz, B. and Varouxakis, G. (eds.), *Utilitarianism and empire* (Oxford: Lexington, 2005), pp. 179–187.

Jones, T. B., 'George Grote and his History of Greece', *The Classical Weekly* 29.8 (1935), pp. 59–61.

Joy, G. C. and McKinney, A. M., 'On a supposed inconsistency in Mill's utilitarianism', *Southwest Philosophical Studies* 14 (1992), pp. 84–91.

Jung, T., 'The politics of time: *Zeitgeist* in early nineteenth-century political discourse', *Contributions to the History of Concepts* 9.1 (2014), pp. 24–49.

Jupp, P., *The governing of Britain, 1688–1848: the executive, Parliament, and the people* (London: Routledge, 2006).

Justman, S., *The hidden text of Mill's liberty* (Maryland: Rowman and Littlefield, 1991).

Kahan, A., *Tocqueville, democracy, and religion: checks and balances for democratic souls* (Oxford: Oxford University Press, 2015).

Kawana, Y., *John Stuart Mill's projected science of society: 1827–1848*, PhD dissertation, University College London (2009).

Kawana, Y., *Logic and society: the political thought of John Stuart Mill, 1827–1848* (London: Palgrave, 2018).

Kent, C., *Brains and numbers: elitism, Comtism, and democracy in mid-Victorian England* (Toronto: University of Toronto Press, 1978).

Kent Wright, J., 'History and historicism' in Porter, T. M. and Ross, D. (eds.), *The Cambridge history of science: the modern social sciences* (Cambridge: Cambridge University Press, 2003), pp. 113–131.

Kierstead, J., 'Grote's Athens: the character of democracy' in Demetriou, K. N. (ed.), *Brill's companion to George Grote and the classical tradition* (Leiden: Brill, 2014), pp. 161–211.

Kiliminster, R., *The sociological revolution: from the Enlightenment to the global age* (London: Routledge, 1998).

Kingstone, H., *Victorian narratives of the recent past: memory, history, fiction* (London: Palgrave, 2017).

Kinzer, B., 'George Grote, the Philosophic Radical and politician' in Demetriou, K. N. (ed.), *Brill's companion to George Grote and the classical tradition* (Leiden: Brill, 2014), pp. 16–47.

Kinzer, B., 'J. S. Mill and the secret ballot', *Historical Reflections* 5.1 (1978), pp. 19–39.

Kinzer, B., *J. S. Mill revisited: biographical and political explorations* (London: Palgrave, 2007).

Kippur, S. A., *Jules Michelet: a study of mind and sensibility* (Albany: State University of New York Press, 1981).

Kitcher, P., 'Mill, education, and the good life' in Eggleston, B., Miller, D., and Weinstein, D. (eds.), *John Stuart Mill and the art of life* (Oxford: Oxford University Press, 2011), pp. 192–215.

Knights, B., *The idea of the clerisy in nineteenth-century Britain* (Cambridge: Cambridge University Press, 1978).

Knowles, A., 'Conjecturing rudeness: James Mill's utilitarian philosophy of history and the British civilising mission' in Watt, C. A. and Mann, M. (eds.), *Civilising missions in colonial and postcolonial South Asia* (London: Anthem, 2011), pp. 37–65.

Knudsen, J., 'The historicist Enlightenment' in Baker, K. M. and Reill, P. (eds.), *What's left of Enlightenment? A postmodern question* (Stanford: Stanford University Press, 2001), pp. 39–50.

Koditschek, T., *Liberalism, imperialism, and the historical imagination: nineteenth-century visions of a greater Britain* (Cambridge: Cambridge University Press, 2011).

Kooy, M. J., 'Romanticism and Coleridge's idea of history', *Journal of the History of Ideas* 60.4 (1999), pp. 717–735.

Kosso, P., 'Philosophy of historiography' in Tucker, A. (ed.), *A companion to the philosophy of history and historiography* (London: Wiley-Blackwell, 2009), pp. 9–26.

Krieger, L., *Ranke: the meaning of history* (Chicago: University of Chicago Press, 1977).

Krieger, L., *Time's reasons: philosophies of history old and new* (Chicago: Chicago University Press, 1989).

Kuklick, B., 'Seven thinkers and how they grew' in Rorty, R., Schneewind, J. B. and Skinner, Q. (eds.), *Philosophy in history: essays on the historiography of philosophy* (Cambridge: Cambridge University Press, 1984), pp. 125–141.

Kurer, O., *John Stuart Mill: the politics of progress* (London: Garland, 1991).

Laborde, C. and Maynor, J., 'The republican contribution to political theory' in Laborde, C. and Maynor, J. (eds.), *Republicanism and political theory* (Oxford: Wiley & Sons, 2009), pp. 1–31.

Lachs, J., 'Mill and Constant: a neglected connection in the history of the idea of liberty', *History of Philosophy Quarterly* 9 (1992), pp. 87–96.

Lane, M., 'Political theory and time' in Baert, P. N. (ed.), *Time in modern intellectual thought* (Amsterdam: Elsevier, 2000), pp. 233–251.

Larsen, T., *John Stuart Mill: a secular life* (Oxford: Oxford University Press, 2018).

Le Rider, J., 'La codification, objet de la controverse Thibaut-Savigny' in Kamecke, G. and Le Rider, J. (eds.), *La codification: perspectives transdisciplinaires* (Paris: Librairie Droz, 2007), pp. 161–179.

Levin, M., *Mill on civilisation and barbarism* (London: Routledge, 2004).

Levine, P. J. A., *The amateur and the professional: antiquarians, historians, and archaeologists in Victorian England 1838–1886* (Cambridge: Cambridge University Press, 1986).

Lewisohn, D., 'Mill and Comte on the methods of social science', *Journal of the History of Ideas* 33 (1972), pp. 315–324.

Lianeri, A., 'Unfounding times: the idea and ideal of ancient history in Western historical thought' in Lianeri, A. (ed.), *The western time of ancient history: historiographical encounters with the Greek and Roman pasts* (Cambridge: Cambridge University Press, 2011), pp. 3–33.

Liddel, P., 'Liberty and obligation in George Grote's Athens', *Polis* 23 (2006), pp. 140–161.

Liddel, P., 'The comparative approach in Grote's <u>History of Greece</u>' in Demetriou, K. N. (ed.), *Brill's companion to George Grote and the classical tradition* (Leiden: Brill, 2014), pp. 211–254.

Liddel, P., *Civic obligation and individual liberty in ancient Athens* (Oxford: Oxford University Press, 2007).

Liebel, H. P., 'The Enlightenment and the rise of historicism in German thought', *Eighteenth-Century Studies* 4.4 (1971), pp. 359–385.

Lieberman, D., 'Adam Smith on justice, rights, and law' in Haakonssen, K. (ed.), *The Cambridge companion to Adam Smith* (Cambridge: Cambridge University Press, 2006), pp. 214–246.

Lieberman, D., 'From Bentham to Benthamism', *The Historical Journal* 28.1 (1985), pp. 199–224.

Lieberman, D., *The province of legislation determined* (Cambridge: Cambridge University Press, 1989).

Lifschitz, A., *Language and Enlightenment: the Berlin debates of the eighteenth century* (Oxford: Oxford University Press, 2012).

Lindsay, A. D., 'Introduction' in Grote, G. (ed. Lindsay, A. D.), *History of Greece* [1846–1856] (London: Dent, 1906), I, pp. vii-xiv.

Lively, J. and Rees, J. (eds.), *Utilitarian logic and politics* (Oxford: Clarendon Press, 1978).

Livingstone, R. W. (ed.), *The legacy of Greece* (Oxford: Clarendon Press, 1921).

Loizides, A., 'Induction, deduction, and James Mill's "Government"', *Modern Intellectual History* (2015), pp. 1–29.

Loizides, A., 'James Mill and George Grote: a defence of "theoretic freedom"' in Demetriou, K. N. (ed.), *Brill's companion to George Grote and the classical tradition* (Leiden: Brill, 2014), pp. 47–85.

Loizides, A., *James Mill's utilitarian logic and politics* (London: Routledge, 2019).

Loizides, A., 'Mill on the method of politics' in Loizides, A. (ed.), *Mill's A system of logic: critical appraisals* (London: Routledge, 2014), pp. 218–246.

Loizides, A., *John Stuart Mill's Platonic heritage: happiness through character* (Lanham: Lexington, 2013).

Long, D. G., *Bentham on liberty: Jeremy Bentham's idea of liberty in relation to his utilitarianism* (Toronto: Toronto University Press, 1977).

Long, D. G., 'Censorial jurisprudence and political radicalism: a reconsideration of the early Bentham', *The Bentham Newsletter* 12 (1988), pp. 4–24.

López, R., 'John Stuart Mill's idea of history: a rhetoric of progress', *Res Publica: Revista de Filosofía Política*, 27 (2012), pp. 63–74.

Loring, R., 'The role of universal jurisprudence in Bentham's legal cosmopolitanism', *Revue d'études benthamiennes* 13 (2014), http://journals.openedition.org/etudes-benthamiennes/749, last accessed on 7 June 2017.

Losman, D. L., 'J. S. Mill on alternative economic systems', *American Journal of Economics and Sociology* 30 (1971), pp. 85–104.

Macedo, S., *Liberal virtues: citizenship, virtue, and community in liberal constitutionalism* (Oxford: Oxford University Press, 1990).

Macgregor Morris, I., 'Navigating the Grotesque; or, rethinking Greek historiography' in Moore, J., Macgregor Morris, I., and Bayliss, A. J. (eds.), *Reinventing history: the Enlightenment origins of ancient history* (London: Institute of Historical Research, 2008), pp. 247–290.

Macintyre, S., Maiguashca, J., and Pók, A. (eds.), *The Oxford history of historical writing* (Oxford: Oxford University Press, 2011–2015), 5 vols.

Macleod, C., 'Mill on history' in Macleod, C. and Miller, D. (eds.), *A companion to Mill* (Oxford: Wiley Blackwell, 2017), pp. 266–279.

Mack, M. P., *Jeremy Bentham: an odyssey of ideas, 1748–1792* (London: Heinemann, 1962).

Majeed, J., 'James Mill's The history of British India: a reevaluation' in Moir, M. I., Peers, D. M., and Zastoupil, L. (eds.), *J. S. Mill's encounter with India* (Toronto: Toronto University Press, 1999), pp. 53–72.

Majeed, J., *Ungoverned imaginings: James Mill's The history of British India and orientalism* (Oxford: Oxford University Press, 1992).

Mandler, P., *The English national character: the history of an idea from Edmund Burke to Tony Blair* (New Haven: Yale University Press, 2006).

Manin, B., *The principles of representative government* (Cambridge: Cambridge University Press, 1997).

Mansfield, H. C. and Winthrop, D., 'Tocqueville's new political science' in Welch, C. B. (ed.), *The Cambridge companion to Tocqueville* (Cambridge: Cambridge University Press, 2006), pp. 81–108.

Manuel, F., *The prophets of Paris: Turgot, Condorcet, Saint-Simon, Fourier, and Comte* (New York: Harper, 1962).

Manuel, F., *The new world of Henri Saint-Simon* (Cambridge: Harvard University Press, 1956).

Marsh, J. L., *Critique, action and liberation* (Albany: State University of New York Press, 1995).

Marshall, D., *Vico and the transformation of rhetoric in early modern Europe* (Cambridge: Cambridge University Press, 2010).

Marwah, I. S. 'Complicating barbarism and civilisation: Mill's complex sociology of human development', *History of Political Thought* 32.2 (2011), pp. 345–366.

Marwah, I. S., *Liberalism, diversity, and domination: Kant, Mill, and the government of difference* (Cambridge: Cambridge University Press, 2019).

Mayer, P., 'Alexis de Tocqueville and John Stuart Mill', *The Listener* 43 (1950), pp. 471–472.

Mazlish, B., *James and John Stuart Mill. Father and son in the Nineteenth Century* (London: Hutchinson, 1975).

McCabe, H., 'Navigating by the North Star: the role of the "ideal" in John Stuart Mill's view of "utopian" schemes and the possibilities of social transformation', *Utilitas* 31 (2019), pp. 291–309.

McCalla, A., 'Romantic Vicos: Vico and providence in Michelet and Ballanche', *Réflexions historiques* 19.3 (1993), pp. 389–408.

McKown, D. B., *Behold the antichrist. Bentham on religion* (New York: Prometheus, 2004).

Mehta, U., *Liberalism and empire: a study in nineteenth-century British liberal thought* (Chicago: University of Chicago Press, 1999).

Meinecke, F., *Historism: the rise of a new historical outlook* (New York: Herder and Herder, 1972).

Melman, B., 'Claiming the nation's past: the invention of an Anglo-Saxon tradition', *Journal of Contemporary History* 26 (1991), pp. 575–595.

Merrill, T. W., *Hume and the politics of Enlightenment* (Cambridge: Cambridge University Press, 2015).

Meyer, A., 'Ferguson's "appropriate stile"' in Heath, E. and Merolle, V. (eds.), *Adam Ferguson: history, progress and human nature* (London: Pickering and Chatto, 2008), pp. 131–146.

Middell, M., 'The French Revolution in the global world of the eighteenth century' in Forest, A. and Middell, M. (eds.), *The Routledge companion to the French Revolution in world history* (London: Routledge, 2016), pp. 23–39.

Mill, A. J., 'John Stuart Mill's visit to Wordsworth, 1831', *The Modern Language Review* 44 (1949), pp. 341–350.

Miller, D., *John Stuart Mill* (Cambridge: Polity Press, 2010).

Millgram, E., *John Stuart Mill and the meaning of life* (Oxford: Oxford University Press, 2019).

Mitchell, A. A., 'Bentham and his school' in Parekh, B. C. (ed.), *Jeremy Bentham: critical assessments* (London: Routledge, 1993), I, pp. 290–317.

Mitchell, H., *Individual choice and the structures of history: Alex de Tocqueville as historian reappraised* (Cambridge: Cambridge University Press, 1996).

Mitchell, R., *Picturing the past: English history in text and image, 1830–1870* (Oxford: Oxford University Press, 2000).

Momigliano, A. (eds. Bowersock, G. W. and Cornell, T. J.), *A. D. Momigliano: studies on modern scholarship* (London: University of California Press, 1994).

Morales, M., *Perfect equality: John Stuart Mill on well-constituted communities* (Maryland: Rowman and Littlefield, 1996).

Mori, J., *Britain in the age of the French Revolution* (London: Routledge, 2000).

Moyer, C. R., 'The idea of history in Thomas and Matthew Arnold', *Modern Philology* 67 (1969), pp. 160–167.

Mueller, I. W., *John Stuart Mill and French thought* (Urbana: University of Illinois Press, 1956).

Muhlack, U., 'German Enlightenment historiography and the rise of historicism' in Bourgault, S. and Sparling, R. (eds.), *A companion to Enlightenment historiography* (Leiden: Brill, 2013), pp. 249–307.

Muhlack, U., 'Universal history and national history: eighteenth- and nineteenth-century German historians and the scholarly community' in Stuchtey, B. and Wende, P. (eds.), *British and German historiography 1750–1950: traditions, perceptions, and transfers* (Oxford: Oxford University Press, 2000), pp. 25–49.

Mulgan, T., 'Utilitarianism and our obligations to future people' in Eggleston, B. and Miller, D. (eds.), *The Cambridge companion to utilitarianism* (Cambridge: Cambridge University Press, 2014), pp. 325–348.

Murray, C. J. (ed.), *Encyclopedia of the Romantic era* (London: Routledge, 2004), 2 vols.

Newbould, I., *Whiggery and reform 1830–41: the politics of government* (California: Stanford University Press, 1990).

Nicholson, P., *The political philosophy of the British Idealists: selected studies* (Cambridge: Cambridge University Press, 1990).

Nickau, K., 'Karl Otfried Müller, Professor der Klassischen Philologie 1819–1840' in Classen, C. J. (ed.), *Die Klassische Altertumswissenschaft an der Georg-August-Universität Göttingen* (Göttingen: Vandenhoeck & Ruprecht, 1989), pp. 27–53.

Nippel, W., *Ancient and modern democracy: two concepts of liberty?* (Cambridge: Cambridge University Press, 2015).

Nippel, W., *Antike oder moderne Freiheit? Die Begründung der Demokratie in Athen und in der Neuzeit* (Berlin: Fischer Taschenbuch Verlag, 2008).

Nisbet, R. A., *History of the idea of progress* (New Brunswick: Transaction, 1980).

Nisbet, R. A., *Metaphor and history: the Western idea of social development* [1969] (London: Transaction, 2009).

Nora, P., 'Introduction' in Nora, P. (ed.), *Rethinking France: les lieux de mémoire* [1984] (Chicago: University of Chicago Press, 2010), IV, pp. vii–xiv.

Noronha-DiVanna, I., *Writing history in the Third Republic* (Newcastle upon Tyne: Cambridge Scholars Publishing, 2010).

O'Brien, K., 'English Enlightenment histories 1750–c.1815' in Rabasa, J. and Woolf, D. R. (eds.), *The Oxford history of historical writing* (Oxford: Oxford University Press, 2012), III, pp. 518–536.

O'Brien, K., *Narratives of Enlightenment: cosmopolitan history from Voltaire to Gibbon* (Cambridge: Cambridge University Press, 1997).

O'Neill, D. I., *The Burke-Wollstonecraft debate: savagery, civilisation, and democracy* (Pennsylvania: Pennsylvania State Press, 2007).

Ober, J., 'What the ancient Greeks can tell us about democracy', *Annual Review of Political Science* 11 (2008), pp. 67–91.

Oexle, O. G., *Geschichtswissenschaft im Zeichen des Historismus: Studien zu Problemgeschichten der Moderne* (Göttingen: Vandenhoeck and Ruprecht, 1996).

Offer, J., *Herbert Spencer and social theory* (London: Palgrave, 2010).

Okie, L., *Augustan historical writing: histories of England in the English Enlightenment* (New York: University Press of America, 1991).

Pagán, V. E., *A companion to Tacitus* (Wiley-Blackwell, 2012).

Palmer, T. G., *Realising freedom: libertarian theory, history, and practice* (Washington: Cato Institute, 2009).

Palmeri, F., *State of nature, stages of society: Enlightenment conjectural history and modern social discourse* (New York: Columbia University Press, 2016).

Pappé, H. O., 'Mill and Tocqueville', *Journal of the History of Ideas* 25.2 (1964), pp. 217–234.

Parker, C., 'English historians and the opposition to positivism', *History and Theory* 22 (1983), pp. 120–145.

Pateman, C., *Participation and democratic theory* (Cambridge: Cambridge University Press, 1970).

Peltonen, M. 'Introduction' in Peltonen, M. (ed.), *The Cambridge companion to Bacon* (Cambridge: Cambridge University Press, 2012), pp. 1–25.

Petit, A., *Le système d'Auguste Comte: de la science à la religion par la philosophie* (Paris: Vrin, 2016).

Pettit, P., *Made with words: Hobbes on language, mind, and politics* (Princeton: Princeton University Press, 2009).

Phillips, M. S., *On historical distance* (New Haven: Yale University Press, 2013).

Phillips, M. S., 'Relocating inwardness: historical distance and the transition from Enlightenment to Romantic historiography', *Modern Language Association* 118.3 (2003), pp. 436–449.

Phillips, M. S., *Society and sentiment: genres of historical writing in Britain, 1740–1820* (New Jersey: Princeton University Press, 2000).

Philp, M., *Reforming ideas in Britain: politics and language in the shadow of the French Revolution* (Cambridge: Cambridge University Press, 2014).

Pick, D., 'Psychoanalysis, history and national culture' in Feldman, D. and Lawrence, J. (eds.), *Structures and transformations in modern British history* (Cambridge: Cambridge University Press, 2011), pp. 210–237.

Pickering, M., 'Auguste Comte and the Saint-Simonians', *French Historical Studies* 18 (1993), pp. 211–236.

Pickering, M., *Auguste Comte: an intellectual biography* (Cambridge: Cambridge University Press, 1993–2009), 3 vols.

Pilbeam, P., *Saint-Simonians in nineteenth-century France: from free love to Algeria* (London: Palgrave Macmillan, 2014).

Pittock, M. G. H., 'Historiography' in Broadie, A. (ed.), *The Cambridge companion to the Scottish Enlightenment* (Cambridge: Cambridge University Press, 2003), pp. 258–280.

Pitts, J., *A turn to empire: the rise of imperial liberalism in Britain and France* (Princeton: Princeton University Press, 2005).

Pitts, J., 'The global in Enlightenment historical thought' in Duara, P., Murthy, V., and Sartori, A. (eds.), *A companion to global historical thought* (Sussex: Wiley Blackwell, 2014), pp. 184–197.

Pocock, J. G. A., *Political thought and history: essays on theory and method* (Cambridge: Cambridge University Press, 2009).

Pocock, J. G. A., 'Adam Smith and history' in Haakonssen, K. (ed.), *The Cambridge companion to Adam Smith* (Cambridge: Cambridge University Press, 2006), pp. 270–288.

Pocock, J. G. A., 'Perceptions of modernity in early modern historical thinking', *Intellectual History Review* 17 (2007), pp. 55–63.

Pocock, J. G. A., *Barbarism and religion* (Cambridge: Cambridge University Press, 1999–2015), 6 vols.

Pompa, L., *Vico: a study of the 'new science'* (Cambridge: Cambridge University Press, 1990).

Popper, K., *The open society and its enemies* [1945] (Princeton: Princeton University Press, 1994).

Popper, K., *The poverty of historicism* [1957] (London: Routledge, 2004).

Porter, T. N., *The rise of statistical thinking 1820–1900* (New Jersey: Princeton University Press, 1986).

Posner, R. A., 'Blackstone and Bentham', *The Journal of Law and Economics* 19.3 (1976), pp. 569–606.

Postema, G., 'The expositor, the censor, and the common law', *Canadian Journal of Philosophy* 9.4 (1979), pp. 643–670.

Potter, E., *Confronting modernity: ancient Athens and modern British political thought c. 1780s–1880s*, PhD dissertation, University of Royal Holloway (2004).

Pradhan, S. V., 'The historiographer of reason: Coleridge's philosophy of history', *Studies in Romanticism* 25.1 (1986), pp. 39–62.

Prest, W., 'William Blackstone and the "free constitution of Britain"' in Galligan, D. (ed.), *Constitutions and the classics: patterns of constitutional thought from Fortescue to Bentham* (Oxford: Oxford University Press, 2014), pp. 191–231.

Preyer, R. O., 'John Stuart Mill on the utility of classical Greece', *Browning Institute Studies* 10 (1982), pp. 41–70.

Preyer, R. O., *Bentham, Coleridge, and the science of history* (Bochum-Langendreer: Verlag Heinrich Pöppinghaus, 1958).

Price, R., 'Historiography, narrative, and the nineteenth century', *Journal of British Studies* 35.2 (1996), pp. 220–256.

Qualter, T. H., 'John Stuart Mill, disciple of de Tocqueville', *Western Political Quarterly* 13 (1960), pp. 880–889.

Quinalt, R., 'The French Revolution of 1830 and parliamentary reform', *History* 79 (1994), pp. 377–393.

Quinn, M., 'Which comes first, Bentham's chicken of utility, or his egg of truth?', *Journal of Bentham Studies* 14 (2012), pp. 1–46.

Raeder, L. C., *John Stuart Mill and the religion of humanity* (Columbia: University of Missouri Press, 2002).

Rawls, J. (ed. Freeman, S.), *Lectures on the history of political philosophy* (Cambridge: Harvard University Press, 2007).

Regan, J., 'No "nonsense upon stilts": James Mill's History of British India and the poetics of Benthamite historiography' in Fermanis, P. and Regan, J. (eds.), *Rethinking British Romantic history* (Oxford: Oxford University Press, 2014), pp. 72–94.

Reill, P. H., 'Barthold Georg Niebuhr and the Enlightenment tradition', *German Studies Review* 3 (1980), pp. 9–26.

Reill, P. H., *The German Enlightenment and the rise of historicism* (California: University of California Press, 1975).

Rendall, J., 'Scottish orientalism: from Robertson to James Mill', *Historical Journal* 25.1 (1982), pp. 43–69.

Richter, C., 'Friedrich Schleiermacher: symbol theory, hermeneutics, and forms of religious communication' in Sockness, B. W. and Gräb, W. (eds.), *Schleiermacher, the study of religion, and the future of theology: a transatlantic dialogue* (Walter de Gruyter, 2010), pp. 375–391.

Riley, J., 'Interpreting Mill's quantitative hedonism', *The Philosophical Quarterly* 53 (2003), pp. 410–18.

Riley, J., *Mill on liberty* (London: Routledge, 1998).

Riley, J. R., 'J. S. Mill's liberal utilitarian assessment of capitalism versus socialism', *Utilitas* 8.1 (1996), pp. 39–71.

Riley, J. R., 'Mill's Greek ideal of individuality' in Demetriou, K. N. and Loizides, A. (eds.), *John Stuart Mill: a British Socrates* (London: Palgrave, 2013), pp. 97–126.

Riley, J. R., 'Mill's neo-Athenian model of liberal democracy' in Urbinati, N. and Zakaras, A. (eds.), *J. S. Mill's political thought: a bicentennial reassessment* (Cambridge: Cambridge University Press, 2007), pp. 221–250.

Roberts, C., *The logic of historical explanation* (Pennsylvania: Penn State Press, 2010).

Roberts, J. T., *Athens on trial: the antidemocratic tradition in Western thought* (Princeton: Princeton University Press, 1994).

Roberts, W., 'Bentham's conception of political change: a liberal approach' in Parekh, B. C. (ed.), *Jeremy Bentham: critical assessments* (London: Routledge, 1993), III, pp. 952–966.

Robson, J. M., *The improvement of mankind: the social and political thought of John Stuart Mill* (Toronto: University of Toronto Press, 1968).

Rosanvallon, P., *Le moment Guizot* (Paris: Bibliotheque des Sciences Humaines, 1985).

Rosen, F., 'The method of reform: J. S. Mill's encounter with Bentham and Coleridge' in Urbinati, N. and Zakaras, A. (eds.), *J. S. Mill's political thought: a bicentennial reassessment* (Cambridge: Cambridge University Press, 2007), pp. 124–147.

Rosen, F., 'The philosophy of error and liberty of thought: J. S. Mill on logical fallacies' in Demetriou, K. N. and Loizides, A. (eds.), *John Stuart Mill: a British Socrates* (London: Palgrave, 2013), pp. 17–49.

Rosen, F., *Classical utilitarianism from Hume to Mill* (London: Routledge, 2003).

Rosen, F., *Jeremy Bentham and representative democracy: a study of The constitutional code* (Clarendon: Oxford, 1983).

Rosen, F., *Mill* (Oxford: Oxford University Press, 2013).

Rosen, S., *The ancients and the moderns: rethinking modernity* (Indianapolis: St Augustine Press, 2002).

Rossi, P., 'Bacon's idea of science' in Peltonen, M. (ed.), *The Cambridge companion to Bacon* (Cambridge: Cambridge University Press, 2012), pp. 25–47.

Rudan, P., 'Society as a code: Bentham and the fabric of order', *History of European Ideas* 42.1 (2016), pp. 39–54.

Rumble, W. E., 'John Austin and his nineteenth-century critics: the case of Sir Henry Summer Maine', *Northern Ireland Legal Quarterly* 39 (1988), pp. 119–149.

Ryan, A., 'Two concepts of democracy: James and John Stuart Mill' in Lively, J. and Reeve, A. (eds.), *Modern political theory from Hobbes to Marx: key debates* (London: Routledge, 1989), pp. 220–248.

Ryan, A., *J. S. Mill* (London: Routledge and Kegan Paul, 1974).

Ryan, A., *The philosophy of John Stuart Mill*, (London: Macmillan, 1987).

Sabine, G. H., 'Hume's contribution to the historical method', *Philosophical Review* 15 (1906), pp. 17–38.

Sato, S., *Edmund Burke as historian: war, order, and civilisation* (Cham: Springer, 2018).

Saxonhouse, A. W., *Free speech and democracy in ancient Athens* (Cambridge: Cambridge University Press, 2006).

Scarre, G., 'Mill on induction and scientific method' in Skorupski, J. (ed.), *The Cambridge companion to Mill* (Cambridge: Cambridge University Press, 1998), pp. 112–138.

Scarre, G., *Logic and reality in the philosophy of John Stuart Mill* (Dordect: Kluwer Academic, 1989).

Scharff, R. C., *Comte after positivism* (Cambridge: Cambridge University Press, 1995).

Schlicke, P., 'Hazlitt, Horne, and the spirit of the age', *Studies in English Literature* 45.4 (2005), pp. 829–851.

Schmidt, C., *David Hume: reason in history* (Pennsylvania: Pennsylvania State University Press, 2003).

Schmidt, M., 'Dugald Stewart, "conjectural history" and the decline of Enlightenment historical writing in the 1790s' in Broich, U., Dickinson, H. T., Hellmuth, E., and Schmidt, M. (eds.), *Reactions to revolutions: the 1790s and their aftermath* (Berlin: Verlag, 2007), pp. 231–263.

Schofield, P., 'Bentham on taste, sex, and religion' in Zhai, X. and Quinn, M. (eds.), *Bentham's theory of law and public opinion* (Cambridge: Cambridge University Press, 2014), pp. 90–119.

Schofield, P., 'Bentham on the identification of interests', *Utilitas* 8 (1996), pp. 223–234.

Schofield, P., 'Jeremy Bentham and nineteenth-century English jurisprudence', *The Journal of Legal History* 12.1 (1991), pp. 58–88.

Schofield, P., 'Jeremy Bentham: legislator of the world', *Current Legal Problems* 51 (1998), pp. 115–147.

Schofield, P., *Bentham: a guide for the perplexed* (London: Continuum, 2009).

Schofield, P., *Utility and democracy: the political thought of Jeremy Bentham* (Oxford: Oxford University Press, 2006).

Schultz, A., *Mind's world: imagination and subjectivity from Descartes to Romanticism* (Seattle: Washington University Press, 2009).

Scott, J., *Commonwealth principles: republican writing on the English Revolution* (Cambridge: Cambridge University Press, 2004).

Sebastiani, S., *The Scottish Enlightenment: race, gender, and the limits of progress* (London: Palgrave, 2013).

Seidman, S., *Liberalism and the origins of European social theory* (Berkeley: University of California Press, 1983).

Sell, A. P. F., *Mill on God: the pervasiveness and elusiveness of Mill's religious thought* (London: Ashgate, 2004).

Sikka, S., *Herder on humanity and cultural difference: enlightened relativism* (Cambridge: Cambridge University Press, 2011).

Simmons, C. A., *Eyes across the channel: French revolutions, party history, and British writing, 1830–1832* (Amsterdam: Harwood, 2000).

Skinner, Q., *Liberty before liberalism* (Cambridge: Cambridge University Press, 1998).

Skinner, Q., *Visions of politics: regarding method* (Cambridge: Cambridge University Press, 2002), 3 vols.

Skorupski, J., *John Stuart Mill* (London: Routledge, 1989).

Skorupski, J., *Why read Mill today?* (London: Routledge, 2006).

Smith, C., 'The Scottish Enlightenment, unintended consequences, and the science of man', *The Journal of Scottish Philosophy* 7.1 (2009), pp. 9–28.

Smith, J., *Fact and feeling: Baconian science and the nineteenth-century literary imagination* (Wisconsin: University of Wisconsin Press, 1994).

Smith, R., *Free will and the human sciences in Britain, 1870–1910* (London: Routledge, 2013).

Smith, R. J., *The Gothic bequest: medieval institutions in British thought, 1688–1863* (Cambridge: Cambridge University Press, 2002).

Snyder, L. J., *Reforming philosophy: a Victorian debate on science and society* (Chicago: University of Chicago Press, 2010).

Sonenscher, M., 'Ideology, social science and general facts in late eighteenth-century French political thought', *History of European Ideas* 35 (2009), pp. 24–37.

Spadafora, D., *The idea of progress in eighteenth-century Britain* (New Haven: Yale University Press, 1990).

Spahn, P., 'George Grote, John Stuart Mill und die antike Demokratie' in Gähde, U. and Schrader, W. H. (eds.), *Der klassische Utilitarianismus* (Berlin: Akademie Verlag, 1991), pp. 145–172.

Sperber, J., *The European revolutions, 1848–1851* (Cambridge: Cambridge University Press, 2005).

Srbik, H. R., *Geist und Geschichte vom deutschen Humanismus bis zur Gegenwart* (Salzberg: Otto Muller Verlag, 1960).

Stanley, A. P., *The life and correspondence of Thomas Arnold* (Boston: Ticknor and Fields, 1868), 2 vols.

Staum, M. S., *Minerva's message: stabilising the French Revolution* (Montreal: McGill-Queen's University Press, 1996).

Stephen, L., *The English utilitarians* [1900] (London: Continuum, 2005), 3 vols.

Stephen, L., *Alexander Pope* (London: Macmillan, 1880).

Stevenson, J., *Popular disturbances in England 1700–1832* (London: Routledge, 1992).

Stewart, L., 'A meaning for machines: modernity, utility, and the eighteenth-century British public', *Journal of Modern History* 70.2 (1998), pp. 259–294.

Stewart, R. S., 'Utilitarianism meets Romanticism: J. S. Mill's theory of imagination', *History of Philosophy* 10.4 (1993), pp. 369–388.

Stokes, E., *The English utilitarians and India* (Oxford: Clarendon Press, 1959).

Stray, S., '"Thucydides or Grote?" Classical disputes and disputed classics in nineteenth-century Cambridge', *Transactions of the American Philological Association* 127 (1974), pp. 363–371.

Stroud, B., 'Hume and the idea of causal necessity', *Philosophical Studies* 33.1 (1978), pp. 39–59.

Stuchtey, B. and Wende, P., 'Towards a comparative history of Anglo-German historiographical traditions and transfers' in Stuchtey, B. and Wende, P. (eds.), *British and German historiography 1750–1950: traditions, perceptions, and transfers* (Oxford: Oxford University Press, 2000), pp. 1–26.

Sullivan, L., *Oakeshott on history* (Exeter: Imprint, 2003).

Thomas, W., 'James Mill's politics: the Essay on government and the movement for reform', *History Journal* 12.2 (1969), pp. 249–284.

Thomas, W., 'James Mill's politics: a rejoinder', *Historical Journal* 14.4 (1971), pp. 735–770.

Thomas, W., 'Introduction' in Mill, J., *The History of British India* (Chicago: University of Chicago Press, 1975).

Thomas, W., *The Philosophic Radicals. Nine studies in theory and practice 1817–1841* (Oxford: Clarendon Press, 1979).

Thompson, D., *John Stuart Mill and representative government* (Princeton: Princeton University Press, 1976).

Tresch, J., *The romantic machine: utopian science and technology after Napoleon* (Chicago: University of Chicago Press, 2012).

Tritle, L. A., 'The Athens of George Grote: historiography and Philosophic Radicalism' in Mellor, R. and Tritle, L. A. (eds.), *Text and tradition: studies in Greek history and historiography in honour of Mortimer Chambers* (California: Regina, 1999), pp. 368–379.

Tucker, A. (ed.), *A companion to the philosophy of history and historiography* (London: Wiley-Blackwell, 2009).

Turk, C., *Coleridge and Mill: A study of influence* (Aldershot: Avery, 1988).

Turner, F. M., 'Antiquity in Victorian contexts', *Browning Institute Studies* 10 (1982), pp. 1–15.

Turner, F. M., *The Greek heritage in Victorian Britain* (Yale: Yale University Press, 1980).

Turner, J., *Philology: the forgotten origins of the modern humanities* (Princeton: Princeton University Press, 2014).

Turner, M. J., *Independent radicalism in early Victorian Britain* (London: Greenwood, 2004).

Turner S. (eds. Cohen, R. S. and Wartowsky, M. W.), *The search for a methodology of social science: Durkheim, Weber, and the nineteenth-century problem of cause, probability, and action* (Dordrecht: Springer, 1986).

Urbinati, N., 'The many heads of the hydra: J. S. Mill on despotism' in Urbinati, N. and Zakaras, A. (eds.), *J. S. Mill's political thought: a bicentennial reassessment* (Cambridge: Cambridge University Press, 2007), pp. 66–97.

Urbinati, N., *Mill on democracy: from the Athenian 'polis' to representative government* (London: University of Chicago Press, 2002).

Valls, A., 'Self-development and the liberal state: the cases of John Stuart Mill and Wilhelm von Humboldt', *The Review of Politics* 61 (1999), pp. 251–274.

Van Holthoon, F. L., 'Hume and the end of history' in Spencer, M. G. (ed.), *David Hume: historical thinker, historical writer* (Pennsylvania: Pennsylvania State Press, 2013), pp. 143–163.

Van Holthoon, F. L., *The road to utopia: a study of John Stuart Mill's social thought* (Assen: Van Gorcum, 1971).

Varouxakis, G., 'French radicalism through the eyes of John Stuart Mill', *History of European Ideas* 30.4 (2004), pp. 433–461.

Varouxakis, G., 'Guizot's historical works and J. S. Mill's reception of Tocqueville', *History of Political Thought* 20.2 (1999), pp. 292–312.

Varouxakis, G., *Mill on nationality* (London: Routledge, 2002).

Varouxakis, G., 'National character in John Stuart Mill's thought', *History of European Ideas* 24.6 (1998), pp. 375–391.

Varouxakis, G., *Victorian political thought on France and the French* (London: Palgrave, 2002).

Vartanian, A., *Science and humanism in the French Enlightenment* (Charlottesville: Rockwood, 1999).

Vernon, R., 'The political self: Auguste Comte and phrenology', *History of European Ideas* 7 (1986), pp. 271–86.

Vieira, R. A., *Time and politics: parliament and the culture of modernity in Britain and the British world* (Oxford: Oxford University Press, 2015).

Vigus, J., *Platonic Coleridge* (London: Legenda, 2009).

Vlassopoulos, K., *Politics: antiquity and its legacy* (Oxford: Oxford University Press, 2009).

Wagner, P., 'Transformations of democracy: towards a history of political thought and practice in long-term perspective' in Arnason, J. P., Raaflaub, K. A., and Wagner, P. (eds.), *The Greek polis and the invention of democracy: a politico-cultural transformation and its interpretations* (Oxford: Wiley-Blackwell, 2013), pp. 47–69.

Walch, J., *Les maîtres de l'histoire 1815–1850: Augustin Thierry, Mignet, Guizot, Thiers, Michelet, Edgar Quinet* (Paris: Champion-Slatkine, 1986).

Wallace, V., 'Benthamite radicalism and its Scots Presbyterian contexts', *Utilitas* 24.1 (2012), pp. 1–25.

Ward, I., *The English constitution: myths and realities* (Oregon: Hart, 2004).

Ward, L., *The politics of liberty in England and Revolutionary America* (Cambridge: Cambridge University Press, 2004).

Watkins, M., *The philosophical progress of Hume's Essays* (Cambridge: Cambridge University Press, 2019).

Wormald, H. G., *Francis Bacon: history, politics, and science, 1561–1626* (Cambridge: Cambridge University Press, 1993).

Webb, S. (ed. Shaw, G. B.), *Fabian essays in socialism* (London: George Allen & Unwin, 1948).

Weinberg, A., *The influence of Auguste Comte on the economics of John Stuart Mill* [1949] (London: E.G. Weinberg, 1982).

Wernick, A., *Auguste Comte and the religion of humanity: the post-theistic program of French social theory* (Cambridge: Cambridge University Press, 2003).

Wernick, A. (ed.), *The Anthem companion to Auguste Comte* (London: Anthem, 2017).

West, H. R., *An introduction to Mill's utilitarian ethics* (Cambridge: Cambridge University Press, 2004).

Whedbee, K. E., 'Reclaiming rhetorical democracy: George Grote's defense of Cleon and the Athenian Demagogues', *Rhetoric Society Quarterly* 34.4 (2004), pp. 71–95.

Whelan, F. J., *Order and artifice in Hume's political philosophy* (New Jersey: Princeton University Press, 1985).

Whitaker, J. K., 'John Stuart Mill's methodology', *Journal of Political Economy* 83 (1975), pp. 1033–1049.

White, H., *Metahistory: the historical imagination in nineteenth-century Europe* (Baltimore: Johns Hopkins University Press, 1973).

Williams, D., *Condorcet and modernity* (Cambridge: Cambridge University Press, 2004).

Williams, G. L., 'J. S. Mill on the Greeks: history put to use', *The Mill newsletter* 17.1 (1982), pp. 1–11.

Williams, J. R., *Jules Michelet: historian as critic of French literature* (Alabama: Summa, 1987).

Winch, D., *Adam's Smith's politics* (Cambridge: Cambridge University Press, 1978).

Winch, D. (ed.), *James Mill: selected economic writings* (Edinburgh: Oliver and Boyd, 1966).

Wintle, M., 'Britain, Belgium, and the Netherlands and the historical imagination in the nineteenth century: an introduction' in Dunthorne, H. and Wintle, M., *The historical imagination in nineteenth-century Britain and the Low Countries* (Leiden: Brill, 2012), pp. 3–19.

Wolloch, N., *History and nature in the Enlightenment: praise of the mastery of nature in eighteenth-century historical literature* (Surrey: Ashgate, 2011).

Wood, I., *The modern origins of the Early Middle Ages* (Oxford: Oxford University Press, 2013).

Wood, N., *Cicero's social and political thought* (California: University of California Press, 1991).

Wright, T. R., *The religion of humanity: the impact of Comtean positivism on Victorian England* (Cambridge: Cambridge University Press, 1986).

Wroth, W. W. and Taylor, J. S., 'William Mitford', *Oxford dictionary of national biography*, www.oxforddnb.com/view/article/18860, accessed on 10 January 2013.

Young, B. W., 'History' in Bevir, M. (ed.), *Historicism and the human sciences* (Cambridge: Cambridge University Press, 2017), pp. 154–186.

Young, B. W., *The Victorian eighteenth century: an intellectual history* (Oxford: Oxford University Press, 2007).

Zakaras, A., *Individuality and mass democracy: Mill, Emerson, and the burdens of citizenship* (Oxford: Oxford University Press, 2009).

Zastoupil, L., 'Moral government: J. S. Mill on Ireland', *The Historical Journal* 26.3 (1983), pp. 707–717.

Index

and James Mill, 59
and Montesquieu, 30, 50
Maurice, F. D., 7, 186
McCulloch, John Ramsay, 216
methodological individualism, 203
Michelet, Jules, 9, 120, 123, 124, 126, 159, 163, 180, 187, 192, 193, 196, 197, 218
Mignet, François, 155, 191
Millar, John, 67, 70, 79, 133, 187
Milman, H. H., 161
Mitchell, A. A., 9
Mitford, William, 33, 91, 95, 96, 97, 99, 102, 126, 127, 129
Molesworth, William, 173
Moltke, Adam, 129
Montesquieu, 16, 31, 40, 47, 48, 57, 149, 160, 222, 223
Moore, John, 82
Müller, Karl Otfried, 94, 137
Murray, John, 103

nationality, idea of, 190
  and history, 5, 159
  and J. S. Mill, 7, 132, 203
  and James Mill, 7
natural law, 16, 46, 49
necessity, problem of, 156, 170, 188, 196, 198, 199, 200, 201, 202, 204, 212
Newton, Isaac, 12, 28, 56, 156
Nichol, John Pringle, 156
Niebuhr, Barthold Georg, 13, 47, 94, 95, 97, 114, 116, 125, 126, 127, 128, 129, 137, 143, 160, 161, 224
nominalism, 17
Norman Conquest, 7, 196

objectivity
  and Bentham, 36
  and Grote, 8, 94
  and J. S. Mill, 130, 131
  and James Mill, 71
  see Hume, David
organicism, 6, 23, 28, 141, 156, 169, 220
orientalism, 65, 77
Owen, Robert, 200

Paine, Thomas, 27
Paley, William, 23, 28, 81
Palgrave, Francis, 6, 110
philology, 16, 17, 94, 98, 100, 127, 128, 129
Philosophic Radicalism, 2, 12, 40, 90, 166
  development of, 26, 43, 80
philosophic Whigs, 12, 13, 19, 61, 209, 222
philosophy of history, 12
  and Bentham, 34, 37
  and Coleridge, 159
  and Comte, 120, 179, 202

conjectural, 5, 66, 67, 68, 70, 220
  and Grote, 86, 95, 96, 97, 98, 114
  and J. S. Mill, 1, 117, 121, 122, 127, 129, 143, 147, 150, 158, 171, 190, 204
  and James Mill, 76, 77
  liberal Anglican, 162
  Saint-Simonian, 164, 171
  Scottish, 16, 32, 57, 60, 70, 124, 144, 154, 187, 219, 223
phrenology, 142, 174
Pitt, William, 83
Plato, 105
Platonism, 157, 161
political economy, 161, 172, 174, 182, 221
  and Adam Smith, 48
  French, 150
  and J. S. Mill, 13, 117, 148, 208, 213, 224
  and James Mill, 83
political obligation
  and Grote, 20, 102, 104, 105, 106, 108
  and J. S. Mill, 112
political reform, 3, 6, 10, 11, 12, 123, 165, 221, 224
  and Bentham, 15, 24, 26, 43, 44, 62
  and Grote, 89
  and J. S. Mill, 118, 142, 148, 160, 207, 208, 209, 210
  and James Mill, 61, 80, 82, 86
political science, 8, 186, 221
  and Bentham, 16, 30
  and the chemical method, 153
  and Coleridge, 158
  evolutionary, 116
  and Grote, 93
  and J. S. Mill, 2, 63, 143, 147, 148, 151, 154, 163, 171, 183, 185, 186, 197, 208, 210
  and James Mill, 63, 64
Popper, Karl, 17, 188
positivism, 1, 15, 16, 144, 149, 151, 162, 169, 173, 174, 175, 176, 178, 187, 219, 224
  see Comte, Auguste
postcolonialism, 77
presentism, 6, 7, 8, 40, 221
  and Grote, 114
  and J. S. Mill, 115, 120, 122, 123, 125, 143, 144
  and James Mill, 8
Priestley, Joseph, 3
problem of necessity, 199
progress, idea of, 11, 186
  and Bentham, 44, 48, 55, 56
  and Coleridge, 148
  and Comte, 96, 97, 175, 176, 177, 180, 188
  and Grote, 106, 184
  and J. S. Mill, 1, 14, 15, 18, 118, 120, 121, 122, 140, 142, 143, 149, 150, 151, 152, 160, 162, 171, 176, 181, 183, 189, 195, 203, 204, 206, 216

For EU product safety concerns, contact us at Calle de José Abascal, 56–1°,
28003 Madrid, Spain or eugpsr@cambridge.org.